UNITED STATES
CORPORATION HISTORIES

GARLAND REFERENCE LIBRARY
OF SOCIAL SCIENCE
(VOL. 807)

UNITED STATES CORPORATION HISTORIES
A Bibliography
1965–1990
A Second Edition

Wahib Nasrallah

GARLAND PUBLISHING, INC. • NEW YORK & LONDON
1991

Library of Congress Cataloging-in-Publication Data

Nasrallah, Wahib, 1945–
    United States corporation histories : a bibliography, 1965–1990 /
Wahib Nasrallah — 2nd ed.
        p.   cm. — (Garland reference library of social science ; vol.
807)
    Includes indexes.
    ISBN 0–8153–0639–3
    1. Corporations—United States—History—Bibliography. I. Title.
II. Series: Garland reference library of social science ; v. 807.
Z7164.T87N37   1991
[HD2785]
016.3387'4'0973—dc20   91–28858
                                                                CIP

Printed on acid-free, 250-year-life paper
Manufactured in the United States of America

CONTENTS

INTRODUCTION

Interest among various corporations to document heritage, tradition, and progress over the years has been increasing. Corporations are finding new values in producing printed accounts of the company's history, and some have created history departments with in-house corporate historians. The value of these accounts can help corporate executives understand long-term strategic issues and can enhance the ability to plan for the future. Public relations benefits to the company remain a strong consideration for producing the company history document. For the business researcher, a proliferation of company histories can mean more data to study industry trends. Some universities, recognizing the educational value to their students, have started to incorporate business history courses in their curricula.

The second revised and enlarged edition of this book extends the time period covered in the first edition to the end of 1990. It also expands the scope of citations to cover 25 collected works of corporate histories listed in appendix A. The present edition also includes newspaper articles, where the theme of the article is a historical treatment of the corporation. More private companies are included in the 2nd edition, as a result of a direct mailing to the largest private companies in the United States.

The bibliography contains books, periodical articles, theses, dissertations, pamphlets and other company-produced literature, corporate histories embedded in annual reports or fact sheets, and articles from national or regional newspapers. It also indexes collected works containing more than one history of a company.

The attempt for a comprehensive work of this nature undoubtedly means listings that are diverse in length and also in quality. For many corporations, especially new and emerging ones, only a newspaper article may exist. For companies such as Tootsie Roll, Topps (baseball cards), or Compaq Computer Company, no scholarly historical works exist. I have chosen to include such material to satisfy a need, and for its informational value.

The focus of the time period is 1965 through 1990. Prior to 1965, company histories are well documented in various bibliographic works. This bibliography includes companies whose histories extended to 1965 or after. Excluded are companies whose history did not extend to 1965 or beyond, even though they may have been published later than 1965.

The process of identifying those histories was a laborious and painstaking one. Bibliographic tools do not allow for direct access under the subject matter, i.e., corporation histories. It was necessary to search the literature using a company name approach to identify those histories in secondary sources. The new technologies of CD-Rom have made databases accessible and affordable for researching this book. In addition, a direct mailing to the largest U.S. corporations was utilized to insure a wide and diversified method of collecting data.

The main body of the bibliography lists corporations alphabetically. A letter by letter approach is used; acronyms are interfiled. "Cross references" are used when the company's popular name is at variance with the official name. "See also" references are used to link name changes and other corporate family relationships.

The index to U.S. corporations' histories by industry, which follows the main text, will aid researchers of industrial history as collective histories of companies in one particular industry can often shed light on the whole industry. The executive officer index allows access to biographical sources cited in the bibliography. An author index is also provided.

United States
Corporation Histories

THE BIBLIOGRAPHY

A&M RECORDS, INC.

"A&M Records at 25--Success Hasn't Spoiled the Magic."
Los Angeles Times, 4 January 1988, sec. IV, p. 1.

Casell, Chuck. *A&M Records; The First 10 Years: A
Fairy Tale*. Hollywood, Calif.: The Company, 1972.
34 p.

A&P
SEE:
GREAT ATLANTIC AND PACIFIC TEA
COMPANY

ABBOTT LABORATORIES

*The Abbott Almanac: 100 Years of Commitment to
Quality Health Care*. Elmsford, NY: Benjamin, 1988.
224 p.

Abbott Laboratories. *Abbott: 1888-1979*. North Chicago,
Ill.: The Company, 1979. 4 p.

Kogan, Herman. *The Long White Line; The Story of
Abbott Laboratories*. New York, N.Y.: Alexander
Hamilton Institute, 1965. 327 p.

"100, 1888-1988; Quality Health Care Worldwide." In
Abbott Laboratories. Annual Report, 23-27. Abbott
Park, Ill.: The Company, 1987.

Sawyers, June. "The Pill Joint That Grew into a Giant Pharmaceutical Firm." *Chicago Tribune*, 21 May 1989, sec. 10, p.10.

ABC
SEE:
AMERICAN BROADCASTING COMPANY

ABERCROMBIE (JAMES SMITHER)

Nicholson, Patrick James. *Mr. Jim: The Biography of James Smither Abercrombie.* Houston, Tex.: Gulf Publishing, 1983. 364 p.

ABINGDON POTTERIES, INC.

Rehl, Norma. *Abingdon Pottery*, ed. by Connie DeAngelo. Milford, N.J.: N. Rehal, 1981. 56 p.

ABLE (RICHARD) AND COMPANY

Newlin, Lyman. "The Rise and Fall of Richard Abel and Company, Inc." *Scholarly Publishing* 7 (January 1975): 55-61.

ACCURAY CORPORATION

Kurstedt, Harold A. "AccuRay Puts Computers to Work." *IE News* 19 (Summer 1984): 1-3+

ACE HARDWARE CORPORATION

Ace Hardware Corporation. *Our 60th Anniversary.* Oak Brook, Ill.: The Company, 1984. 4 p.

ACME-CLEVELAND CORPORATION

Armstrong, Arthur S. *The Persistence of Struggle: The Story of Acme-Cleveland Corporation.* New York, N.Y: Newcomen Society of North America, 1976. 24 p. (Newcomen publication; no. 1040)

ACME MARKETS, INC.

Nicholson, Arnold. *Acme Markets, Inc., 1891-1967, From Corner Grocery to Supermarket Chain.* Philadelphia, Pa.: Acme Markets, 1967.

ACTION INSTRUMENTS, INC.

Kotkin, Joel. "A Call to Action." *Inc.* 5 (November 1983): 85-96.

ADDRESSOGRAPH MULTIGRAPH CORPORATION

Addressograph Multigraph Corporation. *Beginning with Imagination.* Cleveland, Ohio.: The Company, n.d. 11 p.

ADELL CHEMICAL COMPANY (LESTOIL)

Fucini, Joseph J., and Suzy Fucini. "Jacob L. Barowsky, Adell Chemical Company (LESTOIL): 'Television Showed us the Way.'" In *Experience Inc.; Men and Women Who Founded Famous Companies After the Age of 40*, 47-52. New York, N.Y.: Free Press, 1987.

ADMOS SHOE CORPORATION

Kingston, Brett. "Jay Adoni of Admos Shoe Corporation." In *The Dynamos: Who Are They Anyway?*, 105-110. New York, N.Y: Wiley, 1987.

SEE ALSO: BRUNING (CHARLES) COMPANY

AERO MAYFLOWER TRANSIT COMPANY, INC.

Floros, Leo. "The Mayflower Story." *Public Relations Journal* 39 (September 1983): 23-25.

AEROSPACE CORPORATION

Aerospace Corporation. *The Aerospace Corporation, Its People, 1980.* El Segundo, Calif.: The Company, 1980. 256 p.

AETNA LIFE AND CASUALTY

Post, James E. *Risk and Response: Management and Social Change in the American Insurance Industry.* Lexington, Mass.: Lexington Books, 1976. 206 p.

AFFILIATED FUND INC.

Driscoll, Robert S. *The Story of Lord, Abbett and Company and Affiliated Fund, Inc.: A View of the Capital Needs of the U.S. Economy.* New York, N.Y.: Newcomen Society in North America, 1974. (Newcomen publication; no. 999)

AFG INDUSTRIES, INC.

Jones, Billy Mac. *Magic with Sand: A History of AFG Industries, Inc.* Wichita, Kans.: Center for Entrepreneurship, College of Business Administration, Wichita State University, 1984. 172 p.

AGWAY, INC.

Steel, George. *George Steel: Yesterdays (Sound Recordings).* West Chester, Pa.: Chester County District Library Center, 1979. 2 cassettes (Recorded April 12, 1979)

AIR FLORIDA

"Air Florida's Meteoric Rise." *Business Week* (10 November 1980): 141-142.

"Behind the Rise and Fall of Air Florida." *Business Week* (23 July 1984): 122-123+

AIR MIDWEST

Quastler, I.E. *Pioneer of the Third Level: A History of Air Midwest*. San Diego, Calif.: Commuter Airlines Press, 1980. 174 p.

AIR PRODUCTS AND CHEMICAL, INC.

Air Products and Chemicals, Inc. *Who We Are*. Allentown, Pa.: The Company, 1982. 6 p.

"Air Products Begins in 1940 with 'A Better Idea.'" *Air Products Monthly News* (October 1975) Special 35th Anniversary Issue.

Butrica, Andrew J. *Out of This Air: A History of Air Products and Chemicals, Inc., 1940-1990*. San Francisco, Calif.: Greenwood Press, 1990. 336 p.

AIRBORNE EXPRESS

Airborne Express. *History of Airborne Express*. Seattle, Wash.: The Company, 1989. 6 p.

ALABAMA BANCORPORATION

Woods, John W. *Alabama Bancorporation: The Story of Alabama's Largest Banking Institution*. New York, N.Y.: Newcomen Society in North America, 1978. 26 p. (Newcomen publication; no. 1070)

ALABAMA POWER COMPANY

Farley, Joseph M. *Alabama Power Company: Developed for the Service of Alabama*. New York, N.Y.: Newcomen Society of the United States, 1988. 24 p. (Newcomen publication; no. 1313)

ALACHUA GENERAL HOSPITAL, INC.

Rathbun, Frank F. *Proud of Our Past, Proud of Our*

Future: The Story of Alachua General Hospital, Inc.
Gainesville, Fla.: The Hospital, 1978. 79 p.

ALAGO SALES AND MANUFACTURING COMPANY

Persinos, John F. "East Side Story." Inc. 6 (July 1984):
61-64.

THE ALASKA AIRLINES, INC.

Satterfield, Archie. *The Alaska Airlines Story*. Anchorage,
Alaska: Alaska Northwest Publishing Company, 1981.
207 p.

ALBERT KAHN ASSOCIATES, INC.

King, Sol. *Creative--Responsive--Pragmatic. 75 Years of
Professional Practice. Albert Kahn and Associates,
Architects--Engineers*. New York, N.Y.: Newcomen
Society in North America, 1970. 36 p. (Newcomen
address)

ALCO STANDARD CORPORATION

Veale, Tinkham, and R.B. Mundt. *Alco Standard
Corporation, "The Corporate Partnership": A
Commitment to Excellence*. New York, N.Y.:
Newcomen Society in North America, 1980. 29 p.
(Newcomen publication; no. 1131)

ALCOA
SEE:
ALUMINUM COMPANY OF AMERICA

ALCON LABORATORIES, INC.

Alexander, Robert D. *The Story of Alcon Laboratories,
Inc.: Prescription for Success*. New York, N.Y.:
Newcomen Society in North America, 1969. 28 p.
(Newcomen address)

ALEXANDER AIRCRAFT COMPANY

De Vries, John A. *Alexander Eaglerock: A History of Alexander Aircraft Company*. Colorado Springs, Colo.: Century One Press, 1985. 126 p.

ALEXANDER AND BALDWIN, INC.

Alexander and Baldwin, Inc. *Eighty-five Years a Corporation, 1900-1985*. Honolulu: The Company, 1985. 66 p.

ALLEGHENY AIRLINES
SEE:
USAIR

ALLEGHENY INTERNATIONAL, INC.

Buckley, Robert J. *Allegheny International, A New Global Business Enterprise*. New York, N.Y.: Newcomen Society of the United States, 1983. 23 p. (Newcomen publication; no. 1198)

ALLEN-BRADLEY COMPANY

Allen-Bradley Company. *The Allen-Bradley Story*. Milwaukee, Wis.: The Company, 1965. 51 p.

ALLIED BANKSHARES

MacPhee, William. "Gerald Smith of Allied Bankshares." In *Rare Breed: The Entrepreneur, An American Culture*, 133-141. Chicago, Ill.: Probus Publishing Company, 1987.

ALLIED CORPORATION

Cunningham, Mary. *Powerplay: What Really Happened at Bendix*. New York, N.Y.: Linden Press/Simon & Schuster, 1984. 286 p.

Hennessy, Edward L. *Allied Corporation: Strength Through Diversification.* New York, N.Y.: Newcomen Society in North America, 1984. 24 p. (Newcomen publication; no. 1218)

Williams, Kathy. "Ed. Hennessy Reshapes Allied." *Management Accounting* 66 (January 1985): 18-25.

ALLIED STORES CORPORATION

Macioce, Thomas M. *Allied Stores Corporation: 50 Years of Retail Growth.* New York, N.Y.: Newcomen Society in North America, 1979. (Newcomen publication; no. 1100)

ALLIS-CHALMERS CORPORATION

Peterson, Walter Fritio F. *An Industrial Heritage, Allis-Chalmers Corporation.* Milwaukee, Wis.: Milwaukee County Historical Society, 1978. 448 p.

Scott, David Charles. *Managerial Vision and Craftsmanship: To Meet Human Needs: The Story of Allis-Chalmers Corporation.* New York, N.Y.: Newcomen Society in North America, 1979. 18 p. (Newcomen publication; no. 1101)

Wendel, Charles. *The Allis-Chalmers Story.* Sarasota, Fla.: Crestline Pub., 1988. 372 p.

ALLSTATE INSURANCE COMPANY

Boe, Archie R. *Allstate: The Story of the Good Hands Company.* New York, N.Y.: Newcomen Society in North America, 1981. 19 p. (Newcomen publication; no. 1148)

Seldow, Leona. *Allstate: A Study in Entrepreneurial Decision Making That Changed the Tradition-Bound Insurance Industry.* New York, N.Y.: Graduate School of Business Administration, New York University,

1976. 211 p.

SEE ALSO: SEARS, ROEBUCK AND COMPANY

ALLTEL CORPORATION

Case, Weldon W. *ALLTEL Corporation: Twenty-Five Years of Growth and Dedication to Excellence.* New York, N.Y.: Newcomen Society of the United States, 1985. 20 p. (Newcomen publication; no. 1246)

ALPHA BETA COMPANY

Cramer, Esther R. *The Alpha Beta Story; An Illustrated History of a Leading Western Food Retailer.* La Habra, Calif.: Alpha Beta Acme Markets, 1973. 436 p.

ALUMINUM COMPANY OF AMERICA (ALCOA)

"ALCOA Timeline: Significant Developments Over the Past Decade." In *Aluminum Company of America Annual Report*, 10-11. Pittsburgh, Pa.: The Company, 1985.

Graham, Margaret B.W. *R&D for Industry: A Century of Technical Innovation at ALCOA.* Cambridge; New York, N.Y.: Cambridge University Press, 1990. 645 p.

Parry, Charles W. *ALCOA: A Retrospection.* New York, N.Y.: Newcomen Society of the United States, 1985. (Newcomen publication; no. 1249)

Smith, George David. *From Monopoly to Competition: The Transformations of ALCOA, 1888-1986.* Cambridge; New York, N.Y.: Cambridge University Press, 1988. 554 p.

Smith, George David, and John E. Wright. "ALCOA Goes Back to the Future." *Across the Board* 23 (September 1986): 22-31.

AMARILLO NATIONAL BANK

Thompson, Thomas Hazzard. *The Ware Boys: The Story of a Texas Family Bank.* Canyon, Tex.: Staked Plains Press, 1978. 293 p.

AMAX, INC.

AMAX, Inc. *AMAX Today; What We Are, What We Do.* Greenwich, Conn.: The Company, 1984. 20 p.

Born, Allen. *AMAX Century Plus One: A "New" Company Faces the Future.* New York, N.Y.: Newcomen Society of the United States, 1988, c1989. (Newcomen publication; no. 1319)

Levinson, Harry, and Stuart Rosenthal. "Ian K. MacGregor." In *CEO: Corporate Leadership in Action*, 96-136. New York, N.Y.: Basic Books, 1984.

Wilson, Arthur J. *The AMAX Century.* Greenwich, Conn.: The Company, 1987. 41 p.

AMC CORPORATION
SEE:
AMERICAN MOTORS CORPORATION

AMCAST
SEE:
DAYTON MALLEABLE, INC.

AMDAHL CORPORATION

Amdahl Corporation. *The Amdahl Phenomenon.* Sunnyvale, Calif.: The Company, 1983. 13 p.

Amdahl, Gene M. "The Early Chapters of the PCM Story." *Datamation* 25 (February 1979): 112-116.

AMEDCO, INC.

Bettner, Jill. "Till Death Do Us Part." *Forbes* 132 (29 August 1983): 112-113.

AMERICAN AGRONOMICS

Louis, Arthur M. "Squeezing Gold Out of Oranges." *Fortune* 103 (26 January 1981): 78-82.

AMERICAN AIRLINES, INC.

American Airlines, Inc. *American Airlines, Inc.: A Brief History.* Dallas, Tex.: The Company, 1988. 18 p.

American Airlines, Inc. *A Brief History of American Airlines.* Dallas, Tex.: The Company, 1985. 17 p.

Cearley, George Walker. *American Airlines: An Illustrated History.* Dallas, Tex.: G. W. Cearley, Jr., 1981. 100 p.

Serling, Robert J. *Eagle: The Story of American Airlines.* New York, N.Y.: St. Martin's/Marek, 1985. 482 p.

AMERICAN BRASS COMPANY

Brass Valley: The Story of Working People's Lives and Struggles in an American Industrial Region. The Brass Workers History Project: Compiled and Edited by Jeremy Brecher, Jerry Lombardi, and Jan Stakhouse. Philadelphia, Pa.: Temple University Press, 1982. 284 p.

AMERICAN BROADCASTING COMPANY

American Broadcasting Company. *Historical Highlights.* New York, N.Y.: The Company, 1980. 12 p.

MacDonald, J. Fred. *One Nation Under Television: The Rise and Decline of Network TV.* New York, N.Y.:

Pantheon, 1990. 335 p.

Quinlan, Sterling. *Inside ABC: American Broadcasting Company's Rise to Power*. New York, N.Y.: Hastings House, 1979. 290 p.

AMERICAN BRUSH MANUFACTURERS ASSOCIATION

American Brush Manufacturers Association. *The First Fifty Years, 1917-1967*. Philadelphia, Pa.: The Association, 1967. 16 p.

AMERICAN CRYSTAL SUGAR COMPANY

Guide to the Records of the American Crystal Sugar Company. Compiled by: Lydia A. Lucas, and Marion E. Matters. St. Paul: Division of Archives and Manuscripts, Minnesota Historical Society, 1985. 100 p.

THE AMERICAN DISTILLING COMPANY

Brown, Russell R. *The American Distilling Company: A Story of People, Products and Progress*. New York, N.Y.: Newcomen Society in North America, 1965. 24 p. (Newcomen address)

AMERICAN ELECTRIC POWER COMPANY

White, W.S. *American Electric Power: 75 Years of Meeting the Challenge*. New York, N.Y.: Newcomen Society in North America, 1982. 23 p. (Newcomen publication; no. 1175)

AMERICAN EXPRESS COMPANY

American Express Company. *Promises to Pay: The Story of American Express Company*. New York, N.Y.: The Company, 1977. 283 p.

Brock, C. "Undoing the Eighties." *New Yorker* 66 (23 July 1990): 56+

Carrington, Tim. *The Year They Sold Wall Street.* Boston, Mass.: Houghton, 1985. 384 p.

Fritz, David. "Lady Luck: Don't Leave Home Without Her." *Across the Board* 24 (September 1987): 59-59.

Grossman, Peter Z. *American Express: The Unofficial History of the People Who Built the Great Financial Empire.* New York, N.Y.: Crown Publishers, 1987. 389 p.

AMERICAN FARM BUREAU FEDERATION

Berger, Samuel R. *Dollar Harvest; The Story of the Farm Bureau.* Lexington, Mass.: Lexington Books, 1971. 221 p.

AMERICAN FINANCIAL CORPORATION

"UDF: Birth of an Empire; Depression Spawned Big Dreams." *Cincinnati Enquirer,* 6 May 1990, sec. G, p. 1.

AMERICAN GENERAL INSURANCE COMPANY

Woodson, Benjamin W. *"A Financial Services Supermarket": the American General Story.* New York, N.Y.: Newcomen Society in North America, 1974. 32 p. (Newcomen publication; no. 992)

AMERICAN GREETINGS CORPORATION

American Greetings Corporation. *History of American Greetings Corporation.* Cleveland, Ohio: The Company, 1985. 4 p.

Weiss, Morry. *American Greetings Corporation.* New York, N.Y.: Newcomen Society in North America,

1982. 20 p. (Newcomen publication; no. 1164)

AMERICAN HOECHST CORPORATION

Van Vlaandern, Edward. *Pronounced Success, America and Hoechst, 1953-1978.* Bridgewater, N.J.: The Company, 1979. 184 p.

AMERICAN HOSPITAL SUPPLY CORPORATION

Sturdivant, Frederick D. *Growth Through Service: The Story of American Hospital Supply Corporation.* Evanston, Illinois: Northwestern University Press, 1970. 382 p. (Northwestern University studies in business history)

AMERICAN INSTITUTE OF CERTIFIED PUBLIC ACCOUNTANTS

AICPA 100, A Century of Progress in Accounting, 1887-1987. New York, N.Y.: The Institute, 1987. 400 p.

AMERICAN INSTITUTE OF STEEL CONSTRUCTION, INC.

Gillette, Leslie H. *The First 60 Years: The American Institute of Steel Construction, Inc., 1921-1980.* Chicago, Ill.: The Institute, 1980. 179 p.

AMERICAN INTERNATIONAL GROUP, INC.

American International Group, Inc. *History of AIG.* New York, N.Y.: The Company, 1984. 10 p.

AMERICAN MAIZE-PRODUCTS

"75 Years of American Maize-Products Company." In *American Maize-Products Company. Annual Report,* 13-14. Stamford, Conn.: The Company, 1981.

AMERICAN MOTORS CORPORATION

"AMC Looks Back on 25 Years." *Automotive News* (7 May 1979): 6+

"The Story of American Motors." *Wards Quarterly* (Spring 1965): 1-40.

AMERICAN NATURAL BEVERAGE CORPORATION

Kingston, Brett. "Sophia Collier and Connie Best of American Natural Beverage Corporation." In *The Dynamos: Who Are They Anyway?*, 85-89. New York, N.Y.: Wiley, 1987.

THE AMERICAN NATURAL RESOURCES COMPANY

Seder, Arthur R. *The American Natural Resources Company. Seventy-Five Years Old and Building for the Future.* New York, N.Y.: Newcomen Society in North America, 1977. 22 p. (Newcomen publication; no. 1058)

AMERICAN OLEAN TILE COMPANY

Bell, Frederic. *Notes on a 50-Year Revolution, A Profile of the Company Whose Innovations Brought Ceramic Tile into the 20th Century.* Landsdale, Pa.: The Company, 1973. 109 p.

AMERICAN OPTICAL CORPORATION

Wells, Ruth Dyer. *The Wells Family, Founders of the American Optical Company and Old Sturbridge Village.* Southbridge, Mass.: n.p., 1979. 233 p.

AMERICAN PRESIDENT LINES, LTD.

Niven, John. *The American President Lines and Its*

Forebears, 1848-1984: From Paddle Wheelers to Containerships. Newark, N.J.: University of Delaware Press, 1987. 327 p.

AMERICAN SECURITY BANK

Smith, Vicki. *Managing the Corporate Interest; Control and Resistance in an American Bank*. Berkeley, Calif.: University of California Press, 1990. 245 p.

AMERICAN SECURITY LIFE INSURANCE COMPANY

Evett, Alice. *A Man, A Dream, A Company, The History of American Security Life Insurance Company*. San Antonio, Tex.: The Company, 1980. 183 p.

AMERICAN SHIP BUILDING COMPANY

Wright, Richard J. *Freshwater Whales; A History of the American Ship Building Company and Its Predecessors*. Kent: Kent State University Press, 1969. 299 p.

AMERICAN STOCK EXCHANGE

Sobel, Robert. *Amex: A History of the American Stock Exchange, 1921-1971*. New York, N.Y.: Weybright and Talley, 1972. 382 p.

Sobel, Robert. *The Curbstone Brokers; The Origins of the American Stock Exchange*. New York, N.Y.: Macmillan, 1970. 296 p.

AMERICAN TELEPHONE AND TELEGRAPH COMPANY

Bolling, George. *AT&T Aftermath of Antitrust: Preserving Positive Command and Control*. Fort Lesley J. McNair, Washington, D.C.: National Defense University; Washington, D.C.: GPO, 1983. 169 p.

Brooks, John. *Telephone: The First Hundred Years.* New York, N.Y.: Harper and Row, 1976. 369 p.

Coll, Steve. *The Deal of the Century; The Breakup of AT&T.* New York, N.Y.: Simon & Schuster, 1988, c1986. 400 p.

Feldman, Steven Paul. *The Culture of Monopoly Management: An Interpretive Study in an American Utility.* New York, N.Y.: Garland, 1986. 209 p.

Goulden, Joseph C. *Monopoly.* New York, N.Y.: Putnam, 1968. 350 p.

Henck, Fred W., and Bernard Strassburgh. *A Slippery Slope; The Long Road to the Breakup of AT&T.* New York, N.Y.: Greenwood Press, 1988. 277 p.

Kahaner, Larry. *On the Line; The Men of MCI--Who Took on AT&T, Risked Everything, And Won.* New York, N.Y.: Random House, 1986. 327 p.

Kehoe, Thomas Joseph. "Federal Communications Commission Regulation of the American Telephone & Telegraph Company, 1965-1974." Ph.D. diss., New York University, 1978. 282 p.

Kleinfield, Sonny. *The Biggest Company on Earth: A Profile of AT&T.* New York, N.Y.: Holt, Rienhart, and Winston, 1981. 321 p.

Kraus, Constantine Raymond, and Alfred W. Deurig. *The Rape of Ma Bell; The Criminal Wrecking of the Best Telephone System in the World.* Secaucus, N.J.: Lyle Stuart, 1988. 270 p.

Phillips, John Patrick. *Ma Bell's Millions.* New York, N.Y.: Vantage Press, 1970. 141 p.

Schlesinger, Leonard A. *Chronicles of Corporate Change: Management Lessons from AT&T and Its Offspring.*

Lexington, Mass.: Lexington Books, 1987. 254 p.

Schnee, Victor, and Walter J. Gorkiewicz. *The Future of AT&T*. Millburn, N.J.: Probe Research, 1976. 454 p.

Shooshan, Harry M., III. *Disconnecting Bell: The Impact of the AT&T Divestiture*. New York, N.Y.: Pergamon, 1984. 176 p.

Sloan, Bryan. *Bell Is Phony*. Austin, Tex.: Oasis Press, 1976. 73 p.

Sloan, Bryan. *Ma Bell*. New York, N.Y.: Vantage Press, 1983. 44 p.

Smith, George David. *Anatomy of a Business Strategy: Bell, Western Electric, and the Origins of the American Telephone Industry*. Baltimore, Md.: Johns Hopkins University Press, 1985. 208 p.

Sterling, Christopher H. *Decision to Divest, Major Documents in U.S. Vs. AT&T, 1974-1984*. Washington, D.C.: Communications Press, 1986. 3 vols. 2100 p.

Stone, Alan. *Wrong Number: The Breakup of AT&T*. New York, N.Y.: Basic Books, 1989. 381 p.

Stone, K. Aubrey. *I'm Sorry, The Monophony You Have Reached Is Not in Service*. New York, N.Y.: Ballantine Books, 1973. 247 p.

Tarullo, Patsy Ronald. "American Telephone and Telegraph Company, A Survey of Its Development Through Basic Strategy and Structure." Ph.D. diss., University of Pittsburgh, 1976. 373 p.

Temin, Peter, and Louis Galambos. *The Fall of the Bell System; A Study in Prices and Politics*. Cambridge; New York, N.Y.: Cambridge University Press, 1987. 378 p.

Toffler, Alvin. *The Adaptive Corporation.* New York, N.Y.: McGraw-Hill, 1984. 256 p.

Von Auw, Alvin. *Heritage and Destiny: Reflections of the Bell System in Transition.* New York, N.Y.: Praeger, 1983. 496 p.

SEE ALSO: WESTERN ELECTRIC COMPANY

AMERICAN TOBACCO COMPANY

Cunningham, Bill. *On Bended Knees: The Night Rider Story.* Nashville, Tenn.: McClanahan Publishing House, 1983. 224 p.

AMERICAN UNITED LIFE INSURANCE COMPANY

Strange, Georgianne. *From the Days of Knights, A History of the American United Life Insurance Company of Indianapolis, Indiana, 1877-1977.* Indianapolis, Ind.: The Company, 1977. 161 p.

AMERICAN ZINC COMPANY

Norris, James D. *AZN; A History of the American Zinc Company.* Madison: State Historical Society of Wisconsin, 1968. 244 p.

AMFAC, INC.

Simpich, Frederick, Jr. *Dynasty in the Pacific.* New York, N.Y.: McGraw-Hill, 1974. 270 p.

AMOSKEAG MANUFACTURING COMPANY

Hareven, Tamara K. *Amoskeag: Life and Work in an American Factory City.* New York, N.Y.: Pantheon Books, 1978.

Hareven, Tamara K. *Family Time and Industrial Time:*

The Relationship Between the Family and Work in a New England Industrial Community. New York, N.Y.: Cambridge University Press, 1982. 474 p.

AMTORG TRADING CORPORATION

Amtorg Trading Corporation. *Amtorg Trading Corporation: Fiftieth Anniversary.* New York, N.Y.: The Corporation, 1974. 24 p.

Feinstein, J. M. Tather. *Fifty Years of U.S.-Soviet Trade.* New York, N.Y.: Symposium Press, 1974. 256 p.

AMTRAK

Bradley, Rodger. *Amtrak: The U.S. National Railroad Passenger Corporation.* Poole, Eng.: Blandford Press, 1985. 176 p.

Dorin, Patrick C. *Amtrak Trains and Travel.* Seattle, Wash.: Superior Publishing, 1979. 184 p.

Edmonson, Herald A. *Journey to Amtrak, The Year History Rode the Passenger Train.* Milwaukee, Wis.: National Railroad Passenger Corporation, 1972. 104 p.

Hilton, George Woodman. *Amtrak: The National Railroad Passenger Corporation.* Washington: American Enterprise Institute for Public Policy Research, 1980. 80 p. (AEI studies; no.266)

Taibi, John. *Amtrak Heritage, Passenger Trains in the East, 1971-1977.* New York, N.Y., Railroad Heritage Press, 1979. 48 p.

Thomas, William E. *Reprieve for the Iron Horse: The Amtrak Experiment--Its Predecessors and Prospects.* Baton Rouge, La.: Claitor's Publishing Division, 1974. 136 p.

United States. Congress. House. Committee on Energy and

Commerce. Subcommittee on Transportation, Tourism, and Hazardous Materials. *Administration's Proposal to Sell Amtrak: Hearings Before the Subcommittee on Transportation, Tourism, and Hazardous Materials.* 100th Cong., Ist Sess., 9 April 1987. (Y 4.En 2/3: 100-22)

SEE ALSO: PENN CENTRAL COMPANY

AMWAY CORPORATION

Butterfield, Stephen. *Amway: Cult of Free Enterprise.* Boston, Mass.: South End Press, 1985. 185 p.

Conn, Charles P. *The Possible Dream: A Candid Look at Amway.* Old Tappan, N.J.: Revell, 1977. 174 p.

Conn, Charles Paul. *Promises to Keep: The Amway Phenomenon and How It Works.* New York, N.Y.: Putnam, 1985. 128 p.

Conn, Charles Paul. *An Uncommon Freedom.* Old Tappan, N.J.: Revell, 1982. 160 p.

Conn, Charles Paul. *The Winner's Circle.* Old Tappan, N.J.: Revell, 1979. 160 p.

Cross, Wilbur, and Gordon L. Olson. *Commitment to Excellence; The Remarkable Amway Story.* Elmsford, N.Y.: Benjamin, 1986. 175 p.

Radford, Michael J. *A Team of Champions*, ed. by Gerald W. Faust. Sacramento, Calif.: Radford, 1978. 229 p.

ANCHOR HOCKING GLASS CORPORATION

Gushman, John L. *Living Glass: The Story of the Anchor Hocking Glass Corporation.* New York, N.Y.: Newcomen Society in North America, 1965. 24 p. (Newcomen address)

ANDERSEN (ARTHUR) AND COMPANY

Arthur Andersen and Company. *Arthur Andersen and Company, The First Sixty Years, 1913-1973.* Chicago, Ill.: The Company, 1974. 189 p.

Arthur Andersen and Company. *70 Years of Superior Client Service, Innovative Use of New Technologies, Worldwide Expansion and Leadership in the Profession, 1913-1983.* New York, N.Y.: The Company, 1983. 26 p.

Glickauf, Joseph S. *Footsteps Toward Professionalism: The Development of an Administrative Services Practice Over the Past Twenty-Five Years: Addresses and Articles by Joseph S. Glickauf, 1948-1970.* Chicago, Ill.: The Company, 1971. 180 p.

Spacek, Leonard. *The Growth of Arthur Andersen and Company, 1928-1973.* Chicago, Ill.: The Company, 1985. 349 p.

ANDERSON, CLAYTON AND COMPANY

"Anderson Clayton: Eight Decades of Progress." In *Anderson, Clayton and Company. Annual Report,* 4-9. Houston, Tex.: The Company, 1984.

Fleming, Lamar. *Growth of the Business of Anderson, Clayton and Company.* Houston, Tex.: Texas Gulf Coast Historical Association, 1966. 46 p.

ANDERSON CORPORATION

Ruble, Kenneth Douglas. *The Magic Circle: A Story of the Men and Women Who Made Anderson the Most Respected Name in Windows.* Bayport, Minn.: Ruble, 1978. 216 p.

ANDERSON ELECTRIC CORPORATION

Schuler, John Hamilton. *The Anderson Story: A Profile of Growth*. New York, N.Y.: Newcomen Society in North America, 1970. 28 p. (Newcomen address)

SEE ALSO: SQUARE D COMPANY

ANDERSON-TULLY COMPANY

Heavrin, Charles A. *Boxes, Baskets, And Boards: A History of Anderson-Tully Company*. Memphis: Memphis State University Press, 1981. 178 p.

ANGLO AMERICAN CORPORATION OF SOUTH AFRICA, LTD.

Anglo American and the Rise of Modern South Africa. New York, N.Y.: Monthly Review Press, 1984. 352 p.

ANHEUSER-BUSCH COMPANIES, INC.

Anheuser-Busch Companies, Inc. *A-B History of Innovation*. St. Louis, Mo.: The Company, 1987. 4 p.

Anheuser-Busch Companies, Inc. *Fact Book: 1987-1988*. St. Louis, Mo.: The Company, 1988. 65 p.

Cleary, David Powers. "Budweiser Beer; Making Friends Is Our Business." In *Great American Brands: The Success Formulas That Made Them Famous*, 24-35. New York, N.Y.: Fairchild Publications, 1981.

Price, Steven D. *All the King's Horses: The Story of the Budweiser Clydesdales*. New York, N.Y.: Viking Press, 1983. 200 p.

ANTILLES AIR BOATS

Blair, Charles F. *Red Ball in the Sky*. New York, N.Y.: Random House, 1969. 203 p.

Robinson, Douglas H. "Antilles Air Boats of the Virgin Islands: The Commercial Flying Boat 30 Years Later." *American Aviation Historical Society Journal* 18 (Spring 1973): 73-79.

A-P-A TRANSPORT

Levitt, Mortimer. "Arthur Imperatore: Obsessive Drive Converts an Army Truck into a Transportation Empire." In *How to Start Your Own Business Without Losing Your Shirt; Secrets of Seventeen Successful Entrepreneurs*, 53-60. New York, N.Y.: Atheneum, 1988.

APPLE COMPUTER, INC.

Apple Computer, Inc. *The First Decade: A Brief History of Apple Computer, Inc.* Cupertino, Calif.: The Company, 1987. 6 p.

Apple Computer, Inc. *Press Background Information.* Cupertino, Calif.: The Company, 1985. 5 p.

Butcher, Lee. *Accidental Millionaire: The Rise and Fall of Steve John at Apple Computer.* New York, N.Y.: Paragon House, 1988. 224 p.

Moritz, Michael. *Little Kingdom: The Private Story of Apple Computer.* New York, N.Y.: Morrow, 1984. 336 p.

Rose, Frank. *West of Eden: The End of Innocence at Apple Computer.* New York, N.Y.: Viking Penguin, Inc., 1989. 356 p.

Sculley, John. *Odyssey: Pepsi to Apple: A Journey of Adventure, Ideas, And the Future.* New York, N.Y.: Harper, 1987. 450 p.

ARA SERVICES, INC.

Fishman, William S. *ARA Services, Inc. Developing a New Industry: Service Management.* New York, N.Y.: Newcomen Society in North America, 1977. 24 p. (Newcomen publication; no.1056)

ARABIAN AMERICAN OIL COMPANY (ARAMCO)

Kennedy, William J., ed. *Secret History of the Oil Companies in the Middle East.* Salisbury, N.C.: Documentary Publications, 1979. 2 vol. 466 p.

ARCHER DANIELS MIDLAND COMPANY

Archer Daniels Midland Company. Decatur, Ill.: The Company, 1984. 16 p.

ARDEN (ELIZABETH), INC.

Lewis, Alfred A., and Constance Woodworth. *Miss Elizabeth Arden.* New York, N.Y.: Coward, McCann & Geoghegan, 1972. 320 p.

THE ARIZONA BANK

Bean, G. Clarke. *The Spirit of the Arizona Bank.* New York, N.Y.: Newcomen Society in North America, 1972. 31 p. (Newcomen address)

ARIZONA PUBLIC SERVICES COMPANY

Reilly, William P. *Arizona Public Service Company: People, Power and Progress.* New York, N.Y.: Newcomen Society in North America, 1970. 32 p. (Newcomen address)

THE ARIZONA REPUBLIC

Pulliam, Eugene C. *Is There a Fighter in the House?* New York, N.Y.: Newcomen Society in North America,

1966. 24 p. (Newcomen address)

ARMCO STEEL CORPORATION

Armco Steel Corporation. *The American Rolling Mills Company*. Middletown, Ohio: The Company, 1975. 31 p. (*Armco Today* Seventy-Fifth Anniversary Issue)

Verity, C. William. *Faith in Men: The Story of Armco Steel Corporation*. New York: Newcomen Society in North America, 1971. 28 p. (Newcomen address)

ARMOUR AND COMPANY

Shultz, George Pratt. *Strategies for the Displaced Worker: Confronting Economic Change*. Westport, Conn.: Greenwood Press, 1976, c1966. 221 p.

ARMSTRONG RUBBER COMPANY

Walsh, James A. *The Armstrong Rubber Company: Seventy Years of Progress in the Tire Industry*. New York, N.Y.: Newcomen Society in North America, 1982. 19 p. (Newcomen publication; no. 1155)

ARMSTRONG WORLD INDUSTRIES, INC.

Armstrong World Industries, Inc. *Armstrong: A Historical Summary*. Lancaster, Pa.: The Company, 1985. 2 p.

Armstrong World Industries, Inc. *The Story of Armstrong*. Lancaster, Pa.: The Company, 1985. 11 p.

Cleary, David Powers. "Armstrong Floors, Let the Buyer Have Faith." In *Great American Brands: The Success Formulas That Made Them Famous*, 1-6. New York, N.Y.: Fairchild Publications, 1981.

ART METAL, INC.

Yahn, Mildred L. *The Rise and Fall of a Corporation:*

The Story of Art Metal, Inc., 1888-1971. Jamestown, N.Y.: M.L. Yahn, 1983. 170 p.

ARTHUR ANDERSEN AND COMPANY
SEE:
ANDERSEN (ARTHUR) AND COMPANY

ARVIN INDUSTRIES, INC.

Coons, Coke. *Arvin--The First Sixty Years History.* Columbus, Ind.: The Company, 1982. 263 p.

ASHLAND OIL AND REFINING COMPANY, INC.

Scott, Otto J. *The Exception; The Story of Ashland Oil and Refining Company.* New York, N.Y.: McGraw-Hill, 1968. 450 p.

ASSOCIATED GENERAL CONTRACTORS OF AMERICA

Mooney, Booth. *Builders for Progress, The Story of the Associated General Contractors of America.* New York, N.Y.: McGraw-Hill, 1965. 194 p.

ASSOCIATED GROCERS, INC.

"Fifty Years of Excellence, 1934-1984." In *Associated Grocers, Inc. Annual Report*, 4-10. Seattle, Wash.: The Company, 1984.

ASSOCIATES CORPORATION OF NORTH AMERICA

"The Associates History: 1918-1983." *Associates Magazine* (Summer 1983): 1-19. (Sixty-fifth anniversary issue)

ASSOCIATES INVESTMENT COMPANY

Carmichael, O.C., Jr. *New Doors of Achievement: The*

Story of Associates Investment Company. New York, N.Y.: Newcomen Society in North America, 1969. 24 p. (Newcomen address)

AST RESEARCH CORPORATION

Kingston, Brett. "Qureshey, Wong, And Yuen of AST Research, Inc." In *The Dynamos: Who Are They Anyway?*, 113-117. New York, N.Y.: Wiley, 1987.

AT&T
SEE:
AMERICAN TELEPHONE AND TELEGRAPH COMPANY

ATARI, INC.

Cohen, Scott. *ZAP the Rise and Fall of Atari.* New York, N.Y.: McGraw-Hill, 1984. 177 p.

"Former Exec.: Rapid Success Begat Atari Failure." *Marketing News* 19 (10 May 1985): 10-11.

ATKINSON (GUY F.) COMPANY OF CALIFORNIA

Atkinson, Ray N. *Guy F. Atkinson Company of California: A Free Enterprise Success Story.* New York, N.Y.: Newcomen Society of the United States, 1985, c 1986. (Newcomen publication; no. 1266)

ATLANTA BRAVES

Couch, J. Hudson. *The Braves: First Fifteen Years in Atlanta.* Rosewell, Calif.: Other Alligator Creek Company, 1984. 436 p.

Fields, Robert A. *Take Me Out to the Crowd; Ted Turner and the Atlanta Braves.* Huntsville, Ala.: Strodel, 1977. 256 p.

Onigman, Marc. *This Date in Braves History.* New York,

N.Y.: Stein and Day, 1982. 194 p.

SEE ALSO: TURNER BROADCASTING SYSTEMS, INC.

ATLANTA GAS LIGHT COMPANY

Tate, James H. *Keeper of the Flame: The Story of Atlanta Gas Light Company, 1856-1985.* Atlanta, Ga.: The Company, 1985. 342 p.

ATLANTA LIFE INSURANCE COMPANY

Henderson, Alexa Benson. *Atlanta Life Insurance Company: Guardian of Black Economic Dignity.* Tuscaloosa: University of Alabama, 1990. 251 p.

ATLANTA SAW COMPANY

Brown, Edmund D. *1594 Evans Drive, S.W.: A History of Southern Saw Service, Inc. and the Atlanta Saw Company.* Atlanta, Ga.: The Company, 1983. 213 p.

THE ATLANTIC AND PACIFIC TEA COMPANY
SEE:
GREAT ATLANTIC AND PACIFIC TEA COMPANY

ATLANTIC AVIATION CORPORATION

Grangier, M. "Atlantic Aviation: A Front Runner for 50 Years." *Interavia* 32 (September 1977): 897-899.

ATLANTIC MUTUAL INSURANCE COMPANY

Cosgrove, John N. *Gray Days and Gold; A Character Sketch of Atlantic Mutual Insurance Company.* New York, N.Y.: Doremus and Company, 1967. 142 p.

ATLANTIC RECORDING CORPORATION

Gillett, Charlie. *Making Tracks; Atlantic Records and the Growth of a Multi-Billion-Dollar Industry*. New York, N.Y.: E.P.Dutton, 1974. 305 p.

ATLANTIC RICHFIELD COMPANY

Harris, Kenneth. *The Wildcatter: A Portrait of Robert O. Anderson*. New York, N.Y.: Weidenfeld & Nicolson, 1987. 180 p.

Jones, Charles S. *From the Rio Grande to the Arctic: The Story of the Richfield Oil Corporation*. Norman: University of Oklahoma Press, 1972. 364 p.

Shaner, J. Richard. "Arco Retreat a New Element in Normal Marketing Turmoil." *National Petroleum News* 77 (July 1985): 41-42.

ATLANTIC STEEL COMPANY

Kuniansky, Harry R. *A Business History of Atlantic Steel Company, 1901-1968*. New York, N.Y.: Arno Press, 1976. 395 p.

AUSTIN BRIDGE COMPANY

Miller, Shannon. *The First 50 Years, 1918-1968; Austin Bridge Company and Associated Companies*. Dallas, Tex.: Taylor Publishing Company, 1974. 204 p.

THE AUSTIN COMPANY

Greif, Martin. *The New Industrial Landscape: The Story of the Austin Company*. Clinton, N.J.: Main Street Press, 1978. 192 p.

Shirk, Charles A. *The Austin Company: A Century of Results*. New York, N.Y.: Newcomen Society in North America, 1978. 23 p. (Newcomen publication;

no.1085)

AUTOMOBILE CLUB OF SOUTHERN CALIFORNIA

Mathison, Richard R. *Three Cars in Every Garage, A Motorist's History of the Automobile and the Automobile Club in Southern California.* New York, N.Y: Doubleday, 1968. 257 p.

AVCO CORPORATION

Lawrence, Joanne T. *AVCO Corporation: The First Fifty Years.* Greenwich, Conn.: The Company, 1979. 106 p.

AVERY INTERNATIONAL

Avery, R. Stanton. *Avery International: Fifty Years of Progress.* New York, N.Y.: Newcomen Society of the United States, 1985, c1986. 28 p. (Newcomen publication; no. 1265)

AVON PRODUCTS, INC.

"Avon Calling." *Antiques & Collecting Hobbies* (July 1987): 77+

Bender, Marylin. "Avon: Ding-Dong-Down." In *At the Top; Behind the Scenes with the Men and Women Who Run America's Corporate Giants*, 21-42. Garden City, N.Y.: Doubleday, 1975.

Kleinfield, Sonny. *Staying at the Top: The Life of a CEO.* New York, N.Y: New American Library, 1986. 298 p.

AVONDALE MILLS

Smith, James C. *Avondale's Third Generation.* New York, N.Y.: Newcomen Society in North America, 1972. 20 p. (Newcomen address)

AVTEK CORPORATION

"On a Wing and a Prayer." *Inc.* 6 (August 1984): 37-44.

AVX CORPORATION

"How AVX Became No. 1 in Ceramic Capacitors." *Business Week (Industrial Edition)* (29 October 1979): 54J-54P.

AZTEC MANUFACTURING COMPANY

Berman, Phyllis. "Close to the Vest." *Forbes* 127 (27 April 1981): 102-104.

THE BABCOCK AND WILCOX COMPANY

The Babcock and Wilcox Company. *The Babcock and Wilcox Story, 1867-1967, 100 Years of Service to Industry.* New York, N.Y.: The Company, 1967. 80 p.

Nielsen, M. *The Babcock and Wilcox Company, 1867-1967: A Century of Progress.* New York, N.Y.: Newcomen Society in North America, 1967. 28 p. (Newcomen address)

BABSON (DAVID L.) AND COMPANY, INC.

Babson, David L. *David L. Babson and Company, Inc.* Newcomen Society in North America, 1978. 22 p. (Newcomen publication; no. 1094)

BACH REALTY, INC.

Kingston, Brett. "Deborah Lee Charatan of Bach Realty." In *The Dynamos: Who Are They Anyway?*, 153-155. New York, N.Y.: Wiley, 1987.

Taylor, Russel R. "Deborah Lee Charatan; She Made Millions Before Age Thirty." In *Exceptional Entrepreneurial Women*, 41-45. New York, N.Y.:

Quorum Books, 1988.

BACHE HALSEY STUART

Stevens, Mark. "Chicken McLaw: The Boys from Chicago." In *Power of Attorney: The Rise of the Giant Law Firms*, 153-178. New York, N.Y.: McGraw Hill, 1987.

Welles, Chris. "The Botching of Bache." *Institutional Investor* 14 (September 1980): 36-55.

BAKER INTERNATIONAL CORPORATION

Baker International Corporation. *The Baker Story*. Orange, Calif.: The Company, 1979. 33 p.

BALDWIN (D.H.) COMPANY

Baldwin (D.H.) Company. *Baldwin Marks 125 Years of Service to Music*. Cincinnati, Ohio: The Company, 1987. 8 p. (Reprinted from *The Music Trades Magazine*, June 1987)

Thompson, Morley P. *D.H. Baldwin; The Multibank Music Company*. New York, N.Y.: Newcomen Society in North America, 1974. 14 p.

BALDWIN-LIMA-HAMILTON CORPORATION

Dolzall, Gary W., and Stephen F. Dolzall. *Diesels from Eddystone: The Story of Baldwin Diesel Locomotives*. Milwaukee, Wis.: Kalmbach Publishing Company, 1984. 152 p.

Kirkland, John F. *The Diesel Builders: Fairbanks-Morse and Lima-Hamilton*. Glendale, Calif.: Interurban Press, 1985. 111 p.

BALDWIN LOCOMOTIVE WORKS

Dolzall, Gary W., and S. F. Dolzall. *Diesels from Eddystone: The Story of Baldwin Diesel Locomotives.* Milwaukee, Wis.: Kalmbach Publishing Company, 1984. 152 p.

Westing, Fred. *The Locomotives That Baldwin Built.* New York, N.Y.: Bonanza Books, 1966. 191 p.

BALL CORPORATION

Birmingham, Frederic A. *Ball Corporation: The First Century.* Indianapolis, Ind.: Curtis Publishing Company, 1980. 185 p.

Brantley, William F. *A Collector's Guide to Ball Jars.* Color photography by David A. Harris. Muncie, Ind.: R.H. Martin, 1975. 100 p.

Fisher, John W. *Managing Change; How to Grow a Modern Enterprise.* Muncie, Ind.: Ball State University Press, 1986. 184 p. (Ball State University Business History Series, no. 4)

BALLANTINE LABORATORIES, INC.

Voelcker, John. "Ballantine's Katzmann Measures Up." *IEEE Spectrum* 26 (April 1989): 44-47.

BALTIMORE AND OHIO RAILROAD COMPANY

Baltimore and Ohio Railroad Company. *The Story So Far: The Birth and Growth of America's Railroads.* Cleveland, Ohio: The Company, 1977. 32 p.

Bias, Charles V. "The Merger of the Chesapeake and Ohio Railway and the Baltimore and Ohio Railroad Companies." *Journal of the West Virginia Historical Association* 4 (1980): 24-34.

Harwood, Herbert H. *Impossible Challenge: The Baltimore & Ohio Railroad in Maryland.* Baltimore, Md.: Barnard, Roberts, 1979. 497 p.

Jacobs, Timothy. *The History of the Baltimore & Ohio: America's First Railroad.* New York, N.Y.: Crescent Books, Distributed by Crown Publishers, 1989.

Mellander, Deane. *B & O Thunder in the Alleghenies.* Newton, N.J.: Carstens, 1983. 80 p.

Stover, John F. "America's Pioneer Railroad--150 Years of B&O." *Railway Age* 178 (25 April 1977): 46-52.

Stover, John F. *History of the Baltimore and Ohio Railroad.* West Lafayette, Ind.: Purdue University Press, 1987. 419 p.

BALTIMORE ORIOLES

Hawkins, John C. *This Date in Baltimore Orioles and St. Louis Browns History.* New York, N.Y.: Stein and Day, 1983, c1982. 202 p.

Patterson, Ted. *Day by Day in Orioles History.* New York, N.Y.: Leisure Press, 1984. 207 p.

BALTIMORE SUN

Williams, Harold A. *The Baltimore Sun, 1837-1987.* Baltimore, Md.: Johns Hopkins University Press, 1987. 418 p.

BANCOHIO CORPORATION

Searle, Philip F. *BancOhio Corporation Since 1929; Ohio's Leader in the Multibank Holding Company Concept.* New York, N.Y.: Newcomen Society in North America, 1974. 30 p. (Newcomen publication; no. 980)

BANCROFT (JOSEPH) AND SONS COMPANY

Booth, John M. "An Organizational History of the Joseph Bancroft & Company Textile Firm with References to the Chandler." Thesis, University of Pennsylvania, 1973. 239 p.

BANDAG, INC.

Fucini, Joseph J., and Suzy Fucini. "Roy J. Carver, Bandag, Inc.: 'Conceive, Believe, Achieve.'" In *Experience Inc.; Men and Women Who Founded Famous Companies After the Age of 40*, 53-58. New York, N.Y: Free Press, 1987.

BANK OF AMERICA
SEE:
BANKAMERICA CORPORATION

BANK OF BOSTON CORPORATION

U.S. Congress. Senate. Committee on Governmental Affairs. Permanent Subcommittee on Investigations. *Domestic Money Laundering, The First National Bank of Boston: Hearings before the Permanent Subcommittee on Investigations*. 99th Cong., Ist sess., 12 March 1984

Williams, Ben A. *Bank of Boston 200: A History of New England's Leading Bank, 1784-1984*. Boston, Mass.: Houghton Mifflin, 1984. 480 p.

BANK OF NEW MEXICO

Clark, Wilfred A. *History of the Bank of New Mexico: The Past Is Prologue*. New York, N.Y: Newcomen Society in North America, 1972. 23 p. (Newcomen address)

BANK OF NEW YORK

Fitch, Thomas P. "Two Hundred Years of Looking Ahead." *United States Banker* 95 (July 1984): 31-34.

BANK OF VIRGINIA

Bank of Virginia. *Bank of Virginia: A Unique Heritage for the Future*. Richmond: The Bank, 1981. 8 p.

Wessells, John H. *The Bank of Virginia: A History*. Charlottesville: University of Virginia Press, 1973. 192 p.

BANKAMERICA CORPORATION

Hector, Gary. *Breaking the Bank: The Decline of BankAmerica*. Boston, Mass.: Little, Brown & Company, 1988. 363 p.

Johnston, Moira. *Roller Coaster; The Bank of America and the Future of American Banking*. New York, N.Y.: Ticknor & Fields, 1990. 406 p.

THE BANKER MAGAZINE

"Our First 60 Years." *Banker* 136 (January 1986): 79-101.

BANKERS LIFE AND CASUALTY COMPANY

Darby, Edwin. "MacArthur." In *The Fortune Builders*, 117-135. Garden City, N.Y.: Doubleday and Company, Inc., 1986.

Wall, Joseph Frazier. *Policies and People; The First Hundred Years of the Bankers Life*. Englewood Cliffs, N.J.: Prentice Hall, 1979. 192 p.

BANKERS SECURITY LIFE INSURANCE SOCIETY

Schultz, Leslie P. *Pioneering in Life Insurance: The Story of Bankers Security Life Insurance Society.* New York, N.Y.: Newcomen Society in North America, 1967. 28 p. (Newcomen address)

BANKERS TRUST COMPANY

Bankers Trust Company. *Bankers Trust Company: 75 Years.* New York, N.Y.: The Bank, 1978. 60 p.

BANTAM BOOKS, INC.

Peterson, Clarence. *The Bantam Story: Thirty Years of Paperback Publishing.* New York, N.Y.: Bantam Books, 1975. 167 p.

Peterson, Clarence. *The Bantam Story; Twenty-Five Years of Paperback Publishing.* New York, N.Y.: Bantam Books, 1970. 118 p.

BAR HARBOR BANKING AND TRUST COMPANY

Marmon, Edward Lee. *Taking Care of Business Down East; The History of the Bar Harbor Banking and Trust Company, 1887-1987.* Boston, Mass.: Graphic Chronologies, 1987. 168 p.

BARBER-GREENE COMPANY

Barber-Greene Company. *Our First Five Decades.* Aurora, Illinois: The Company, 1966. 63 p.

BARNETT BANK OF JACKSONVILLE

Barnett Bank of Jacksonville. *Barnett: A Century of Tradition.* Jacksonville, Fla.: The Bank, 1977. 31 p.

BARNEYS NEW YORK

Stern, E. "Behold the Rising Sons." *GQ* 60 (March 1990):
300+

BARONS OIL LTD.

Zwarun, Suzanne. "The Best Little Oil Company in the
West." *Canadian Business* 58 (October 1985): 38-43,
135-137.

BAROUH-EATON ALLEN CORPORATION

Richman, Tom. "One Man's Family." *Inc.* 5 (November
1983): 151-156.

BARRY (R.G.) CORPORATION

R.G. Barry Corporation. *Thirty Years of Progress
Through People*. Columbus: The Company, 1977. 5 p.
(Also published in the 1977 March/April issue of *It's
The Barry's* the company magazine)

BARTON-MALLOW COMPANY

Maibach, Ben C., Jr. *Barton-Mallow over 60 Years Old*.
Detroit, Mich.: The Company, 1986. 51 p.

BASKAHEGAN COMPANY

Milliken, Roger, Jr. *Forest for the Trees: A History of the
Baskahegan Company*. Augusta, Maine: R. Milliken,
1983. 140 p.

BASS (D.C.) AND SONS CONSTRUCTION

Bass, Henry Benjamin. *The First 75 Years: D.C. Bass &
Sons Construction Company, 1893-1968*. Oklahoma
City, Okla.: Colorgraphics, 1969. 114 p.

BASS PRO SHOPS

MacPhee, William. "John L. Morris of Bass Pro Shops." In *Rare Breed: The Entrepreneur, An American Culture*, 105-114. Chicago, Ill.: Probus Publishing Company, 1987.

BATTELLE MEMORIAL INSTITUTE

Boehm, George A., and A. Groner. *Science in the Service of Mankind: The Battelle Story*. Lexington, Mass.: Lexington Books, 1972. 132 p.

Fawcett, Sherwood L. *Battelle Memorial Institute: On The Cutting Edge of the Future*. New York, N.Y.: Newcomen Society in North America, 1980. 28 p. (Newcomen publication; no. 1113)

BAXTER INTERNATIONAL

Baxter International. *Baxter: A History of Health-Care Leadership*. Deerfield, Ill.: The Company, 1985. 2 p.

Baxter International. *Over Half a Century of Innovating for Life*. Deerfield, Ill.: The Company, 1981. 7 p.

BAYBANKS

Crozier, William M. *BayBanks*. New York, N.Y.: Newcomen Society of the United States, 1988, c1989. 19 p. (Newcomen publication; no. 1320)

BAYFRONT MEDICAL CENTER

Albright, James W. *Bayfront Medical Center: Caring for the Community*. New York, N.Y.: Newcomen Society of the United States, 1989. 21 p. (Newcomen publication; no. 1340)

BE&K, INC.

BE&K, Inc. *History*. Birmingham, Ala.: The Company, 1988. 3 p.

BEAN (L.L.), INC.

Gorman, Leon A. *L.L. Bean, Inc.: Outdoor Specialties by Mail From Maine*. New York, N.Y.: Newcomen Society in North America, 1981. 23 p. (Newcomen publication; no. 1154)

Montgomery, M.R. *In Search of L.L. Bean*. New York, N.Y.: New American Library, 1985, c1984. 244 p.

BEARINGS, INC.

Bruening, Joseph M. *Keeping Industry in Motion for Fifty Years: The Story of Bearings, Inc.* New York, N.Y.: Newcomen Society in North America, 1973. 15 p.

BEATRICE FOOD COMPANY

Beatrice Food Company. *The Beatrice Food Story*. Chicago, Ill.: The Company, 1977. 16 p.

Gazel, Neil R. *Beatrice: From Buildup Through Breakup*. Urbana: University of Illinois Press, 1990. 264 p.

BEAUTY STORE AND MORE

"King: Grooming for Success." *Chain Store Age Executive* 63 (March 1987): 43-46.

BECHTEL GROUP, INC.

Dowie, Mark. "The Bechtel File [History and Current Operations of the Engineering and Construction Firm]." *Mother Jones* 3 (September/October 1978): 28-38.

Ingram, Robert Lockwood. *The Bechtel Story; Seventy Years of Accomplishment in Engineering and Construction*. San Francisco, Calif.: The Company, 1968. 157 p.

McCartney, Laton. *Friends in High Places: The Bechtel Story; The Most Secret Corporation and How It Engineered the World*. New York, N.Y.: Simon & Schuster, 1988. 273 p.

THE BECK ENGRAVING COMPANY, INC.

Beck, George P. *The Economy of Excellence: The Story of the Beck Engraving Company*. New York, N.Y.: Newcomen Society in North America, 1966. 24 p. (Newcomen address)

BECKMAN INSTRUMENTS, INC.

Beckman, Arnold O. *Beckman Instruments, Inc.: "There Is No Satisfactory Substitute for Excellence."* New York, N.Y.: Newcomen Society in North America, 1976. 38 p. (Newcomen publication; no. 1032)

Stephens, Harrison. *Golden Past, Golden Future: The First Fifty Years of Beckman Instruments, Inc.* Claremont, Calif.: Claremont University Center, 1985. 144 p.

BEDFORD-STUYVESANT RESTORATION CORPORATION

Stein, Barry. *Rebuilding Bedford-Stuyvesant: Community Economic Development in the Ghetto*. Cambridge, Mass.: Center for Community Economic Development, 1975. 37 p.

BEECH AIRCRAFT CORPORATION

Hedrick, Frank E. *Pageantry of Flight: The Story of Beech Aircraft Corporation*. New York, N.Y.:

Newcomen Society in North America, 1967. 34 p. (Newcomen address)

McDaniel, William Herbert. *The History of Beech.* Wichita, Kan.: McCormick-Armstrong Company, Publishing Division, 1971. 336 p.

BEKINS VAN LINES COMPANY

Whiteson, Leon. "Bekins: A Storehouse of History." *Los Angeles Times*, 1 March 1989, sec. V, p. 5.

BELK STORES SERVICES

Covington, Howard E. *Belk: A Century of Retail Leadership.* Chapel Hill, N.C.: University of North Carolina Press, 1988. 308 p.

BELL AND BECKWITH

Brickey, Homer. *Master Manipulator.* New York, N.Y.: AMACOM, 1985. 161 p.

BELL AND HOWELL COMPANY

Robinson, Jack Fay. *Bell & Howell Company: A 75-Year History.* Chicago, Ill.: The Company, 1982. 175 p.

BELL TELEPHONE LABORATORIES, INC.

Bernstein, Jeremy. *Three Degrees Above Zero: Bell Labs in the Information Age.* New York, N.Y.: Scribner's, 1984. 241 p.

Gregor, Arthur. *Bell Laboratories; Inside the World's Largest Communication Center.* New York, N.Y.: Scribner, 1972. 125 p.

Mabon, Prescott C. *Mission Communications, The Story of Bell Laboratories.* Murray Hill, N.J.: The Labs, 1975. 198 p.

Morton, Jack Andrew. *Organizing for Innovation; A Systems Approach to Technical Management.* New York, N.Y.: McGraw-Hill, 1971. 171 p.

Mueser, Roland. *Bell Laboratories Innovation in Telecommunications, 1925-1977.* Prepared by members of the technical staff, Bell Laboratories, Inc. Murray Hill, N.J.: Technical Documentation Dept., Bell Laboratories, 1979. 227 p.

BENDEL (HENRI) ASSOCIATES

Taylor, Russel R. "Geraldine Stutz; She Bought the Store." In *Exceptional Entrepreneurial Women*, 33-39. New York, N.Y.: Quorum Books, 1988.

THE BENDIX CORPORATION

Cunningham, Mary. *Powerplay: What Really Happened at Bendix.* New York, N.Y.: Linden Press/Simon & Schuster, 1984. 286 p.

Fontaine, A.P. *Where Ideas Unlock the Future: The Story of the Bendix Corporation.* New York, N.Y.: Newcomen Society in North America, 1967. 28 p. (Newcomen address)

Hartz, Peter F. *Merger; The Exclusive Inside Story of the Bendix-Martin-Marietta Takeover War.* New York, N.Y.: Morrow, 1985. 418 p.

Lambert, Hope. *Till Death Do Us Part: Bendix vs Martin Marietta.* San Diego, Calif.: Harcourt Brace Jovanovich, 1983. 264 p.

Sloan, Allan. *Three Plus One Equals Billions: The Bendix-Martin Marietta War.* New York, N.Y.: Arbor House, 1983. 270 p.

BENEFICIAL CORPORATION

Williams, George M. *You're Good for More: The Story of Beneficial Corporation, 1913-1975.* s.l.: Haddon Craftsmen, 1977. 338 p.

BENHAM-BLAIR AND AFFILIATES, INC.

Benham, David Blair. *One Good Job Leads to Another: The Story of Benham-Blair and Affiliates, Inc.* New York, N.Y.: Newcomen Society in North America, 1979. 24 p. (Newcomen publication; no. 1108)

BENIHANA NATIONAL CORPORATION

McCallum, Jack. *Making It in America: The Life and Times of Rocky Aoki, Benihana's Pioneer.* New York, N.Y.: Dodd Mead and Company, 1985. 165 p.

BENTON AND BOWLES, INC.

Danzig, Fred. "Benton & Bowles, At 50, Likes Quiet Consistency." *Advertising Age* 50 (16 July 1979): 3+

BERRY (L.M.) AND COMPANY

Berry, Loren M. *L.M. Berry and Company 1910-1971: A People Company.* New York, N.Y.: Newcomen Society in North America, 1971. 24 p. (Newcomen address)

BESSEMER AND LAKE ERIE RAILROAD COMPANY

Beaver, Roy C. *Bessemer & Lake Erie Railroad, 1819-1969.* San Marino, Calif.: Golden West Books, 1969. 184 p.

BEST (A.M.) COMPANY, INC.

Fenske, Doris. "The Birth of a Magazine." *Best's Review (Property/Casualty)* 91 (June 1990): 20-24.

BETHLEHEM STEEL CORPORATION

Bethlehem Steel Corporation. *A Brief History of Bethlehem Steel Corporation*. Bethlehem, Pa.: The Company, 1988. 13 p.

Bethlehem Steel Corporation. *Recollections: In Celebration of 75 Years*. Bethlehem, Pa.: The Company, 1979. 33 p.

Hessen, Robert. *Steel Titan: The Life of Charles M. Schwab*. New York, N.Y.: Oxford University Press, 1975. 350 p.

Leary, Thomas E. *From Fire to Rust: Business, Technology and Work at the Lackawanna Steel Plant, 1899-1983*. Buffalo, N.Y.: Buffalo and Erie County Historical Society, 1987. 134 p.

Martin, Edmund F. *Promise for the Future*. New York, N.Y.: Newcomen Society in North America, 1967. 16 p. (Newcomen address)

Sethi, S. Prakash. *Bethlehem Steel Corporation: Advocacy or Idea/Issue Advertising Campaign*. Richardson, Tex.: Center for Business and Social Policy, University of Texas at Dallas, 1982. 65 p. (Special report / UTD Center for Research in Business and Social Policy)

Strohmeyer, John. *Crisis in Bethlehem; Big Steel's Struggle to Survive*. New York, N.Y.: Penguin Books, 1986. 244 p.

BIG SKY OF MONTANA, INC.

Thompson, Layton S. *Increased Tax Base and Increased Costs of Public Services Resulting Directly from Economic Development: A Case Study Involving Big Sky of Montana, Inc.* Bozeman: Montana Agricultural Experiment Station, Montana State University, 1976.

34 p.

BINGHAM FAMILY
SEE:
LOUISVILLE COURIER JOURNAL

BINNEY AND SMITH, INC.

"Crayola's True Colors." *Town & Country* (December 1987): 94+

BIRDS EYE FROZEN FOODS

Cleary, David Powers. "Birds Eye Frozen Foods; You've Got a Great Idea--If You Can Make It Work." In *Great American Brands: The Success Formulas That Made Them Famous*, 7-12. New York, N.Y: Fairchild Publications, 1981.

THE BIRMINGHAM NEWS

Hanson, Clarence B., Jr. *The Story of the Birmingham News: A Good Newspaper.* New York, N.Y: Newcomen Society in North America, 1967. 24 p. (Newcomen address)

BIRTCHER REALTY CORPORATION

St. George, Karen. "Birtcher Continues Its Tradition As a Family Business; Attention to Detail Still Held Sacred After 50 Years." *National Real Estate Investor* 31 (April 1989): 93-96, 179.

BISSELL CARPET SWEEPERS

Cleary, David Powers. "Bissell Carpet Sweepers; To Live Up to Our Ideals, We Must Keep Clean." In *Great American Brands: The Success Formulas That Made Them Famous*, 13-18. New York, N.Y: Fairchild Publications, 1981.

BIXLER'S

Buchholz, Barbara B., and Margaret Crane. "Bixler's, Easton, PA." In *Corporate Blood Lines: The Future of the Family Firm*, 78-91. New York, N.Y.: Carol Publishing Group, 1989.

BLACK AND DECKER MANUFACTURING COMPANY

Black and Decker Manufacturing Company. *Highlights of Progress*. Towson, Md.: The Company, 1981. 30 p.

Cleary, David Powers. "Black & Decker Power Tools; No Idea Is Worth Anything Unless You Have the Guts to Back It Up." In *Great American Brands: The Success Formulas That Made Them Famous*, 19-23. New York, N.Y.: Fairchild Publications, 1981.

Scott, Otto J. *The Powered Hand: History of the Black and Decker Manufacturing Company*. New York, N.Y.: McGraw Hill, 1972.

BLACK AND VEATCH, INC.

Robinson, Thomas B. *Black and Veatch: Consulting Engineers; A Back-Sight at 63 Years of Growth*. New York, N.Y.: Newcomen Society in North America, 1970. 31 p. (Newcomen address)

BLACK CLAWSON COMPANY

Landegger, Karl F. *Growing with the Paper Industry Since 1853: The Parsons and Whittemore Organization and the Black Clawson Company*. New York, N.Y.: Newcomen Society in North America, 1968. 24 p. (Newcomen address)

BLACK ENTERPRISE
SEE:
GRAVES (EARL G.) LTD.

BLAKE-LAMB FUNERAL HOMES

Buchholz, Barbara B., and Margaret Crane. "Blake-Lamb Funeral Homes, Oak Park, IL." In *Corporate Blood Lines: The Future of the Family Firm*, 212-228. New York, N.Y.: Carol Publishing Group, 1989.

BLISS AND LAUGHLIN INDUSTRIES

Robbins, Frederic J. *"The Performance of Change": The Story of Bliss and Laughlin Industries.* New York, N.Y.: Newcomen Society in North America, 1968. 28 p. (Newcomen address)

BLOCK (H&R)

Goldwasser, Thomas. "H&R Block: Helping People with Taxing Issues." In *Family Pride; Profiles of Five of America's Best-Run Family Businesses*, 125-162. New York, N.Y.: Dodd, Mead and Company, 1986.

BLOOMINGDALE'S

Brady, Maxine. *Bloomingdale's.* New York, N.Y.: Harcourt Brace Jovanovich, 1980. 229 p.

Stevens, Mark. *"Like No Other Store in the World": The Inside Story of Bloomingdale's.* New York, N.Y.: Crowell, 1979. 224 p.

BLOUNT, INC.

Blount, Winton M. *The Blount Story: "American Enterprise at Its Best."* New York, N.Y.: Newcomen Society in North America, 1980. 23 p. (Newcomen publication; no. 1114)

BLUE CROSS AND BLUE SHIELD CORPORATION
SEE:
HOSPITAL CORPORATION OF AMERICA

BLUMENFELD SPORTS NET (BSN)

Heller, Matthew. "The Up & Comers: The Renegade Man." *Forbes* 136 (18 November 1985): 66-67.

BOB EVANS FARMS

Bob Evans Farms. *The Bob Evans Story*. Columbus, Ohio: The Company, 1985. 4 p.

Bob Evans Farms. *The Bob Evans Story*. Columbus, Ohio: The Company, 1986. 4 p.

BOBBS-MERRILL COMPANY

O'Bar, Jack. *Origins and History of the Bobbs-Merrill Company*. Urbana: Graduate School of Library and Information Science, University of Illinois, 1985.

BODINE CORPORATION

Bodine, Richard P. *A Man and His Machines: The Story of Alfred Van Sante Bodine and the Bodine Corporation*. New York, N.Y.: Newcomen Society in North America, 1982. 34 p. (Newcomen publication; no. 1183)

BOEHM PORCELAIN STUDIOS

MacPhee, William. "Helen F. Boehm of the Boehm Porcelain Studios." In *Rare Breed: The Entrepreneur, An American Culture*, 49-65. Chicago, Ill.: Probus Publishing Company, 1987.

THE BOEING COMPANY

The Boeing Company. *Background Information*. Seattle, Wash.: The Company, 1984. 31 p.

Boyne, Walter J. *Boeing B-52, A Documentary History*. London, England: Jane's Pub. Co. Ltd., 1981. 160 p.

Hardy, Michael John. *Boeing.* New York, N.Y.: Beufort Books, 1984, c1982. 86 p.

Ingells, Douglas J. *747: Story of the Boeing Super Jet.* Fallbrook, Calif.: Aero Pub., 1970. 272 p.

Kuter, Laurence S. *The Great Gamble: The Boeing 747; The Boeing-Pan AM Project to Develop, Produce, And Introduce the 747.* University, Ala.: University of Alabama Press, 1973. 134 p.

Mansfield, Harold. *Vision, the Story of Boeing; A Saga of the Sky and the New Horizons of Space.* New York, N.Y.: Popular Library, 1966. 383 p.

Munson, Kenneth G. *Boeing.* New York, N.Y.: Arco Publishing Company, 1971. 144 p.

Norris, William. *Willful Misconduct: An Untold Story.* New York, N.Y.: Norton, 1984. 290 p.

BOISE CASCADE CORPORATION

Boschken, Herman L. *Corporate Power and the Mismarketing of Urban Development: Boise Cascade Recreation Communities.* New York, N.Y.: Praeger, 1974. 283 p.

Churchill, Samuel. *Don't Call Me Ma.* Garden City, N.Y.: Doubleday, 1977. 201 p.

BOOK-OF-THE-MONTH CLUB

Kaplan, J. "Inside the Club." *New York Times Magazine* (11 June 1989): 62+

THE BOOKSTOP

Buchholz, Barbara B., and Margaret Crane. "Bookstop, Austin, TX." In *Corporate Blood Lines: The Future of the Family Firm*, 145-159. New York, N.Y.: Carol

Publishing Group, 1989.

BORDEN COMPANY

Wade, Mary Dodson. *Milk, Meat, Biscuits and the Terraqueous Machine; The Story of Gail Borden.* Austin, Tex.: Eakin Press, 1987. 49 p.

BORLAND INTERNATIONAL

Kingston, Brett. "Philippe Kahn of Borland International." In *The Dynamos: Who Are They Anyway?*, 123-127. New York, N.Y.: Wiley, 1987.

BORMAN'S, INC.

Borman's, Inc. *Farmer Jack's 50th Birthday, 1927-1977.* Detroit, Mich.: The Company, 1977. 12 p.

BOSTON BANK OF COMMERCE

Patterson, Gregg. "B.E. Bank of the Year: Banking on Boston." *Black Enterprise* 16 (June 1986): 150-154.

BOSTON CELTICS

Henshaw, Tom. *The Boston Celtics: A Championship Tradition.* Englewood Cliffs, N.J.: Prentice-Hall, 1974. 127 p.

Tyan, Bob. *Boston Celtics: The History, Legends and Images of America's Most Celebrated Team.* Reading, Mass.: Addison-Wesley, 1989.

BOSTON EDISON COMPANY

Boston Edison Company. *Centennial: 1886-1986; One Hundred Years in Review.* Boston, Mass.: The Company, 1986. 14 p.

THE BOSTON GLOBE

Lyons, Louis M. *Newspaper Story: One Hundred Years of the Boston Globe.* Cambridge, Mass.: Belknap Press, 1971. 482 p.

BOSTON RED SOX

Clark, Ellery H. *Boston Red Sox: Seventy-Fifth Anniversary History, 1901-1975.* Hicksville, N.Y.: Exposition Press, 1975. 168 p.

Frommer, Harvey. *Baseball's Greatest Rivalry: The New York Yankees and Boston Red Sox.* New York, N.Y.: Atheneum, 1982. 159 p.

Honig, Donald. *The Boston Red Sox: An Illustrated History.* Englewood Cliffs, N.J.: Prentice-Hall, 1990. 256 p.

Valenti, Dan. *From Florida to Fenway.* Pittsfield, Mass.: Literations, 1982. 141 p.

Walton, Ed. *Red Sox Triumphs and Tragedies: A Continuation of Day by Day Listings and Events in the History of the Boston American League Baseball Team.* New York, N.Y.: Stein and Day, 1980. 380 p.

BOVAY ENGINEERS, INC.

Bovay, Harry E., Jr. *Bovay Engineers, Inc.: The Cutting Edge of Technology.* New York, N.Y.: Newcomen Society in North America, 1982. 23 p. (Newcomen publication; no. 1166)

BOWERY SAVINGS BANK

Schisgall, Oscar. *The Bowery Savings Bank of New York; A Social and Financial History.* New York, N.Y.: AMACOM, 1984. 402 p.

Schisgall, Oscar. *Out of One Small Chest: A Social and Financial History of the Bowery Savings Bank.* New York, N.Y.: AMACOM, 1975. 312 p.

BOWMAN (E.G.) COMPANY

Iverem, E. "Wall Street Success Story." *Essence* (October 1988): 130+

BOYERTOWN AUTO BODY WORKS

Hafer, Erminie Shaeffer. *A Century of Vehicle Craftsmanship.* Boyertown, Pa.: Hafer Foundation, 1972. 264 p.

BRADLEY (MILTON) COMPANY

Shea, James J., Jr. *The Milton Bradley Story.* New York, N.Y.: Newcomen Society in North America, 1973. 24 p. (Newcomen address)

BRAINRESERVE

Taylor, Russel R. "Faith Popcorn; She Discerns the Future." In *Exceptional Entrepreneurial Women*, 25-31. New York, N.Y.: Quorum Books, 1988.

BRANIFF AIRWAYS

Braniff, Inc. *Braniff's First 50 Years, 1928-1978.* Dallas, Tex.: The Company, 1978. 16 p.

Nance, John J. *Splash of Colors: The Self-Destruction of Braniff International.* New York, N.Y.: Morrow, 1984. 426 p.

BRIGGS AND STRATTON CORPORATION

Briggs and Stratton Corporation. *The History of Briggs & Stratton Corporation.* Milwaukee, Wis.: The Company, 197?. 10 p.

Briggs and Stratton Corporation. *The History of Briggs & Stratton Corporation.* Milwaukee: The Company, 1985. 25 p.

BRIGHTON FINANCIAL PLANNING, INC.

White, Richard T. "A Slow Blossoming." *Financial Planning* 14 (July 1985): 171-173.

BRINK'S, INC.

Behn, Noel. *Big Stick-Up at Brink's!* New York, N.Y.: Putnam, 1977. 384 p.

BROADMOOR HOTEL, INC.

Tutt, William Thayer. *The Broadmoor Story.* New York, N.Y.: Newcomen Society in North America, 1969. 24 p. (Newcomen address)

BROCKWAY GLASS COMPANY, INC.

Brockway Glass Company, Inc. *A History of Brockway, Inc.* Brockway, Pa.: The Company, 1985. 14 p.

Brockway Glass Company, Inc. *Brockway: Serving Growth Industries for 75 Years.* Brockway, Pa.: The Company, 1982. 17 p.

BROOKLYN UNION GAS

Larson, Elwin S. *Brooklyn Union Gas: Fueling Growth and Change in New York City.* New York, N.Y.: Newcomen Society of the United States, 1987. 23 p. (Newcomen publication; no. 1286)

BROWN BROTHERS, HARRIMAN AND COMPANY

Finn, Edwin A., Jr., and Jack Willoughby. "Living in the Past." *Forbes* 142 (11 July 1988): 64-72.

Kouwenhoven, John A. *Partners in Banking, An Historical Portrait of a Great Private Bank, Brown Brothers Harriman and Company*. New York, N.Y.: Doubleday, 1968. 248 p.

BROWN-FORMAN DISTILLERS CORPORATION

Lucas, William F. *"Nothing Better in the Market": Brown-Forman's Century of Quality 1870-1970*. New York, N.Y.: Newcomen Society in North America, 1970. 32 p. (Newcomen address)

Hallgarten & Company, New York. *The Distilling Industry in the United States, With Particular Reference to Brown-Forman Distillers Corporation, Distillers Corporation-Seagrams Limited, Hiram Walker-Gooderham and Worts Limited*. New York, N.Y.: Hallgarten & Co., 1968. 68 p.

Pearce, John E. *Nothing Better in the Market*. Louisville: The Company, 1970. 96 p. (Double golden 100th anniversary)

BROWN GROUP, INC.

Brown Group, Inc. *The First Hundred Years*. St. Louis, Mo.: The Company, 1978. 72 p.

Cleary, David Powers. "Buster Brown Shoes; Kids of Six Today Are Smarter Than They Used to Be at Twelve." In *Great American Brands: The Success Formulas That Made Them Famous*, 36-39. New York, N.Y.: Fairchild Publications, 1981.

BROWN (K.J.) AND COMPANY

Geelhoed, E. Bruce. *Bringing Wall Street to Main Street: The Story of K.J. Brown and Company, Inc., 1931-1981*. Muncie, Ind.: Bureau of Business and Research, College of Business, and Department of History, Ball State University, 1981. 59 p. (Ball State

University Business History Series; no.1)

BROWNING-FERRIS INDUSTRIES

Browning-Ferris Industries. *BFI Corporate History*. Houston, Tex.: The Company, 1985. 6 p.

Browning-Ferris Industries. *50 Years of People*. Houston, Tex.: The Company, 1975. 4 p.

Gilder, George. "The Dynamics of Entrepreneurship." In *The Spirit of Enterprise*, 245-258. New York, N.Y.: Simon and Schuster, 1984.

BRUNING (CHARLES) COMPANY

Addressograph Multigraph Corporation. *Today at Bruning*. Mt. Prospect, Ill.: Charles Bruning Company, 1966. 14 p.

SEE ALSO: ADDRESSOGRAPH MULTIGRAPH CORPORATION

BRUNO'S, INC.

Bruno, Joseph S. *All the Best for 57 Years*. New York, N.Y.: Newcomen Society of the United States, c1989, 1990. 24 p. (Newcomen publication; no. 1335)

BRUNSON, DOROTHY

Taylor, Russel R. "Dorothy Brunson; Revolutionary of Radio." In *Exceptional Entrepreneurial Women*, 103-109. New York, N.Y.: Quorum Books, 1988.

BRUNSWICK CORPORATION

Murphy, H. Lee. "Oldest Sporting-Goods Maker Builds on Its Athletic Foundation." *Illinois Business* (Autumn 1984): 62-63.

BRYAN FOODS, INC.

Bryan, George W. *The Bryan Foods Story.* New York, N.Y.: Newcomen Society in North America, 1983. 17 p. (Newcomen publication; no. 1193)

BUCKEYE FEDERAL SAVINGS AND LOAN ASSOCIATION

Guthrie, William S. *The Buckeye; A Community Institution.* New York, N.Y.: Newcomen Society in North America, 1970. 31 p.

BUCKEYE INTERNATIONAL

Blackford, Mansel G. *A Portrait Cast in Steel: Buckeye International and Columbus, Ohio, 1881-1980.* Westport, Conn.: Greenwood Press, 1982. 225 p.

BUCYRUS-ERIE COMPANY

Anderson, George. *One Hundred Booming Years: A History of Bucyrus-Erie Company, 1880-1980.* South Milwaukee, Wis.: The Company, 1980. 303 p.

THE BUDD COMPANY

Kerr, James W. *Illustrated Treasury of Budd Railway Passenger Cars: World's Foremost Builder of Railway Passenger Cars, 1931-1981, Fiftieth Anniversary.* Alburg, Vt.: Delta Publishing Associates Division, DPA-LTA Enterprises, 1981. 250 p.

Richard, Gilbert F. *"Budd on the Move": Innovation for a Nation on Wheels.* New York, N.Y.: Newcomen Society in North America, 1975. 20 p. (Newcomen publication; no. 1008)

BUDWEISER BEER
SEE:
ANHEUSER-BUSCH

BUFFALO BILLS

Pitoniak, Scott. *The Buffalo Bills Official Trivia Book.* New York: St. Martin, 1989. 128 p.

BUFFALO SAVINGS BANK

Harder, William H. *The Life and Times of Buffalo Savings Bank: Through 125 Years.* New York, N.Y.: Newcomen Society in North America, 1971. 24 p. (Newcomen address)

BUILDINGS; THE CONSTRUCTION AND BUILDING MANAGEMENT JOURNAL

"Our First 75 Years." *Buildings* 75 (September 1981): 50-63+

BURGER KING CORPORATION

Alexander, Larry D., and Thomas W. Ripp. "Burger King's Battle for the Burgers." *Journal of Management Case Studies* 3 (Spring 1987): 27-47.

BURLINGTON INDUSTRIES, INC.

Burlington Industries, Inc. *A Portrait of the World's Largest and Most Diversified Textile Company.* New York, N.Y.: The Company, 1966. 49 p.

BURLINGTON NORTHERN, INC.

Dorin, Patrick C. *Everything West: The Burlington Route.* Seattle, Wash.: Superior Publishing Company, 1976. 171 p.

BURNETT (LEO) COMPANY

"Special Report: 50 Years of Reaching for the Stars - Leo Burnett, 1935-1985." *Advertising Age* 56 (1 August 1985): 15-48.

BURPEE (W. ATLEE) COMPANY

Pechter, Kerry. "Profile of a Hardy American Perennial: The W. Atlee Burpee Company is Back in Private Hands and Hoping to Cultivate Once Again the Entrepreneurial Spirit of D.B." *Across the Board* 24 (June 1987): 59-62.

Seipp, C. "Growth Enterprise." *Discover* 11 (August 1990): 72+

BURROUGHS CORPORATION

MacDonald, Ray W. *Strategy for Growth: The Story of Burroughs Corporation*. New York, N.Y.: Newcomen Society in North America, 1978. 28 p. (Newcomen publication; no.1076)

BURROUGHS WELLCOME COMPANY

Coe, Fred A. *Burroughs Wellcome Company, 1880-1980: Pioneer of Pharmaceutical Research*. New York, N.Y.: Newcomen Society in North America, 1980. 24 p. (Newcomen publication; no. 1127)

BUSINESS MEN'S ASSURANCE COMPANY OF AMERICA

Grant, William Downing. *Aiming High: The 75-Year Story of Business Men's Assurance Company of America*. New York, N.Y.: Newcomen Society of the United States, 1984. 28 p. (Newcomen publication; no. 1217)

Grant, W.D. *From Jalopies to Jets--Sixty Exciting Years of Growth: The Story of Business Men's Assurance Company*. New York, N.Y.: Newcomen Society in North America, 1969. 28 p. (Newcomen address)

BUSINESSLAND, INC.

Fucini, Joseph J., and Suzy Fucini. "David A. Norman, Businessland, Inc.: 'There Was an Opportunity to Build a Very Large Company Very Quickly in a Whole New Industry.'" In *Experience Inc.; Men and Women Who Founded Famous Companies After the Age of 40*, 105-111. New York, N.Y.: Free Press, 1987.

BUSTER BROWN SHOES
SEE:
BROWN GROUP, INC.

BUTCHER AND COMPANY

Butcher, Jonathan. *Butcher and Company: Serving the American Investment Community for 75 Years*. New York, N.Y.: Newcomen Society of the United States, 1985. 20 p. (Newcomen publication; no. 1235)

BUTCHER, JACOB F.

Adams, James Ring. "The Butcher Revels." In *The Big Fix: Inside the S&L Scandal: How an Unholy Alliance of Politics and Money Destroyed America's Banking System*, 87-124. New York, N.Y.: Wiley, 1990.

CABOT CORPORATION

"Cabot Centenial." In *Cabot Corporation. Annual Report*, 2-22. Boston, Mass.: The Company, 1982.

Cabot Corporation. *Cabot 100*. Boston, Mass.: The Company, 1982. 16 p.

CADE INDUSTRIES

Kingston, Brett. "John Cade of Cade Industries/EDAC Technologies." In *The Dynamos: Who Are They Anyway?*, 189-194. New York, N.Y.: Wiley, 1987.

CAJUN ELECTRIC POWER COOPERATIVE, INC.

Cajun Electric Power Cooperative, Inc. *Cajun Overview*. Baton Rouge, La.: The Company, 1987. 7 p.

CALCOT, LTD.

Calcot, Ltd. *The First Fifty Years*. Bakersfield, Calif.: The Company, 1977. 12 p.

CALDWELL AND COMPANY

McFerrin, John Berry. *Caldwell and Company, A Southern Financial Empire*. Nashville, Tenn.: Vanderbilt University Press, 1969. 284 p.

CALDWELL (J.E.) AND COMPANY

Green, Joseph Hugh. *Jewelers to Philadelphia and the World: 125 Years on Chestnut Street*. New York, N.Y.: Newcomen Society in North America, 1965. 24 p. (Newcomen address)

Meyer, Linde. *The J.E. Caldwell Story: When Once Bought, Worth Keeping*. New York, N.Y.: Newcomen Society of the United States, c1989, 1990. 24 p. (Newcomen publication; no. 1334)

CALFED, INC.

CalFed, Inc. *Historical Highlights*. Los Angeles, Calif.: The Company, 1989. 8 p.

SEE ALSO: CALIFORNIA FEDERAL SAVINGS AND LOAN ASSOCIATION

CALIBRAKE, INC.

Richman, Tom. "Private Lives: Profiles from the Inc. 500--#319: Calibrake, Inc." *Inc.* 7 (December 1985): 72, 77.

THE CALIFORNIA AERO COMPANY

Cull, George E. "The LARK-95." *American Aviation Historical Society. Journal* 25, no.4 (1980): 277-280.

CALIFORNIA ANGELS

Newhan, Ross. *The California Angels.* New York, N.Y.: Simon and Schuster, 1982. 191 p.

CALIFORNIA FEDERAL SAVINGS AND LOAN ASSOCIATION

Edgerton, J. Howard. *The Story of California Federal Savings.* New York, N.Y.: Newcomen Society in North America, 1969. 24 p. (Newcomen address)

SEE ALSO: CALFED, INC.

CALUMET AND HECLA, INC.

Robson, Paul W. *Calumet and Hecla: Pioneer, Producer, and Pacemaker.* New York, N.Y.: Newcomen Society in North America, 1966. 28 p. (Newcomen address)

CAMEL CIGARETTES
SEE:
REYNOLDS (R.J.) INDUSTRIES

CAMP DRESSER AND MCKEE, INC.

Lawler, Joseph C. *Camp Dresser and McKee, Inc.: 30 Years of Environmental Consulting.* New York, N.Y.: Newcomen Society in North America, 1977. 26 p. (Newcomen Publication; no. 1057)

CAMPBELL SOUP COMPANY

Briggs, Jean A., and Barbara Rudolph. "Mmm, Mmm, Not So Good." *Forbes* 128 (7 December 1981): 44-46.

Campbell Soup Company. *Chronology*. Camden, N.J.: The Company, 1985. 7 p.

Cleary, David Powers. "Campbell's Soup; We Blend the Best with Careful Pains in Skillful Combination, And Everything We Make Contains Our Business Reputation." In *Great American Brands: The Success Formulas That Made Them Famous*, 53-59. New York, N.Y.: Fairchild Publications, 1981.

CAPITAL NATIONAL BANK

Heaney, Christopher K. "A Bank Grows in Manhattan." *ABA Banking Journal* 78 (September 1986): 35-37.

CARBORUNDUM COMPANY

Wendel, William H. *The Scratch Heard 'Round the World: The Story of the Carborundum Company*. New York, N.Y.: Newcomen Society in North America, 1965. 24 p.

CARDIAC PACEMAKERS, INC. (CPI)

Pine, Carol, and Susan Mundale. "Manuel Villafana." In *Self-Made: The Stories of 12 Minnesota Entrepreneurs*, 161-172. Minneapolis, Minn.: Dorn Books, 1982.

CAREERTRACK, INC.

Kingston, Brett. "James Calano and Jeff Salzman of Careertrack." In *The Dynamos: Who Are They Anyway?*, 97-100. New York, N.Y.: Wiley, 1987.

CARGILL, INC.

Cargill, Inc. *Cargill*. Minneapolis, Minn.: The Company, 1977. 26 p.

CARLSON COMPANIES, INC.

Pine, Carol, and Susan Mundale. "Curt Carlson: Stamped in Gold." In *Self-Made: The Stories of 12 Minnesota Entrepreneurs*, 209-223. Minneapolis, Minn.: Dorn Books, 1982.

CARNATION COMPANY

Marshall, James Leslie. *Elbridge A. Stuart, Founder of Carnation Company*. 2nd ed., Los Angeles, Calif.: The Company, 1970.

Weaver, John Downing. *Carnation: The First 75 Years. 1899-1974*. Los Angeles, Calif.: The Company, 1974. 253 p.

CARRIER CORPORATION

Mellow, Craig. "The Coolest Company in America." *Across the Board* 22 (July/August 1985): 11-14.

CARTER HAWLEY HALE STORES, INC.

Carter Hawley Hale Stores, Inc. *Carter Hawley Hale*. Los Angeles, Calif.: The Company, 1989. 5 p.

Carter Hawley Hale Stores, Inc. *Corporate History Highlights*. Los Angeles, Calif.: The Company, 1988. 5 p.

CARTER-WALLACE, INC.

Palmer, Jay. "Who Needs Hype? Not Carter-Wallace, As Its Record Demonstrates." *Barron's* 68 (29 February 1988): 13, 60.

CASCADE AIRWAYS

Steenblik, Jean W. "Cascade Comes of Age." *Air Line Pilot* 51 (May 1982): 17-20.

CASCO NORTHERN BANK, N.A.

Daigle, John M. *Casco Northern Bank, N.A.: The Chronicle of a Bank.* New York, N.Y.: Newcomen Society in North America, 1984. 28 p. (Newcomen publication; no. 1224)

CASE INTERNATIONAL COMPANY

Cosgrove, Tom. "Excavation: Case Likes It Down and Dirty." *ENR* 225 (20 September 1990): 34, 37.

CASTLE AND COOKE, INC.

Castle and Cooke, Inc. *Castle and Cooke, Incorporated: From Land and Sea.* Honolulu, Hawaii: The Company, 1966.

Taylor, Frank J. *From Land and Sea: The Story of Castle and Cooke of Hawaii.* San Francisco, Calif.: Chronicle Books, 1976. 288 p.

SEE ALSO: STANDARD FRUIT AND STEAMSHIP COMPANY

CASTO TRAVEL

Taylor, Russel R. "Maryles Casto: 'Never Say No.'" In *Exceptional Entrepreneurial Women*, 73-78. New York, N.Y.: Quorum Books, 1988.

CATERPILLAR TRACTOR COMPANY

Benjamin Holt: The Story of the Caterpillar Tractor. Edited by Walter A. Payne. Stockton, Calif.: University of the Pacific, 1982. 102 p.

Caterpillar Tractor Company. *Century of Change.* Peoria, Ill.: The Company, 1984. 59 p. (*Caterpillar World* special historical edition)

Naumann, William L. *The Story of Caterpillar Tractor Company.* New York, N.Y: Newcomen Society in North America, 1977. 23 p. (Newcomen publication; no.1060)

Payne, Walter A. *Benjamin Holt: The Story of the Caterpillar Tractor.* Stockton, Calif.: University of the Pacific, 1982. 102 p. (Holt-Atherton Pacific Center for Western Studies, series 2, no. 1)

Zinman, Michael. *The History of the Decline and Fall of the Caterpillar Tractor Company: A Modern Business Saga.* 2nd ed., Croton-on-Hudson, N.Y.: North River Press, 1988.

CBS
SEE:
COLUMBIA BROADCASTING COMPANY

CCT, INC. (CONCEPTS IN COMPUTER TECHNOLOGY)

Kingston, Brett. "Jashua Beren of CCT, Inc." In *The Dynamos: Who Are They Anyway?*, 207-215. New York, N.Y.: Wiley, 1987.

CELANESE CORPORATION OF AMERICA

Hall, Richard W. *Putting Down Roots, Twenty-Five Years of Celanese in Mexico.* New York, N.Y.: Vantage Press, 1969. 128 p.

CENTEX CORPORATION

Centex Corporation. *Centex Corporation.* Dallas, Tex.: The Company, n.d. 16 p.

CENTRAL HUDSON GAS AND ELECTRIC CORPORATION

Central Hudson Gas and Electric Corporation. *Central Hudson's 75 Years of Service*. Poughkeepsie, N.Y.: The Company, 1975. 15 p.

CENTRAL ILLINOIS PUBLIC SERVICE COMPANY

Central Illinois Public Service Company. *It Started with a Streetcar; Central Illinois Public Service Company, 1902-1979*. Springfield, Ill.: The Company, 1979. 20 p.

CENTRAL NATIONAL BANK OF CLEVELAND

Jollie, Rose Marie. *On the Grow with Cleveland*. Cleveland, Ohio: The Bank, 1965. 110 p.

CENTRAL PACIFIC RAILWAY COMPANY

Best, Gerald M. *Iron Horses to Promontory Railroad: Central Pacific-Union Pacific*. San Marino, Calif.: Golden West Books, 1969. 207 p.

CENTRAL POWER AND LIGHT COMPANY

Central Power and Light Company. *CPL 60th Anniversary: From Ice to Atoms*. Corpus Christi, Tex.: The Company, 1977. 17 p.

Central Power and Light Company. *The First 50 Years*. Corpus Christi, Tex.: CPL, 1967. 38 p.

CENTRAL SOYA COMPANY, INC.

Central Soya Company, Inc. *Central Soya: People and Perspective--Fifty Years of Growth and a Future to Share*. Fort Wayne, Ind.: The Company, 1984. 21 p.

McMillan, Harold W. *Mr. Moe and Central Soya: The Foodpower Story.* New York, N.Y.: Newcomen Society in North America, 1967. 28 p. (Newcomen address)

CENTRAL VERMONT PUBLIC SERVICE CORPORATION

Cree, Albert A. *The Story of Central Vermont Public Service Corporation.* Rutland, Vt.: The Company, 1966.

CERTAIN-TEED CORPORATION

Meyer, Malcolm. *Total Commitment to a Better Environment: The Story of Certain-Teed Products Corporation.* New York, N.Y.: Newcomen Society in North America, 1972. 16 p. (Newcomen address)

CF&I STEEL CORPORATION

Scamehorn, Howard Lee. *Pioneer Steelmaker in the West: The Colorado Fuel and Iron Company, 1872-1903.* Boulder, Colo.: Pruett Publishing Company, 1976. 231 p. (The latter part of the book includes an update of current history)

CFS CONTINENTAL

Bowman, Jim. *More Than a Coffee Company: The Story of CFS Continental.* Chicago, Ill.: Chicago Review Press, 1986. 207 p.

CHAMPION AWARDS, INC.

Copetas, A. Craig. "Private Lives: Profiles from the Inc. 500--#147: Champion Awards, Inc." *Inc.* 7 (December 1985): 92, 94.

CHAMPION BRIDGE COMPANY

Miars, David H. *A Century of Bridges; The History of the Champion Bridge Company and the Development of Industrial Manufacturing in Wilmington, Ohio.* Wilmington, Ohio: Cox Print Company, 1972. 47 p.

CHAMPION HOME BUILDERS COMPANY

Champion Home Builders Company. *The Story of Champion Home Builders.* Dryden, Mich.: The Company, 1971. 21 p.

CHANCE (A.B.) COMPANY

Chance, F. Gano. *The Ideas That Guide Us: The Story of the A.B. Chance Company, Centralia, Missouri.* New York, N.Y.: Newcomen Society in North America, 1968. 20 p. (Newcomen address)

CHARLESTOWN SAVINGS BANK

Loughlin, Terry. "A Case History: The Charlestown Celebrates." *Bank Marketing* 12 (October 1980): 24-26.

CHARLOTTE PIPE AND FOUNDRY COMPANY

Smith, Beth Laney. *A Foundry, Volume 1: Being the Story of Charlotte Pipe and Foundry Company, Founded November 1, 1907.* Charlotte, N.C.: Laney-Smith, 1977. 86 p.

THE CHARTER COMPANY

Mason, Raymond K. *The History of the Charter Company: Its Challenges and Opportunities.* New York, N.Y.: Newcomen Society in North America, 1983. 13 p. (Newcomen publication; no. 1189)

CHASE HOTEL

Lobbia, J.A. "Chased into History." *Chicago Tribune*, 24 September 1989, sec. 5, p. 7.

CHASE MANHATTAN CORPORATION

Hill, Roy. "Chase Manhattan Rings up Change." *International Management* 35 (August 1980): 14-18.

"History of Chase, 1799-1982." *Chase News* 25 (March 1982) 1-8. (Special edition)

Miller, Richard B. "Chase Manhattan--The Rockefeller Years...And the Years Ahead." *Bankers Magazine* 164 (March/April 1981): 54-64.

Wilson, John Donald. *Chase: The Chase Manhattan Bank, N.A., 1945-1985*. Boston, Mass.: Harvard Business School Press, 1986. 432 p.

CHASEN (N.) AND SON

Kahn, Joseph P. "Private Lives: Profiles from the Inc. 500--#435: N. Chasen & Son Inc." *Inc.* 7 (December 1985): 69-72.

CHELSEA MILLING COMPANY

Koselka, Rita. "A Family Affair." *Forbes* 145 (11 June 1990): 83-87.

CHEMICAL BANKING CORPORATION

Chemical Bank. *Chemical Bank, 1823-1983*. New York, N.Y: The Bank, 1983. 20 p. (Special edition of the *Chemical Chronicle*)

Chemical Banking Corporation. *History of Chemical New York Corporation*. New York, N.Y.: The Company, 1984. 2 p.

Glasberg, Davita Silfen. "Corporate Power and Control: The Case of Leasco Corporation Versus Chemical Bank." *Social Problems* 29 (December 1981): 104-116.

Glasberg, Davita Silfen. *The Power of Collective Purse Strings: The Effects of Bank Hegemony on Corporations and the State.* Berkeley, Calif.: University of California Press, 1989. 239 p.

CHEMLAWN SERVICES CORPORATION

Nayak, P. Ranganath, and John M. Ketteringham. "Chemlawn: Dick Duke's Lonely Battle." In *Breakthroughs!*, 74-101. New York, N.Y: Rawson Associates, 1986.

THE CHESAPEAKE AND OHIO RAILWAY

Bias, Charles V. "The Merger of the Chesapeake and Ohio Railway and the Baltimore and Ohio Railroad Companies." *Journal of the West Virginia Historical Association* 4 (1980): 24-34.

Dorin, Patrick C. *The Chesapeake and Ohio Railway, George Washington's Railroad.* Seattle, Wash.: Superior Pub., 1981. 232 p.

THE CHESAPEAKE AND POTOMAC TELEPHONE COMPANY OF MARYLAND

Cromwell, Joseph H. *The C&P Story: Service in Action: Maryland.* Washington, D.C.: The Company, 1981. 241, 65 p.

THE CHESAPEAKE AND POTOMAC TELEPHONE COMPANY OF VIRGINIA

Cromwell, Joseph H. *The C&P Story: Service in Action: Virginia.* Washington, D.C.: The Company, 1981. 201, 65 p.

THE CHESAPEAKE AND POTOMAC TELEPHONE COMPANY OF WASHINGTON, D.C.

The C&P Story: Service in Action. Washington, D.C.: The Company, 1981. 144, 82 p.

THE CHESAPEAKE AND POTOMAC TELEPHONE COMPANY OF WEST VIRGINIA

The C&P Story: Service in Action: West Virginia. Washington, D.C.: The Company, 1981. 110, 65 p.

THE CHESAPEAKE CORPORATION OF VIRGINIA

Dill, Alonzo Thomas. *Chesapeake: Pioneer Papermaker; A History of the Company and Its Community.* Charlottesville, Va.: University Press of Virginia, 1968. 356 p.

CHESEBROUGH-POND'S, INC.

Chesebrough-Pond's, Inc. *The First Hundred Years.* Greenwich, Conn: The Company, 1980. 6 p. (Special centennial issue of *Chesebrough-Pond's World*)

THE CHESSIE SYSTEM, INC.

Bias, Charles V. "Chessie's Growth: Success and Failure, 1966-1973." *West Virginia History* 44 (January 1982): 41-53.

CHEVRON CHEMICAL COMPANY - ORTHO DIVISION

Gardner, Leo R. *The First Thirty Years: The Early History of the Company Now Known As Ortho Division, Chevron Chemical Company.* San Francisco, Calif.: The Company, 1978. 45 p.

CHEVY CHASE SAVINGS AND LOAN, INC.

Walsh, Sharon Warren. "Chevy Chase Savings Bank: A Giant Born in a Trailer." *Washington Post*, 30 January 1989, sec. WBIZ, p. 1.

CHIAT/DAY

Kessler, Stephen. *Chiat/Day: The First Twenty Years*. New York, N.Y.: Rizzoli, 1990. 349 p.

CHICAGO AND ALTON RAILROAD COMPANY

Matejka, Michael. *Bloomington's C&A Shops; Our Lives Remembered*. Bloomington, Ill.: McLean County Historical Society, 1987. 161 p.

CHICAGO AND NORTH WESTERN RAILWAY COMPANY

Dorin, Patrick C. *Chicago and North Western Power; Modern Steam and Diesel, 1900-1971*. Seattle, Wash.: Superior Publishing Company, 1972. 192 p.

Olmsted, Robert P. *Prairie Rails*. Woodridge, Ill.: McMillan Pub., 1979. 168 p.

CHICAGO BEARS

Whittingham, Richard. *The Chicago Bears: An Illustrated History*. Chicago, Ill.: Rand McNally, 1982. 268 p.

CHICAGO, BURLINGTON AND QUINCY RAILROAD COMPANY

Dorin, Patrick C. *Everything West: The Burlington Route*. Seattle, Wash.: Superior Publishing Company, 1976. 171 p.

CHICAGO CUBS

Ahrens, Art, and Eddie Gold. *Day by Day in Chicago Cubs History*. El Cerrito, Calif.: Leisure Press, 1982. 352 p.

Colletti, Ned. *You Gotta Have Heart: Dallas Green's Rebuilding of the Cubs*. South Bend, Ind.: Diamond Communications, 1985. 272 p.

Gold, Eddie, and Art Ahrens. *The Renewal Era Cubs, 1985-1990*. Chicago, Ill.: Bonus Books, 1990. 180 p.

Langford, Jim. *The Game Is Never Over: An Appreciative History of the Chicago Cubs*. 2nd, revised edition. South Bend, Ind.: Icarus Press, 1982. 264 p.

The New Era Cubs, Nineteen Forty-One to Nineteen Eighty-Five. Chicago, Ill.: Bonus Books, 1985. 288 p.

CHICAGO, INDIANAPOLIS AND LOUISVILLE RAILWAY

Hilton, George Woodman. *Monon Route*. Berkeley: Howell North Books, 1978. 323 p.

CHICAGO RESEARCH AND TRADING GROUP

Ritchie, Mark A. *God in the Pits: Confessions of a Commodities Trader*. New York, N.Y.: Macmillan, 1989. 271 p.

CHICAGO TRIBUNE

Geis, Joseph. *The Colonel of Chicago*. New York, N.Y.: Dutton, 1979. 261 p.

Wendt, Lloyd. *Chicago Tribune: The Rise of a Great American Newspaper*. Chicago, Ill.: Rand McNally, 1979. 861 p.

CHICAGO WHITE SOX

Berke, Art, and Paul Schmidt. *This Date in Chicago White Sox History*. Briarcliff Manor, N.Y.: Stein and Day, 1982. 177 p.

Lindberg, Richard. *Who's on Third: The Chicago White Sox Story*. South Bend, Ind.: Icarus Press, 1983. 287 p.

Vanderberg, Bob. *Sox: From Lane & Fain to Zisk & Fisk*. 2nd ed. Chicago, Ill.: Chicago Review Press, 1984. 384 p.

CHIC-FIL-A CORPORATION

Cathy, S. Truett. *It's Easier to Succeed Than to Fail*. Nashville, Tenn.: Oliver-Nelson, 1989. 192 p.

CHISOS MINING COMPANY

Ragsdale, Kenneth Baxter. *Quicksilver: Terlinqua and the Chisos Mining Company*. Forward by Joe B. Frantz. College Station: Texas A&M University Press, 1976. 327 p.

CHRYSLER CORPORATION

Abodaher, David J. *Iacocca*. New York, N.Y: Macmillan, 1982. 319 p.

Ansari, Abdolreza. "The Crisis of the Automobile Industry and National Adjustment Policy, A Comparative Study of British Leyland and Chrysler." Ph.D. diss., Indiana University, 1986. 285 p.

Butler, Don. *The Plymouth-DeSoto Story*. Sarasota, Fla.: Crestline Pub., 1978. 405 p.

Chrysler Corporation. *Historical Summary*. Detroit, Mich.: The Company, 1985. 9 p.

Dammann, George H. *Seventy Years of Chrysler*. Glen Ellyn, Ill.: Crestline Publications, 1974. 382 p.

Gallaway, Edward A. *Accountability*. Philadelphia, Pa.: Dorrance, 1975. 99 p.

Gallaway, Edward A. *Masters of Deception: A Corporate Giant Confronted by Its Stockholders*. Bryn Mawr, Pa.: Dorrance, 1985. 216 p.

Gordon, Maynard M. *Iacocca Management Technique; A Profile of the Chrysler Chairman's Unique Key to Business Success*. New York, N.Y.: Dodd, Mead, 1985. 154 p.

Iacocca, Lee A., and W. Novak. *Iacocca: An Autobiography*. New York, N.Y.: Bantam Books, 1984. 352 p.

Jefferys, Steve. *Management and Managed; Fifty Years of Crisis at Chrysler*. Cambridge; New York, N.Y.: Cambridge University Press, 1986. 290 p.

Langworth, Richard M., and Jan P. Norbye. *The Complete History of Chrysler Corporation, 1924-1985*. New York, N.Y.: Beekman House, 1985. 384 p.

Marcy, Sam. *Chrysler and the UAW, A Critical Evaluation of the Union Leadership's Strategy and Alternative Plans to Meet the Autoworkers' Needs*. Atlanta, Ga.: World View Pub., 1981. 28 p.

Moritz, Michael, and B. Seaman. *Going for Broke: The Chrysler Story*. Garden City, N.Y.: Doubleday, 1981. 374 p.

Reich, Robert B., and John D. Donahue. *New Deals: The Chrysler Revival and the American System*. New York, N.Y.: Times Books, 1985. 352 p.

Samra, Rise Jane. "The Changing Image of the Chrysler

Corporation, 1979-1980; A Dramatistic Analysis."
Ph.D. diss., University of Arizona, 1985. 170 p.

Stuart, Reginald. *Bailout: The Story Behind America's Billion Dollar Gamble on the New Chrysler Corporation.* South Bend, Ind.: Icarus Books, 1980. 210 p.

Thorpe, Judith Mosier. "The Role of Persuasion for a Corporate Spokesman, An Analysis of the Arguments Lee Iacocca Presented on Behalf of Chrysler Corporation to the American Consumer and to the Congress from 1979-1982 (Toulmin, Media, Advertisements)." Ph.D. diss., Ohio State University, 1986. 228 p.

Wyden, Peter. *The Unknown Iacocca.* New York, N.Y.: Morrow, 1987. 416 p.

CHRYSLER CORPORATION - DODGE DIVISION

Latham, Caroline. *Dodge Dynasty: The Car and the Family That Rocked Detroit.* San Diego, Calif.: Harcourt Brace Jovanovich, 1989. 360 p.

Pitrone, Jean M., and J.P. Elwart. *The Dodges, The Auto Family Fortune and Misfortune.* South Bend, Ind.: Icarus Press, 1981. 316 p.

CIANBRO CORPORATION

Cianchette, Ival R. *Cianbro: The Constructors.* New York, N.Y.: Newcomen Society in North America, 1984. 20 p. (Newcomen publication; no. 1199)

CINCINNATI BELL, INC.

Cincinnati Bell, Inc. *Cincinnati Bell Centennial, 1873-1973.* Cincinnati, Ohio: The Company, Inc., 1973.

CINCINNATI BENGALS

Collett, Ritter. *Super Stripes: Paul Brown & the Super Bowl Bengals*. Dayton: Landfall Press, 1982. 221 p.

Snyder, John, and Floyd Conner. *Day by Day in Cincinnati Bengals History*. New York, N.Y.: Leisure Press, 1984. 368 p.

THE CINCINNATI COUNTRY CLUB

The Cincinnati Country Club, 1903-1965. Cincinnati, Ohio: The Club, 1965. 76 p.

THE CINCINNATI ENQUIRER

Pale, Francis L. *The Cincinnati Enquirer: The Shadows of Its Publishers*. New York, N.Y.: Newcomen Society in North America, 1966. 28 p. (Newcomen address)

CINCINNATI FINANCIAL CORPORATION

Curry, Robert P. *Prospectus Fulfilled: The Cincinnati Financial Corporation*. Cincinnati, Ohio: The Company, 1984. 73 p.

Schiff, John J. *Cincinnati Financial Corporation: Keeping Every Promise*. New York, N.Y.: Newcomen Society in North America, 1978. 20 p. (Newcomen publication; no. 1083)

CINCINNATI GAS AND ELECTRIC COMPANY

Cincinnati Gas and Electric Company. *History*. Cincinnati, Ohio: The Company, 1984. 11 p.

CINCINNATI MILACRON

Cincinnati Milacron. *Cincinnati Milacron, 1884-1984; Finding Better Ways*. Cincinnati, The Company, 1984. 288 p.

CINCINNATI POST

Stevens, George E. "A History of the Cincinnati Post." Thesis, University of Minnesota, 1968. 422 p.

THE CINCINNATI REDS

Anderson, Sparky. *The Main Spark: Sparky Anderson and the Cincinnati Reds.* Garden City, N.Y.: Doubleday, 1978. 239 p.

Collett, Ritter. *The Cincinnati Reds: A Pictorial History of Professional Baseball's Oldest Team.* Virginia Beach, Va.: Jordan-Powers Corp., 1976. 192 p.

Conner, Floyd, and John Snyder. *Day by Day in Cincinnati Reds History.* New York, N.Y.: Leisure Press, 1983. 300 p.

Lawson, Earl. *Cincinnati Seasons: My Thirty-Four Years with the Reds.* South Bend, Ind.: Diamond Communications, 1987. 218 p.

Lewis, Dottie L. *Baseball in Cincinnati from Wooden Fences to Astroturf.* Cincinnati, Ohio: Cincinnati Historical Society, 1988. 64 p.

Rathgeber, Bob. *Cincinnati Reds Scrapbook.* Virginia Beach, Va.: JCP Corp. of Virginia, 1982. 151 p.

Walker, Robert H. *Cincinnati and the Big Red Machine.* Bloomington, Ind.: Indiana University Press, 1988. 176 p.

Wheeler, Lonnie, and John Baskin. *The Cincinnati Game.* Wilmington, Ohio: Orange Frazer, 1988. 270 p.

C.I.T. FINANCIAL CORPORATION

Wilson, William L. *Full Faith and Credit: The Story of C.I.T. Financial Corporation, 1908-1975.* New York,

N.Y.: Random House, 1976. 376 p.

CITICORP

Citicorp. *The Citicorp Story*. New York, N.Y.: The Company, 1986. 5 p.

Cleveland, Harold Van B. *Citibank, 1812-1970*. Cambridge: Harvard University Press, 1986. 512 p. (Harvard studies in business history; no. 37)

Hutchinson, Robert A. *Off the Books. Citibank and the World's Biggest Money Game*. New York, N.Y.: Morrow, 1986. 416 p.

Levinson, Harry, and Stuart Rosenthal. "Walter B. Wriston." In *CEO: Corporate Leadership in Action*, 56-95. New York, N.Y.: Basic Books, 1984.

"The First Sixteen Decades." *Citicorp Magazine* no.2 (1972): 17-27. (160th anniversary issue)

CITIZENS FEDERAL SAVINGS AND LOAN ASSOCIATION OF DAYTON

Kerby, Jerry L. *"Where Rainbows Begin": The Story of Citizens Federal Savings and Loan Association of Dayton*. New York, N.Y.: Newcomen Society in North America, 1984. 32 p. (Newcomen publication; no. 1214)

CITIZENS GAS AND COKE UTILITY

Rumer, Thomas A. "Corporate History--One Company's Approach." *Public Utilities Fortnightly* 114 (19 July 1984): 19-22.

CITY NATIONAL BANK AND TRUST COMPANY OF ROCKFORD

Garson, Bill. *The Knight on Broadway: The Story of City*

National Bank and Trust Company of Rockford and Sir Greenback--The Bank's Financial Symbol. Rockford, Ill.: The Bank, 1978. 171 p.

CITY PUBLIC SERVICE

City Public Service. *45 Years of Municipal Ownership: 1942-1987.* San Antonio, Tex.: The Company, 1987. 29 p.

CITY SECURITIES CORPORATION

Gaelhoed, E. Bruce. *Indiana's Investment Banker, The Story of City Securities Corporation.* Muncie, Ind.: Bureau of Business Research, Ball State University, 1985. 150 p. (Ball State University. Business history series, no. 3)

THE CLARK COUNTY STATE BANK

Haffner, Gerald O., and Albert M. Helzer. *The Clark County State Bank and Its Years of Service.* Unpublished paper, 1983. 15 p. (On file at the CommerceAmerica Corporation, Jeffersonville, Ind.)

CLARK EQUIPMENT COMPANY

French, Robert W. *Living Together, Buchnan and Clark 1904-1975.* 1976. 194 p.

Phillips, Bert E. *Plus Faith Unlimited: The Story of Clark Equipment Company.* New York, N.Y.: Newcomen Society in North America, 1978. 32 p. (Newcomen publication; no. 1087)

CLARK ESTATES, INC.

Barrett, William P. "The Clarks of Cooperstown." *Forbes* 144 (18 September 1989): 76-82.

CLARK (J.L.) MANUFACTURING COMPANY

Nelson, William C. *Clark Manufacturing Company: A Model of American Enterprise.* New York, N.Y.: Newcomen Society in North America, 1981. 20 p. (Newcomen publication; no. 1136)

CLEVELAND BROWNS

Borst, Bill, and Jim Scott. *The Browns Through the Years.* St. Louis, Mo.: Krank Press, 1987. 20 p.

Clary, Jack T. *Cleveland Browns.* New York, N.Y.: Macmillan, 1973. 191 p.

Eckhouse, Morris. *Day by Day in Cleveland Browns History.* New York, N.Y.: Leisure Press, 1984. 528 p.

Levy, William V. *Sam, Sipe & Company: The History of the Cleveland Browns.* Cleveland, Ohio: J.T. Zubal and P.D. Dole, Publishers, 1981. 237 p.

THE CLEVELAND-CLIFFS IRON COMPANY

Harrison, H. Stuart. *The Cleveland-Cliffs Iron Company.* New York, N.Y.: Newcomen Society in North America, 1974. 32 p. (Newcomen publication; no. 1004)

THE CLEVELAND INDIANS

Eckhouse, Morris. *Day by Day in Cleveland Indians History.* New York, N.Y.: Leisure Press, 1983. 400 p.

CLIFFS NOTES, INC.

Hillegass, Clifton K. *Cliffs Notes, Inc.: Quality of Product--Service--Policy.* New York, N.Y.: Newcomen Society of the United States, 1985, c1986. 28 p. (Newcomen publication; no. 1257)

CLOROX COMPANY

The Clorox Company Backgrounder. *Backgrounder: The Clorox Company, 1913-1988*. Oakland, Calif.: The Company, 1989. 2 p.

Shetterly, Robert B. *Renaissance of the Clorox Company*. New York, N.Y.: Newcomen Society in North America, 1973. 16 p. (Newcomen address)

CLOW CORPORATION

Rinehart, Raymond G. *Clow Corporation: 100 Years of Service to the Water and Waste Water Industries*. New York, N.Y.: Newcomen Society in North America, 1978. 24 p. (Newcomen publication; no. 1092)

CLUETT, PEABODY AND COMPANY, INC.

Cluett, Peabody and Company, Inc. *The Cluett Experience: A History of Cluett, Peabody & Company, Inc.* New York, N.Y.: The Company, 1976.

CNA INSURANCE COMPANIES

Donahue, Richard J. "Continental Assurance, Without Aches, Turns 75." *National Underwriter (Life/Health)* 90 (2 August 1986): 30.

CNN
SEE:
TURNER BROADCASTING SYSTEM

COACHMEN INDUSTRIES, INC.

Coachmen Industries, Inc. *An Overview*. Middlebury, Ind.: The Company, 1983?. 14 p.

Coachmen Industries, Inc. *Milestones*. Middlebury, Ind.: The Company, 1984. 3 p.

COAP PLANNING COMPANY, INC.

Taylor, Nick. "The COAP Experience." *Financial Planning* 14 (September 1985): 71-78.

COCA-COLA BOTTLING COMPANY OF CHATTANOOGA

Harrison, Desales. *"Footprints On the Sands of Time": A History of Two Men and the Fulfillment of a Dream.* New York, N.Y.: Newcomen Society in North America, 1969. 24 p. (Newcomen address)

COCA-COLA BOTTLING COMPANY OF WEST POINT-LAGRANGE, GEORGIA

Henry, Waights G. *Tributary to a Golden Stream: The Story of the Coca-Cola Bottling Company of West Point-LaGrange, Georgia.* New York, N.Y.: Newcomen Society in North America, 1982. 22 p. (Newcomen publication; no. 1182)

COCA-COLA BOTTLING COMPANY UNITED, INC.

Johnson, Crawford T. *Coca-Cola Bottling Company United, Inc.: A Pause to Reflect.* New York, N.Y.: Newcomen Society of the United States, 1987, c1988. (Newcomen publication; no. 1298)

COCA-COLA COMPANY

Cleary, David Powers. "Coca-Cola; There Is No Limit to What a Man Can Do or Where He Can Go." In *Great American Brands: The Success Formulas That Made Them Famous*, 60-74. New York, N.Y.: Fairchild Publications, 1981.

Coca-Cola Company. *Portrait of a Business, The Coca-Cola Bottling Company.* Atlanta, Ga.: Coca-Cola Company, 1968. 19 p.

Coke's First 100 Years--And a Look Into the Future.
Great Neck, N.Y.: Beverage World/Keller
International Publishing Corporation, 1986. 352.

Hoy, Ann H. *Coca-Cola; The First Hundred Years.*
Atlanta, Ga.: The Company, 1986. 159 p.

Louis, J.C. *The Cola Wars.* New York, N.Y.: Everest
House, 1980. 386 p.

Oliver, Thomas. *The Real Coke, The Real Story.* New
York, N.Y.: Random House, 1986. 195 p.

Rowland, Sanders, and B. Terrell. *Papa Coke: Sixty-Five
Years Selling Coca-Cola.* Ashville, N.C.: Bright
Mountain Books, 1986. 236 p.

Steinbach Palazzini, Fiora. *Coca-Cola Superstar.* New
York, N.Y.: Barron's, 1989, c1988. 142 p. (Translated
from the Italian)

Tedlow, Richard S. "The Great Cola Wars: Coke Vs.
Pepsi." In *New and Improved: The Story of Mass
Marketing in America*, 22-111. New York, N.Y.: Basic
Books, 1990.

Watters, Pat. *Coca-Cola.* Garden City, N.Y.: Doubleday,
1978. 288 p.

COHERENT, INC.

Chakravarty, Subrata N. "We Prefer to Follow." *Forbes*
127 (13 April 1981): 83-86.

COLD SPRING GRANITE COMPANY

Dominik, John J. *Cold Spring Granite: A History.* Cold
Spring, Minn.: The Company, 1982. 123 p.

COLDWELL BANKER REAL ESTATE GROUP, INC.

Levy, Jo Ann L. *Behind the Western Skyline: Coldwell Banker: The First 75 Years.* Los Angeles, Calif.: The Company, 1981. 210 p.

COLECO INDUSTRIES, INC.

Coleco Industries, Inc. *Coleco, 1932-1982.* Hartford, Conn.: The Company, 1982. 53 p.

Hoffman, William. *Fantasy: The Incredible Cabbage Patch Phenomenon.* Dallas, Tex.: Taylor Publishing Company, 1984. 217 p.

COLEMAN COMPANY, INC.

Jones, Lawrence M. *The Coleman Story: The Ability to Cope With Change.* New York, N.Y.: Newcomen Society in North America, 1975. 28 p. (Newcomen publication; no. 1010)

COLES EXPRESS

Cole, Galen L. *The Cole Family of Business: Serving Maine and New England for 72 Years.* New York, N.Y.: Newcomen Society of the United States, 1989. 28 p. (Newcomen publication; no. 1329)

COLGATE-PALMOLIVE COMPANY

Foster, David R. *The Story of Colgate-Palmolive: One Hundred and Sixty-Nine Years of Progress.* New York, N.Y.: Newcomen Society in North America, 1975. 40 p. (Newcomen publication; no. 1022)

Menzies, Hugh D. "The Changing of the Guard at Colgate." *Fortune* 100 (24 September 1979): 92+

COLLINS RADIO COMPANY

Braband, Ken C. *The First 50 Years: A History of Collins Radio Company and the Collins Divisions of Rockwell International.* Cedar Rapids, Iowa: Communications Dept., Avionics Group, Rockwell International, 1983. 218 p.

COLONIAL PIPELINE COMPANY

Colonial Pipeline Company. *The Quest for Excellence; Colonial Pipeline Company, 1962-1987.* Atlanta, Ga.: The Company, 1987. 21 p.

COLORADO MOUNTAIN CLUB

Kingery, Hugh E. *The Colorado Mountain Club; The First Seventy-Five Years of a Highly Individual Corporation, 1912-1987.* Evergreen, Colo.: Cordillera Press, 1988. 125 p.

COLT INDUSTRIES, INC.

"The Colt Story." *American Rifleman* (January 1986): 32+

Wilson, Robert Laurence. *The Colt Heritage: The Official History of Colt Firearms from 1836 to the Present.* New York, N.Y.: Simon & Schuster, 1979. 358 p.

Wilson, Robert Laurence. *The Rampant Colt: The Story of a Trademark.* Spencer, Ind.: T. Haas, 1969. 107 p.

COLUMBIA BROADCASTING SYSTEM, INC.

Boyer, Peter J. *Who Killed CBS? The Undoing of America's Number One News Network.* New York, N.Y.: Random House, 1988. 361 p.

Joyce, Ed. *Prime Time and Bad Times, A Personal Drama of Network Television.* New York, N.Y.:

Doubleday, 1988. 432 p.

Leonard, Bill. *In the Storm of the Eye, A Lifetime at CBS.* New York, N.Y.: Putnam Publishing Group, 1987. 256 p.

MacDonald, J. Fred. *One Nation Under Television: The Rise and Decline of Network TV.* New York, N.Y.: Pantheon, 1990. 335 p.

Metz, Robert. *CBS: Reflections in a Bloodshot Eye.* Chicago, Ill.: Playboy Press, 1975. 428 p.

Paley, William Samuel. *As It Happened, A Memoir.* Garden City, N.Y.: Doubleday, 1979. 418 p.

Paper, Lewis J. *Empire, The Life and Times of William Paley.* New York, St. Martin, 1987. 384 p.

Slater, Robert. *This--Is CBS: A Chronicle of 60 Years.* Englewood Cliffs, N.J.: Prentice-Hall, 1988. 354 p.

COLUMBIA GAS SYSTEM SERVICE CORPORATION

Columbia Gas System Service Corporation. *A History of the Columbia Gas System: The First 50 Years.* Wilmington, Del.: The Company, 1976. 22 p.

COLUMBIA MANUFACTURING COMPANY

Cleary, David Powers. "Columbia Bicycles; Could It Have Become 'The First General Motors'?" In *Great American Brands: The Success Formulas That Made Them Famous*, 75-79. New York, N.Y.: Fairchild Publications, 1981.

COLUMBIA PICTURES

McClintick, David. *Indecent Exposure: A True Story of Hollywood and Wall Street.* New York, N.Y.: Morrow,

1982. 544 p.

Yule, Andrew. *Fast Fade: David Puttnam, Columbia Pictures, And the Battle for Hollywood.* New York, N.Y: Delacorte Press, 1989. 376 p.

COLUMBUS AND SOUTHERN OHIO ELECTRIC COMPANY

Columbus and Southern Ohio Electric Company. *A Brief History.* Columbus, Ohio: The Company, 1978? 24 p.

COLUMBUS MUTUAL LIFE INSURANCE COMPANY

Gingher, Paul R. *Running Mates: The Story of State Automotive Mutual Insurance Company and Columbus Mutual Life Insurance Company.* New York, N.Y.: Newcomen Society in North America, 1978. 30 p. (Newcomen publication; no. 1090)

COMAIR, INC.

Comair, Inc. *History of Comair.* Cincinnati, Ohio: The Company, 1985. 3 p.

COMBINED INSURANCE COMPANY OF AMERICA

Shook, Robert L. "W. Clement Stone." In *The Entrepreneurs: Twelve Who Took Risks and Succeeded,* 19-39. New York, N.Y: Harper & Row, 1980.

COMBUSTION ENGINEERING, INC.

Santry, Arthur J. *Combustion Engineering Today, A Presentation at the Luncheon Meeting of the Security Analysts of San Francisco.* San Francisco, Calif.: The Company, 1967.

"75 Years of Excellence." *Combustion Engineering World* (October/November 1987): 1-16. (Special issue of the Company's Magazine)

COMDISCO, INC.

Blumenthal, Marcia. "Comdisco Thriving in Used Equipment Market." *Computerworld* 15 (12 January 1981): 61-62.

COMMAND-AIRE CORPORATION

Davisson, Budd. "Forgotten Success; The Command-Aire Aircraft Company." *Air Progress* 46 (October 1984): 70-75.

COMMERCE TRUST COMPANY

Kemper, James M. *A Bank and Its Community: The Story of Commerce Trust Company.* New York, N.Y.: Newcomen Society in North America, 1966. 24 p. (Newcomen address)

COMMODORE RECORDS

McDonough, John. "Marking Time." *Chicago Tribune*, 25 February 1990, sec. 13, p. 28.

COMMONWEALTH COMPANIES, INC.

Brice, James. *Three Generations, A History of Commonwealth Companies, Inc.* Oakland, Calif.: J. Brice, 1982. 342 p.

COMMONWEALTH EDISON COMPANY

Commonwealth Edison Company. *A History of Electric Service in Chicagoland.* Chicago, Ill.: The Company, 1983. 20 p.

Hogan, John. *Spirit Capable: The Story of Commonwealth*

Edison. Chicago, Ill.: Mobium Press, 1986. 450 p.

COMMONWEALTH LIFE INSURANCE COMPANY

Gerard, Victor B. *Commonwealth Life Insurance Company: A History of the Development Years.* Louisville, Ky.: The Company, 1985. 165 p.

COMMUNICATIONS SATELLITE CORPORATION

Communication Satellite Corporation. *Twenty Years Via Satellite: A Chronology of Events of Communications Satellite Corporation, 1962-1985.* Washington, D.C.: The Company, 1985. 32 p.

COMMUNITY PUBLIC SERVICE COMPANY

Smith, Bennett. *Community Public Service Company, Its History, People, And Places.* Fort Worth, Tex.: Smith, 1975. 711 p.

COMPAQ COMPUTER CORPORATION

Bane, Michael. "PC Leadership Shoe Fits, And Compaq Wears it Well." *Chicago Tribune*, 19 March 1989, sec. 20, p. 14.

COMPUTER MEMORIES, INC.

Pitta, Julie. "The Checkered Past of Computer Memories." *Computerworld* 22 (31 October 1988): 91, 94-95.

COMPUTER SCIENCES CORPORATION

"CSC: The First 25 Years, 1959-1984; Excellence in Action." *CSC News* 15, no.3 (April 1984). Anniversary issue.

COMPUTERLAND CORPORATION

Fucini, Joseph J., and Suzy Fucini. "William H. Millard,

Computerland Corporation: 'Anybody Had the Opportunity to Observe This Phenomenon.'" In *Experience Inc.; Men and Women Who Founded Famous Companies After the Age of 40*, 82-88. New York, N.Y.: Free Press, 1987.

Littman, Jonathan. *Once Upon a Time in Computerland: The Amazing, Billion-Dollar Tale of Bill Millard*. Los Angeles, Calif.: Price Stern Sloan, 1987. 296 p.

CONDEC CORPORATION

Chakravarty, Subrata N. "Springtime for an Ugly Duckling." *Forbes* 127 (27 April 1981): 58, 60-61.

CONFEDERATION LIFE INSURANCE COMPANY

Davidson, J. Craig. *The Confederation Life People Story*. New York, N.Y.: Newcomen Society in North America, 1971. 24 p. (Newcomen address)

CONNECTICUT MUTUAL LIFE INSURANCE COMPANY

Cahn, William. *A Matter of Life and Death: The Connecticut Mutual Story*. New York, N.Y.: Random House, 1970. 309 p.

CONNELL BROS. COMPANY, LTD.

Connell Bros. Company, Ltd. *A Century of Success*. San Francisco, Calif.: The Company, 1987. 12 p.

CONOCO
SEE:
CONTINENTAL OIL COMPANY

CONRAIL
SEE:
CONSOLIDATED RAIL CORPORATION

CONSOLIDATED AIRCRAFT CORPORATION

Wagner, William. *Reuben Fleet: And the Story of Consolidated Aircraft.* Fallbrook, Calif.: Aero Publishers, 1976. 324 p.

CONSOLIDATED EDISON COMPANY OF NEW YORK, INC.

Axelrod, Regina S. *Conflict Between Energy and Urban Environment: Consolidated Edison Versus the City of New York.* Washington, D.C.: University Press of America, 1982. 198 p.

Luce, Charles F. *155 Years of Technological Excellence.* New York, N.Y.: Newcomen Society in North America, 1978. 24 p. (Newcomen publication; no. 1095)

Lurkis, Alexander. *The Power Brink, Con Edison, A Centennial of Electricity.* New York, N.Y.: Icare Press, 1982. 200 p.

Talbot, Allan R. *Power Along the Hudson, The Storm King Case and the Birth of Environmentalism.* New York, N.Y.: Dutton, 1972. 244 p.

CONSOLIDATED FOODS

Cummings, Nathan. *Consolidated Foods: Blueprint for the Construction of a Diversified Company.* New York, N.Y.: Newcomen Society in North America, 1965. 24 p. (Newcomen address)

CONSOLIDATED FREIGHTWAYS, INC.

Consolidated Freightways, Inc. *Consolidated Freightways, Inc. Fact Book and Financial Review 1961-1970.* San Francisco, Calif.: The Company, 1970.

Consolidated Freightways, Inc. *Consolidated Freightways,*

Inc.: The First 50 Years, 1929-1979. Researched and written by Mirriam Stein; edited by W.J. Grant. San Francisco, Calif.: The Company, 1979. 64 p.

CONSOLIDATED NATURAL GAS COMPANY

Tankersley, G. J. *The Story of Consolidated Natural Gas Company: Innovation, Ingenuity, And Accomplishment.* New York, N.Y.: Newcomen Society in North America, 1980. 23 p. (Newcomen publication; no. 1118)

CONSOLIDATED RAIL CORPORATION (CONRAIL)

Crane, L. Stanley. *Rise from the Wreckage: A Brief History of Conrail.* New York, N.Y.: Newcomen Society of the United States, 1988. 44 p. (Newcomen publication; no. 1305)

CONSUMER WATER COMPANY

Parker, John Van C. *Consumer Water Company: "Not Just Another Utility."* New York, N.Y.: Newcomen Society of the United States, 1988. 24 p. (Newcomen publication; no. 1311)

CONSUMERS POWER COMPANY

Bush, George. *Future Builders: The Story of Michigan's Consumers Power Company.* New York, N.Y.: McGraw-Hill, 1973. 603 p.

Consumers Power Company. *100 Years of Service, 1886-1986.* Jackson, Mich.: The Company, 1986. 30 p.

CONTEXT MANAGEMENT CORPORATION

Berger, Harvey. "Success Story: Context Management Corporation." *Computers & Electronics* 22 (April 1984): 52-53+

CONTINENTAL AIRLINES CORPORATION

Davies, Ronald E.G. *Continental Air Lines: The First Fifty Years, 1934-1984.* The Woodlands, Tex.: Pioneer Publications, Inc., 1984. 191 p.

Murphy, Michael E. *The Airline That Pride Almost Bought: The Struggle to Take Over Continental Airlines.* New York, N.Y.: Franklin Watts, 1986. 289 p.

Serling, Robert J. *Maverick: The Story of Robert Six and Continental Airlines.* Garden City, N.Y.: Doubleday, 1974. 351 p.

Wagner, William. *Continental; Its Motors and Its People.* Fallbrook, Calif.: Aero Publishers, 1983. 256 p.

CONTINENTAL ASSURANCE COMPANY

Donahue, Richard J. "Continental Assurance, Without Aches, Turns 75." *National Underwriter (Life/Health)* 90 (2 August 1986): 30.

CONTINENTAL ILLINOIS CORPORATION

McCollom, James P. *Continental Affair: The Rise and Fall of the Continental Illinois Bank.* New York, N.Y.: Dodd, Mead, 1987. 393 p.

U.S. Congress. House. Committee on Banking, Finance, and Urban Affairs. *Inquiry into Continental Illinois Corporation and Continental Illinois National Bank: Hearings Before the Committee on Banking, Finance, and Urban Affairs.* 98th Cong., 2d Sess., 18 September- 4 October 1984. (Y 4.B 22/1:98-111)

CONTINENTAL INSURANCE COMPANY

Kelchburg, Ann, and Ronald G. Mullins. *A History of the Continental Insurance Company.* New York, N.Y.:

Corporate Communications Dept., Continental Corporation, 1979. 126 p.

CONTINENTAL MOTORS CORPORATION

Wagner, William. *Continental: Its Motors and Its People.* Washington, D.C.: Armed Forces Journal International; Fallbrook, Calif.: Aero Publishers, 1983. 240 p.

CONTINENTAL OIL COMPANY

Continental Oil Company. *CONOCO: The First One Hundred Years: Building on the Past for the Future.* New York, N.Y.: Special Marketing Division, Dell Publishing Company, 1975. 238 p.

Continental Oil Company. *Historical Brief--Continental Oil Company, 1875-1970.* Stamford, Conn.: The Company, 1970.

CONTINENTAL TELEPHONE CORPORATION

"A Special Report; The Talking Machine and Bit Streams." In *Continental Telephone Corporation. Annual Report*, 9-14. Atlanta, Ga.: The Corporation, 1978.

CONTROL DATA CORPORATION

Fucini, Joseph J., and Suzy Fucini. "William C. Norris, Control Data Corporation: 'Address Society's Unmet Needs As Profitable Business Opportunities.'" In *Experience Inc.; Men and Women Who Founded Famous Companies After the Age of 40*, 112-118. New York, N.Y.: Free Press, 1987.

Lundstrom, David E. *A Few Good Men from Univac.* Cambridge, Mass.: MIT Press, 1987. 227 p. (MIT Press series in the history of computing)

Pine, Carol, and Susan Mundale. "William Norris; There

Ain't No Backin' Up." In *Self-Made: The Stories of 12 Minnesota Entrepreneurs*, 101-124. Minneapolis, Minn.: Dorn Books, 1982.

Raimondi, Donna. "From Code Busters to Mainframes: The History of CDC." *Computerworld* 19 (15 July 1985): 93, 98-99.

Worthy, James C. *William C. Norris: Portrait of a Maverick*. Cambridge, Mass.: Ballinger, 1987. 240 p.

CONVERGENT TECHNOLOGIES

Hills, Stephanie M. "Networking Helps Convergent Emerge from Its Dark Hours." *Data Communications* 15 (March 1986): 87-96.

COOPER INDUSTRIES

Keller, David N. *Cooper Industries, 1833-1983*. Athens, Ohio: Ohio University Press, 1983. 400 p.

COOPER TIRE AND RUBBER COMPANY

Cooper Tire and Rubber Company. *A History of Cooper*. Findlay, Ohio: The Company, 1985. 7 p.

COORS (ADOLPH) COMPANY

Adolph Coors Company. *The Adolph Coors Story*. Golden, Colo.: The Company, 1984. 32 p.

COPPER RANGE COMPANY

Boyd, James. *Copper Range Company: The Story of Man's Oldest and Newest Metal*. New York, N.Y.: Newcomen Society in North America, 1970. 24 p. (Newcomen address)

COR-AGO COMPANY

Monette, Clarence J., and G. Walton Smith. *Cor-Ago: A Lake Linden Medicine Company*. Lake Linden, Mich.: Monette, 1974. 23 p.

CORNELL HOTEL AND RESTAURANT ADMINISTRATION QUARTERLY

"A History of the Quarterly." *Cornell Hotel and Restaurant Administration Quarterly* 26 (May 1985): 102-103.

CORNING GLASS WORKS

Houghton, James R. "The Role of Technology in Restructuring a Company." *Research Management* 26 (November/December 1983): 9-16.

Scanlon, Sally. "How Corning Process Systems Refused to Go Down the Tube." *Sales & Marketing Management* 126 (2 February 1981): 25-28.

CORPORATION FOR ENTERTAINMENT AND LEARNING

"20 Years of Entertainment and Learning." *Broadcasting* 105 (25 July 1983): 95-96.

CORROON AND BLACK CORPORATION

Corroon and Black Corporation. *A History of Corroon and Black Corporation*. New York, N.Y.: The Company, 1988. 12 p.

COTTER AND COMPANY

Kantowicz, Edward R. *True Value: John Cotter; 70 Years of Hardware*. Chicago, Ill.: Regnery Books, 1986. 270 p.

COTTON PRODUCERS ASSOCIATION, ATLANTA

Dimsdale, Parks B. *A History of the Cotton Producers Association*. Atlanta, Ga.: The Association, 1970. 231 p.

COWARD, MCCANN AND GEOGHEGAN

Weyr, Thomas. "Coward, McCann & Geoghegan: Fifty Years in the Business of Books." *Publishers Weekly* 213 (3 April 1978): 33-36.

COX BROADCASTING CORPORATION

Cox Broadcasting Corporation. *Cox Broadcasting Corporation: General Information*. Atlanta, Ga.: Cox Broadcasting Corporation, 1979. 14 p.

Howard, Herbert H. "Cox Broadcasting Corporation: A Group-Ownership Case Study [History of One of the Oldest and Largest of the Group Owners in Radio and Television, Which Maintains Headquarters in Atlanta]." *Journal of Broadcasting* 20 (Spring 1976): 209-232.

CPT CORPORATION

Pine, Carol, and Susan Mundale. "Dean Scheff; A Jury of One." In *Self-Made: The Stories of 12 Minnesota Entrepreneurs*, 193-206. Minneapolis, Minn.: Dorn Books, 1982.

CR INDUSTRIES

Mark, Norman. *The CR Century: Images of American Business*. Elgin, Ill.: The Company, 1978. 190 p.

CRANE AND COMPANY

Pierce, Wadsworth R. *First 175 Years of Crane Papermaking*. Dalton, Mass.: The Company, 1977.

76 p.

CRAY COMPUTER CORPORATION

Markoff, John. "Cray's Future Without Cray." *New York Times*, 21 May 1989, sec. 3, p. 1.

CRAYOLA CRAYONS
SEE:
BINNEY AND SMITH, INC.

CROCKER-CITIZENS NATIONAL BANK

Bloom, Monroe A. *A Century of Pioneering; A Brief History of Crocker-Citizens National Bank.* San Francisco, Calif.: The Bank, 1970. 48 p.

CROCKER NATIONAL CORPORATION

Edwards, Raoul D. "Crocker National--The Turnaround Under Wilcox." *United States Banker* 90 (October 1979): 32+

CROWLEY MARITIME CORPORATION

Crowley, Thomas B. *Crowley Maritime Corporation: San Francisco Bay Tugboats to International Transportation Fleet.* An Interview Conducted by Miriam Feingold Stein, 1973-1975. Berkeley, Calif.: Regional Oral History Office, The Bancroft Library, University of California at Berkeley, 1983.

CROWN AMERICAN CORPORATION

Crown American Corporation. *Frank J. Pasquerilla, Chairman of the Board & Chief Executive Officer, Crown American Corporation.* Johnstown, Pa.: The Company, 1988. 7 p.

CROWN ZELLERBACH CORPORATION

Crown Zellerbach. *It's a Beginning: Crown Zellerbach's First One Hundred Years*. San Francisco, Calif.: The Company, 1970. 10 p.

CRUCIBLE STEEL CORPORATION

Kaufmann, Dwight W. *Crucible; The Story of a Steel Company*. Pittsburgh, Pa.: D.W. Kaufmann, 1986. 298 p.

CTS CORPORATION

Soltow, James H. *Ninety Years; A History of CTS Corporation, 1896-1986*. Elkhart, Ind.: The Company, 1988. 128 p.

CUBIC CORPORATION

Seidenman, Paul, and David J. Spanovich. "Cultivating Companies for Long-Term Growth: The Cubic Case." *Business Horizons* 29 (March/April 1986): 52-55.

CUISINART

Fucini, Joseph J., and Suzy Fucini. "Carl G. Sontheimer, Cuisinart, Inc.: 'If You Aren't Passionate--Don't Even Bother.'" In *Experience Inc.; Men and Women Who Founded Famous Companies After the Age of 40*, 215-220. New York, N.Y.: Free Press, 1987.

Kleinfield, N.R. "How Cuisinart Lost Its Edge." *New York Times*, 15 April 1990, sec. 6, p. 46.

CULLIGAN INTERNATIONAL COMPANY

"Hey, Culligan." *Chicago Tribune*, 31 July 1988, sec. 18, p. 1.

CUMBERLAND FARMS, INC.

"From Yesterday--To Today." *Cumberland Farms Milky Way* (December 1986): 2-3.

CUMMINGS AND LOCKWOOD

Drake, Philip M. *Cummings & Lockwood: A 75-Year Reputation of Hard-Earned Excellence.* New York, N.Y.: Newcomen Society of the United States, 1984. 22 p. (Newcomen publication; no. 1225)

CUMMINS ENGINE COMPANY, INC.

Bender, Marylin. "Black Executives in New Role at Cummins Engine." In *At the Top; Behind the Scenes with the Men and Women Who Run America's Corporate Giants*, 331-356. Garden City, N.Y.: Doubleday, 1975.

Flanigan, James. "Modern Tale of Old-Fashioned Business Values." *Los Angeles Times*, 23 July 1989, sec. IV, p. 1.

CUNA MUTUAL INSURANCE SOCIETY

Eikel, Charles F. *The Debt Shall Die with the Debtor; The CUNA Mutual Insurance Society Story.* New York, N.Y.: Newcomen Society in North America, 1972. 47 p. (Newcomen address)

CUNARD STEAMSHIP COMPANY, LTD.

Hyde, Francis Edwin. *Cunard and the North Atlantic, 1840-1973: A History of Shipping and Financial Management.* Atlantic Highlands, N.J.: Humanities Press, 1975, c1974.

CURTIS PUBLISHING COMPANY

Ackerman, Martin S. *The Curtis Affair.* Los Angeles,

Calif.: Nash, 1970. 202 p.

Culligan, Mathew J. *The Curtis-Culligan Story; From Cyrus to Horace, To Joe.* New York, N.Y.: Crown Publishing, 1970. 224 p.

Friedrich, Otto. *Decline and Fall: The Struggle for Power at a Great American Magazine, The Saturday Evening Post.* New York, N.Y.: Harper & Row, 1970. 499 p.

Goulden, Joseph C. *The Curtis Caper.* New York, N.Y.: G.P. Putnam's Sons, 1965. 281 p.

Woods, James Playsted. *The Curtis Magazines.* New York, N.Y.: Ronald Press Company, 1971. 297 p.

THE CUSTOM SHOP

Levitt, Mortimer. "The Custom Shop----." In *How to Start Your Own Business Without Losing Your Shirt; Secrets of Seventeen Successful Entrepreneurs*, 1-51. New York, N.Y.: Atheneum, 1988.

CUTLER-HAMMER, INC.

Cutler-Hammer, Inc. *A History of Cutler-Hammer, Inc., 1892-1967.* Milwaukee, Wis.: The Company, 1967. 82 p.

Cutler-Hammer, Inc. *An American Dream, A Commemorative History of Cutler-Hammer, Inc., 1892-1978.* Milwaukee, Wis.: The Company, 1979. 94 p.

CYPRUS MINERALS COMPANY

Barr, Kenneth J. *Cyprus Minerals Company: People Make the Difference.* New York, N.Y.: Newcomen Society of the United States, c1990. 20 p. (Newcomen publication; no. 1346)

DA VINCI SYSTEMS

Mardesich, Jodi. "Da Vinci's Renaissance Men: Life Imitates Art." *InfoWorld* 12 (20 August 1990): 44-47.

DAIRYMEN, INC.

"Dairymen 20 Years, 1968-1988." In *Dairymen, Inc. Annual Report*, 1-6. Louisville, Ky.: The Company, 1988.

DALLAS COWBOYS

Meyers, Jeff. *Dallas Cowboys.* New York, N.Y.: Macmillan, 1974. 192 p.

Stowers, Carlton. *Journey to Triumph: 110 Dallas Cowboys Tell Their Stories.* Dallas, Tex.: Taylor Publishing Company, 1982. 260 p.

Whittingham, Richard. *The Dallas Cowboys: An Illustrated History.* New York, N.Y.: Harper & Row, 1981. 224 p.

Wolfe, Jane. *The Murchisons: The Rise and Fall of a Texas Dynasty.* New York, N.Y.: St. Martin's Press, 1989. 505 p.

DAN RIVER, INC.

Cross, Malcolm A. *Dan River Runs Deep: An Informal History of a Major Textile Company, 1950-1981.* New York, N.Y.: The Total Book, 1982. 293 p.

DANA CORPORATION

McPherson, René C. *Dana: Toward the Year 2000.* New York, N.Y.: Newcomen Society in North America, 1973. 24 p.

DARIGOLD, INC.

Darigold, Inc. *The Darigold Story*. Seattle, Wash.: The Company, 1984. 14 p.

DARLING-DELAWARE COMPANY, INC.

Dainty, Ralph B. *Darling-Delaware Centenary, 1882-1982*. Chicago, Ill.: The Company, 1981. 229 p.

DARTNELL CORPORATION

Lewis, Leslie L., and R.S. Minor. *The Dartnell Story*. Chicago, Ill.: The Company, 1984. 148 p.

DATA CARD CORPORATION

Fucini, Joseph J., and Suzy Fucini. "Willis K. Drake, Data Card Corporation: 'Support Good Ideas with a Solid Corporate Structure.'" In *Experience Inc.; Men and Women Who Founded Famous Companies After the Age of 40*, 136-142. New York, N.Y.: Free Press, 1987.

DATA GENERAL CORPORATION

Kidder, Tracy. *The Soul of a New Machine*. Boston, Mass.: Little, Brown, 1981. 292 p.

DATACO, INC.

Petersen, Debbie. "Disaster Planning: Out of the Ashes." *American Printer* 205 (September 1990): 56-58.

DATUM, INC.

"When Firm Outgrows Founder." *Inc.* 1 (December 1979): 72-78.

DAVEY TREE EXPERT COMPANY

Pfleger, Robert E. *Green Leaves: A History of the Davey Tree Expert Company.* Chester, Conn.: Pequot Press, 1970. 194 p.

DAVIS (F.A.) COMPANY

Craven, Robert H. *F.A. Davis Company: 1879-1979; A Very Personal Account.* Philadelphia, Pa.: The Company, 1979. 90 p.

DAY AND ZIMMERMANN, INC.

Day and Zimmermann, Inc. *Sixty Five Years With the Men of Day and Zimmermann.* Philadelphia, Pa.: The Company, 1966. 44 p.

Yoh, Harold L. *Day & Zimmermann, Inc.: Dedicated to Excellence for Eighty Years, 1901-1981.* New York, N.Y.: Newcomen Society in North America, 1981. 27 p. (Newcomen publication; no. 1144)

DAYCO CORPORATION

Fisher, David G. *Dayco History.* Springfield, Mo.: The Company, 1984. 26 p.

DAYTON, COVINGTON, AND PIQUA TRACTION COMPANY

Gordon, William Reed, and Richard M. Wagner. *The Overlook Route: The Dayton, Covington and Piqua Traction Company.* Wyoming, Ohio: Trolley Talk, 1972. 52 p.

DAYTON MALLEABLE, INC.

Miske, Jack C. "Amcast--New Company with a 117-Year History." *Foundry Management and Technology* 112 (April 1984): 52-55.

Miske, Jack C. "Dayton Malleable Inc.--A Company Shaping Change." *Foundry Management and Technology* 109 (November 1981): F1-F16.

Torley, John F. *Dayton Malleable, Inc.: A Story of Progress.* New York, N.Y.: Newcomen Society in North America, 1976. 20 p. (Newcomen publication; no. 1037)

DAYTON RELIABLE TOOL AND MANUFACTURING COMPANY

Fraze, Ermal C. *Dayton Reliable Tool & Manufacturing Company.* New York, N.Y.: Newcomen Society of the United States, 1987, c1989. 18 p. (Newcomen publication; no. 1302)

DDB NEEDHAM WORLDWIDE, INC.

Millman, Nancy. In *Emperors of Adland; Inside the Advertising Revolution*, 57-158. New York, N.Y.: Warner Books, 1988.

Stevenson, Dick. "Up and Down with Doyle Dane Bernbach." *Ad Forum* 5 (October 1984): 10-17, 69-72.

DE LOREAN MOTOR COMPANY

De Lorean, John Z. *De Lorean.* Grand Rapids, Mich.: Zondervan Publishing House, 1985. 349 p.

Fallon, Ivan, and J. Strodes. *Dream Maker: The Rise and Fall of John Z. De Lorean.* New York, N.Y.: Putnam, 1983. 455 p.

Haddad, William F. *Hard Driving: My Years with John De Lorean.* New York, N.Y.: Random House, 1985. 193 p.

Lamm, John, and M. Knepper. *De Lorean: Stainless Steel Illusion.* Santa Ana, Calif.: Newport Press, 1983.

160 p.

Levin, Hillel. *Grand Delusions; The Cosmic Career of John De Lorean.* New York, N.Y.: Viking Press, 1983. 336 p.

Levin, Hillel. *John De Lorean: The Maverick Mogul.* London, Eng.: Orbis Publishing Company, 1983. 268 p.

Shook, Robert L. "John Z. De Lorean." In *The Entrepreneurs: Twelve Who Took Risks and Succeeded,* 157-171. New York, N.Y.: Harper & Row, 1980.

DEAK-PERERA GROUP

Deak, Nicholas L. *Deak-Perera Group: Story of the Nation's Oldest and Largest Foreign Money Exchange Firm.* New York, N.Y.: Newcomen Society in North America, 1975. 24 p. (Newcomen publication; no. 1015)

DEC
SEE:
DIGITAL EQUIPMENT CORPORATION

DEERE AND COMPANY

Broehl, Wayne G. *John Deere's Company; A History of Deere & Company and Its Times.* New York, N.Y.: Doubleday, 1984. 880 p.

Huber, Donald S., and Ralph C. Hughes. *How Johnny Popper Replaced the Horse; A History of John Deere's Two-Cylinder Tractors.* Moline, Ill.: The Company, 1988. 160 p.

Nelson, Selmer, and Nadine Nelson. *Grossenburg's Fifty Years with John Deere.* Freeman, S.D.: Pine Hill Press, 1987. 167 p.

Trumm, Eldon. *Evolution of the John Deere Toy.* Worthington, Iowa: E. Trumm, 1982. 136 p.

DEERFOOT FARMS COMPANY

Doucette, Paul A. *Deerfoot; "The Aristocrat of Farms."* Westport, Conn.: National Association of Milk Bottle Collectors, 1987. 38 p.

DEL MONTE CORPORATION

Braznell, William. *California's Finest: The History of Del Monte Corporation and the Del Monte Brand.* San Francisco, Calif.: Del Monte, 1982. 168 p.

Eames, Alfred W. *"The Business of Feeding People": The Story of Del Monte Corporation.* New York, N.Y.: Newcomen Society in North America, 1974. 22 p. (Newcomen publication; no. 985)

DELAWARE AND HUDSON RAILROAD

Zimmermann, Karl R. *A Decade of D&H.* Oradell, N.J.: Delford Press, 1978. 79 p.

DELTA AIR LINES, INC.

Davis, Sidney. *Delta Air Lines: Debunking the Myth.* Atlanta, Ga.: Peachtree, 1988. 191 p.

Delta Air Lines, Inc. *Delta--Highlights of Our History.* Atlanta, Ga.: The Company, 1983. 5 p.

Delta Air Lines, Inc. *Delta--Highlights of Our History.* Atlanta, Ga.: The Company, 1987. 4 p.

Lewis, Walter David, and Wesley Phillips Newton. *Delta: The History of an Airline.* Athens, Ga.: University of Georgia Press, 1979. 503 p.

Lewis, Walter David, and Wesley Phillips Newton. "The

Delta-C&S Merger: A Case Study in Airline Consolidation and Federal Regulation." *Business History Review* 53 (Summer 1979): 161-179.

DELTA NATURAL GAS COMPANY, INC.

Delta Natural Gas Company, Inc. *Historical Summary.* Winchester, Ky.: The Company, 1985. 4 p.

"Historical Summary." In *Delta Natural Gas Company. Annual Report*, 1-4. Winchester, Ky.: The Company, 1984.

THE DELTA QUEEN STEAMBOAT COMPANY

August Perez and Associates. *The Delta Queen: Last of the Paddlewheel Palaces.* Gretna, La.: Pelican Publishing Company, 1973. 96 p.

Greene, Letha C. *Long Live the Delta Queen.* New York, N.Y.: Hastings House, 1973. 174 p.

DELTA STEAMSHIP LINES

Beargie, T. "Delta Steamship Lines: 1919-1985." *American Shipping* 27 (March 1985): 48.

DENVER AND RIO GRANDE WESTERN RAILROAD COMPANY

Farewell, R.C. *Rio Grande; Ruler of the Rockies.* Glendale, Calif.: Trans-Anglo Books, 1987. 168 p.

DENVER BRONCOS

Connor, Dick. *The Denver Broncos.* Englewood Cliffs, N.J.: Prentice Hall, 1974. 127 p.

The Denver Broncos. Denver, Colo.: R.R. Donnelley & Sons, 1982. 111 p.

Hession, Joseph, and Michael Spence. *Broncos: Three Decades of Football*. San Francisco, Calif.: Foghorn Press, 1987. 200 p.

DENVER TRAMWAY CORPORATION

Luskey, Sam. *101 Years Young; The Tramway Saga*. Denver, Colo.: Printed by A.B. Hirschfeld Press, 1968. 95 p.

DEPOSIT GUARANTEE BANK AND TRUST COMPANY OF JACKSON

McMullan, W.P. *From Mississippi Soil--A People and a Bank. The Story of Deposit Guaranty Bank and Trust Company of Jackson*. New York, N.Y.: Newcomen Society in North America, 1965. 24 p. (Newcomen address)

DEPOSITORS CORPORATION

Haselton, Wallace M. *Busy Building Maine: The Story of Depositors Corporation*. New York, N.Y.: Newcomen Society in North America, 1971. 24 p.

DETROIT BANK AND TRUST COMPANY

Woodford, Arthur. *Detroit and Its Bank; the Story of Detroit Bank and Trust Company*. Detroit, Mich.: Wayne State University Press, 1974. 298 p.

DETROIT EDISON COMPANY

McCarthy, Walter J. *Detroit Edison Generates More Than Electricity*. New York, N.Y.: Newcomen Society in North America, 1983. 24 p. (Newcomen publication; no. 1180)

Miller, Raymond Curtis. *The Force of Energy: A Business History of the Detroit Edison Company*. East Lansing: Michigan State University Press, 1971. 363 p.

DETROIT TIGERS

Astor, Gerald, and Joe Falls. *The Detroit Tigers: An Illustrated History.* New York, N.Y.: Walker & Company, 1989. 256 p.

Falls, Joe. *Detroit Tigers.* New York, N.Y.: Macmillan, 1975. 192 p.

Falls, Joe. *The Detroit Tigers: An Illustrated History.* Englewood Cliffs, N.J.: Prentice Hall, 1990. 224 p.

Hawkins, John C. *This Date in Detroit Tigers History: A Day by Day Listing of the Events in the History of the Detroit Tigers Baseball Team.* New York, N.Y.: Stein and Day, 1981. 239 p.

Smith, Fred T. *Fifty Years with the Tigers.* Lathrup Village, Mich.: The Author, 1984. 250 p.

Sullivan, George. *The Detroit Tigers: The Complete Record of Detroit Tigers Baseball.* New York, N.Y.: Collier Books, 1985. 432 p.

DEXTER CORPORATION

Coffin, David Linwood. *The History of the Dexter Corporation, 1767-1967.* New York, N.Y.: Newcomen Society in North America, 1967. 24 p. (Newcomen address)

DI GIORGIO FRUIT CORPORATION

Galarza, Ernesto. *Spiders in the House and Workers in the Field.* South Bend, Indiana: University of Notre Dame Press, 1970. 306 p.

DIAMOND MATCH COMPANY

Stephens, Kent. *Matches, Flumes, and Rails: The Diamond Match Company in the High Sierra.* 2nd ed.

Corona Del Mar, Calif.: Transanglo Books, 1981. 176 p.

DIAMOND SHAMROCK

Bricker, William H. *Partners by Choice and Fortune: The Story of Diamond Shamrock.* New York, N.Y.: Newcomen Society in North America, 1977. 27 p. (Newcomen publication; no. 1064)

DICKERSON (CHARLES W.) FIELD MUSIC, INC.

Boddie, David L. *We've Come a Long Way Together: The Story of a Drum Corps.* New Rochelle, N.Y.: The Company, 1981. 135 p.

DIETRICH-POST COMPANY

"CEO Profile: The Case for Succession Planning." *Small Business Report* 10 (February 1985): 79-83.

DIGITAL EQUIPMENT CORPORATION

Olsen, Kenneth H. *Digital Equipment Corporation, The First Twenty-Five Years.* New York, N.Y.: Newcomen Society in North America, 1983. 19 p. (Newcomen publication; no. 1179)

Rifkin, Glenn. *The Ultimate Entrepreneur: The Story of Ken Olsen and Digital Equipment Corporation.* Chicago, Ill.: Contemporary Books, 1988. 332 p.

Rifkin, Glenn, and George Harrar, "The Ultimate Entrepreneur: How DEC Passed Up the PC Boom." *Computerworld* 22 (3 October 1988): 1, 97-99.

DILLARD'S DEPARTMENT STORES, INC.

Buchholz, Barbara B., and Margaret Crane. "Dillard Department Stores Inc., Little Rock, AR." In *Corporate Blood Lines: The Future of the Family*

Firm, 60-77. New York, N.Y.: Carol Publishing Group, 1989.

Rosenberg, Leon Joseph. *Dillard's, The First Fifty Years*. Fayetteville, Ark.: University of Arkansas Press, 1988. 141 p.

DINERS CLUB

Fucini, Joseph J., and Suzy Fucini. "Ralph E. Schneider, Diners Club: 'I Had a Good Idea and Worked Hard, But I Was Very Lucky, Too.'" In *Experience Inc.; Men and Women Who Founded Famous Companies After the Age of 40*, 96-101. New York, N.Y.: Free Press, 1987.

DISCOVERY TOYS

Taylor, Russel R. "Lane Nemeth: 'Learning Should Be Fun.'" In *Exceptional Entrepreneurial Women*, 79-85. New York, N.Y.: Quorum Books, 1988.

DISNEY (WALT) PRODUCTIONS

Hollis, Richard, and Brian Sibley. *The Disney Studio Story*. New York, N.Y.: Crown, 1988. 256 p.

Mosley, Leonard. *Disney's World: A Biography*. New York, N.Y.: Stein & Day, 1985. 330 p.

Thomas, Bob. *Walt Disney: An American Original*. New York, N.Y.: Simon and Schuster, 1976. 379 p.

DIXON (JOSEPH) CRUCIBLE COMPANY

"History a By-Product of the Joseph Dixon Crucible Company." *New Jersey Business* 13 (June 1967): 34-38.

DOMINO'S PIZZA

Monaghan, Thomas S. *Pizza Tiger*. New York, N.Y.: Random House, 1986. 336 p.

Whalen, Bernie. "'People-Oriented' Marketing Delivers a Lot of Dough for Domino's." *Marketing News* (16 March 1984): 4-5.

DONNELLEY (R.R.) AND SONS

Donnelley, Gaylord. *To Be a Good Printer: Our Commitments*. Chicago, Ill.: Lakeside Press, 1977. 110 p.

DORSEY LABORATORIES

Lavin, Joseph J. *Dorsey Laboratories: People--The Key to Growth and Success*. New York, N.Y.: Newcomen Society of the United States, 1984. 28 p. (Newcomen publication; no. 1216)

DOSKOCIL COMPANIES, INC.

Bork, Robert H., Jr. "The Up and Comers: On Top of the Pizza." *Forbes* 134 (22 October 1984): 115, 118.

DOUGLAS AIRCRAFT COMPANY

Ingells, Douglas J. *The Plane That Changed the World, A Biography of the DC-3*. Fallbrook, Calif.: Aero Publishers, Inc., 1966. 256 p.

DOW CHEMICAL COMPANY

Duerksen, Christopher J. *Dow vs. California: A Turning Point in the Envirobusiness Struggle*. Washington: Conservation Foundation, 1982. 151 p.

Griswold, Thomas. *The Time of My Life*. Midland, Mich.: Northwood Institute, 1973. 201 p.

Mann, Charles C., and Daniel Forbes. "The Town of Dow." *Business Month* 130 (December 1987): 59-68.

Seward, William. *East From Brozosport.* Midland, Mich.: Dow Chemical Company, 1974. 191 p.

Sorey, Gordon Kent. *The Foreign Policy of a Multinational Enterprise: An Analysis of the Policy Interactions of Dow Chemical Company and the United States.* New York, N.Y.: Arno Press, 1980, c1976. 156 p.

Thompson, Stanley J. *The S/B Latex Story: Recollections of "Can Do" at Dow.* Midland, Mich.: The Company, 1980. 326 p.

Whitehead, Don. *The Dow Story: The History of Dow Chemical Company.* New York, N.Y.: McGraw-Hill, 1968. 298 p.

SEE ALSO: MERRELL DOW PHARMACEUTICALS

DOW CORNING CORPORATION

Warrick, Earl L. *Forty Years of Firsts: The Recollections of a Dow Corning Pioneer.* New York, N.Y.: McGraw-Hill, 1990. 330 p.

DOW, JONES AND COMPANY

Caliam, Carnegie Samuel. *The Gospel According to the Wall Street Journal.* Atlanta, Ga.: John Knox Press, 1975. 114 p.

"Celebrating Our First Century." In *Dow Jones And Company. Annual Report*, 5-15. New York, N.Y.: The Company, 1981.

Neilson, Winthrop, and Frances Neilson. *What's News-- Dow Jones: Story of the Wall Street Journal.* Radnor, Pa.: Chilton Book Company, 1973. 171 p.

Rosenberg, Jerry M. *Inside the Wall Street Journal: The History and the Power of Dow Jones & Company and America's Most Influential Newspaper.* New York, N.Y.: Macmillan, 1982. 328 p.

Wendt, Lloyd. *The Wall Street Journal: The Story of Dow Jones & the Nation's Business Newspaper.* Chicago, Ill.: Rand McNally, 1982. 448 p.

DOYLE DANE BERNBACH
SEE:
DDB NEEDHAM WORLDWIDE, INC.

DR. PEPPER COMPANY

Ellis, Harry E. *Dr. Pepper, king of Beverages.* Dallas, Tex.: The Company, 1979. 268 p.

Dr. Pepper Company. *Dr. Pepper's Phos-Ferrates.* Dallas, Tex.: The Company, 1972. 18 p.

Jabbonsky, Larry. "Still Out of the Ordinary After All These Years." *Beverage World* 103 (October 1984): 59-64.

Morgan, Monty Brown. "The Dr. Pepper Company: A Case Study." Report (M.B.A.). Austin: University of Texas at Austin, 1981. 121 p.

DRAVO CORPORATION

Dravo Corporation. *A Company of Uncommon Enterprise: The Story of Dravo Corporation, 1891-1966.* Pittsburgh, Pa.: The Company, 1974. 176 p.

DRESSER INDUSTRIES, INC.

Payne, Darwin. *Initiative in Energy: Dresser Industries, Inc., 1880-1978.* New York, N.Y.: Simon & Schuster, 1979. 415 p.

DREXEL BURNHAM LAMBERT

Drexel Burnham Lambert. *Fiftieth Anniversary*. New York, N.Y.: The Company, 1984. 68 p.

Stone, Dan G. *April Fools: An Insider's Account of the Rise and Collapse of Drexel Burnham*. New York, N.Y.: Donald I. Fine, 1990. 256 p.

DRUG EMPORIUM, INC.

Wilber, Philip I. *Drug Emporium, Inc.: Taking Care of Customers Needs*. New York, N.Y.: Newcomen Society of the United States, c1989, 1990. 16 p. (Newcomen publication; no. 1337)

DRYSDALE GOVERNMENT SECURITIES, INC.

U.S. Congress. Senate. Committee on Banking, Housing, And Urban Affairs. Subcommittee on Securities. *Disturbances in the U.S. Securities Market: Hearings Before the Subcommittee on Securities*. 97th Cong., 2d Sess., 25 May 1982.

DU PONT DE NEMOURS (E.I.) AND COMPANY

Chambless, William. *Haskell Laboratory for Toxicology and Industrial Research: Fifty Years of Research and Service*. Wilmington, Del.: Du Pont Company, 1985. 96 p.

Chandler, Alfred D., and Stephen Salsbury. *Pierre S. Du Pont and the Making of the Modern Corporation*. New York, N.Y.: Harper and Row, 1971. 722 p.

Colby, Gerald. *Du Pont Dynasty: Behind the Nylon Curtain*. Secaucus, N.J.: Lyle Stuart, 1984. 960 p.

Duke, Marc. *The Du Ponts: Portrait of a Dynasty*. New York, N.Y.: Saturday Review Press/E.P.Dutton, 1976. 340 p.

Hounshell, David A., and John K. Smith. *Science and Corporate Strategy: Du Pont R&D, 1902-1980*. New York, N.Y.: Cambridge University Press, 1988. 756 p.

Mosley, Leonard. *Blood Relations: The Rise and Fall of the Du Ponts of Delaware*. New York, N.Y.: Atheneum, 1980. 426 p.

Munyan, Mary G. *Du Pont--The Story of a Company Town*. Puyallup, Wash.: Valley Press, 1972. 240 p.

Taylor, Graham D. *Du Pont and the International Chemical Industry*. Boston, Mass.: Twayne Publishers, 1984. 251 p.

Wall, Joseph Frazier. *Alfred I. Du Pont: The Man and His Family*. New York, N.Y.: Oxford University Press, 1990. 685 p.

Williams, Jon M., and D.T. Muir. *Corporate Images: Photography and the Du Pont Company, 1865-1972*. Wilmington: Hagley Museum and Library, 1984. 72 p.

Wingate, Phillip Jerome. *The Colorful Du Pont Company*. Wilmington: Serendipity Press, 1982. 213 p.

Zilg, Gerald C. *Du Pont: Behind the Nylon Curtain*. Englewood Cliffs, N.J.: Prentice-Hall, 1974. 623 p.

DUDLEY-ANDERSON-YUTZY PUBLIC RELATIONS, INC.

Hartman, Curtis. "Selling the Brooklyn Bridge." *Inc.* 5 (November 1983): 58-70.

DUKE POWER COMPANY

Horn, Carol. *The Duke Power Story 1904-1973*. New York, N.Y.: Newcomen Society in North America, 1973. 17 p. (Newcomen publication; no. 969)

Johnson, John W. *Insuring Against Disaster, The Nuclear Industry on Trial.* Macon, Ga.: Mercer University Press, 1986. 284 p.

Lee, William S. *Duke Power Company: The Roots That Nourish the Future.* New York, N.Y.: Newcomen Society of the United States, 1986, c1987. 22 p. (Newcomen publication; no. 1279)

Maynor, Joe. *Duke Power, The First Seventy-Five Years.* Albany, N.Y.: Delmar, 1980. 180 p.

DULUTH, MISSABLE AND IRON RANGE RAILWAY COMPANY

King, Frank A. *The Missable Road: The Duluth, Missable and Iron Range Railway.* San Marino, Calif.: Golden West Books, 1972. 224 p.

DUNCAN ELECTRIC COMPANY

Duncan Electric Company. *Duncan History.* Lafayette, Ind.: The Company, 1980. 27 p.

DUNES HOTELS AND CASINOS, INC.

"Looking for Mr. Good Deal." *Forbes* 128 (7 December 1981): 51, 54.

EAST AUGUSTA MUTUAL FIRE INSURANCE COMPANY

East Augusta Mutual Fire Insurance Company. *Centennial: The East Augusta Mutual Fire Insurance Company: Organization and Growth, 1870-1970.* Verona, Va.: McClure Printing Company, 1970. 111 p.

EAST OHIO GAS COMPANY

Kelso, J. Richard. *The Spirit of Progress: The Story of the East Ohio Gas Company and the People Who*

Made It. New York, N.Y.: Newcomen Society of the United States, 1988. 24 p. (Newcomen publication; no. 1317)

EAST RIVER SAVINGS BANK

Murphy, Austin S. *East River Savings Bank: 125 Years of Service to the People and the City of New York.* New York, N.Y.: Newcomen Society in North America, 1973. 26 p. (Newcomen address)

EAST TEXAS CHAMBER OF COMMERCE

The First Fifty Years: A History of Commerce. Edited by Howard W. Rosser. Longview, Texas: East Texas Magazine, 1976. 213 p.

EASTERN AIRLINES, INC.

Bernstein, Aaron. *Grounded; Frank Lorenzo and the Destruction of Eastern Airlines.* New York, N.Y.: Simon and Schuster, 1990. 320 p.

Cearley, George Walker, Jr. *Eastern Air Lines: An Illustrated History.* Dallas, Tex.: G.W. Cearely, Jr., 1985. 96 p.

Elder, Robb, and Sarah Elder. *Crash.* New York, N.Y.: Atheneum, 1977. 253 p. (About the 1972 accident)

Hall, Floyd D. *Sunrise at Eastern: Re-Birth of a Pioneer Airline.* New York, N.Y.: Newcomen Society in North America, 1965. 32 p.

Renaud, Vern. *Sketches of an Airline.* Long Valley, N.J.: Renaud Enterprises, 1969. 31 p.

Serling, Robert J. *From the Captain to the Colonel: An Informal History of Eastern Airlines.* New York, N.Y.: Dial Press, 1980. 535 p.

Smith, Frank K. *Legacy of Wings: The Story of Harold F. Pitcairn.* New York, N.Y.: Jason Aronson, 1981. 371 p.

Stockton, William. *Final Approach, The Crash of Eastern 212.* Garden City, N.Y.: Doubleday, 1977. 276 p.

THE EASTERN COMPANY

McMillen, Russell G. *The Eastern Company Since 1858: From Farm Tools to Yachting Instruments.* New York, N.Y.: Newcomen Society in North America, 1971. 24 p.

EASTERN GAS AND FUEL ASSOCIATES

EG&G, Inc. *40 Years of Leadership in Science & Technology Worldwide; A History of the Company.* Wellesley, Mass.: The Company, 1987. 37 p. (40th anniversary commemorative edition of *EGGINK*)

EG&G, Inc. *History.* Boston, Mass.: The Company, 1985. 3 p.

"50 Years: A Retrospective." In *Eastern Gas and Fuel Associates. Annual Report, Special Section.* Boston, Mass.: The Company, 1979.

EASTMAN KODAK COMPANY
SEE:
KODAK (EASTMAN) COMPANY

EATON CORPORATION

Scobel, Donald N. *Creative Worklife.* Houston, Tex.: Gulf Publishing Company, 1981. 244 p.

EATON YALE AND TOWNE, INC.

Ludvigsen, E.L. *Eaton Yale and Towne: A Corporate Portrait.* New York, N.Y.: Newcomen Society in North

America, 1968. 20 p. (Newcomen address)

EBASCO SERVICES, INC.

Wallace, William. *Ebasco Services Incorporated: The Saga of Electric Power; Meeting the Challenge of Change.* New York, N.Y.: Newcomen Society of the United States, 1986. 28 p. (Newcomen publication; no. 1268)

EBONY MAGAZINE
SEE:
JOHNSON PUBLISHING

EBSCO INDUSTRIES, INC.

EBSCO Industries, Inc. *The EBSCO Story.* Birmingham, Ala.: The Company, 1988. 80 p.

ECHLIN, INC.

It's Been an Exciting Ride!: Jack Echlin's Story of Echlin, Inc., As Told to Christopher Gilson. Branford, Conn.: The Company, 1989. 124 p.

Mancheski, Frederick J. *The Echlin Manufacturing Company: Its First Fifty Years.* New York, N.Y.: Newcomen Society in North America, 1975. 18 p. (Newcomen publication; no. 1024)

ECKERD (JACK) CORPORATION

Eckerd, Jack. *Eckerd.* Old Tappan, N.J.: Fleming H. Revell Company, 1987. 190 p.

ECONOMICS LABORATORY, INC.

Lanners, Fred T. *Products and Services for a Cleaner World: The Story of Economics Laboratory, Inc.* New York, N.Y.: Newcomen Society in North America, 1981. 24 p. (Newcomen publication; no. 1152)

EDAC TECHNOLOGIES
SEE:
CADE INDUSTRIES

EDS
SEE:
ELECTRONIC DATA SYSTEMS CORPORATION

EG&G, INC.
SEE:
EASTERN GAS AND FUEL ASSOCIATES

EGGHEAD DISCOUNT SOFTWARE

Gantz, John. "Egghead's Success Defies Conventional Wisdom." *InfoWorld* 10 (25 July 1988): 34+

EL PASO COMPANY

Mangan, Frank. *The Pipeliners*. El Paso, Tex.: Guynes Press, 1977. 353 p.

ELANO CORPORATION

Nutler, Ervin J. *The Elano Story: An Engineer's Free Enterprise Dream*. New York, N.Y.: Newcomen Society in North America, 1982. 24 p. (Newcomen publication; no. 1168)

ELDER-BEERMAN STORES CORPORATION

Gutmann, Max. *The Elder-Beerman Stores Corporation: A Tradition of Success*. New York, N.Y.: Newcomen Society of the United States, 1986. 21 p. (Newcomen publication; no. 1267)

ELECTRONIC DATA SYSTEMS CORPORATION

Levin, Doron P. *Irreconcilable Differences; Ross Perot Versus General Motors*. Boston, Mass.: Little Brown & Company, 1989. 357 p.

Mason, Todd. *Perot: An Unauthorized Biography.*
Homewood, Ill.: Dow Jones-Irwin, 1990. 316 p.

Meyer, Michael. "Living Theater." In *The Alexander
Complex; The Dreams That Drive the Great
Businessmen*, 55-103. New York, N.Y.: Times Books,
1989.

Sorge, M., and M. Krebs. "23 Years of EDS." *Automotive
News* (18 March 1985): 28.

ELECTRONIC NEWS

"25th Anniversary Issue." *Electronic News* 28 (25 January
1982): sec. 2, 1-95.

ELECTROPAC COMPANY, INC.

Goodman, Gerson. "The Company He Keeps." *D&B
Reports* 33 (September/October 1985): 24-26.

ELI BRIDGE COMPANY

Horan, K. "Big Wheel." *Modern Maturity* (June/July
1989): 78+

ELIZABETHTOWN WATER COMPANY

Carlisle, Robert D.B. *Water Ways: A History of the
Elizabethtown Water Company.* Elizabeth, N.J.: The
Company, 1982. 285 p.

ELLAM (PATRICK), INC.

Ellam, Patrick. *Wind Song: Our Ten Years in the Yacht
Delivery Business.* Camden, Maine: International
Marine Publishing Company, 1976. 222 p.

ELYACHAR REAL ESTATE

Buchholz, Barbara B., and Margaret Crane. "Elyachar

Real Estate, New York, N.Y. and Sarasota, FL." In *Corporate Blood Lines: The Future of the Family Firm*, 193-211. New York, N.Y.: Carol Publishing Group, 1989.

EMERSON ELECTRIC COMPANY

Snead, William Scott. *Emerson Electric Company, 1890-1965: The History of an Industrial Pioneer.* New York, N.Y.: Newcomen Society in North America, 1965. 28 p. (Newcomen address)

EMERY AIR FREIGHT CORPORATION

"Landmarks in Emery History." In *Emery Air Freight Corporation. 1984 Factbook*, 16. Wilton, Conn.: The Company, 1984.

EMPIRE AIRLINES

Davis, Lou W. "Some Said It Couldn't Be Done, But Empire Is Doing It." *Air Transport World* XIX (October 1982): 91-92+

EMPIRE SAVINGS AND LOAN

Adams, James Ring. "The Making of an Outcast." In *The Big Fix: Inside the S&L Scandal: How an Unholy Alliance of Politics and Money Destroyed America's Banking System*, 195-209. New York, N.Y.: Wiley, 1990.

EMPLOYEE INSURANCE OF WAUSAU MUTUAL COMPANY

Schlueter, Clyde F. *The Wausau Story of Employers Insurance of Wausau.* New York, N.Y.: Newcomen Society in North America, 1974. 24 p. (Newcomen publication; no. 998)

ENDICOTT JOHNSON CORPORATION

White, Eli G. *The Awakening of a Company: The Story of Endicott Johnson Corporation*. New York, N.Y.: Newcomen Society in North America, 1967. 24 p. (Newcomen address)

ENVIRONMENTAL SYSTEMS COMPANY

MacPhee, William. "Melvyn Bell of Environmental Systems Company." In *Rare Breed: The Entrepreneur, An American Culture*, 39-46. Chicago, Ill.: Probus Publishing Company, 1987.

EQUIFAX, INC.

Equifax, Inc. *A History of Equifax, Inc.* Atlanta, Ga.: The Company, 1985. 2 p.

EQUITABLE LIFE ASSURANCE SOCIETY OF THE UNITED STATES

Burley, Roscoe Carlyle. *The Equitable Life Assurance Society of the United States, 1859-1964*. New York, N.Y.: Appleton-Century-Crofts, 1967. 2 vol. 1475 p.

Equitable Life Assurance Society of the United States. *The Equitable Story*. New York, N.Y.: The Society, 197?. 20 p.

EQUITABLE LIFE INSURANCE COMPANY OF IOWA

Pease, George Sexton. *Patriarch of the Prairie, The Story of Equitable of Iowa, 1867-1967*. New York, N.Y.: Appleton-Century-Crofts, 1967. 260 p.

EQUITY FUNDING CORPORATION OF AMERICA

Dirks, Raymond L., and Leonard Gross. *The Great Wall Street Scandal*. New York, N.Y.: McGraw-Hill, 1974.

295 p.

Seidler, Lee J., Frederick Andrews, and Marc J. Epstein. *The Equity Funding Papers, The Anatomy of a Fraud.* Santa Barbara, Calif.: Wiley, 1977. 578 p.

ERIE INSURANCE EXCHANGE

Hirt, A. Orth. *The Story of Erie Insurance Exchange.* New York, Newcomen Society in North America, 1971. 32 p. (Newcomen address)

ERIE RAILROAD

Carleton, Paul. *The Erie Railroad Story.* Dunnellon, Fla.: D. Carleton Railbooks, 1988. 223 p.

E.S.M. GOVERNMENT SECURITIES
SEE:
HOME STATE SAVINGS BANK

ESTEE LAUDER
SEE:
LAUDER (ESTEE)

ESTEY ORGAN COMPANY

Whiting, Robert B. *Estey Reed Organs on Parade: A Pictorial Review of the Many Parlour, Cabinet, Boudoir, Philharmonic, And Other Types of Reed Organs Made Over a 100-Year Period by the Famous Estey Organ Company, Together with a Brief Corporate History.* Vestal, N.Y.: Vestal Press, 1981. 150 p.

ETHYL CORPORATION

Robert, Joseph C. *Ethyl: A History of the Corporation and the People Who Made It.* Charlottesville: University Press of Virginia, 1983. 448 p.

THE EVENING GAZETTE

Stoddard, Robert W. *The Evening Gazette: 100 Years--A Consistent Story*. New York, Newcomen Society in North America, 1966. 24 p. (Newcomen address)

EX-CELL-O CORPORATION

Giblin, Edward J., and E.P. Casey. *Innovative Products Through People: The Story of Ex-Cell-O Corporation*. New York, N.Y.: Newcomen Society in North America, 1982. 28 p. (Newcomen publication; no. 1162)

EXXON CORPORATION

Exxon Corporation. *The Other Dimensions of Business: A Report on Exxon's Participation in Areas of Public Interest*. New York, N.Y.: The Company, 1977. 44 p.

"Milestones in 90 Years of Company History." *Lamp* 54 (Winter 1972): 24-27.

Wall, Bennett H. *Growth in a Changing Environment: A History of Standard Oil Company (New Jersey), Exxon Corporation, 1950-1975*. New York, N.Y.: McGraw Hill, 1988. 1020 p.

SEE ALSO: STANDARD OIL COMPANY OF NEW JERSEY

FABER-CASTELL CORPORATION

Willis, Rod. "Getting the Lead Out; Providing the Leverage: Faber-Castell's Wiedenmayer and Jorgensen: Pencilling in the Future." *Management Review* 76 (August 1987): 12-15.

FAIRBANKS-MORSE CORPORATION

Kirkland, John F. *The Diesel Builders: Fairbanks-Morse*

and Lima-Hamilton. Glendale, Calif.: Interurban Press, 1985. 111 p.

THE FAMOUS AMOS CHOCOLATE CHIP COOKIE COMPANY

Amos, Wally, and Leroy Robinson. *The Famous Amos Story: The Face That Launched a Thousand Chips.* Garden City, N.Y.: Doubleday, 1983. 201 p.

FANNIE MAY CANDY SHOPS, INC.

Gorman, John. "Fannie May Thrives with Fresh Approach." *Chicago Tribune,* 15 December 1986, Sec. 4, P. 1.

FANSTEEL, INC.

Tennyson, Jon R. *$2500 and a Dream: The Fansteel Story.* Chicago, Ill.: The Company, 1982. 118 p.

FARAH MANUFACTURING COMPANY

Coyle, Laurie, Gail Hershatter, and Emily Honig. *Women at Farah: An Unfinished Story.* El Paso, Tex.: REFORMA, El Paso Chapter, 1979. 66 p.

FARM AND HOME SAVINGS AND LOAN ASSOCIATION

Farm and Home Savings and Loan Association. *Portrait of an Era; 1893-1968, 75 Years of Growth.* Nevada, Mo.: The Company, 1968.

FARMERS AND MECHANICS NATIONAL BANK, FREDERICK, MD.

Cahn, Louis F. *Sesqui Centennial History, 1817-1967, Farmers and Mechanics National Bank, Frederick, Maryland.* Frederick, Md.: The Bank, 1967. 48 p.

FARMERS AND MERCHANTS BANK OF LOS ANGELES

Cleland, Robert Glass, and Frank B. Putnam. *Isais W. Hellman and the Farmers and Merchants Bank.* San Marino, Calif.: Huntington Library, 1965. 136 p.

FARMLAND INDUSTRIES, INC.

Anderson, John F. *"Make No Little Plans,--": The Story of Farmland Industries, Inc.* New York, N.Y: Newcomen Society in North America, 1980. 20 p. (Newcomen publication; no. 1120)

Farmland Industries, Inc. *This Is Farmland Industries; The Story of a Farmer-Owned Business.* Kansas City, Mo.: The Company, 1984. 12 p.

Fite, Gilbert Courtland. *Beyond the Fence Rows: A History of Farmland Industries, Incorporated, 1929-1978.* Columbia: University of Missouri Press, 1978. 404 p.

FCX, INC.

Knight, Eugene S. *FCX at Five-O, 1934-1984: A Half-Century of Service to Farm People of the Carolinas.* Raleigh, N.C.: The Company, 1984. 123 p.

FEDERAL DEPOSIT INSURANCE CORPORATION

Federal Deposit Insurance Corporation. *Federal Deposit Insurance Corporation, The First Fifty Years, A History of the FDIC, 1933-1983.* Washington, D.C.: FDIC, 1984. 148 p.

Waddell, Harry. "The FDIC's Fifty Years." *ABA Bank Journal* 75 (October 1983): 38-52.

FEDERAL EXPRESS CORPORATION

Feldman, Joan M. "Federal Express: Big, Bigger and Biggest." *Air Transport* 22 (November 1985): 46-54.

Kanner, Barbara. "Story of a Brilliant Commercial." *New York* 14 (26 October 1981): 19-20+

Linden, Eugene. "Frederick W. Smith of Federal Express: He Didn't Get There Overnight." *Inc.* (April 1984): 89.

Nayak, P. Ranganath, and John M. Ketteringham. "Federal Express: The Knights on the Last White Horse." In *Breakthroughs!*, 314-342. New York, N.Y.: Rawson Associates, 1986.

Ponder, Ronny. *Federal Express: The Small Package Airline*. Memphis, Tenn.: The Company, 1977. 17 p.

Sigafoos, Robert Alan. *Absolutely Positively Overnight: The Unofficial Corporate History of Federal Express*. 2nd ed., Memphis, Tenn.: St. Luke's Press, 1988. 190 p.

Sigafoos, Robert Alan. *Absolutely Positively Overnight!: Wall Street's Darling Inside and Up Close*. Memphis: St. Luke's Press, 1983. 189 p.

Sobel, Robert, and David B. Sicilia. "Fred Smith and Federal Express." In *The Entrepreneurs: An American Adventure*, 42-48. Boston, Mass.: Houghton Mifflin Company, 1986.

FEDERAL PAPER BOARD COMPANY, INC.

Kennedy, John R. *No Room for Discouragement: The Story of Federal Paper Board Company*. New York, N.Y.: Newcomen Society in North America, 1967. 24 p. (Newcomen address)

FEDERATED DEPARTMENT STORES

Federated Department Stores. *A History*. Cincinnati, Ohio: The Company, 1984. 31 p.

"Federated History Deep-Woven; Lazarus Company Planted Seed." *Cincinnati Post*, 2 March 1988, sec. B, p. 5.

Gottschalk, Alfred. *Fred Lazarus, Jr., 1884-1973*. Cincinnati, Ohio: Hebrew Union College, 1973. 55 p.

THE FELLOWS GEAR SHAPER COMPANY

Miller, Edward W. *Ingenuity and Courage: A Personalized History of the Fellows Gear Shaper Company*. New York, N.Y.: Newcomen Society in North America, 1966. 24 p. (Newcomen address)

FERRACUTE MACHINE COMPANY

Cox, Arthur J., and Thomas Malim. *Ferracute: The History of an American Enterprise*. Bridgeton, N.J.: A.J. Cox, 1985. 197 p.

FESTERSEN (FRED) AND ASSOCIATES, INC.

Younger, Jack. "A Tough Way to Get Started in the Agency Business." *Rough Notes* 132 (November 1989): 18-24.

FIDELITY-PHILADELPHIA TRUST COMPANY

Fidelity Philadelphia Trust Company. *A Tribute to the Year 1866*. Philadelphia, Pa.: The Company, 1966. 26 p.

FIDELITY UNION LIFE INSURANCE COMPANY

Fidelity Union Life Insurance Company. Dallas, Tex.: The Company, 1972.

Neville, Dorothy. *Carr P. Collins: Man on the Move.* Dallas, Tex.: Park Press, 1963. 185 p.

FIDUCIARY TRUST COMPANY OF NEW YORK

Fowler, Harry W. *Fiduciary Trust Company of New York, N.Y: Investment Management Specialists--For Individuals, Corporations, Institutions.* New York, N.Y.: Newcomen Society in North America, 1974. 23 p. (Newcomen publication; no. 1013)

FIELD ENTERPRISES EDUCATIONAL CORPORATION

Darby, Edwin. "Field." In *The Fortune Builders*, 17-94. Garden City, N.Y.: Doubleday and Company, Inc., 1986.

Phalin, Howard V. *The Pursuit of Excellence.* Chicago, Ill.: The Company, 1968. 190 p.

FIELDCREST MILLS, INC.

Fieldcrest Mills, Inc. *Fieldcrest: Promise and Pride; Challenge and Achievement.* Eden, N.C.: The Company, 1978. 59 p.

FIGGIE INTERNATIONAL HOLDINGS, INC.

Figgie, Harry E., Jr. *A Dream Comes True: The Story of Figgie International.* New York, N.Y.: Newcomen Society of the United States, 1986. 22 p. (Newcomen publication; no. 1264)

"Reflections." In *Figgie International Holdings, Inc. Annual Report*, 4-23. Willoughby, Ohio: The Company, 1983.

FINANCIAL EXECUTIVES INSTITUTE

Haase, Paul. *Financial Executives Institute: The First*

Forty Years. New York, N.Y.: The Institute, 1971. 264 p.

FINANCIAL GENERAL BANKSHARES, INC.

Olmsted, George Hamden. *The Story of Financial General Bankshares and the Importance of Financial Institutions in a Free Enterprise Society*. New York, N.Y.: Newcomen Society in North America, 1976. 20 p. (Newcomen publication; no. 1042)

FINANCIAL NEWS NETWORK

Block, Alex Ben. "Oh, Lucky Man!" *Forbes* 136 (16 December 1985): 70-77.

FINANCIAL SERVICES CORPORATION

"Manager-Employee Team to Buy FSC." *Atlanta Journal*, 13 May 1989, sec. B, p. 1.

FINLEY, KUMBLE, WAGNER, HEINE, UNDERBERG, MANLEY AND CASEY

Stevens, Mark. "Breaking 'The Code': Finley, Kumble and the Cult of the Rainmakers." In *Power of Attorney: The Rise of the Giant Law Firms*, 37-67. New York, N.Y.: McGraw Hill, 1987.

FIRESTONE TIRE AND RUBBER COMPANY

Firestone Tire and Rubber Company. *Historical Highlights of the Firestone Tire and Rubber Company*. Akron, Ohio: The Company, 1984. 7 p.

THE FIRESTONE VINEYARD

Buchholz, Barbara B., and Margaret Crane. "The Firestone Vineyard, Los Olivos, CA." In *Corporate Blood Lines: The Future of the Family Firm*, 111-126. New York, N.Y.: Carol Publishing Group, 1989.

FIRST ALABAMA BANCSHARES

Plummer, Frank. *First Alabama Bankshares: An Outstanding Record of Performance*. New York, N.Y.: Newcomen Society in North America, 1984. 24 p. (Newcomen publication; no. 1202)

FIRST AMERICAN NATIONAL SECURITIES

Rudnitsky, Howard. "Art Williams and His Part-Time Army." *Forbes* 135 (3 June 1985): 104-108.

FIRST AND MERCHANTS NATIONAL BANK, RICHMOND

Williams, Frances Leigh. *A Century of Service; Prologue to the Future, A History of the First & Merchants National Bank*. Richmond: The Bank, 1965. 141 p.

FIRST BANK SYSTEM, INC.

First Bank System, Inc. *A History of First Bank System, Inc.* Minneapolis, Minn.: The Bank, 1985. 3 p.

First Bank System, Inc. *The First Fifty Years*. Minneapolis, Minn.: The Bank, 1979. 14 p.

FIRST EXECUTIVE LIFE

Lauterbach, Jeffrey R. "Nouveau Giant." *Financial Planning* 14 (July 1985): 70-77.

FIRST FEDERAL SAVINGS AND LOAN ASSOCIATION OF JACKSON

Scott, Tom B. *Making Change: The Story of First Federal Savings and Loan Association of Jackson*. New York, N.Y.: Newcomen Society in North America, 1970. 24 p. (Newcomen address)

FIRST FEDERAL SAVINGS AND LOAN ASSOCIATION OF MINNEAPOLIS

Lund, Doniver Adolph. *50 Years, A History of First Federal, Minneapolis.* Minneapolis, Minn.: The Company, 1976. 95 p.

FIRST FEDERAL SAVINGS AND LOAN ASSOCIATION OF ST. PETERSBURG

Thomson, Lila. *The Biography of Business.* St. Petersburg, Fla.: The Company, 1969. 174 p.

FIRST FIDELITY BANCORPORATION

First Fidelity Bancorporation. *History of First Fidelity Bancorporation.* Newark, N.J.: The Company, 1985. 4 p.

FIRST HAWAIIAN BANK

"First Hawaiian Bank: 125 Years." In *First Hawaiian, Inc. Annual Report,* I-XI. Honolulu: The Bank, 1983.

FIRST MISSISSIPPI CORPORATION

Williams, J. Kelly. *First Mississippi Corporation: The First Twenty Five Years.* New York, N.Y.: Newcomen Society in North America, 1982. 24 p. (Newcomen publication; no. 1174)

FIRST NATIONAL BANK AND TRUST COMPANY OF ESCANABA, MI

First National Bank and Trust Company of Escanaba. *100 Years of Service.* Escanaba, Mich.: The Bank, 1971. 58 p.

FIRST NATIONAL BANK AND TRUST COMPANY OF WYOMING

Dowdy, Auburn W. *The First 100 Years: The First National Bank and Trust Company of Wyoming*. New York, N.Y.: Newcomen Society in North America, 1982. 24 p. (Newcomen publication; no. 1166)

FIRST NATIONAL BANK IN HOUSTON

Kirkland, William A. *Old Bank--New Bank: The First National Bank, Houston, 1866-1956*. Houston, Tex.: Pacesetter Press, 1975. 115 p.

FIRST NATIONAL BANK OF BELLEVILLE

First National Bank of Belleville. *The First 100 Years*. Belleville, Ill.: The Bank, 1974. 95 p.

FIRST NATIONAL BANK OF BILOXI

Holt, Hazel. *75th Anniversary; First National Bank of Biloxi, 1893-1968*. Biloxi, Miss.: The Bank, 1968. 56 p.

FIRST NATIONAL BANK OF BOSTON
SEE:
BANK OF BOSTON CORPORATION

FIRST NATIONAL BANK OF COMMERCE

White, Joseph C. *Eulogies in Bronze: The Story of First National Bank of Commerce*. New Orleans, La.: The Bank, 1983. 79 p.

FIRST NATIONAL BANK OF DENVER

Adams, Eugene H. *The Pioneer Western Bank: First of Denver, 1860-1980*. Denver, Colo.: First Interstate Bank of Denver: State Historical Society of Colorado, Colorado Heritage Center, 1984.

FIRST NATIONAL BANK OF FARGO

First National Bank of Fargo, N.D. *First National Bank of Fargo, 1878-1978: A Century of Service to the Community*. Fargo, N.D.: The Bank, 1978. 8 p.

FIRST NATIONAL BANK OF FORT WORTH

Mason, Paul. *The First: The Story of Fort Worth's Oldest National Bank*. New York, N.Y.: Newcomen Society in North America, 1977. 23 p. (Newcomen publication; no. 1062)

FIRST NATIONAL BANK OF GENEVA

Wood, William C. *The First 65 Years*. Geneva, Ill.: The Bank, 1972. 49 p.

FIRST NATIONAL BANK OF GRAND ISLAND

Lund, Doniver. *A Great Tradition: The Centennial History of the First National Bank of Grand Island*. Grand Island, Nebr.: The Bank, 1980. 140 p.

FIRST NATIONAL BANK OF MOBILE

Mathews, Charles Elijah. *Highlights of 100 Years in Mobile*. Mobile, Ala.: The Bank, 1965. 169 p.

FIRST NATIONAL BANK OF PLATTEVILLE

Dobson, Linda. *The First National Bank of Platteville, Eighty-One Years of Progress*. Platteville, Wis.: The Bank, 1972. 16 p.

FIRST NATIONAL BANK OF TUSCALOOSA

The First National Bank of Tuscaloosa. *The First National Bank of Tuscaloosa: Growing With You, Caring for You*. Tuscaloosa, Ala.: The Bank, 1971. 12 p.

FIRST NATIONAL CITY BANK

First National City Bank. *Citibank, Nader and the Facts.* New York, N.Y: Citibank, 1974. 92 p.

Leinsdorf, David, and Donald Etra. *Citibank; Ralph Nader's Study Group Report on First National City Bank.* New York, N.Y.: Grossman Publishers, 1973. 406 p.

FIRST OF AMERICA BANK CORPORATION

First of America Bank Corporation. *History of First of America Bank Corporation.* Kalamazoo, Mich.: The Company, 1989. 9 p.

Slater, Robert Bruce. "The Savvy Crew from Kalamazoo." *Bankers Monthly* 107 (September 1990): 21-28.

FIRST PENNSYLVANIA BANK, N.A.

First Pennsylvania Bank N.A. *The Bank, 1781-1976: A Short History of First Pennsylvania Bank.* Philadelphia, Pa.: The Bank, 1976. 96 p.

Foltz, N. "200 Years Ago, America Needed a Bank." *Banking* 67 (March 1975): 102+

FIRST REALTY RESERVE

Kingston, Brett. "Jeffrey Britz of First Realty Reserve." In *The Dynamos: Who Are They Anyway?*, 165-170. New York, N.Y.: Wiley, 1987.

FIRST SECURITY CORPORATION

Eccles, George S. *First Security Corporation: The First Fifty Years, 1928-1978.* New York, N.Y.: Newcomen Society in North America, 1978. 21 p. (Newcomen publication; no. 1089)

Hyman, Sidney. *Challenge and Response: The First Security Corporation First Fifty Years, 1928-1978.* Salt Lake City, Utah: Graduate School of Business, University of Utah, 1978. 462 p.

FIRST TRUST AND DEPOSIT COMPANY, SYRACUSE, N.Y.

Schramm, Henry W. *The Dynamic Years: A History of First Trust and Deposit Company.* Syracuse, N.Y.: The Company, 1976. 131 p.

FIRST UNION CORPORATION

Cameron, Charles Clifford. *First Union Corporation, A Bank Holding Company: A Tradition of Leadership.* New York, N.Y.: Newcomen Society in North America, 1980. 30 p. (Newcomen publication; no. 1111)

FITCH MILLER AND TOURSE

Patterson, Gregory A. "Fitch Miller & Tourse Does the Possible." *Boston Globe*, 21 June 1988, p. 2.

FITNESS FINDERS, INC.

Waters, Craig R. "Fleshing Out an Empire." *Inc.* 6 (October 1984): 53-61.

FLORIDA EAST COAST RAILWAY (FEC)

"Ed. Ball's Tantalizing Railroad." *Financial World* 150 (1 April 1981): 30-31.

FLORIDA POWER CORPORATION

Parsons, Al. *Lightning in the Sun; A History of Florida Power Corporation, 1899-1974.* St. Petersburg, Fla.: The Company, 1974. 199 p.

FLOUR CORPORATION

Flour, J. Robert. *Flour Corporation: A 65-Year History.* New York, N.Y.: Newcomen Society in North America, 1978. 30 p. (Newcomen publication; no. 1074)

FLUKE (JOHN) MANUFACTURING COMPANY

"Thumbnail History of the John Fluke Mfg. Co., Inc." In *John Fluke Mfg. Co., Inc. General Information*, 16. Everett, Wash.: The Company, 1985.

FMC CORPORATION

Early, Stewart. "Issues and Alternatives: Key to FMC's Strategic Planning System." *Planning Review* 18 (May/June 1990): 26-33.

FOOD LION, INC.

Food Lion, Inc. *The Food Lion Story.* Salisbury, N.C.: The Company, n.d. 6 p.

FORBES MAGAZINE

Jones, Arthur. *Malcolm Forbes: Peripatetic Millionaire.* New York, N.Y.: Harper & Row, 1977. 211 p.

Winans, Christopher. *Malcolm Forbes: The Man Who Had Everything.* New York, N.Y.: St. Martin's Press, 1990. 227 p.

FORD, BACON AND DAVIS, INC.

Ford, Bacon and Davis, Inc. *For Human Needs: The Story of Ford, Bacon & Davis.* New York, N.Y.: The Company, 1967. 223 p.

FORD MOTOR COMPANY

Beynon, H. *Working for Ford*. London, Eng.: Allen Lane, 1973. 336 p.

Bryan, Ford Richardson. *Beyond the Model T: The Other Ventures of Henry Ford*. Detroit, Mich.: Wayne State University Press, 1990. 204 p.

Cleary, David Powers. "Ford Cars; Somewhere Along the Line, There's Always Something More. Our Job Is to Find It, Refine It, and Get the Public Accustomed to It." In *Great American Brands: The Success Formulas That Made Them Famous*, 87-111. New York, N.Y.: Fairchild Publications, 1981.

Colier, Peter. *The Fords: An American Epic*. New York, N.Y.: Simon & Schuster, 1987. 496 p.

Dammann, George H. *50 Years of Lincoln-Mercury*. Glen Ellyn, Ill.: Crestline Publications, 1971. 320 p.

Dammann, George H. *Illustrated History of Ford*. Glen Ellyn, Ill.: Crestline Publications, 1971. 320 p.

Dassbach, Carl H.A. *Global Enterprises and the World Economy: Ford, General Motors, and IBM, The Emergence of the Transnational Enterprise*. New York, N.Y.: Garland, 1989. 576 p.

Dominiques, Henry. *The Ford Agency: A Pictorial History*. Osceola, Wis.: Motorbooks International, 1981. 131 p.

Doody, Alton F. *Reinventing the Wheels: Ford's Spectacular Comeback*. Cambridge, Mass.: Ballinger, 1988. 136 p.

Ford Motor Company. *An American Legend*. Dearborn, Mich.: The Company, 1988. 7 p.

Friedman, Henry, and Sander Meredeen. *The Dynamics of Industrial Conflict: Lessons from Ford.* London: Croom Helm, 1980. 386 p.

Gawronski, F.W. "By Land, Air, Sea; Automotive Transportation Is Not the Only Mode at Ford." *Automotive News* (16 June 1978): 196-201.

Gordon, Maynard M. *Iacocca Management Technique; A Profile of the Chrysler Chairman's Unique Key to Business Success.* New York, N.Y.: Dodd, Mead, 1985. 154 p.

Hayes, Walter. *Henry: A Life of Henry Ford II.* New York, N.Y.: Grove Weidenfeld, 1990. 285 p.

Herndon, Booton. *Ford; An Unconventional Biography of the Men and Their Times.* New York: Weybright and Talley, 1969. 408 p.

Kimes, Beverly Rae. *The Cars That Henry Ford Built, 75th Anniversary Tribute to America's Most Remembered Automobiles.* Princeton, N.J.: Princeton Publications, distributed by E.P. Dutton, 1978. 136 p.

Lacey, Robert. *Ford: The Man and the Machine.* Boston, Mass.: Little Brown, 1986. 778 p.

Lasky, Victor. *Never Complain, Never Explain: The Story of Henry Ford II.* New York, N.Y.: R. Marck Publishers, 1981. 307 p.

Lewis, David Lanier. *Ford Country.* Sidney, Ohio: Amos Press, 1987. 184 p.

"75 Years of Ford Motor Company." *Automotive News* (16 June 1978): 1-275. (Special issue)

Sorenson, Lorin. *The American Ford: From the Fordiana Series.* St. Helena, Calif.: Silverado Publishing Company, 1975. 263 p.

Sorenson, Lorin. *The Ford Road, 75th Anniversary, Ford Motor Company, 1903-1978.* St. Helena, Calif.: Silverado Publishing Company, 1978. 191 p.

Strobel, Lee Patrick. *Reckless Homicide?: Ford's Trial.* South Bend, Ind.: And Books, 1980. 286 p.

Tedlow, Richard S. "Putting America on Wheels: Ford Vs. General Motors." In *New and Improved: The Story of Mass Marketing in America*, 112-181. New York, N.Y.: Basic Books, 1990.

FOREMOST-MCKESSON, INC.

Morison, William W. *The Story of Foremost-McKesson, Inc.* New York, Newcomen Society in North America, 1978. 30 p. (Newcomen publication; no. 1086)

FORESTVILLE MANUFACTURING COMPANY

Roberts, Kenneth, and Snowdon Taylor. *Jonathan Clark Brown and the Forestville Manufacturing Company.* Fritzwilliam, N.H.: Ken Roberts Publishing Company, 1988. 120 p.

THE FORSCHNER GROUP

Levitt, Mortimer. "Mike Weatherly: Carving Out a Fortune With the Swiss Army Knife." In *How to Start Your Own Business Without Losing Your Shirt; Secrets of Seventeen Successful Entrepreneurs*, 120-132. New York, N.Y.: Atheneum, 1988.

FORT WORTH NATIONAL BANK

Bond, Lewis H. *Century One: 1873-1973: A City... And the Bank That Bears Its Name. The Story of the Fort Worth National Bank.* New York, N.Y.: Newcomen Society in North America, 1973. 21 p. (Newcomen publication; no. 976)

FORT WORTH STAR-TELEGRAM

Meek, Phillip J. *Fort Worth Star-Telegram: "Where the West Begins."* New York, N.Y.: Newcomen Society in North America, 1981. 28 p. (Newcomen publication; no. 1145)

FOSS COMPANY

Skalley, Michael. *Foss: Ninety Years of Towboating.* Seattle, Wash.: Superior, 1981. 312 p.

FOSTER WHEELER CORPORATION

Azzato, Louis E. *Foster Wheeler Corporation: Meeting Industrial Change Worldwide.* New York, N.Y.: Newcomen Society of the United States, 1985. 24 p. (Newcomen publication; no. 1237)

Foster Wheeler Corporation. *Foster Wheeler History.* The Company, n.d. 4 p.

FOSTORIA GLASS COMPANY

McGrain, Patrick. *Fostoria--The Popular Years.* Frederick, Md.: The Weathermans, 1972. 320 p.

Weatherman, Hazel Marie. *Fostoria, Its First Fifty Years.* Springfield, Mo.: The Weathermans, 1972. 320 p.

THE FOURTH NATIONAL BANK AND TRUST COMPANY

Kincade, Arthur W. *Ad Astra Per Aspera: To the Stars Through Difficulties; The Story of the Fourth National Bank and Trust Company, Wichita, Kansas.* New York, N.Y.: Newcomen Society in North America, 1969. 32 p. (Newcomen address)

FOX PHOTO, INC.

Buchholz, Barbara B., and Margaret Crane. "Fox Photo, Inc., San Antonio, TX." In *Corporate Blood Lines: The Future of the Family Firm*, 160-174. New York, N.Y.: Carol Publishing Group, 1989.

FRANKLIN NATIONAL BANK

Ross, Walter Sanford. *People's Banker: The Story of Arthur T. Roth and the Franklin National Bank*. New Canaan, Conn.: Keats Publishing, 1987. 288 p.

Spero, Joan Edelman. *The Failure of the Franklin National Bank: Challenge to the International Banking System*. New York, N.Y.: Columbia University Press, 1980. 235 p. (Published for the Council on Foreign Relations)

FREESE AND NICHOLS, INC.

Nichols, James R. *Freese and Nichols, Inc.: An Engineering Institution*. New York, N.Y.: Newcomen Society In North America, 1983. 28 p. (Newcomen publication; no. 1171)

FRIENDSWOOD DEVELOPMENT COMPANY

Field, Alan M. "Independence Builds Character." *Forbes* 136 (21 October 1985): 135.

FRITO-LAY, INC.

Frito-Lay, Inc. *The Story of Frito-Lay, Inc.* Plano, Tex.: The Company, 1965. 1 p.

SEE ALSO: PEPSICO, INC.

FRONTIER AIRLINES

Frontier Airlines. *Frontier Airlines: Historical Highlights*.

Denver, Colo.: The Company, 1985. 4 p.

FRONTIER NURSING SERVICES, INC.

Breckinridge, Mary. *Wide Neighborhoods, A Story of the Frontier Nursing Service.* Lexington, Ky.: University Press of Kentucky, 1981. 371 p.

FRUEHAUF CORPORATION

Fruehauf Corporation. *Fruehauf's History.* Detroit, Mich.: The Company, 1983. 7 p.

FUQUA INDUSTRIES, INC.

Fuqua, J.B. *The Story of Fuqua Industries, Inc.* New York, N.Y.: Newcomen Society in North America, 1973. 18 p.

GAF CORPORATION

Marder, William. *Anthony, The Man, The Company, The Cameras; An American Photographic Pioneer: 140 Year History of a Company From Anthony to Ansco to GAF.* Plantation, Fla.: Pine Ridge Publishing Company, 1982. 384 p.

GALBREATH (JOHN W.) AND COMPANY

Shook, Robert L. "John W. Galbreath." In *The Entrepreneurs: Twelve Who Took Risks and Succeeded*, 1-17. New York, N.Y.: Harper & Row, 1980.

THE GANNETT COMPANY

Cose, Ellis. "The Chains: Gannett and Knight-Ridder." In *The Press*, 281-356. New York, N.Y.: William Morrow, 1989.

Neuharth, Allen. *Confessions of an S.O.B.* New York,

N.Y.: Doubleday, 1989. 372 p.

THE GARLOCK PACKING COMPANY

Waples, R.M., Sr., and R.M. Waples, Jr. *Garlock: The First Eighty-Eight Years, 1887-1975*. Palmyra, N.Y.: Garlock, Inc., 1976. 105 p.

GARRETT CORPORATION

Schoneberger, William A., and Robert R.H. Scholl. *Out of Thin Air: Garrett's First 50 Years*. Los Angeles, Calif.: The Company, 1985.

GARRETT (ROBERT) AND SONS, INC.

Williams, Harold A. *Robert Garrett and Sons, Inc.; Origin and Development, 1840-1965*. Baltimore, Md.: The Company, 1965. 102 p.

GARROW AND ASSOCIATES

Whitaker, Sarah Tait. "Garrow Builds Future on History." *Atlanta Constitution*, 7 May 1990, sec. XJ, p. 7.

GASTON, SNOW AND ELY, BARTLETT

Gaston, Snow & Ely, Bartlett. A Brief History. New York, Newcomen Society in North America, 1979. 32 p. (Newcomen publication; no. 1103)

GATX (GENERAL AMERICAN TRANSPORTATION CORPORATION)

Ruderman, Gary S. "Truck Innovation Marks 50 Years." *Automotive News* (13 August 1984): 16+

Scanlin, J.R. *GATX (General American Transportation Corporation): Meeting the Changing Needs of Industry*. New York, N.Y.: Newcomen Society in North America, 1970. 32 p. (Newcomen address)

GEFFEN RECORDS

Scoppa, Bud. "Taking It from the Streets." *Los Angeles Times*, 18 February 1990, sec. CAL, p. 67.

GELCO CORPORATION

"Historical Highlights." In *Gelco Corporation. 1982 Fact Book*, 4-5. Eden Prairie, Minn.: The Company, 1982.

GELDERMANN, INC.

Szala, Ginger. "Geldermann, Inc." *Futures; The Magazine of Commodities & Options (Profiles Issue)* 17 (July 1988): 18-23.

GENENTECH, INC.

Barker, Robert. "Taking Stock of Genentech: Are the Investors Overestimating Its Promise?" *Barron's* 65 (4 March 1985): 6-7, 24.

Benner, Susan. "Genentech: Life Under a Microscope." *Inc.* 3 (May 1981): 62-68.

Meyer, Michael. "The Builder." In *The Alexander Complex: The Dreams That Drive the Great Businessmen*, 159-193. New York, N.Y.: Times Books, 1989.

GENERAL DYNAMICS CORPORATION

Boulware, Lemuel R. *The Truth About Boulwarism; Trying to Do Right Voluntarily*. Washington, D.C.: BNA, 1969. 180 p.

Franklin, Roger. *The Defender: The Story of General Dynamics*. New York, N.Y.: Harper, 1986. 385 p.

Goodwin, Jacob B. *Brotherhood of Arms: General Dynamics and the Business of Defending America*.

New York, N.Y.: Times Books, 1985. 384 p.

Mendenhall, Charles A. *Delta Wings: Convair's High-Speed Planes of the Fifties and Sixties.* Osceola, Wis.: Motorbooks International, 1983. 175 p.

Tyler, Patrick. *Running Critical: The Silent War, Rickover, and General Dynamics.* New York, N.Y.: Harper, 1986. 374 p.

GENERAL ELECTRIC COMPANY

Cox, James A. *A Century of Light.* New York, N.Y.: Rutledge Books, 1979. 224 p.

General Electric Company. *A Century of Progress, The General Electric Story: 1876-1978, A Photo History in Four Volumes.* Schenectady, N.Y.: Hall of History Foundation, 1981. 4 Vols. in 1.

General Electric Company. *GE 100, 1878-1978.* Fairfield, Conn.: The Company, 1978. 52 p.

Greenwood, Ronald G. *Managerial Decentralization; A Study of the General Electric Philosophy.* Lexington, Mass.: Lexington Books, 1974. 176 p.

Kerr, O.M. *Illustrated History of General Electric Locomotives.* Montreal, Canada/Alburg, Vt.: Delta Pub., 1979. 96 p.

Levinson, Harry, and Stuart Rosenthal. "Reginald H. Jones." In *CEO: Corporate Leadership in Action,* 16-55. New York, N.Y.: Basic Books, 1984.

Liebhafsky, H.A. *Silicones Under the Monogram: A Story of Industrial Research.* New York, N.Y.: Wiley, 1978. 381 p.

Schatz, Ronald W. *The Electrical Workers: A History of Labor at General Electric and Westinghouse,*

1923-1960. Urbana, Ill.: University of Illinois Press, 1983. 279 p.

Wise, George. *Willis R. Whitney, General Electric and the Origins of U.S. Industrial Research*. New York, N.Y.: Columbia University Press, 1985. 400 p.

GENERAL FOODS CORPORATION

Bender, Marylin. "Did Success Breed Failure at General Foods?" In *At the Top; Behind the Scenes with the Men and Women Who Run America's Corporate Giants*, 43-66. Garden City, N.Y.: Doubleday, 1975.

Cleary, David Powers. "Maxwell House Coffee; Good to the Last Drop." In *Great American Brands: The Success Formulas That Made Them Famous*, 217-222. New York, N.Y.: Fairchild Publications, 1981.

Ferguson, James Leonard. *General Foods Corporation: A Chronicle of Consumer Satisfaction*. New York, N.Y.: Newcomen Society of the United States, 1985. 24 p. (Newcomen publication; no. 1238)

GENERAL FOODS CORPORATION - JELL-O DIVISION

Whitman, Edmund S. *Plant Relocation; A Case Study of a Move*. New York, N.Y.: American Management Association, 1966. 158 p.

GENERAL MILL SUPPLIES, INC.

Frichtl, Paul. "At General Mill Supplies--Surrounded by Adversity, Management Shows Its Mettle." *Industrial Distribution* 75 (May 1986): 125-132.

GENERAL MILLS, INC.

General Mills, Inc. *General Mills: A Collected History*. Minneapolis, Minn.: The Company, 1980. 9 p.

Kennedy, Gerald S. *Minutes and Moments in the Life of General Mills.* Minneapolis, Minn.: The Company, 1971. 270 p.

Wojahn, Ellen. *Playing by Different Rules.* New York, N.Y.: American Management Association, 1988. 306 p.

GENERAL MOTORS CORPORATION

Bender, Marylin. "The Energy Trauma at General Motors." In *At the Top; Behind the Scenes with the Men and Women Who Run America's Corporate Giants,* 167-210. Garden City, N.Y.: Doubleday, 1975.

Berry, Bryan H. "GM at 75: The Making of a Giant." *Chilton's Iron Age* 226 (5 December 1983): 28-50.

Cray, Ed. *Chrome Colossus: General Motors and Its Times.* New York, N.Y: McGraw-Hill, 1980. 615 p.

Dassbach, Carl H.A. *Global Enterprises and the World Economy: Ford, General Motors, and IBM, The Emergence of the Transnational Enterprise.* New York, N.Y.: Garland, 1989. 576 p.

De Lorean, John Z. *On a Clear Day You Can See General Motors: John Z. de Lorean's Look Inside the Automotive Giant.* Grosse Pointe, Mich.: Wright Enterprises, 1979. 237 p.

El-Messidi, Kathy Groehn. *The Story Behind the 30-Year Honeymoon of GM and the UAW.* New York, N.Y.: Nellon Publishing Company, 1980. 120 p.

Fleming, Al. "Lund Looks Back on 40 Years at GM." *Automotive News* (29 October 1984): 6+

General Motors, The First 75 Years. New York, N.Y.: Crown Publishers, 1983. 223 p.

General Motors, The First 75 Years of Transportation Products. Princeton, N.J.: Automobile Quarterly Publications, 1983. 223 p.

"GM 75th Anniversary Issue." *Automotive News* (16 September 1983): 1-434.

Gunnell, John. *75 Years of Pontiac-Oakland.* Sarasota, Fla.: Crestline Publications, 1982. 528 p.

Guston, L.R. "From Recklessness to Global Auto Dominance in 75 Years." *Wards Auto World* 19 (November 1983): 21-24.

Keller, Maryann. *Rude Awakening: The Rise, Fall, and Struggle for Recovery of General Motors.* New York, N.Y.: Morrow, 1989. 275 p.

Kerr, James W. *General Motors Phenomenal SD40 Series Diesel-Electric Locomotives.* Montreal, Canada: Delta Publications, 1980. 100 p.

Langworth, Richard M., and Jan P. Norbye. *Complete History of General Motors, 1908-1986.* Skokie, Ill.: Publications International, 1986. 416 p.

Lee, Albert. *Call Me Roger.* Chicago, Ill.: Contemporary Books, 1988. 324 p.

Levin, Doran P. *Irreconcilable Differences: Ross Perot Versus General Motors.* Boston, Mass.: Little Brown & Company, 1989. 357 p.

"Reminiscing with GM's Retiring Bob Lund." *Wards Automotive World* 20 (December 1984): 21.

Serrin, William. *The Company and the Union; The "Civilized Relationship" of the General Motors Corporation and the United Automobile Workers.* New York, N.Y.: Knopf, 1973, c1972. 308 p.

Siuru, William D., Jr. "From Self-Starters to Tail Fins and Turbochargers: GM's 80 Years of Innovation." *Mechanical Engineering* 110 (March 1988): 46-50.

Smith, Roger B. *Building on 75 Years of Excellence: The General Motors Story.* New York, N.Y.: Newcomen Society in North America, 1984. 22 p. (Newcomen publication; no. 1208)

Tedlow, Richard S. "Putting America on Wheels: Ford Vs. General Motors." In *New and Improved: The Story of Mass Marketing in America,* 112-181. New York, N.Y.: Basic Books, 1990.

Yates, Brock W. *The Decline and Fall of the American Automobile Industry.* New York, N.Y.: Empire Books, Distributed by Harper & Row, 1983. 301 p. (About the J-Cars)

GENERAL MOTORS CORPORATION - BUICK MOTOR DIVISION

Dammann, George H. *Seventy Years of Buick.* Glen Ellyn, Ill.: Crestline Publications, 1973. 360 p.

Dunham, Terry B., and Lawrence R. Gustin. *The Buick: A Complete History.* Princeton, N.J.: Princeton Publishing, 1985. 444 p.

Gawronski, Francis. "The Car That Built a City." *Automotive News* (16 September 1983): 107-114.

GENERAL MOTORS CORPORATION - CADILLAC MOTOR DIVISION

Gawronski, Frank. "Detroit's Oldest Auto Manufacturer." *Automotive News* (16 September 1983): 97-106.

Hendry, Maurice D. *Cadillac, Standard of the World, The Complete History.* New York, N.Y.: Bonanza Books, 1983. 487 p.

McCall, Walter Miller Pearce. *80 Years of Cadillac LaSalle*. Sarasota, Fla.: Crestline Publishing Company, 1982. 447 p.

GENERAL MOTORS CORPORATION - CHEVROLET MOTOR DIVISION

Barmash, Isadore. *More Than They Bargained for: The Rise and Fall of Korvettes*. New York, N.Y.: Lebhar-Friedman Books, Chain Store Publishing Corporation, 1981. 301 p.

Dammann, George H. *Sixty Years of Chevrolet*. Glen Ellyn, Ill.: Crestline Publishing, 1972. 319 p.

Kimes, Beverly Rae, and Robert C. Ackerson. *Chevrolet, A History from 1911*. Kutztown, Pa.: Automobile Quarterly Pub., Distributed by Princeton Pub., 1984. 195 p.

King, Jenny L. "A Bow Tie for Everyman." *Automotive News* (16 September 1983): 127-142.

GENERAL MOTORS CORPORATION - DELCO ELECTRONICS DIVISION

Rowand, Roger. "From Radios to Rockets." *Automotive News* (16 September 1983): 289-290.

GENERAL MOTORS CORPORATION - FISHER BODY DIVISION

Fleming, Al. "Body by Fisher." *Automotive News* (16 September 1983): 143-154.

GENERAL MOTORS CORPORATION - GMC TRUCK AND CAR DIVISION

Walsh, Jack. "They Just Keep Trucking Along." *Automotive News* (16 September 1983): 259-260.

GENERAL MOTORS CORPORATION - OLDSMOBILE DIVISION

Casteele, Dennis. *The Cars of Oldsmobile*. Sarasota, Fla.: Crestline Publications, 1981. 415 p.

Kimes, Beverly Rae. *Oldsmobile; The First Seventy Five Years*. New York, N.Y: Automotive Quarterly, 1972. 72 p.

Sorge, Marjorie. "Ransome's Merry Oldsmobile." *Automotive News* (16 September 1983): 81-95.

THE GENERAL RADIO COMPANY

Sinclair, Donald B. *The General Radio Company: 1915-1965*. New York, N.Y: Newcomen Society in North America, 1965. 32 p.

Thiessen, Arthur E. *A History of the General Radio Company*. West Concord, Mass.: The Company, 1965. 116 p.

GENERAL TELEPHONE COMPANY OF FLORIDA

Cooper, Dennis R. *The People Machine; An Illustrated History of the Telephone on the Central West Coast of Florida*. Tampa, Fla.: The Company, 1971. 301 p.

GENERAL TELEPHONE DIRECTORY COMPANY

Briggs, Don F. *WES: Portrait of a Man in Motion*. St. Petersburg Beach, Fla.: Briggs, 1978. 179 p.

GENERAL TIRE AND RUBBER COMPANY

Oneill, Dennis J. *A Whale of a Territory: The Story of Bill O'Neill*. New York, N.Y.: McGraw-Hill, 1966. 249 p.

GENESCO, INC.

Genesco, Inc. *Genesco's Business Past and Present.* Nashville, Tenn.: The Company, n.d. 5 p. (History through 1982)

Jarman, W. Maxey. *The Genesco: Formula for Growth--People--Products.* New York, N.Y.: Newcomen Society in North America, 1969. 22 p. (Newcomen address)

GEORGIA-PACIFIC CORPORATION

Cheatham, Owen R. *The Georgia-Pacific Story.* New York, N.Y.: Newcomen Society in North America, 1966. 28 p. (Newcomen address)

Ross, John R. *Maverick, The Story of Georgia-Pacific.* Portland, Oreg.: The Company, 1978, c1980. 318 p.

GERBER PRODUCTS COMPANY

Cleary, David Powers. "Gerber Baby Foods; We Had to Be Expert About Babies As Well As Baby Foods." In *Great American Brands: The Success Formulas That Made Them Famous,* 112-119. New York, N.Y.: Fairchild Publications, 1981.

Gerber Products Company. *Fifty Years of Caring: Our Golden Anniversary Year, 1928-1978.* Fremont, Mich.: The Company, 1978. 26 p.

Gordon, Mitchell. "Reborn Gerber: More Women Are Entering Peak Child-Bearing Years." *Barron's* 61 (19 January 1981): 37, 49.

GETTY OIL COMPANY

Coll, Steve. *The Taking of Getty Oil: The Full Story of the Most Spectacular--And Catastrophic--Takeover of All Time.* New York, N.Y.: Atheneum, 1987. 528 p.

Dechair, Somerset Struben. *Getty on Getty: A Man in a Billion*. London: Cassel, 1989. 170 p.

Getty, Jean Paul. *As I See It: The Autobiography of J. Paul Getty*. London: W.H. Allen, 1976. 361 p.

Getty Oil Company. *Getty Oil Company*. Los Angeles, Calif.: Petroleum Information Corporation, 1971.

Lenzner, Robert. *The Great Getty: The Life and Loves of J. Paul Getty, Richest Man in the World*. New York, N.Y.: Crown Publishers, 1985. 283 p.

Lund, Robina. *The Getty I Knew*. Kansas City, Kans.: Sheed Andrews and McMeel, 1977. 183 p.

Miller, Russell. *The House of Getty*. New York, N.Y.: Henry Holt, 1986. 361 p.

Miscellaneous Pamphlets on the Company Compiled at Normandale Community College. Bloomington, Minn.: Normandale Community College, 1977.

GIBBONS GREEN VAN AMERONGEN

Kepper, Bruce. "Partner of Gibbons Green to Start L.A. Banking Firm." *Los Angeles Times*, 5 May 1989, sec. IV, P. 3.

GIBBS AND HILL, INC.

Johnson, Barclay G. *Before the Colors Fade: A Personal History of Gibbs & Hill, Inc., 1911-1971*. New York, N.Y.: Gibbs & Hill, 1975. 110 p.

GIBRALTAR SAVINGS AND LOAN ASSOCIATION

"A History of Gibraltar Savings; A Federal Savings and Loan Association." *Gibraltar Journal* 4 (September 1982): 1-8.

GIBSON GREETING CARDS, INC.

Gibson Greeting Cards, Inc. *Gibson, 1850-1975: Our 125th Anniversary*. Cincinnati, Ohio: The Company, 1975. 16 p.

GIFFORD-HILL AND COMPANY, INC.

Gifford, P.W. *The Gifford-Hill Story*. New York, N.Y.: Newcomen Society in North America, 1968. 20 p. (Newcomen address)

"So We've Made 200 Years--Now What?" *Gifford-Hill Times* 8, no.7 (July 1976): 1-3.

GILBERT AND BENNETT MANUFACTURING COMPANY

Miller, Raymond Curtis, and Phillip H. Knowles. *Gilbert and Bennett Manufacturing Company, 1818-1968, 150th Anniversary*. Georgetown, Conn., 1968. 93 p.

GILLETTE COMPANY

Adams, Russell B. *King C. Gillette, The Man and His Wonderful Shaving Device*. Boston, Mass.: Little, Brown, 1978. 311 p.

Cleary, David Powers. "Gillette Razors; I Was a Dreamer--I Didn't Know Enough to Quit." In *Great American Brands: The Success Formulas That Made Them Famous*, 120-127. New York, N.Y.: Fairchild Publications, 1981.

Flaherty, Robert J. "The Patient Honing of Gillette." *Forbes* 127 (16 February 1981): 83-87.

Gillette Company. *The Gillette Company, 1901-1976*. Boston, Mass.: The Company, 1977. 32 p.

GILPIN (HENRY B.) COMPANY

Allen, James Elbert. *The Story of the Henry B. Gilpin Company.* New York, N.Y.: Newcomen Society in North America, 1977. 24 p. (Newcomen publication; no. 1063)

GLEN ELLEN WINERY

Berger, Dan. "Family-Owned Glen Ellen Puts a Premium on Quality--Unreservedly." *Los Angeles Times*, 12 April 1990, sec. H, p. 18.

Buchholz, Barbara B., and Margaret Crane. "Glen Ellen Winery, Glen Ellen, CA." In *Corporate Blood Lines: The Future of the Family Firm*, 245-266. New York, N.Y.: Carol Publishing Group, 1989.

Weisman, Katherine. "Mike Benziger's Fighting Varietals." *Forbes* 145 (19 February 1990): 134, 137.

GLEN RAVEN MILLS, INC.

Gant, Margaret Elizabeth. *The Ravens Story.* S.l.: The Company, 1979. 225 p.

GLENDALE FEDERAL SAVINGS AND LOAN

Edwards, Raymond D. *Glendale Federal: A One-Stop Financial Services Center: Now in Our 50th Year.* New York, N.Y.: Newcomen Society of the United States, 1984. 20 p. (Newcomen publication; no. 1219)

Glendale Federal Savings and Loan. *Past, Present and Future.* Glendale, Calif.: The Company, 1987. 8 p.

GOLD BOND STAMPS
SEE:
CARLSON COMPANIES, INC.

GOLD KIST, INC.

Martin, Harold H. *A Good Man--A Great Dream: D.W. Brooks of Gold Kist.* Atlanta, Ga.: The Company, 1982. 196 p.

GOLDEN GATE AIRLINES

Kistner, Rocky. "California or Bust: Birth and Growth of Golden Gate Airlines." *Professional Pilot* 14 (May 1980): 35-39.

GOLDMAN, SACHS AND COMPANY

United States. Federal Reserve Board. *Informal Hearings Concerning the Proposed Investment by the Sumitomo Bank, Ltd. in Goldman Sachs & Company.* Washington, D.C.: Neal R. Gross Court Reporters and Transcribers, 1986. 205 p.

GOODRICH TRANSIT COMPANY

Elliot, James L. *Red Stacks Over the Horizon; The Story of the Goodrich Steamboat Line.* Grand Rapids, Mich.: William B. Erdman Publishing Company, 1967. 314 p.

GOODTAB MANAGEMENT COMPANY

Kingston, Brett. "Robert Goodman of Goodtab Management Company." In *The Dynamos: Who Are They Anyway?*, 157-163. New York, N.Y.: Wiley, 1987.

GOODYEAR AIRCRAFT CORPORATION

Hansen, Zenon C.R. *The Goodyear Airships.* Bloomington, Ill.: Airship International Press, 1977. 110 p.

GOODYEAR TIRE AND RUBBER COMPANY

Cleary, David Powers. "Goodyear Tires; It is Harder to Stay Ahead Than to Get Ahead." In *Great American Brands: The Success Formulas That Made Them Famous*, 128-148. New York, N.Y.: Fairchild Publications, 1981.

O'Reilly, Maurice. *The Goodyear Story*. Edited by James T. Keating. Elmsford, N.Y.: Benjamin Company, 1983. 223 p.

GORE (W.L.) AND ASSOCIATES, INC.

Fucini, Joseph J., and Suzy Fucini. "Wilbert L. Gore, W.L. Gore and Associates, Inc.: 'We Don't Manage People Here--They Manage Themselves.'" In *Experience Inc.; Men and Women Who Founded Famous Companies After the Age of 40*, 143-149. New York, N.Y.: Free Press, 1987.

GORHAM MANUFACTURING COMPANY

Barol, B. "Chantilly." *American Heritage* (November 1989): 26+

Carpenter, Charles Hope, Jr. *Gorham Silver, 1831-1981*. New York, N.Y.: Mead, 1982. 332 p.

GOSS PRINTING PRESS COMPANY

Kogan, Herman. *Proud of Our Past, Committed to the Future*. Chicago, Ill.: Mobium Press, 1985. 171 p. (Cover title: *Goss: 100 Years, 1885-1985...*)

GOULD, INC.

Ylvisaker, William T. *Integrated Technology: The Story of Gould, Inc.* New York, N.Y.: Newcomen Society in North America, 1972. 16 p. (Newcomen address)

GOUTERMAN AND SHEFFEY, INC.

Wynn, Jack. "Diamonds in the Rough." *Venture* 8 (February 1986): 85-86.

GOVERNMENT EMPLOYEES INSURANCE COMPANY

Byrne, John J. *Government Employees Insurance Company, The First Forty Years.* New York, N.Y.: Newcomen Society in North America, 1981. 27 p. (Newcomen publication; no. 1125)

Davidson, Lorimer A. *The Government Employees Insurance Company, 1936-1966: A Brief History.* New York, N.Y.: Newcomen Society in North America, 1966. 32 p. (Newcomen address)

GRABAR ELECTRIC COMPANY, INC.

Warburton, Frederick R. *Wiring the World: Forty Years in Nuts & Bolts.* St. Petersburg, Fla.: Valkyrie Press, 1980. 351 p.

GRACE (W.R.) AND COMPANY

Grace (W.R.) and Company. *What Is Grace?* New York, N.Y.: The Company, 1982. 3 p. (Reprinted from: *Chemical Week*, 29 September, 1982)

GRACE'S MARKETPLACE

Buchholz, Barbara B., and Margaret Crane. "Grace's Marketplace, New York, NY." In *Corporate Blood Lines: The Future of the Family Firm*, 43-59. New York, N.Y.: Carol Publishing Group, 1989.

GRAINGER (W.W.) , INC.

W.W. Grainger, Inc. *50 Years of Growth, 1927-1977.* Chicago, Ill.: The Company, 1977. 16 p.

GRAND HOTEL

Woodfill, W. Stewart. *Grand Hotel: The Story of an Institution*. New York, N.Y.: Newcomen Society in North America, 1969. 28 p. (Newcomen address)

GRANGE MUTUAL CASUALTY COMPANY

Reid, J. Frederick. *Grange Mutual, 1935-1985: A Growing Partnership in Protection*. New York, N.Y.: Newcomen Society of the United States, 1985, c1986. 16 p. (Newcomen publication; no. 1259)

GRANVILLE AIRPLANE COMPANY

Mendenhall, Charles A. *The Gee Bee Racers, A Legacy of Speed*. North Branch, Minn.: Specialty Press, 1979. 173 p.

GRAVES (EARL G.) LTD.

Whigham, Marjorie. "20 Years of Black Enterprise: A Portrait of Earl G. Graves Ltd." *Black Enterprise* 21 (August 1990): 63-71.

GREAT AMERICAN SALVAGE COMPANY

Levitt, Mortimer. "Steve Israel: Architectural Artifacts from Junk." In *How to Start Your Own Business Without Losing Your Shirt; Secrets of Seventeen Successful Entrepreneurs*, 113-119. New York, N.Y.: Atheneum, 1988.

GREAT ATLANTIC AND PACIFIC TEA COMPANY

Hoyt, Edwin P. *That Wonderful A&P!* New York, N.Y.: Hawthorn Books, 1969. 279 p.

Mueller, Robert W. *A&P; Past, Present and Future*. New York, N.Y.: Progressive Grocer Magazine, 1971. 173 p. (Based on the A&P study written by the editors of

Progressive Grocer Magazine in cooperation with the Great Atlantic and Pacific Tea Company)

Tedlow, Richard S. "Stocking America's Pantries: The Rise and Fall of A&P." In *New and Improved: The Story of Mass Marketing in America*, 182-258. New York, N.Y.: Basic Books, 1990.

Walsh, William I. *Rise and Decline of the Great Atlantic and Pacific Tea Company.* Secaucus, N.J.: Lyle Stuart, 1986. 254 p.

GREAT LAKES CHEMICAL CORPORATION

Kampen, Emerson. *Great Lakes Chemical Corporation: A History of Innovation and Success.* New York, N.Y.: Newcomen Society of the United States, 1989. 16 p. (Newcomen publication; no. 1324)

Wells, Grant J. "Great Lakes Chemical Corporation-- Mixing Good Management, Research, and Opportunity." *Ball State Business Review* 12 (1985): 2-11.

GREAT WESTERN SUGARLANDS

May, William John. *The Great Western Sugarlands: The History of the Great Western Sugar Company and the Economic Development of the Great Plains.* New York, N.Y.: Garland, 1989. 471 p.

GREDE FOUNDRIES, INC.

Miner, Craig. *Grede of Milwaukee.* Wichita, Kan.: Watermark Press, 1989. 253 p.

GREEN BAY PACKERS

Torinus, John B. *The Packer Legend: An Inside Look.* Neshkoro, Wis.: Landmark Press, 1982. 251 p.

GREENWOOD MILLS

Wideman, Frank J. *"Fabric with the Character of Quality": The Story of Greenwood Mills.* New York, N.Y.: Newcomen Society in North America, 1980. 24 p. (Newcomen publication; no. 1126)

THE GRENADA BANK

Kennington, Robert E. *Grenada Bank: The Story of a $180,000,000 Small Town Bank.* New York, N.Y.: Newcomen Society in North America, 1975. 23 p. (Newcomen publication; no. 996)

GREYHOUND CORPORATION

Greyhound Corporation. *An Era of Excellence: The History of Greyhound.* Chicago, Ill.: Greyhound Corporation, 1967. 18 p.

Jackson, Carlton. *Hounds of the Road: A History of the Greyhound Bus Company.* Bowling Green: Bowling Green University Popular Press, 1984. 214 p.

Quirt, John. "How Greyhound Made a U-Turn." *Fortune* 101 (24 March 1980): 139-140.

Schisgall, Oscar. *The Greyhound Story; From Hibbing to Everywhere.* New York, N.Y.: Doubleday, 1985. 309 p.

GRIFFIN WHEEL COMPANY

Karow, Thomas R. *Griffin Wheel Company First Hundred Years, 1877-1977.* [s.l., s.n.] 1977. 79 p.

GRIGSBY BRANDFORD POWELL, INC.

Branch, E. "How High Is Up." *Black Enterprise* 21 (October 1990): 96+

GROLIER, INC.

Grolier, Inc. *A Brief History of Grolier*. Danbury, Conn.: The Company, 1984. 4 p.

GROSS, KELLY AND COMPANY, INC.

Kelly, Daniel T. *The Buffalo Head; A Century of Mercantile Pioneering in the Southwest*. Santa Fe, N. Mex.: Vergara Publishing Company, 1972. 288 p.

GROSSENBURG IMPLEMENT, INC.
SEE:
DEERE AND COMPANY

GROVE FARM COMPANY, INC.

Krauss, Bob. *Grove Farm Plantation; The Biography of a Hawaiian Sugar Plantation*. Palo Alto, Calif.: Pacific Books, 1965. 400 p.

GRUMMAN CORPORATION

Grumman Corporation. *Grumman: 50 Years*. Bethpage, N.Y.: The Company, 1978. 32 p.

Gunston, Bill. *Grumman: Sixty Years of Excellence*. New York, N.Y.: Orion Books, 1988. 159 p.

Thruelsen, Richard. *The Grumman Story*. New York, N.Y.: Praeger, 1976. 401 p.

GS&A GROUP, INC.

Shook, Robert L. "Joseph Sugarman." In *The Entrepreneurs: Twelve Who Took Risks and Succeeded*, 115-125. New York, N.Y.: Harper & Row, 1980.

GTC ENTERTAINMENT

Carter, Bill. "Tinker Looks Beyond 'USA Today on TV.'" *New York Times*, 27 November 1989, sec. D, p. 8.

GUARANTEE MUTUAL LIFE COMPANY

Conley, Eugene A. *Guarantee Mutual Life Company: A Promise Fulfilled During 75 Years, 1901-1976.* New York, N.Y.: Newcomen Society in North America, 1976. 20 p. (Newcomen publication; no. 1038)

GUILFORD TRANSPORTATION INDUSTRIES, INC.

Bushnell, Davis. "No Easy Ride for Billerica-Based Rail Company." *Boston Globe*, 8 July 1990, sec. NW, p. 13.

GULF AND WESTERN INDUSTRIES

Bluhdorn, Charles G. *The Gulf-Western Story.* New York, N.Y.: Newcomen Society in North America, 1973. 23 p.

GULF OIL CORPORATION

Gulf Oil Corporation: A Capsule History. Pittsburgh, Pa.: The Corporation, 1980. 25 p.

McCloy, John Jay. *The Great Oil Spill: The Inside Report, Gulf Oil's Bribery and Political Chicanery.* New York, N.Y.: Chelsea House Publishers, 1976. 374 p.

National Council of Churches of Christ in the United States of America. Corporate Information Center. *Gulf Oil: Portuguese Ally in Angola.* New York, N.Y.: The Council, 1972. 26 p.

United Church of Christ. Ohio Conference. *Background*

Information Passed at the Seventh Annual Meeting.
Columbus, Ohio, 1970. 45 p.

GULF STATES TOYOTA

Gulf States Toyota. *Gulf States Toyota, 1969-1989.*
Houston, Tex.: The Company, 1989. 17 p.

H&R BLOCK
SEE:
BLOCK (H&R)

HACKENSACK WATER COMPANY

Leiby, Adrian Coulter. *Hackensack Water Company:
1869-1969.* River Edge, N.J.: Bergen County
Historical Society, 1969. 231 p.

HAGERSTOWN AND FREDERICK RAILWAY
COMPANY

Harwood, Herbert H., Jr. *Blue Ridge Trolley: The
Hagerstown and Frederick Railway.* San Marino,
Calif.: Golden West Books, 1970. 144 p.

HAGGAR COMPANY

Spiegel, Joy G. *That Haggar Man; A Biographical
Portrait.* New York, N.Y.: Random House, 1979.
149 p.

HALCON INTERNATIONAL, INC.

Landau, Ralph. *Halcon International, Inc.: An
Entrepreneurial Chemical Company.* New York, N.Y.:
Newcomen Society in North America, 1978. 32 p.
(Newcomen publication; no. 1088)

HALLE BROS COMPANY

Wood, James M. *Halle's: Memoirs of a Family*

Department Store, 1891-1982. Cleveland, Ohio: Geranium Press, 1987. 223 p.

HALLMARK CARDS, INC.

Cleary, David Powers. "Hallmark Cards; Good Taste is Good Business." In *Great American Brands: The Success Formulas That Made Them Famous*, 149-157. New York, N.Y.: Fairchild Publications, 1981.

Goldwasser, Thomas. "Hallmark: Caring Enough to Send the Very Best." In *Family Pride; Profiles of Five of America's Best-Run Family Businesses*, 7-44. New York, N.Y.: Dodd, Mead and Company, 1986.

Hall, Joyce C. *When You Care Enough.* Kansas City, Mo.: The Company, 1979. 269 p.

HAMILTON COUNTY STATE BANK

"Hamilton County State Bank: A Dream Realized." *NIP* (April 1984): 36+

HAMMERMILL PAPER COMPANY

Hammermill Paper Company. *Hammermill: An Industrial Pioneer with Ongoing Pride in Quality and Innovation.* Erie, Pa.: The Company, 1982. 17 p.

Laslie, Donald S. *Hammermill: A Revolution in Papermaking.* New York, N.Y.: Newcomen Society in North America, 1965. 24 p. (Newcomen address)

McQuillen, Michael J., and William P. Garvey. *The Best Known Name in Paper: Hammermill, A History of the Company.* Erie, Pa.: The Company, 1985. 206 p.

THE HANCOCK BANK

Seal, Leo W. *The Hancock Bank: Leading the Way on Mississippi's Gulf Coast.* New York, N.Y.: Newcomen

Society of the United States, 1987, c1988. 24 p.
(Newcomen publication; no. 1287)

HARBERT CORPORATION

Harbert, John M., III. *Harbert: "A Story of Continuous Beginnings. "* New York, N.Y.: Newcomen Society in North America, 1982. 24 p. (Newcomen publication; no. 1161)

HARD ROCK CAFE

Cobb, Nathan. "Rock and Hard Places." *Boston Globe*, 4 June 1989, sec. BGM, p. 23.

HARDEE'S FOOD SYSTEMS, INC.

Waters, Craig R. "Franchise Capital of America." *Inc.* 6 (September 1984): 99-108.

HARDWICK CLOTHES, INC.

Hardwick Clothes, Inc. *The History of Hardwick Clothes, Inc.* Cleveland, Ohio: The Company, 1980. 67 p.

HARLEY-DAVIDSON MOTOR COMPANY

Hendry, Maurice D. *Harley-Davidson.* New York, N.Y.: Ballantine Books, 1972. 157 p.

Reid, Peter C. *Well Made in America; Lessons from Harley-Davidson on Being the Best.* New York, N.Y.: McGraw-Hill, 1989. 226 p.

Sucher, Harry V. *Harley-Davidson: The Milwaukee Marvel.* 3rd rev. ed., Sparkford, Somerset: Haynes, 1985. 328 p.

Wright, David. *The Harley-Davidson Motor Company: An Official Eighty-Year History.* Osceola, Wis.: Motorbooks International, 1987. 288 p.

HARNISCHFEGER CORPORATION

Harnischfeger Corporation. *A Centennial History*. New York, N.Y.: Newcomen Society of the United States, 1985. 24 p. (Newcomen publication; no. 1234)

Harnischfeger Corporation. *A Centennial History of the Harnischfeger Corporation*. Milwaukee, Wis.: The Company, 1984. 30 p.

HARPER AND ROW, PUBLISHERS, INC.

Exman, Eugene. *The House of Harper: One Hundred and Fifty Years of Publishing*. New York, N.Y.: Harper & Row, 1967. 31 p.

Nevins, Allan. *The Price of Survival*. New York, N.Y.: Harper & Row, 1967. 31 p.

HARRIS TRUST AND SAVINGS BANK

Harris Trust and Savings Bank. *History*. Chicago, Ill.: The Bank, 1979. 2 p.

HART SCHAFFNER AND MARX

Cleary, David Powers. "Hart Schaffner & Marx Suits; The Clothes a Man Wears Are to Some Extent a True Index of His Character and Taste, But They Are Also an Influence Upon His Character and Taste." In *Great American Brands: The Success Formulas That Made Them Famous*, 158-165. New York, N.Y.: Fairchild Publications, 1981.

THE HARTER BANK AND TRUST COMPANY

Root, John B. *One Hundred Years of the Harter Bank and Trust Company*. New York, N.Y.: Newcomen Society in North America, 1967. 24 p. (Newcomen address)

HARTFORD COURANT

Kreig, Andrew. *Spiked; How Chain Management Corrupted America's Oldest Newspaper.* Old Saybrook, Conn.: Peregrine Press, 1987. 237 p.

HARTFORD NATIONAL BANK AND TRUST COMPANY

Enders, Ostrom. *Hartford National Bank and Trust Company: Three Stories of Its One Hundred and Seventy-Five Years.* New York, N.Y.: Newcomen Society in North America, 1967. 24 p. (Newcomen address)

HARTFORD STEAM BOILER INSPECTION AND INSURANCE COMPANY

Wilde, Wilson. *"--In the Pursuit of Greater Safety, Reliability, and Efficiency": The Story of the Hartford Steam Boiler Inspection and Insurance Company.* New York, N.Y.: Newcomen Society in North America, 1978. 24 p. (Newcomen publication; no. 1067)

HARTMARX CORPORATION

"A Tradition of Growth: 1887-1978." In *Hartmarx Corporation. Annual Report*, 1-2. Chicago, Ill.: The Company, 1986.

HARZA ENGINEERING COMPANY

Harza Engineering Company: Developing Water Resources Worldwide, 1920-1983. New York, N.Y.: Newcomen Society in North America, 1984. 24 p. (Newcomen publication; no. 1213)

HASBRO, INC.

Gilbert, Nathaniel. "Stephen Hassenfeld: More Than a Family Affair." *Management Review* 76 (September 1987): 19-21.

HASKELL LABORATORY
SEE:
DU PONT...

HASKINS AND SELLS

Foye, Arthur B. *Haskins and Sells, Our First Seventy Five Years; 1895-1970.* New York, N.Y.: The Company, 1970. 192 p.

HAVERTY FURNITURE COMPANIES, INC.

Harte, Susan. "Stopping to Smell the Roses." *Atlanta Constitution*, 1 August 1990, sec. D, p. 1.

HAWAIIAN AIRLINES

Nelson, M. "Hawaiian Air." *Exxon Air World* 29 (Fall 1975): 58-61.

HAWAIIAN TELEPHONE COMPANY

Bendix, Bud. *Serving Hawaii, The First 100 Years: The 100th Anniversary of Hawaiian Telephone Company.* Honolulu, Hawaii: The Company, 1983. 88 p.

HAYES MICROCOMPUTER PRODUCTS, INC.

Blankenhorn, Dana. "Hayes Faces Fight with IBM and AT&T." *Data Communications* 15 (February 1986): 85-92.

HAZELTINE CORPORATION

Wheeler, Harold Alden. *The Early Days of Wheeler and*

Hazeltine Corporation--Profiles in Radio and Electronics. Greenlawn, N.Y.: The Company, 1982. 432 p.

HCB CONTRACTORS

HCB Contractors. *HCB 75th, 1912-1987.* Dallas, Tex.: The Company, 1987. 7 p.

HEARST CORPORATION

Bennack, Frank A. *The Hearst Corporation: 100 Years of Making Communications History.* New York, N.Y.: Newcomen Society of the United States, 1987. 20 p. (Newcomen publication; no. 1301)

Chaney, Lindsay, and Michael Cieply. *The Hearsts: Family and Empire: The Later Years.* New York, N.Y.: Simon & Schuster, 1981. 416 p.

HEBREW NATIONAL KOSHER FOODS, INC.

Berman, Phyllis. "Why Pastrami and Soap Didn't Mix." *Forbes* 136 (2 December 1985): 134-138.

HEDERMAN BROTHERS

Hederman, Robert M., Jr. *The Hederman Story: A Saga of the Printed Word in Mississippi.* New York, N.Y.: Newcomen Society in North America, 1966. 28 p. (Newcomen address)

HEILEMAN (G.) BREWING COMPANY, INC.

G. Heileman Brewing Company, Inc. *The House of Heileman Story: A Short History.* La Crosse, Wis.: The Company, 1985. 8 p.

HEINZ (H.J.) COMPANY

Alberts, Robert C. *The Good Provider: H.J. Heinz and*

His 57 Varieties. Boston, Mass.: Houghton Mifflin, 1973. 297 p.

HELDOR INDUSTRIES

Curtis, Carol E. "The Up & Comers: Splashing the Competition." *Forbes* 134 (22 October 1984): 126, 130.

HELMSLEY-NOYES COMPANY, INC.

Moss, Michael. *Palace Coup: The Inside Story of Harry and Leona Helmsley.* New York, N.Y.: Doubleday, 1989. 346 p.

HENDERSON ADVERTISING

Cummings, Bart. "Southerner's Pride Builds Ad Agency." *Advertising Age* 55 (20 August 1984): 34, 36.

HENDERSON STEEL AND MANUFACTURING COMPANY

Hassinger, Bernice Shield. *Henderson Steel, Birmingham's First Steel.* Birmingham, Ala.: Hassinger, 1978. 45 p.

THE HENNEGAN COMPANY

Hennegan & Company. *Hennegan & Company: Lithographers, Engineers, Printers, Designers.* Cincinnati, Ohio: The Company, 1975. 14 p.

HENNINGSON, DURHAM AND RICHARDSON

Durham, Charles W. *Henningson, Durham and Richardson: Offering Professional Design Services Since 1917.* New York, N.Y.: Newcomen Society in North America, 1978. 32 p. (Newcomen publication; no. 1082)

HERBALIFE INTERNATIONAL

Hartman, Curtis. "Inc. 500: Unbridled Growth." *Inc.* 7 (December 1985): 100-106.

HERCULES, INC.

Brown, Werner C. *Hercules, Inc.* New York, N.Y.: Newcomen Society in North America, 1977. 24 p. (Newcomen publication; no. 1078)

"Hercules Milestones." In *Hercules, Inc. Worldwide Research Products Processes*, 24. Wilmington, Del.: The Company, 1987.

Miller, Carolyn. "Hercules Marks 75th Anniversary." *Hercules Mixer, The Hercules Employee Magazine* no.1 (1988): 1-8.

HERRESHOFF MANUFACTURING COMPANY

Bray, Maynard. *Herreshoff of Bristol: A Photographic History of America's Greatest Yacht and Boat Builders*. Brooklin, Maine: WoodenBoat Publications, 1989. 241 p.

HERSHEY FOODS CORPORATION

Cleary, David Powers. "Hershey's Milk Chocolate Bars; You Must Do Things in a Large Way." In *Great American Brands: The Success Formulas That Made Them Famous*, 166-171. New York, N.Y.: Fairchild Publications, 1981.

Hershey Foods Corporation. *Hershey Foods Corporation: A Profile*. Hershey, Penn.: The Company, 1983. 14 p.

HESSTON CORPORATION

Jones, Billy Mac. *Factory on the Plains; Lyle Yost and the Hesston Corporation*. Wichita, Kans.: Center of

Entrepreneurship, W. Frank Barton School of Business Administration, Wichita State University, 1987. 237 p.

HEUBLEIN CORPORATION

"The Education of Hicks Waldron." *Forbes* 126 (8 December 1980): 98, 103, 105.

HEWLETT PACKARD COMPANY

Perry, Tekla S. "When the Car Was Out, The Business Was 'In.'" *IEEE Spectrum* 25 (April 1988): 44-45.

HEXCEL CORPORATION

Hexcel Corporation. *Background Information*. Dublin, Calif.: The Company, 1975. 6 p.

HIALEAH BANK

Adams, James Ring. "The Road to Washington." In *The Big Fix: Inside the S&L Scandal: How an Unholy Alliance of Politics and Money Destroyed America's Banking System*, 71-86. New York, N.Y.: Wiley, 1990.

HIGH TOR VINEYARDS

Crosby, Everett. *Vintage Years: The Story of High Tor Vineyards*. New York, N.Y.: Harper & Row, 1973. 227 p.

HILL HOLLIDAY CONNORS COSMOPULOS

Alter, Stewart. "HHCC Agency of the Year." *Advertising Age* 57 (28 April 1986): 36, 44.

HILLENBRAND INDUSTRIES

Bettner, Jill. "Till Death Do Us Part." *Forbes* 132 (29 August 1983): 112-113.

Dalglish, Garven. *Of This Man: The Biography of William A. Hillenbrand*. Canaan, N.H.: Phoenix Publishing Company, 1982. 250 p.

Hillenbrand Industries. *Hillenbrand Industries: Above All Leadership*. Batesville, Ind.: The Company, 1985. 26 p.

HILLS BROTHERS COFFEE, INC.

Wilson, Thomas Carroll. *A Background Story of Hills Bros. Coffee, Inc., As Presented by T. Carroll Wilson, Philadelphia District Sales Meeting, September 9, 1966*. San Francisco, Calif.: Printed by the James H. Barry Co., 1967. 80 p.

HINKLEY AND SINGLEY

Hunter, Wilbur Harvey. *A Baltimore Law Firm; A Brief History of Hinkley and Singley and Its Predecessors, 1817-1967*. Baltimore, Md.: Press of Schneidereith, 1967. 38 p.

Cleary, David Powers. "Kitchenaid Dishwashers; 'If Nobody Else Is Going to Invent a Dishwashing Machine, I'll Do It Myself.'" In *Great American Brands: The Success Formulas That Made Them Famous*, 192-196. New York, N.Y.: Fairchild Publications, 1981.

HOE (R) AND COMPANY

Comparato, Frank E. *Chronicles of Genius and Folly: R. Hoe & Company and the Printing Press As a Service to Democracy*. Culver City, Calif.: Labyrinthos, 1979. 846 p.

HOLIDAY HOUSE

Freedman, Russell. *Holiday House: The First Fifty Years*. New York, N.Y.: Holiday House, 1985. 152 p.

HOLIDAY INNS OF AMERICA, INC.

Bender, Marylin. "The Hospitality Crusade: Holiday Inns." In *At the Top; Behind the Scenes With the Men and Women Who Run America's Corporate Giants*, 144-164. Garden City, N.Y.: Doubleday, 1975.

Helyar, June. "Altered Landscape: The Holiday Inns Trip: A Breeze for Decades; Bumpy Ride in the 80's." *Wall Street Journal* 209 (11 February 1987): 1+

Wilson, Kemmons. *The Holiday Inn Story*. New York, N.Y.: Newcomen Society in North America, 1968. 24 p. (Newcomen address)

HOLLINS (WILLIAM) AND COMPANY, LTD.

Wells, Frederick Arthur. *Hollins and Viyella; A Study in Business History*. New York, N.Y.: A.M. Kelly, 1968. 264 p.

THE HOME INSURANCE COMPANY

Tullis, Robert H. *The Home Insurance Company: Men of Vision During 125 Years*. New York, N.Y.: Newcomen Society in North America, 1978. 24 p. (Newcomen publication; no. 1081)

HOME SHOPPING NETWORK, INC.

Fucini, Joseph J., and Suzy Fucini. "Lowell W. Paxson, Roy M. Speer, Home Shopping Network, Inc.: 'We Knew We Were on a Rocket.'" In *Experience Inc.; Men and Women Who Founded Famous Companies After the Age of 40*, 89-95. New York, N.Y.: Free Press, 1987.

HOMESTAKE MINING COMPANY

Cash, Joseph H. *Working the Homestake*. Ames, Iowa: Iowa State University Press, 1973. 141 p.

Fielder, Mildred. *The Treasure of Homestake Gold.* Aberdeen, S.D.: North Plains Press, 1970. 478 p.

Johnson, Jerry W. *Regional Impact Via Multiplier Analysis of Primary Industries: A Case Study: Homestake Mining Company, Lead, South Dakota.* Vermillion, S.D.: Business Research Bureau, School of Business, University of South Dakota, 1974. 38 p.

Palmer, Jay. "Good As Gold: Homestake's New Mines, Finances Glitter." *Barron's* 68 (30 May 1988): 14-15, 18.

HOME-STAKE PRODUCTION COMPANY

McClintick, David. *Stealing from the Rich: The Home-Stake Oil Swindle.* New York, N.Y.: M. Evans, 1977. 338 p.

HOME STATE SAVINGS BANK

Adams, James Ring. "The Friends of Marvin Warner." In *The Big Fix: Inside the S&L Scandal: How an Unholy Alliance of Politics and Money Destroyed America's Banking System*, 145-179. New York, N.Y.: Wiley, 1990.

HONDA MOTOR COMPANY
SEE:
AMERICAN HONDA MOTOR COMPANY

HONEYWELL, INC.

Henkel, Tom. "Research, Acquisitions Tell Honeywell's Tale." *Computerworld* 19 (9 September 1985): 95, 98-99.

Honeywell, Inc. *The First 100 Years.* Minneapolis, Minn.: The Company, 1985. 36 p.

Spencer, Edson W. *Honeywell: After 100 Years.* New York, N.Y.: Newcomen Society of the United States, 1985, c1986. 24 p. (Newcomen publication; no. 1258)

HOOK-SUPERX, INC.

Bertman, Toni. "SupeRx, The First 25 Years." *HSInsight* 1 (Spring 1987): 10-12.

Karzos, Joan. "Past 30 Years Most Dynamic for Hook Chain." *HSInsight* 1 (Spring 1987): 7-9.

THE HOOVER COMPANY

The Hoover Company. *A Proud Past--An Exciting Future.* North Canton, Ohio: The Company, n.d. 10 p.

THE HORCHOW COLLECTION

Shook, Robert L. "S. Roger Horchow." In *The Entrepreneurs: Twelve Who Took Risks and Succeeded*, 67-79. New York, N.Y.: Harper & Row, 1980.

HORIZON AIR

Wenger, LoraLee. "Horizon: A Winner in the .Pacific Northwest." *Rolls-Royce Magazine* 7 (June 1985): 22+

HORMEL (GEORGE A.) AND COMPANY

Dougherty, Richard. *In Quest of Quality: Hormel's First 75 Years.* Austin, Minn.: The Company, 1966. 357 p.

Hage, Dave. *No Retreat No Surrender: Labor's War at Hormel.* New York, N.Y.: William Morrow & Company, 1989. 398 p.

HORSMAN DOLLS, INC.

Gibbs, Patikii. *Horsman Dolls, 1950-1970.* Paducah, Ky.: Collector Books, 1985. 263 p.

HOSPITAL CORPORATION OF AMERICA

Hospital Corporation of America. *Fifteen Years of Growing Through Caring.* Nashville, Tenn.: The Company, 1983. 5 p.

HOUDAILLE INDUSTRIES

Holland, Max. *When the Machine Stopped: A Cautionary Tale from Industrial America.* Boston, Mass.: Harvard Business School Press, 1989. 335 p.

SEE ALSO: IBEX CORPORATION

HOUGHTON MIFFLIN COMPANY

Ballou, Ellen B. *The Building of the House of Houghton.* Boston, Mass.: Houghton Mifflin Company, 1970. 695 p.

Miller, Harold T. *Houghton Mifflin Company.* New York, N.Y.: Newcomen Society in North America, 1984. 19 p. (Newcomen publication; no. 1211)

HOUSEHOLD FINANCE CORPORATION

Kogan, Herman. *Lending Is Our Business; The Story of Household Finance Corporation.* Chicago, Ill.: The Company, 1965. 147 p.

HOUSTON LIGHTING AND POWER COMPANY

Budd, Millie. *The Light Company; Houston and the Houston Lighting & Power Company, A Century of Growth.* Houston, Tex.: Gulf Publishing Company, 1987.

HOWARD CLOCK PRODUCTS

Koselka, Rita. "Made in the U.S.A." *Forbes* 139 (15 June 1987): 80-87.

HOWARD JOHNSON

Merwin, John. "The Sad Case of the Dwindling Orange Roofs." Forbes 136 (30 December 1985): 75-79.

HOWARD SHIP YARD AND DOCK COMPANY

Fishbaugh, Charles Preston. *From Paddle Wheels to Propellers; The Howard Ship Yard of Jeffersonville in the Story of Steam Navigation on the Western Rivers.* Indianapolis, Ind.: Indiana Historical Society, 1970. 240 p.

HUBBARD CONSTRUCTION COMPANY

Powers, Ormund. *One Man, One Mule, One Shovel.* Winter Park, Fla.: Anna Publications, 1982. 314 p.

HUBBELL, INC.

Hubbell, Inc. *Hubbell 100; Second Century of Solutions.* Orange, Conn.: The Company, 1988. 24 p.

HUBER (J.M.) CORPORATION

Weiss, Catherine. *One Hundred Years of Huber: 1883-1983.* Edison, N.J.: The Company, 1983. 116 p.

HUDEPOHL BREWING COMPANY

Hudepohl Brewing Company. *Brewing in Cincinnati, 1885-1985: 100 Years of the Hudepohl Brewing Company.* Cincinnati, Ohio: The Company, 1985. 20 p.

HUDSON OIL COMPANY

Shook, Robert L. "Mary Hudson." In *The Entrepreneurs: Twelve Who Took Risks and Succeeded*, 41-52. New York, N.Y.: Harper & Row, 1980.

HUGHES AIRCRAFT COMPANY

Bain, Trevor. *Defense Manpower and Contract Termination*. Tucson, Ariz.: Division of Economic and Business Research, College of Business and Public Administration, University of Arizona, 1968. 59 p.

Davenport, Joe. *The Empire of Howard Hughes*. San Francisco, Calif.: Peace and Pieces Foundation, 1975. 81 p.

Drosnin, Michael. *Citizen Hughes*. New York, N.Y.: Holt, Rinehart and Winston, 1985. 532 p.

Garrison, Omar V. *Howard Hughes in Las Vegas*. New York, N.Y.: Lyle Stuart, 1967. 384 p.

"Hughes Aircraft: From Hobby Shop to Aerospace Giant." *Los Angeles Times*, 6 June 1985, sec. IV, p. 1.

Smith, George F. "The Early Laser Years at Hughes Aircraft Company." *IEEE Journal of Quantum Electronics* 20 (June 1984): 577-584.

HUGHES TOOL COMPANY

Gordon, Mitchell. "Howard Hughes Legacy--His Old Tool Company Has Hit Pay Dirt." *Barron's* 61 (16 November 1981): 9, 26-30, 42.

"Historical Issue." *Hughes Rigway* 14 (Fall 1976): 1-24.

HUMANA, INC.

Arnell, Peter, and Ted Bickford. *A Tower for Louisville,*

The Humana Competition. New York, N.Y.: Rizzoli, 1982. 117 p.

Humana. *History of Humana.* Louisville, Ky.: The Company, 1989. 4 p.

HUMMEL INDUSTRIES, INC.

Baird, Nancy Disher. *Tradition and Progress; A History of Hummel Industries, Inc.* Cincinnati, Ohio: The Company, 1981. 98 p.

HUNT INTERNATIONAL RESOURCES CORPORATION

Burst, Arois. *Three Families of H.L. Hunt.* New York, N.Y.: Weidenfeld & Nicolson, 1988. 256 p.

Hurt, Harry. *Texas Rich: The Hunt Dynasty, From the Early Oil Days Through the Silver Crash.* New York, N.Y.: W.W. Norton, 1981. 446 p.

Tuccille, Jerome. *Kingdom: The Story of the Hunt Family of Texas.* Ottawa, Ill.: Jameson Books, 1984. 384 p.

HUNT (J.B.) TRANSPORT, INC.

MacPhee, William. "J.B. Hunt of J.B. Hunt Transport, Inc." In *Rare Breed: The Entrepreneur, An American Culture*, 69-75. Chicago, Ill.: Probus Publishing Company, 1987.

HUNTINGTON BANCSHARES, INC.

Fultz, Claire E. *Huntington: A Family and a Bank.* Columbus: The Bank, 1985. 92 p.

HUNTINGTON NATIONAL BANK OF COLUMBUS

Fultz, Clair E. *"The Huntington": A Story of the Huntington National Bank of Columbus.* New York,

N.Y.: Newcomen Society in North America, 1966. 32 p. (Newcomen address)

HUNTSMAN CHEMICAL CORPORATION

Marth, Del. "A Plan for All Seasons." *Nation's Business* 72 (September 1984): 85-86.

HUSKY OIL COMPANY

Harlow, Howard Reed. "A Profile of Growth: Husky Oil Ltd. Strategy and Tactics from 1938-1972." Ph.D. diss., University of Nebraska, 1973. 329 p.

HUTTON (E.F.) GROUP, INC.

Carpenter, Donna Sammons. *The Fall of the House of Hutton.* New York, N.Y.: Holt, 1989. 322 p.

Fromson, Brett Duval. "The Slow Death of E.F. Hutton." *Fortune* 117 (29 February 1988): 82-88.

"Hutton's Rich History Marred by Hard Times." *Los Angeles Times*, 3 December 1987, sec. IV, p. 1.

Stevens, Mark. *Sudden Death: The Rise and Fall of E.F. Hutton.* New York, N.Y.: New American Library, 1989. 298 p.

HYATT CORPORATION

Darby, Edwin. "Pritzker." In *The Fortune Builders*, 95-116. Garden City, N.Y.: Doubleday and Company, Inc., 1986.

HYWELL, INC.

Kain, Susan. "Vicki Sherwood, Founder and Owner, Hywell, Inc." *The Executive Female* (July/August 1984): 12-13.

I CAN'T BELIEVE IT'S YOGURT

Kingston, Brett. "Julie Brice of I Can't Believe It's Yogurt." In *The Dynamos: Who Are They Anyway?*, 91-94. New York, N.Y.: Wiley, 1987.

IBM
SEE:
INTERNATIONAL BUSINESS MACHINES CORPORATION

IC INDUSTRIES

Johnson, William B. *IC Industries*. New York, N.Y.: Newcomen Society in North America, 1973. 27 p. (Newcomen publication; no. 971)

IDAHO FIRST NATIONAL BANK

Idaho First National Bank. *A National Bank 100 Years: 1867-1967*. Boise, Idaho: The Bank, 1967.

IDEX CORPORATION

Sherrod, Pamela. "For a New Firm, IDEX Has Stocked Up Some History." *Chicago Tribune*, 13 August 1989, sec. 7, p. 1.

ILLINOIS CENTRAL INDUSTRIES
SEE:
IC INDUSTRIES

ILLINOIS CENTRAL RAILROAD

Stover, John F. *History of the Illinois Central Railroad*. New York, N.Y.: Macmillan Publishing Company, 1975. 575 p.

ILLINOIS POWER COMPANY

Illinois Power Company. *A History of Illinois Power*

Company. Decatur, Ill.: The Company, 1972. 6 p. (Published in 1972 company magazine)

Punch, Counterpunch: 60 Minutes vs. Illinois Power Company. Washington, D.C.: The Media Institute, 1981. 46 p.

ILLINOIS TOOL WORKS, INC.

Illinois Tool Works, Inc. *History.* Chicago, Ill.: The Company, 1982. 5 p.

IMAGINE FILMS ENTERTAINMENT

Fabrikant, Geraldine. "Tiny Studio but Big-Budget Films." *New York Times*, 22 December 1990, sec. A, p. 35.

IMPERIAL GLASS CORPORATION

Edwards, Bill. *Imperial Carnival Glass: The Early Years.* Paducah, Ky.: Collector Books, 1980. 128 p.

INDEPENDENT LIFE AND ACCIDENT INSURANCE COMPANY

Bryan, Jacob F. *The First Fifty Years of Independent Life.* New York, Newcomen Society in North America, 1970. 28 p. (Newcomen address)

INDIANA GAS COMPANY

Heiney, J. W. *The Story of Indiana Gas Company, Inc.* New York, N.Y.: Newcomen Society in North America, 1972. 28 p. (Newcomen address)

INDIANAPOLIS POWER AND LIGHT COMPANY

Todd, Zone G. *Electrifying Indianapolis: The Story of Indianapolis Power and Light Company.* New York, N.Y.: Newcomen Society in North America, 1977. 30 p. (Newcomen publication; no. 1077)

INDIANAPOLIS WATER COMPANY

Giffin, Marjie Gates. *Water Runs Downhill: A History of the Indianapolis Water Company and Other Centenarians.* Indianapolis, Ind.: The Company, 1981. 251 p.

Giffin, Marjie Gates. *Water Runs Downhill: A History of the Indianapolis Water Company and Other Centenarians.* New York, N.Y.: Newcomen Society in North America, 1981. 66 p. (Newcomen publication; no. 1149)

INDUSTRIAL NATIONAL BANK OF RHODE ISLAND

Weston, Frank. *The Passing Years, 1791-1966.* Text by Frank Weston. Presidential Portrait by Stacy Tolman and Others. Providence: The Bank, 1966. 144 p.

INDUSTRIAL SERVICES OF AMERICA; INC.

Industrial Services of America, Inc. *History.* Louisville: The Company, 1985. 2 p.

INGALLS SHIPBUILDING
SEE:
LITTON INDUSTRIES

INGERSOLL-RAND COMPANY

Koether, George. *The Building of Men, Machines, And a Company.* Woodcliff Lake, N.J.: Ingersoll-Rand, 1971. 107 p.

INLAND STEEL COMPANY

Rowand, R. "Inland's Always Been a Technological Pioneer." *Automotive News* (26 November 1979): 8+

SEE ALSO: GENERAL MOTORS CORPORATION

INSURANCE COMPANY OF NORTH AMERICA

Carr, William H.A. *Perils: Named and Unnamed; The Story of the Insurance Company of North America.* New York, N.Y.: McGraw-Hill, 1967. 424 p.

INTERCO, INC.

Interco, Inc. *Interco, 1911-1980.* St. Louis, Mo.: The Company, 1980. 8 p.

INTER-CONTINENTAL HOTELS

Hampton, Max. *Throw Away the Key.* Indianapolis, Ind.: Bobbs-Merrill, 1966. 256 p.

INTERGRAPH CORPORATION

Graves, Benjamin B., and Ralph E. Geiger, Jr. "Intergraph, Inc." *Journal of Management Case Studies* 3 (Fall 1987): 215-230.

INTERLEAF, INC.

Perry, Robert. "Interleaf: Gray-Flannel Success." *High-Tech Marketing* 4 (August 1987): 36-39, 52.

INTERNATIONAL BUSINESS MACHINES CORPORATION

Applied Management Services. *Inside IBM.* Medford, N.Y.: AMS, 1983. 135 p.

Chposky, James. *Blue Magic: The People, Power and Politics Behind the IBM Personal Computer.* New York, N.Y.: Facts on File, 1989. 228 p.

Dassbach, Carl H.A. *Global Enterprises and the World Economy: Ford, General Motors, and IBM, The Emergence of the Transnational Enterprise.* New York, N.Y.: Garland, 1989. 576 p.

Fisher, Franklin M. *Folded, Spindled, And Mutilated: Economic Analysis and U.S. vs. IBM.* Cambridge, Mass.: MIT Press, 1983. 443 p.

Fisher, Franklin M. *IBM and the U.S. Data Processing Industry; An Academic History.* New York, N.Y.: Praeger, 1983. 532 p.

Fishman, Katherine Davis. *The Computer Establishment.* New York, N.Y.: Harper and Row, 1981. 468 p.

Foy, Nancy S. *The Sun Never Sets on IBM.* New York, N.Y.: W. Morrow, 1975. 218 p.

Gropelli, Angelico A. "The Growth Process in the Computer Industry." Ph.D. diss., New York University, 1970. 302 p.

Killen, Michael. *IBM--The Making of the Common View.* Boston, Mass.: Harcourt Brace Jovanovich, 1988. 284 p.

Levinson, Harry, and Stuart Rosenthal. "Thomas J. Watson, Jr." In *CEO: Corporate Leadership in Action*, 178-218. New York, N.Y.: Basic Books, 1984.

Maisonrouge, Jacques. *Inside IBM: A Personal Story.* New York, N.Y.: McGraw-Hill, 1989, c1985. 316 p. (Translated from the French by Nina Rootes)

Malik, Rex. *And Tomorrow--The World: Inside IBM.* London, Eng.: Millington, 1975. 496 p.

Mercer, David. *Global IBM: Leadership in Multinational Management.* New York, N.Y.: Dodd, Mead, 1988. 374 p.

Mercer, David. *IBM; How the World's Most Successful Corporation Is Managed.* London: K. Page, 1987. 306 p.

Mobley, Lou. *Beyond IBM*. New York, N.Y.: McGraw-Hill, 1989. 253 p.

Rodgers, Francis G., with Robert L. Shook. *The IBM Way: Insights into the World's Most Successful Marketing Organization*. New York, N.Y.: Harper & Row, 1986. 235 p.

Rodgers, William. *Think, A Biography of the Watsons and IBM*. New York, N.Y.: Stein and Day, 1969. 320 p.

Simmons, W.W. *Inside IBM: The Watson Years: A Personal Memoir*. Bryn Mawr, Pa.: Dorrance, 1988. 202 p.

Sobel, Robert. *IBM. Colossus in Transition*. New York, N.Y.: Times Books, 1981. 360 p.

Sobel, Robert. *IBM Vs. Japan, The Struggle for the Future*. New York, N.Y.: Stein and Day, 1986. 262 p.

Watson, Thomas. *Father Son and Company; My Life at IBM and Beyond*. New York, N.Y.: Bantam Books, 1990. 468 p.

Watson, Thomas J., Jr. "The Greatest Capitalist in History." *Fortune* 116 (31 August 1987): 24-35.

Weil, Ulric. *Computer Company Valuations: IBM and Its Major Competitors*. New York, N.Y.: Morgan Stanley & Company, 1979, c1980. 28 p.

INTERNATIONAL HARVESTER COMPANY

Marsh, Barbara. *A Corporate Tragedy: The Agony of International Harvester Company*. Garden City, N.Y.: Doubleday, 1985. 312 p.

Ozanne, Robert. *A Century of Labor-Management Relations at McCormick and International Harvester*.

Madison: University of Wisconsin Press, 1967. 300 p.

Wendel, C.H. *150 Years of International Harvester.*
Sarasota, Fla.: Crestline Publishers, 1981. 416 p.

INTERNATIONAL MINERALS AND CHEMICAL CORPORATION.

Ware, Thomas M. *So Little Soil--So Little Time: The Story of International Minerals and Chemical Corporation.* New York, N.Y.: Newcomen Society in North America, 1967. 24 p. (Newcomen address)

INTERNATIONAL MULTIFOODS

International Multifoods. *A History of International Multifoods.* Minneapolis, Minn.: The Company, 1988. 4 p.

INTERNATIONAL SILVER COMPANY

International Silver Company. *Sketch of the International Silver Company.* Meriden, Conn.: The Company, 1969.

INTERNATIONAL TELEPHONE AND TELEGRAPH CORPORATION

Burns, Thomas S. *Tales of ITT; An Insider's Report.* Boston, Mass.: Houghton Mifflin, 1974. 246 p.

Goolrick, Robert M. *Public Policy Toward Corporate Growth: The ITT Merger Cases.* Forward by John V. Tunney. Port Washington, N.Y.: Kennikat Press, 1978. 212 p.

National Council of Churches of Christ in the United States of America. Corporate Information Center. *IT&T: Apartheid and Business in Southern Africa.* New York, 1972. 37 p.

Sampson, Anthony. *The Sovereign State of ITT.* New York, N.Y.: Stein and Day, 1973. 323 p.

Schoenberg, Robert J. *Geneen.* New York, N.Y.: Norton, 1985. 429 p.

Sobel, Robert. *ITT: The Management of Opportunity.* New York, N.Y.: Times Books, 1982. 421 p.

United States. Congress. Senate. Committee on Foreign Relations. Subcommittee on Multinational Corporations. *The International Telephone and Telegraph Company and Chile, 1970-71: Report to the Committee on Foreign Relations, United States Senate.* Washington, D.C.: U.S. Government Printing Office, 1973. 20 p. (93rd Congress, 1st Session Committee Print)

INTERNATIONAL UTILITIES CORPORATION

Seabrook, John M. *International Utilities Corporation: A Binational Past and a Multinational Future.* New York, N.Y.: Newcomen Society in North America, 1969. 28 p. (Newcomen address).

THE INTERPUBLIC GROUP OF COMPANIES

"An Empire Linked by an 'Economic Umbilical Cord.'" *New York Times,* 30 September 1990, sec. 3, p. 6.

Millman, Nancy. In *Emperors of Adland; Inside the Advertising Revolution,* 39-56. New York, N.Y.: Warner Books, 1988.

INTERSTATE PUBLIC SERVICE COMPANY

Marlette, Jerry. *Interstate; A History of Interstate Public Service Rail Operations.* Polo, Ill.: Transportation Trails, 1988.

INVESTORS OVERSEAS SERVICES

Cantor, Bert. *The Bernie Cornfeld Story.* New York, N.Y.: L. Stuart, 1970. 320 p.

Herzog, Arthur. *Vesco: From Wall Street to Castro's Cuba, The Rise, Fall, and Exile of the King of White Collar Crime.* New York, N.Y.: Doubleday, 1987. 380 p.

Hutchinson, Robert A. *Vesco.* New York, N.Y.: Praeger, 1974. 376 p.

Raw, Charles, B. Page, and G. Hodgson. *"Do You Sincerely Want to Be Rich?" The Full Story of Bernard Cornfeld and IOS.* New York, N.Y.: Viking Press, 1971. 400 p.

IOWA BEEF PROCESSORS, INC.

Kwitny, Jonathan. "Troubled Packer: Iowa Beef Processors, Inc.'s History of Shady Characters Far Outruns '74 Case." *Wall Street Journal*, 17 December 1976, p. 1+

Tinstman, Dale C., and R.L. Peterson. *Iowa Beef Processors, Inc.: An Entire Industry Revolutionized.* New York, N.Y.: Newcomen Society in North America, 1981. 17 p. (Newcomen publication; no. 1137)

IRWIN UNION BANK AND TRUST COMPANY

Irwin Union Bank and Trust Company. *History.* Columbus, Ind.: The Company, 1985. 3 p.

ISCO, INC.

Hron, Frederic. "Flying on Instruments." *Nation's Business* 73 (July 1985): 46-48.

ITHACA STREET RAILWAY COMPANY

Kerr, Richard D. *Ithaca Street Railway Company*. Forty Fort, Pa.: H.E. Cox, 1972. 48 p.

ITT
SEE:
INTERNATIONAL TELEPHONE AND TELEGRAPH COMPANY

IVEY (J.B.) AND COMPANY

Ivey, George M. *J.B. Ivey and Company: A 75th Anniversary Address, 1900-1975*. New York, N.Y.: Newcomen Society in North America, 1975. 18 p. (Newcomen publication; no. 1016)

IVORY SOAP
SEE:
PROCTER AND GAMBLE COMPANY

J.C. PENNEY COMPANY, INC.
SEE:
PENNEY (J.C.) COMPANY, INC.

J WALTER THOMPSON
SEE:
JWT GROUP, INC.

JACOB (M.) AND SONS

Posner, Bruce G. "The 100-Year-Old Start-Up." *Inc.* 7 (September 1985): 79-85.

JACOBS ENGINEERING GROUP, INC.

Jacobs, Joseph J. *Jacobs Engineering Group, Inc.: A Story of Pride, Reputation and Integrity*. New York, N.Y.: Newcomen Society in North America, 1980. 22 p. (Newcomen publication; no. 1122)

JANTZEN, INC.

Cleary, David Powers. "Jantzen Swim Suits; A Good Business." In *Great American Brands: The Success Formulas That Made Them Famous*, 182-191. New York, N.Y.: Fairchild Publications, 1981.

JENNIE-O FOODS

Pine, Carol, and Susan Mundale. "Earl Olson; Betting on the Bird." In *Self-Made: The Stories of 12 Minnesota Entrepreneurs*, 175-190. Minneapolis, Minn.: Dorn Books, 1982.

JENO'S, INC.

Pine, Carol, and Susan Mundale. "Jeno Paulucci; The Kid with the Argentine Bananas." In *Self-Made: The Stories of 12 Minnesota Entrepreneurs*, 19-37. Minneapolis, Minn.: Dorn Books, 1982.

JERGENS (ANDREW) COMPANY

Erwin, Paul F. *With Lotions of Love*. Cincinnati, Ohio: The Author, 1965. 107 p.

JIM WALTERS CORPORATION
SEE:
WALTERS (JIM) CORPORATION

JITNEY JUNGLE STORES OF AMERICA

Holman, William H. *"Save a Nickel on a Quarter": The Story of Jitney Jungle Stores of America*. New York, N.Y.: Newcomen Society in North America, 1974. 30 p.

JOHNS-MANVILLE COMPANY
SEE:
MANVILLE CORPORATION

JOHNSON AND JOHNSON, INC.

Foster, Lawrence G. *A Company That Cares; One Hundred Year Illustrated History of Johnson and Johnson.* New Brunswick, N.J.: The Company, 1986. 175 p.

Johnson & Johnson, Inc. *Brief History of Johnson & Johnson.* New Brunswick, N.J.: The Company, 1981. 8 p.

Update, Johnson & Johnson Company. Washington, D.C.: Investor Responsibility Research Center, 1984. 18 p.

JOHNSON AND TOWERS

Dennis, E. "J&T: A Diesel Dynasty." *Motor Boating & Sailing* 166 (November 1990): 39.

JOHNSON PUBLISHING

Johnson, John Harold. *Succeeding Against the Odds.* New York, N.Y.: Warner Books, 1989. 372 p.

Sobel, Robert, and David B. Sicilia. "John H. Johnson: Apostle of the Black Middle Class." In *The Entrepreneurs: An American Adventure*, 32-37. Boston, Mass.: Houghton Mifflin Company, 1986.

JOHNSON (S.C.) AND SONS, INC.

Goldwasser, Thomas. "Johnson Wax: 100 Years and Still Shining." In *Family Pride; Profiles of Five of America's Best-Run Family Businesses*, 163-202. New York, N.Y.: Dodd, Mead and Company, 1986.

JOHNSON WAX
SEE:
JOHNSON (S.C.) AND SONS, INC.

JONES AND LAUGHLIN STEEL CORPORATION

Cortner, Richard C. *The Jones & Laughlin Case*. New York, N.Y.: Knopf, 1970. 191 p.

JONES, DAY, REAVIS AND POQUE

Stevens, Mark. "Today Cleveland, Tomorrow the World." In *Power of Attorney: The Rise of the Giant Law Firms*, 129-152. New York, N.Y.: McGraw Hill, 1987.

JONES (J.A.) CONSTRUCTION COMPANY

Jones, Edwin L. *J.A. Jones Construction Company: 75 Year's Growth in Construction*. New York, N.Y.: Newcomen Society in North America, 1965. 28 p. (Newcomen address)

JONESBORO, LAKE CITY AND EASTERN RAILROAD

Drew, Lee A. *The JLC&E: The History of an Arkansas Railroad*. State University: Arkansas State University Press, 1968. 121 p.

JORDAN COMPANY

Kingston, Brett. "Jay Jordan of the Jordan Company." In *The Dynamos: Who Are They Anyway?*, 177-187. New York, N.Y.: Wiley, 1987.

JOY LINE

Dunbaugh, Edwin. *The Era of the Joy Line: A Saga of Steamboating on Long Island Sound*. Westport, Conn.: Greenwood Press, 1981.

JOY MANUFACTURING COMPANY

"A Tribute to Joseph Francis Joy; Born September 13,

1883." *Communiqué* (September 1983). 15 p. (Special commemorative issue)

Drain, James A. *Machines That Change the Way the World Works: A Tale of Joy*. New York, N.Y.: Newcomen Society in North America, 1968. 24 p. (Newcomen address)

J.P. INDUSTRIES

Fucini, Joseph J., and Suzy Fucini. "John Psarouthakis: 'Define a Problem Before Trying to Solve It.'" In *Experience Inc.; Men and Women Who Founded Famous Companies After the Age of 40*, 167-172. New York, N.Y.: Free Press, 1987.

JWT GROUP, INC.

Winski, Joseph M. "JWT at 125; Agency Keeps Its Sense of Tradition in a Fast-Changing Environment." *Advertising Age* 60 (27 November 1989): 47-65.

K MART
SEE:
KRESGE (S.S.) COMPANY

KAISER ALUMINUM AND CHEMICAL CORPORATION

Heiner, Albert P. *Henry J. Kaiser, American Empire Building; An Insider's View*. New York, N.Y.: Peter Lang, 1990. 450 p.

Kaiser Industries Corporation. *The Kaiser Story*. Oakland, Calif.: The Company, 1968. 72 p.

Stein, Mimi. *A Special Difference: A History of Kaiser Aluminum & Chemical Corporation*. Oakland, Calif.: The Company, 1980. 191 p.

KAMAN CORPORATION

Kaman, Charles H. *Kaman Corporation: An American Story.* New York, N.Y.: Newcomen Society in North America, 1983. 24 p. (Newcomen publication; no. 1200)

Kaman, Charles H. *Kaman: Our Early Years.* Indianapolis, Ind.: Curtis Publishing Company, 1985. 175 p.

KANSAS CITY CHIEFS

Connor, Dick. *Kansas City Chiefs.* New York, N.Y.: Macmillan, 1974. 192 p.

KANSAS CITY POWER AND LIGHT COMPANY

Olson, Robert A. *Kansas City Power and Light Company: The First Ninety Years.* New York, N.Y.: Newcomen Society in North America, 1972. 24 p. (Newcomen address)

KANSAS CITY SOUTHERN RAILWAY COMPANY

Bryant, Keith L. *Arthur E. Stilwell: Promoter with a Hunch.* Nashville, Tenn.: Vanderbilt University Press, 1971. 256 p.

KANSAS CITY STAR

Kansas City Star. *The First 100 Years: A Man, A Newspaper and a City.* Centennial Sections, Sunday, September 14, 1980. Kansas City, Mo.: Kansas City Star, 1980. 192 p.

KANSAS GAS AND ELECTRIC COMPANY

Cadman, Wilson K. *Kansas Gas and Electric Company.* New York, N.Y.: Newcomen Society of the United States, 1989. 28 p. (Newcomen publication; no. 1330)

KANSAS POWER AND LIGHT COMPANY

Jeffrey, Balfour S. *The Kansas Power and Light Company: Through Fifty Years to the Electric Economy.* New York, N.Y.: Newcomen Society in North America, 1975. 29 p. (Newcomen publication; no. 1005)

KATZ COMMUNICATIONS

"Katz 100th Anniversary." *Television/Radio Age* (November 1988). Special supplement.

KAUFMAN AND BROAD, INC.

"Two Decades As a Public Company; Special Report." *Spectrum* (September 1981): 7-10.

KEESHIN TRANSPORT SYSTEM, INC.

Keeshin, John Lewis. *No Fears, Hidden Tears, A Memoir of Four Score Years: The Autobiography of John Lewis Keeshin.* Chicago, Ill.: The Company, 1983. 240 p.

KELLER MANUFACTURING COMPANY

Kaufman, Charles N. *The History of the Keller Manufacturing Company.* New York, N.Y.: Arno Press, 1976, c1966.

KELLEY DRYE AND WARREN

Lunny, Robert M. *Kelley Drye & Warren; An Informal History, 1836-1984.* New York, N.Y.: The Company, 1985. 246 p.

KELLEY-SPRINGFIELD TIRE COMPANY

Jackson, Kenneth A. *Kelly-Springfield Story.* Cumberland, Md.: The Company, 1988. 279 p.

KELLOGG COMPANY

Gorman, John. "Kellogg: An All-American Success Story." *Chicago Tribune*, 14 April 1986, sec. 4, p. 1.

Kellogg Company. *The History of Kellogg's*. Battle Creek, Mich.: The Company, 1982. 3 p.

THE KELLOGG (L.D.) LUMBER COMPANY

Kellogg, Walter W. *The Kellogg Story: 50 Years in Southern Hardwoods*. Monroe, La.: The Company, 1969. 179 p.

THE KELLWOOD COMPANY

The Kellwood Company. *Kellwood: A History*. St. Louis, Mo.: The Company, 1981. 20 p.

THE KEMPER GROUP

The Kemper Group. *Presenting the Kemper Group*. Long Grove, Ill.: The Company, 1983. 20 p.

KENNAMETAL, INC.

McKenna, Donald C. *The Roots of Kennametal: Or Philip McKenna and How He Grew*. Latrobe, Pa.: The Company, 1974. 32 p.

KENNER PRODUCTS
SEE:
TONKA CORPORATION

KENRICK (ARCHIBALD) AND SONS

Church, Roy A. *Kenricks in Hardware; A Family Business, 1791-1966*. New York, N.Y.: A.M. Kelley Publishers, 1969. 340 p.

KENTUCKY CENTRAL LIFE INSURANCE COMPANY

"Kentucky Central, State's Oldest Life Insurer, Now One of the Nation's Largest." *Kincaid Towers* (1980): 16-21.

KENTUCKY FINANCE COMPANY, INC.

"Kincaid Started Kentucky Finance Company from Scratch." *Kincaid Towers* (1980): 36-39.

KENTUCKY FRIED CHICKEN

Klemm, Edward G., Jr. *Claudia, The Story of Colonel Harland Sanders' Wife*. Los Angeles, Calif.: Crescent Pub., 1980. 95 p.

Pearce, John E. *The Colonel: The Captivating Biography of the Dynamic Founder of Fast-Food Empire*. Garden City, N.Y.: Doubleday, 1982. 225 p.

Sanders, Harland. *The Incredible Colonel*. Carol Stream, Ill.: Creation House, 1974. 144 p.

Sanders, Harland. *Life As I Have Known It Has Been Finger Lickin' Good*. Carol Stream, Ill.: Creation House, 1974. 144 p.

KENTUCKY HILLS INDUSTRIES

Ross, Smith G. *Come Go with Me*. Pine Knot, Ky.: The Company, 1977. 152 p.

KENTUCKY UTILITIES COMPANY

Kentucky Utilities Company. *A Pictorial History*. Lexington, Ky.: The Company, 1987. 24 p. (Kentucky Utilities' 75th anniversary)

KERITE COMPANY

Rudd, Theodore O. *A Century of Cable Making: The Kerite Company, 1854-1966.* New York, N.Y.: Newcomen Society in North America, 1966. 28 p. (Newcomen address)

KERR-MCGEE CORPORATION

Ezell, John Samuel. *Innovations in Energy: The Story of Kerr-McGee.* Norman: University of Oklahoma Press, 1979. 542 p.

Kerr-McGee Corporation. *Diversification Marks 60 Years of Operations; A Brief History of Kerr-McGee Corp.* Oklahoma City, Okla.: The Company, 1989. 2 p.

McGee, Dean A. *Evolution into Total Energy: The Story of Kerr-McGee Corporation.* New York, N.Y.: Newcomen Society in North America, 1971. 24 p. (Newcomen Address)

KERR-MCGEE NUCLEAR CORPORATION

Kohn, Howard. *Who Killed Karen Silkwood?* New York, N.Y.: Summit Books, 1981. 462 p.

Rashke, Richard L. *The Killing of Karen Silkwood: The Story Behind the Kerr-McGee Plutonium Case.* Boston, Mass.: Houghton Mifflin, 1981. 407 p.

KEWANEE OIL COMPANY

Kewanee Oil Company. *Kewanee Oil Company, 1871-1971: 100 Years of Beginning.* Bryn Mawr, Pa.: The Company, 1971. 34 p.

KEY BANKS, INC.
SEE:
KEYCORP

KEYCORP

Key Banks, Inc. *Key Banks, Inc.: A Short History.*
Albany, N.Y.: The Company, 1985. 4 p.

Key Banks, Inc. *Key Banks, Inc.: Milestones.* Albany,
N.Y.: The Company, 1985. 3 p.

KeyCorp. *History and Milestones.* Albany, N.Y.: The
Company, 1990. 9 p.

KIDDER, PEABODY, AND COMPANY

Carosso, Vincent P. *More Than a Century of Investment
Banking: The Kidder, Peabody & Company Story.*
New York, N.Y.: McGraw-Hill, 1979. 212 p.

KIEWIT (PETER) SONS, INC.

Limprecht, Hollis. *The Kiewit Story: Remarkable Man,
Remarkable Company.* Omaha, Nebr.: H.J.
Limprecht: Omaha World-Herald Company, 1981.
294 p.

KIMBALL INTERNATIONAL

Wells, Grant J. "Kimball International--Playing a Sound
Tune." *Ball State Business Review* 11 (1982): 7-14.

KIMBERLY-CLARK CORPORATION

Cleary, David Powers. "Kleenex Tissue; Don't Put a Cold
in Your Pocket." In *Great American Brands: The
Success Formulas That Made Them Famous*, 197-
201. New York, N.Y.: Fairchild Publications, 1981.

KIMMINS CORPORATION

Leonard, Burr. "The Up and Comers: Demolition Demon."
Forbes 139 (20 April 1987): 61-62.

KINDER-CARE LEARNING CENTERS, INC.

Fucini, Joseph J., and Suzy Fucini. "Perry Mendel, Kinder-Care Learning Centers, Inc.: 'An Idea Will Remain Just an Idea Until Someone Moves on It.'" In *Experience Inc.; Men and Women Who Founded Famous Companies After the Age of 40*, 75-81. New York, N.Y.: Free Press, 1987.

KING RANCH, INC.

Denhardt, Robert Moorman. *The King Ranch Quarter Horses, And Something of the Ranch and the Men That Bred Them*. Norman, Okla.: University of Oklahoma Press, 1970. 256 p.

Frost, Dick. *The King Ranch Papers: An Unauthorized and Irreverent History of the World's Largest Landholders, The Kleberg Family*. Chicago, Ill.: Acquarius Rising Press, 1985. 185 p.

KITCHENAID DISHWASHERS
SEE:
HOBART CORPORATION

KLEID COMPANY, INC.

Hoke, Pete. "First Lady of Direct Marketing Blazing New Trails at Saatchi." *Direct Marketing* 48 (October 1985): 110-127.

KLIPSCH LOUDSPEAKERS SYSTEMS

MacPhee, William. "Paul Klipsch of Klipsch Loudspeaker Systems." In *Rare Breed: The Entrepreneur, An American Culture*, 79-88. Chicago, Ill.: Probus Publishing Company, 1987.

KNIGHT-RIDDER NEWSPAPERS

Cose, Ellis. "The Chains: Gannett and Knight-Ridder." In

The Press, 281-356. New York, N.Y.: Morrow, 1989.

Knight-Ridder Newspapers. *"The Press Is Many Things, But Its First Responsibility Is to Print the News Without Fear or Favor."* Miami, Fla.: The Company, 1984. 2 p.

KNOX INDUSTRIAL SUPPLIES

"Knox Celebrates 50 Years of Teamwork." *Industrial Distribution* 72 (November 1982): 81+

KOCH MATADOR CATTLE COMPANY

Lincoln, John. *Rich Grass and Sweet Water; Ranch Life With the Koch Matador Cattle Company.* College Station, Tex.: Texas A&M University Press, 1989.

KODAK (EASTMAN) COMPANY

Eastman Kodak Company. *A Brief History.* Rochester, N.Y.: The Company, 1983. 11 p.

Eastman Kodak Company. *Kodak Milestones.* Rochester, N.Y.: The Company, 1982. 32 p.

KOHLER COMPANY

Bender, Marylin. "The Kohlers of Wisconsin." In *At the Top; Behind the Scenes with the Men and Women Who Run America's Corporate Giants*, 248-268. Garden City, N.Y.: Doubleday, 1975.

Kohler Company. *Bold Craftsmen.* Kohler, Wis.: The Company, 1973. 40 p.

Mahnke, Susan. "Kohler of Kohler." *Wisconsin Trails* (Spring 1979): 36-39.

Milbourne, Claire. "Kohler--A Commitment to Planning." *Wisconsin Architect* (November 1982): 8-15.

KOPPERS COMPANY, INC.

Koppers Company, Inc. *Koppers; The Evolution of the Company and Its Markets*. Pittsburgh, Pa.: The Company, 197?. 7 p.

KOSS CORPORATION

Buchholz, Barbara B., and Margaret Crane. "Koss Corporation, Milwaukee, WI." In *Corporate Blood Lines: The Future of the Family Firm*, 175-192. New York, N.Y.: Carol Publishing Group, 1989.

KRESGE (S.S) COMPANY

Kresge, Stanley Sebastian. *The S.S. Kresge Story*. Racine, Wis.: Western Publishing Company, 1979. 373 p.

KROFTA WATERS, INC.

Gilder, George. "The Man Who Wanted to Clean the Water." In *The Spirit of Enterprise*, 71-92. New York, N.Y.: Simon and Schuster, 1984.

THE KROGER COMPANY

"The Kroger story." *Dallas Times Herald Sunday Magazine* (18 June 1967): 1-16.

Laycock, George. *The Kroger Story: A Century of Innovation*. Cincinnati, Ohio: The Company, 1983. 143 p.

KRUEGER (W.A.) COMPANY

Wells, Robert W., and Robert A. Klaus. *We Have with Us Today; W.A. Krueger Company, 1934-1974*. Scottsdale, Ariz.: The Company, 1974. 219 p.

KUHN, LOEB AND COMPANY

Kuhn, Loeb and Company. *A Century of Investment Banking*. New York, N.Y.: The Company, 1967. 52 p.

KWIK-KOPY CORPORATION

Palmer, Peggy. *An American Original: The Story of Kwik-Kopy Printing*. Houston, Tex.: D. Armstrong Co., 1981. 138 p.

LACKAWANNA STEEL COMPANY

Leary, Thomas E. *From Fire to Rust: Business, Technology and Work at the Lackawanna Steel Plant, 1899-1983*. Buffalo, N.Y.: Buffalo and Erie County Historical Society, 1987. 134 p.

LAFARGE CORPORATION

"The Lafarge Corporation Story." In *Lafarge Corporation. Annual Report*, 4-5. Dallas, Tex.: The Company, 1983.

LAKER AIRWAYS

Banks, Howard. *The Rise and Fall of Freddie Laker*. Winchester, Mass.: Faber and Faber, 1982. 155 p.

Eglin, Roger, and B. Ritchie. *Fly Me, I'm Freddie!: The Life and Times of the Man Who Broke the Airline Cartel and Made Air Travel Available to Everyone*. New York, N.Y.: Rawson, Wade, 1980. 238 p.

LAMSON AND SESSIONS COMPANY

Case, George S., Jr. *Lamson and Sessions--Starting a Second Century of Industrial Fastener Development and Production*. New York, N.Y.: Newcomen Society in North America, 1965. 24 p. (Newcomen address)

LANCE, INC.

Van Every, Philip Lance. *The History of Lance*. New York, N.Y.: Newcomen Society in North America, 1974. 16 p. (Newcomen publication; no. 1002)

LAND O'LAKES CREAMERIES, INC.

Land O'Lakes, Inc. *Guideposts for the Future: History of Land O'Lakes*. Minneapolis, Minn.: The Company, 1982?. 11 p.

Ruble, Kenneth Douglas. *Land O'Lakes: Farmers Make it Happen*. Minneapolis, 1973. 205 p.

LANE COMPANY

Cleary, David Powers. "Lane Cedar Chests; Make a Good Product, And Sell with an Idea." In *Great American Brands: The Success Formulas That Made Them Famous*, 202-210. New York, N.Y.: Fairchild Publications, 1981.

LANE (KENNETH JAY), INC.

Levitt, Mortimer. "Kenneth Jay Lane: An Eye for Fashion Trends Finds a Gold Mine in Rhinestones." In *How to Start Your Own Business Without Losing Your Shirt; Secrets of Seventeen Successful Entrepreneurs*, 77-84. New York, N.Y.: Atheneum, 1988.

LANE PUBLISHING COMPANY

Holt, Patricia. "Lane Publishing Company Celebrates a Half-Century in the West." *Publishers Weekly* 215 (12 March 1979): 37+

Lane, L.W., Jr. *The Sunset Story: "To Serve the Westerner--And No One Else--."* New York, N.Y.: Newcomen Society in North America, 1973. 29 p. (Newcomen address)

LANNON MANUFACTURING COMPANY

Hamilton, Neil A. *Visions of Worth; The Life of G.S. Lannon, Jr., Independent Entrepreneur.* Solon, Iowa: Preservation Publishing Company, 1988. 242 p.

LASKY COMPANY

Lasky Company. *The First 50 Years.* Newark, N.J.: The Company, 1967. 32 p.

LAUDER (ESTEE)

Bender, Marylin. "Estee Lauder: A Family Affair." In *At the Top; Behind the Scenes with the Men and Women Who Run America's Corporate Giants*, 213-233. Garden City, N.Y.: Doubleday, 1975.

Israel, Lee. *Estee Lauder: Beyond the Magic: An Unauthorized Biography.* New York, N.Y.: Macmillan, 1985. 186 p.

Lauder, Estee. *Estee: A Success Story.* New York, N.Y.: Random House, 1985. 222 p.

Taylor, Russel R. "Estee Lauder; High Priestess of Cosmetics." In *Exceptional Entrepreneurial Women*, 111-119. New York, N.Y.: Quorum Books, 1988.

LAWRY'S FOODS, INC.

Frank, Richard Nathan. *Lawry's Foods, Inc.: A Blending of Dreams.* New York, N.Y.: Newcomen Society of the United States, 1987. (Newcomen publication; no. 1299)

LAZZARA OPTICAL

Buchholz, Barbara B., and Margaret Crane. "Lazzara Optical, Villa Park, IL." In *Corporate Blood Lines: The Future of the Family Firm*, 29-42. New York,

N.Y.: Carol Publishing Group, 1989.

LEA AND FEBIGER

Bussy, R. Kenneth. *Two Hundred Years of Publishing: A History of the Oldest Publishing Company in the United States, Lea & Febiger, 1785-1985.* Philadelphia, Pa.: Lea & Febiger, 1985. 126 p.

LEAR, INC.

Boesen, Victor. *They Said It Couldn't Be Done, The Incredible Story of Bill Lear.* Garden City, N.Y.: Doubleday, 1971. 204 p.

LEAR SIEGLER, INC.

Brooks, John G. *Planning for Growth and Profit: The Success Story of Lear Siegler, Inc.* New York, N.Y.: Newcomen Society in North America, 1970. 28 p. (Newcomen address)

LEASCO DATA PROCESSING EQUIPMENT CORPORATION

Glasberg, Davita Silfen. "Corporate Power and Control: The Case of Leasco Corporation Versus Chemical Bank." *Social Problems* 29 (December 1981): 104-116.

Glasberg, Davita Silfen. *The Power of Collective Purse Strings: The Effects of Bank Hegemony on Corporations and the State.* Berkeley, Calif.: University of California Press, 1989. 239 p.

LEATHER LOFT STORES

"Entrepreneur Is into Leather to the Tune of $30 Million in Sales." *Chain Store Age Executive* 61 (November 1985): 110-112.

LEAVELL COMPANY

Lynde, Bill. *The Leavell Story: The Man and His Work, 1933-1983.* El Paso, Tex.: Guynes Print Company, 1983. 83 p.

LEDDY (M.L.) BOAT AND SADDLERY

Livingston, P. "M.L. Leddy's Boat & Saddlery." *Western Horseman* (May 1989): 116+

LEE AND SHEPARD, PUBLISHERS

Kilgour, Raymond Lincoln. *Lee and Shepard, Publishers for the People.* Hamden, Conn.: Shoe String Press, 1965. 306 p.

LEHIGH COAL AND NAVIGATION

Parton, W. Julian. *Death of a Great Company; Reflections on the Decline and Fall of the Lehigh Coal and Navigation Company.* Easton, Pa.: Center for Canal History, 1986. 161 p.

LEHMAN BROTHERS KUHN LOEB

Auletta, Ken. *Greed and Glory on Wall Street: The Fall of the House of Lehman.* New York, N.Y.: Random House, 1986. 253 p.

Bender, Marylin. "The White Knight at Lehman Brothers." In *At the Top; Behind the Scenes with the Men and Women Who Run America's Corporate Giants,* 67-94. Garden City, N.Y.: Doubleday, 1975.

SEE ALSO: KUHN, LOEB AND COMPANY

LEISY BREWING COMPANY

Leisy, Bruce R. *A History of the Leisy Brewing Companies.* North Newton, Kan.: Mennonite Press,

1975. 106 p.

LELAND O'BRIEN RUBINSTEIN ASSOCIATES

Szymczak, Patricia M. "Leland; O'Brien; Rubinstein." *Futures; The Magazine of Commodities and Options (Profiles Issue)* 17 (July 1988): 41-42.

LENNOX INDUSTRIES, INC.

Lennox Industries, Inc. *The Story of Lennox*. Dallas, Tex.: The Company, 1989. 11 p.

Lennox Industries, Inc. *The Story of Lennox Industries, Inc.--Continuing Success Based on 90 Years of Innovation*. Dallas, Tex.: The Company, 1985. 12 p. (Reprint of an article from *Contracting Business*, September, 1985)

LEONARD (STEW)

Levitt, Mortimer. "Stew Leonard: Selling Milk and Groceries in a 'Magic Kingdom' Setting." In *How to Start Your Own Business Without Losing Your Shirt; Secrets of Seventeen Successful Entrepreneurs*, 85-95. New York, N.Y.: Atheneum, 1988.

LEPAGE (F.R.) BAKERY, INC.

Lepage, Regis A. *Seventy Years of Quality: The F.R. Lepage Bakery, Inc. Story*. New York, N.Y.: Newcomen Society in North America, 1973. 20 p.

LEUCADIA NATIONAL

Rosenberg, Hilary. "Elusive Leucadia: A Hard Look at a Little-Known Financial Firm." *Barron's* 65 (11 November 1985): 6-7, 24.

LEVI STRAUSS AND COMPANY

Cleary, David Powers. "Levi's Jeans: The Cowboy's Tailor." In *Great American Brands: The Success Formulas That Made Them Famous*, 211-216. New York, N.Y.: Fairchild Publications, 1981.

Cray, Ed. *Levi's*. Boston, Mass.: Houghton Mifflin, 1978. 286 p.

Grether, E.T. "Four Men and a Company: Levi Strauss Since World War I." *California Management Review* 20 (Fall 1977): 14-20.

Taitz, Emily, and Sondra Henry. *Everyone Wears His Name; A Biography of Levi Strauss*. Minneapolis, Minn.: Dillon Press, 1989. 128 p.

Van Steenwyk, Elizabeth. *Levi Strauss; The Blue Jeans Man*. New York, N.Y.: Walker, 1988. 96 p.

LEVINE AND COMPANY

Frantz, Douglas. *Levine and Company: Wall Street's Insider Trading Scandal*. New York, N.Y.: Holt, 1987. 370 p.

LEVITZ FURNITURE CORPORATION

Martindale, Wight. *We Do It Every Day: The Story Behind the Success of Levitz Furniture*. New York, N.Y.: Fairchild Publications, 1972. 150 p.

LEWIS GROCER COMPANY

Lewis, Morris, Jr. *Wholesaler--Retailer: The Story of Lewis Grocer Company and Sunflower Food Stores*. New York, N.Y.: Newcomen Society in North America, 1975. 21 p. (Newcomen publication; no. 1021)

THE LIBERTY CORPORATION

Hipp, Francis M. *The Liberty Corporation: A Success Story of the Changing South.* New York, N.Y.: Newcomen Society in North America, 1982. 20 p. (Newcomen publication; no. 1157)

LIBERTY NATIONAL LIFE INSURANCE COMPANY

Camp, Ehney A., Jr. *A History of the Investment Division of Liberty National Life Insurance Company.* University, Ala.: University of Alabama Press, 1978. 125 p.

LIFE INSURANCE COMPANY OF VIRGINIA

Sanford, James K., and Robert B. Lancaster. *Century One, One Hundred Years of the Life Insurance Company of Virginia.* Richmond: The Company, 1971. 120 p.

LIFE MAGAZINE

Wainwright, Loudon. *The Great American Magazine: An Inside History of Life.* New York, N.Y.: Knopf, 1986. 443 p.

LIFETIME CORPORATION

Paris, E. "A Business Even the Patients Like." *Forbes* 145 (14 May 1990): 104+

LIGGERT GROUP, INC.

Liggert Group. *The Companies of Your Pleasure.* Montvale, N.J.: The Company, 1977. 32 p.

LILLIAN VERNON
SEE:
VERNON (LILLIAN)

LILLY (ELI) AND COMPANY

Kahn, E.J. *All in a Century: The First 100 Years of Eli Lilly and Company.* West Cornwall, Conn.: Kahn, 1975. 211 p.

Madison, James H. *Eli Lilly, A Life, 1885-1977.* Indianapolis, Ind.: Indiana Historical Society, 1989. 342 p.

THE LIMITED, INC.

The Limited, Inc. *Fact Book: 1989.* Columbus, Ohio: The Company, 1989. 6 p.

The Limited, Inc. *The Pursuit of Excellence.* Columbus, Ohio: The Company, 1985. 4 p.

LIMONIERA COMPANY

Blanchard, Dean Hobbs. *Of California's First Citrus Empire: A Rainbow Arches from Maine to Ventura County.* Santa Paula, Calif.: D.H. Blanchard, 1983.

LINCOLN PROPERTY COMPANY

O'Reilly, Brian. "This Builder Wants It All--Without Risk." *Fortune* 113 (12 May 1986): 50-57.

LINCOLN SAVINGS AND LOAN

Adams, James Ring. "Nemesis." In *The Big Fix: Inside the S&L Scandal: How an Unholy Alliance of Politics and Money Destroyed America's Banking System,* 234-254. New York, N.Y.: Wiley, 1990.

THE LINCOLN TELEPHONE AND TELEGRAPH COMPANY

Geist, James E. *The Lincoln Telephone and Telegraph Company: The Great Independent.* New York, N.Y.:

Newcomen Society in North America, 1979. 21 p.
(Newcomen publication; no. 1104)

LINCOLNVILLE TELEPHONE COMPANY

Lehner, J. Christopher. "And the Child Grew: The Life
and Times of Lincolnville Telephone Company." *Rural
Telecommunications* 6 (Summer 1987): 22-24.

LING-TEMCO-VOUGHT, INC.

Brown, Stanley H. *Ling: The Rise, Fall and Return of a
Texas Titan.* New York, N.Y.: Atheneum, 1972.
308 p.

Jacobs, Donald. "An Account and Evaluation of James
Ling's Rise and Fall with Ling-Temco-Vought." Ph.D.
diss., University of Nebraska, 1977. 208 p.

LIONEL TRAIN COMPANY

Hollander, Ron. *All Aboard!: The Story of Joshua Lionel
Cowen and His Lionel Train Company.* New York,
N.Y.: Workman Pub., 1981. 253 p.

LIONS CLUB OF SPRINGFIELD, IL.

Lions Club of Springfield, Illinois. *50th Anniversary,
1919-1969.* Springfield, Ill.: The Club, 1969.

LIPPINCOTT (J.B.) COMPANY

Lippincott, J.B. Company. *The Author and His Audience;
With a Chronology of Major Events in the Publishing
History of J.B. Lippincott.* Philadelphia, Pa.: The
Company, 1967. 79 p.

LITTLE (ARTHUR D.)

Kahn, Ely Jacques. *The Problem Sowers: A History of
Arthur D. Little, Inc.* Boston, Mass.: Little, Brown &

Co., 1986. 250 p.

Magee, John F. *Arthur D. Little, Inc.: At the Moving Frontier.* New York, N.Y.: Newcomen Society of the United States, 1986. 21 p. (Newcomen publication; no. 1261)

THE LITTLETON SAVINGS BANK

McLaughlin, Ambrose P. *To Rise Above a Village We Need a Bank!: The Story of the Littleton Savings Bank, 1868-1968.* New York, N.Y.: Newcomen Society in North America, 1968. 24 p. (Newcomen address)

LITTON INDUSTRIES, INC.

Lay, Beirne. *Someone Has to Make it Happen: The Inside Story of Tex Thornton, The Man Who Built Litton Industries.* Englewood Cliffs, N.J.: Prentice-Hall, 1969. 204 p.

O'Green, Fred W. *Putting Technology to Work: The Story of Litton Industries.* New York, N.Y.: Newcomen Society of the United States, 1988, c1989. 24 p. (Newcomen publication; no. 1318)

Rosenberg, Ann. *The Technological Warlords.* New York, N.Y.: Computer People for Peace, 1971. 29 p.

St. Pé , Jerry. *A Salute to American Spirit: The Story of Ingalls Shipbuilding, Division of Litton.* New York, N.Y.: Newcomen Society of the United States, 1988, c1989. 23 p. (Newcomen publication; no. 1306)

LIVINGSTON MUTUAL INSURANCE COMPANY

Sipperley, Leonard. *One Hundred Years of Fire Insurance, Being a History of the Livingston Mutual Insurance Company, Dansville, New York, 1877-1977.* Edited by David Parish. Dansville, N.Y.: The

Company, 1977. 34 p.

LOCKHEED AIRCRAFT CORPORATION

"A History of Lockheed." *Lockheed Horizons* 12 (1983) 1-156. (Special issue)

Anderson, Roy A. *A Look at Lockheed*. New York, N.Y.: Newcomen Society in North America, 1983. 52 p. (Newcomen publication; no. 1186).

Boulton, David. *The Grease Machine*. New York, N.Y.: Harper & Row, 1978. 289 p.

Ingells, Douglas J. *L-1011 TriStar and the Lockheed Story*. Fallbrook, Calif.: Aero Pub., 1973. 256 p.

Lockheed Aircraft Corporation. *Days of Trial and Triumph, A Pictorial History of Lockheed*. Burbank, Calif.: The Company, 1969. 108 p.

Siuru, Bill, and Allan Lockheed. "Lockheed: A Legacy of Speed." *Mechanical Engineering* 112 (May 1990): 60-64.

Yenne, Bill. *Lockheed*. New York, N.Y.: Crescent Books, Distributed by Crown Pub., 1987. 255 p.

LOCKHEED-GEORGIA COMPANY

Rice, Berkely. *The C-5A Scandal; An Inside Story of the Military-Industrial Complex*. Boston, Mass.: Houghton Mifflin, 1971. 238 p.

LOCKWOOD GREENE ENGINEERS, INC.

Heiser, William J. *Lockwood Greene, 1958-1968, Another Period in the History of An Engineering Business*, New York, N.Y.: The Company, 1970. 255 p.

LOCTITE CORPORATION

Butterworth, Kenneth W. *The Loctite Story*. New York, N.Y.: Newcomen Society of the United States, 1989. c1988. 24 p. (Newcomen publication; no. 1312)

Fucini, Joseph J., and Suzy Fucini. "Vernon K. Krieble, Loctite Corporation: 'Work is Too Much Fun to Give Up.'" In *Experience Inc.; Men and Women Who Founded Famous Companies After the Age of 40*, 200-206. New York, N.Y.: Free Press, 1987.

Grant, Ellsworth S. *Drop by Drop: The Loctite Story, 1953-1980*. Newington, Conn.: The Company, 1983. 156 p.

LOEHMANNS, INC.

Millstein, Alan G. "Loehmann's: Can the Gypsy Rose Lee of Discounting Find a New Gimmick in the '90s?" *Bobbin* 31 (February 1990): 34-38.

LONE STAR GAS COMPANY

The Lone Star Gas Company. *The First Seventy-Five Years: A Pictorial History of the Lone Star Gas Company, 1909-1984*. Dallas, Tex.: The Company, 1984. 116 p.

LONG ISLAND LIGHTING COMPANY

Grossman, Karl. *Power Crazy*. New York, N.Y.: Grove Press, 1986. 372 p.

Zorpette, Glenn, and Karen Fitzgerald. "The Shoreham Saga/The First Decade: Great Expectations/Regulation and Retrenchment/Power Politics." *IEEE Spectrum* 24 (November 1987): 24-37.

LORD, ABBET AND COMPANY

Driscoll, Robert S. *The Story of Lord, Abbet and Company and Affiliated Fund, Inc.: A View of the Capital Needs of the U.S. Economy.* New York, N.Y.: Newcomen Society in North America, 1974. (Newcomen publication; no. 999)

LORD CORPORATION

Lord, Thomas. *Lord Corporation: A Story of Innovation, Invention, And Learning.* New York, N.Y.: Newcomen Society in North America, 1974. 34 p. (Newcomen publication; no. 982)

LOS ANGELES DODGERS

Gewecke, Clifford George. *Day by Day in Dodgers History.* New York, N.Y.: Leisure Press, 1984. 336 p.

Schoor, Gene. *A Pictorial History of the Dodgers: Brooklyn to Los Angeles.* New York, N.Y.: Macmillan, 1984. 480 p.

Whittingham, Richard. *The Los Angeles Dodgers: An Illustrated History.* New York, N.Y.: Harper & Row, 1982. 256 p.

LOS ANGELES RAIDERS

Hession, Joseph, and Steve Cassady. *The Raiders from Oakland to Los Angeles.* San Francisco, Calif.: Foghorn Press, 1987. 200 p.

LOS ANGELES RAMS

Bisheff, Steve. *Los Angeles Rams.* New York, N.Y.: Macmillan, 1973. 192 p.

Hession, Joseph. *The Rams: Five Decades of Football.* San Francisco, Calif.: Foghorn Press, 1987. 200 p.

LOS ANGELES TIMES

Cose, Ellis. "The Contender: Times Mirror." In *The Press*, 120-184. New York, N.Y.: Morrow, 1989.

Didion, J. "Letter from Los Angeles." *New Yorker* 66 (26 February 1990): 87+

Gottlieb, Robert, and Irene Wolt. *Thinking Big: The Story of the Los Angeles Times, Its Publishers and Their Influence on Southern California.* New York, N.Y.: Putnam, 1977. 603 p.

Hart, Jack R. *The Information Empire: The Rise of the Los Angeles Times and Times Mirror Corporation.* Washington, D.C.: University Press of America, 1981. 410 p.

LOS ANGELES WEEKLY

Clifford, Frank. "LA Weekly's Adolescence Proves a Troubling One." *Los Angeles Times*, 6 March 1990, sec. A, p. 1.

LOUISIANA-PACIFIC

Louisiana-Pacific. *The L-P Originals.* Portland: The Company, 1983. 19 p. (Special tenth anniversary issue of *Momentum*, the company's magazine)

LOUISIANA POWER AND LIGHT COMPANY

Louisiana Power and Light Company. *50 Years of Service, 1927-1977.* New Orleans, La.: The Company, 1977. 77 p.

LOUISVILLE AND NASHVILLE RAILROAD COMPANY

Klein, Maury. *History of the Louisville and Nashville Railroad.* New York, N.Y.: Macmillan, 1972. 572 p.

LOUISVILLE COURIER JOURNAL

Chandler, David Leon. *The Binghams of Louisville: The Dark History Behind One of America's Great Fortunes*. New York, N.Y.: Crown, 1987. 292 p.

LTV CORPORATION

LTV Corporation. *A History of the LTV Corporation*. Dallas, Tex.: The Company, 1984. 3 p.

LTV Corporation. *LTV Looking Ahead*. Dallas, Tex.: The Company, 1980. 71 p.

LUBRIZOL CORPORATION

Smalheer, Calvin V. *The Story of Lubrizol*. Cleveland, Ohio: The Company, 1972. 88 p.

LUCAS INDUSTRIES

Nockolds, Harold. *Lucas: The First Hundred Years*. North Pomfret, Vt.: David & Charles, 1976-1978. 2 v.

LUCKMAN PARTNERSHIP, INC.

Luckman, Charles. *Twice in a Lifetime: From Soap to Skyscrapers*. New York, N.Y.: W.W. Norton, 1988. 416 p.

LUDWIG (DANIEL)

Meyer, Michael. "Obsession." In *The Alexander Complex: The Dreams That Drive the Great Businessmen*, 237-250. New York, N.Y.: Times Books, 1989.

LUFKIN INDUSTRIES, INC.

Jackson, Elaine. *From Sawdust to Oil; A History of Lufkin Industries, Inc.* Lufkin, Tex.: Gulf Publishing Company, 1982. 241 p.

Poland, Robert L. *Lufkin Industries, Inc.: Unique in the South*. New York, N.Y.: Newcomen Society in North America, 1972. 31 p. (Newcomen address)

LUKENS, INC.

DiOrio, Eugene L. *Lukens: Remarkable Past--Promising Future*. Coatesville, Pa.: The Company, 1985. 31 p.

LUMBERMENS MERCHANDISING CORPORATION

Lumbermens Merchandising Corporation. *Lumbermens Merchandising Corporation Corporate Chronicle, 1935-1988*. Wayne, Pa.: The Company, 1988. 40 p.

THE LUNKENHEIMER COMPANY

Laux, James M. "The One Great Name in Valves; A History of the Lunkenheimer Company." *Queen City Heritage* 41 (Spring 1983): 17-38.

LUSCOMBE AIRPLANE CORPORATION

Swick, John C. *The Luscombe Story; Every Cloud Has a Silvaire Lining: A Story About the History of the Luscombe Airplanes and of the Designer, Don Luscombe*. Terre Haute, Ind.: Sunshine House, 1987. 216 p.

MCCANN-ERICKSON WORLDWIDE
SEE:
THE INTERPUBLIC GROUP OF COMPANIES

MCCLURE'S MAGAZINE

Wilson, Harold S. *McClure's Magazine and the Muckrakers*. Princeton, N.J.: Princeton University Press, 1970. 347 p.

MCCORMICK AND COMPANY, INC.

McCormick and Company, Inc. *This Is McCormick.* Hunt Valley, Md.: The Company, 1984. 5 p.

MCCRORY CORPORATION

Barmash, Isadore. *For the Good of the Company, Work and Interplay in a Major American Corporation.* New York, N.Y.: Grosset & Dunlap, 1976. 299 p.

Chain Store Age. *Evolution of a Revolution.* New York, N.Y.: Chain Store Age, 1970. 100 p.

MACDONALD (E.F.) COMPANY

MacDonald, Elton F. *Money Isn't Everything!: The Story of the E.F. MacDonald Company.* New York, N.Y.: Newcomen Society in North America, 1966. 24 p. (Newcomen address)

MCDONALD'S CORPORATION

Boas, Max, and Steve Chain. *Big Mac: The Unauthorized Story of McDonald's.* New York, N.Y.: New American Library, 1977, c1976. 185 p.

DiBlase, Donna. "McDonald's Folds History into Personalized Booklet." *Business Insurance* 20 (4 August 1986): 16-17.

Kroc, Ray, with Robert Anderson. *Grinding It Out: The Making of McDonald's.* Chicago, Ill.: H. Regenery, 1977. 201 p.

Kroc, Ray, with Robert Anderson. *Grinding It Out: The Making of McDonald's.* New York, N.Y.: St. Martins Press, 1987. 218 p.

Love, John F. *McDonald's: A Corporate Biography.* New York, N.Y.: Bantam, 1984.

Love, John F. *McDonald's: Behind the Arches.* New York, N.Y.: Bantam Books, 1986. 480 p.

McDonald's Corporation. *McDonald's History Listing.* Oak Brook, Ill.: The Company, 1985. 6 p.

MCDONNELL DOUGLAS CORPORATION

Francillon, René J. *McDonnell Douglas Aircraft Since 1920.* Annapolis, Md.: Naval Institute Press, c1979, 1988.

Francillon, René J. *McDonnell Douglas Aircraft Since 1920.* London: Putnam, 1979. 721 p.

Ingells, Douglas J. *The McDonnell Douglas Story.* Fallbrook, Calif.: Aero Publishers, 1979.

McDonnell Douglas Corporation. *McDonnell Douglas Corporation, 1920-1970; 50 Years of Service to the Community, The Nation and the World.* St. Louis, Mo.: The Company, 1970. 48 p.

Pisney, Raymond F. "James S. McDonnell and His Company: A Vision of Flight and Space." *Gateway Heritage* 2 (June 1981): 2-17.

Yenne, Bill. *McDonnell Douglas: A Tale of Two Giants.* New York, N.Y.: Crescent Books, 1985. 256 p.

MCGRAW-EDISON COMPANY

Williams, Edward Joseph. *Partners in Success: The Story of McGraw-Edison Company.* New York, N.Y.: Newcomen Society in North America, 1978. 20 p. (Newcomen publication; no. 1072)

MCGRAW-HILL BOOK COMPANY

McGraw-Hill Book Company. *Imprint: The McGraw-Hill Book Company Story--Learning, Information, And*

Entertainment. New York, N.Y.: The Company, 1967. 55 p.

MACGREGOR GOLF COMPANY

Kaplan, Jim. *MacGregor Golf: History, Catalogs*. Glencoe, Ill.: Vintage Golf, 1980. 400 p.

MACK TRUCKS, INC.

Hansen, Zenon C.R. *The Legend of the Bulldog*. New York, N.Y.: Newcomen Society in North America, 1974. 43 p. (Newcomen publication; no. 988)

Montiville, John B. *Mack: A Living Legend of the Highway*. Tucson, Ariz.: Aztex Corporation, 1981. 219 p.

MCILHENNY COMPANY

Thwaite, Jean. "Sense of History Peppers Tour of Tabasco Company." *Atlanta Constitution*, 12 November 1987, sec. W, p. 1.

MCKIM, MEAD AND WHITE

Roth, Leland M. *McKim, Mead & White, Architects*. New York, N.Y.: Harper & Row, 1983. 441 p.

MACLEAN-HUNTER

Chalmers, Floyd S. *A Gentleman of the Press: The Story of Colonel John Bayne Maclean and the Publishing Empire He Founded*. Garden City, N.Y.: Doubleday, 1969. 368 p.

MACMILLAN BLOEDEL LIMITED

MacKay, Donald. *Empire of Wood; The MacMillan Bloedel Story*. Seattle, Wash.: University of Washington Press, 1982. 361 p.

MCMILLEN, INC.

Brown, Erica. *Sixty Years of Interior Design: The World of McMillen*. New York, N.Y.: Viking Press, 1982. 319 p.

MCNAIR LAW FIRM, P.A.

McNair, Robert E. *McNair Law Firm, P.A.: Right People, Right Place, Right Time*. New York, N.Y.: Newcomen Society of the United States, 1989. 20 p. (Newcomen publication; no. 1331)

MCNALLY PITTSBURGH

McNally, Edward T. *The McNally Story*. New York, N.Y.: Newcomen Society in North America, 1973. 35 p.

Mahan, Ernest. *The History of McNally Pittsburgh*. Wichita, Kan.: McCormick-Armstrong Company, 1972. 270 p.

MACNEAL-SCHWENDLER CORPORATION

MacNeal, Richard. *The MacNeal-Schwendler Corporation; The First Twenty Years*. Los Angeles, Calif.: R.H. MacNeal, 1988. 202 p.

MCRAE'S DEPARTMENT STORES

McRae, Richard Duncan. *Main Entrance in Mississippi: The McRae Story*. New York, N.Y.: Newcomen Society in North America, 1971. 21 p. (Newcomen address).

MACY (R.H.) AND COMPANY, INC.

Barmash, Isadore. *Macy's for Sale*. New York, N.Y.: Weidenfeld & Nicolson, 1989. 172 p.

Johnson, Curtiss S. *America's First Lady Boss; A Wisp of a Girl, Macy's and Romance.* New York, N.Y.: Taplinger, 1965. 164 p.

Macy (R.H.) and Company, Inc. *Macy's New York, N.Y.: 125th Anniversary, 1858-1983.* New York, N.Y.: The Company, 1983. 4 p.

MADERA SUGAR PINE COMPANY

Johnston, Hank. *Thunder in the Mountains; The Life and Times of Madera Sugar Pine.* Los Angeles, Calif.: Trans-Anglo Books, 1968. 128 p.

MADISON BANK AND TRUST COMPANY

Madison Bank & Trust Company. *Sesqui-Centennial; 150 Years of Progress in Banking, 1833-1983.* Madison, Ind.: The Bank, 1983. 12 p. (Published as a supplement to the *Madison Courier*, June 21, 1983)

MAGIC CHEF, INC.

Rymer, S.B. *The Magic Chef Story.* New York, N.Y.: Newcomen Society in North America, 1979. 24 p. (Newcomen publication; no. 1117)

MAGNETEK, INC.

MagneTek, Inc. *MagneTek; A History in the Making.* Los Angeles, Calif.: The Company, 1988. 6 p.

MAHON (R.C.) COMPANY

Mahon (R.C.) Company. *A Picture Story of the R.C. Mahon Company.* Detroit, Mich.: The Company, 1971. 44 p.

MAIDENFORM, INC.

Morris, Michele. "The Mother Figure of Maidenform."

Working Woman 12 (April 1987): 82-88.

MAIN (C.T.) CORPORATION

Hall, W.M. *Chas T. Main, Inc.: A Professional Legacy.* New York, N.Y.: Newcomen Society in North America, 1975. 31 p. (Newcomen publication; no. 1025)

MAINE CENTRAL RAILROAD

Miller, E. Spencer. *Maine Central Railroad, 1940-1978.* New York, N.Y.: Newcomen Society in North America, 1979. 52 p. (Newcomen publication; no. 1110)

MAINE PUBLIC SERVICE COMPANY

Stetson, C. Hazen. *From Logs to Electricity, A History of the Maine Public Service Company.* Presque Island, Me.: The Company, 1984. 232 p.

MAKERS MARK DISTILLERY, INC.

"Bill Samuels Makes His Mark." *Inc. Supplement* (Spring 1990): 48-50.

MALRITE COMMUNICATIONS GROUP

Gorisek, Sue. "How to Make $100 Million in Broadcasting." *Forbes* 136 (28 October 1985): 348-354.

MANHATTAN LIFE INSURANCE COMPANY

Buck, Wendell. *From Quill Pens to Computers: An Account of the First One Hundred and Twenty-Five Years of the Manhattan Life Insurance Company of New York.* New York, N.Y.: The Company, 1975. 156 p.

MANISCHEWITZ (B.) COMPANY

Manischewitz (B.) Company. *History*. Jersey City, N.J.: The Company, n.d. 2 p.

MANSIONS AND MILLIONAIRES, INC.

Travis, Arlene, and Carole Aronson. *Mansions and Millionaires: Their Story, Their Style*. Greenvale, N.Y.: The Company, 1983. 119 p.

MANVILLE CORPORATION

Brodeur, Paul. *An Industry on Trial*. New York, N.Y.: Pantheon Books, 1984.

Goodwin, W. Richard. *The Johns-Manville Story*. New York, N.Y.: Newcomen Society in North America, 1972. 16 p. (Newcomen address)

Johns-Manville Corporation. *Johns-Manville People: An Odyssey of Progress*. Denver, Colo.: The Company, 1976. 32 p.

MAPCO, INC.

Jarman, Rufus. *The Energy Merchants*. New York, N.Y.: Rosen Press, 1977. 279 p.

Thomas, Robert E. *From a Dream to a "Scrappy" Little Pipeline to a National Leader in Energy*. New York, N.Y.: Newcomen Society in North America, 1976. 19 p. (Newcomen publication; no. 1039)

MARANTZ COMPANY, INC.

Fucini, Joseph J., and Suzy Fucini. "Joseph S. Tushinsky, Superscope, Inc.: 'I Knew That the Sony Tape Recorder Couldn't Miss This Country.'" In *Experience Inc.; Men and Women Who Founded Famous Companies After the Age of 40*, 37-42. New York,

N.Y.: Free Press, 1987.

MARATHON OIL COMPANY

Marathon Oil Company. *One Hundred Years on the Frontier*. Findlay, Ohio: The Company, 1987. 136 p. (Commemorative edition of *Marathon World*)

MARINE MIDLAND BANKS, INC.

Buckwalter, Nancy. "Building the 'New Marine.'" *United States Banker* 94 (August 1983): 48-50.

MARINE SHALE PROCESSORS, INC.

"Toxic Waste Handler Under Fire." *Los Angeles Times*, 29 June 1989, sec. IV, p. 2.

MARKETING CORPORATION OF AMERICA

Levitt, Mortimer. "James McManus: A Money-Making Smorgasbord of Marketing, Advertising, And Management Innovations." In *How to Start Your Own Business Without Losing Your Shirt; Secrets of Seventeen Successful Entrepreneurs*, 143-156. New York, N.Y.: Atheneum, 1988.

MARLIN FIREARMS COMPANY

Brophy, William S. *Marlin Firearms; A History of the Guns and the Company That Made Them*. Harrisburg, Pa.: Stackpole Books, 1989. 696 p.

Kenna, Frank. *The Marlin Story*. New York, N.Y.: Newcomen Society in North America, 1975. 24 p. (Newcomen publication; no. 1011)

MARRIOTT CORPORATION

Goldwasser, Thomas. "Marriott: A Hamburger Stand Becomes a Food and Lodging Empire." In *Family*

Pride; Profiles of Five of America's Best-Run Family Businesses, 85-124. New York, N.Y.: Dodd, Mead and Company, 1986.

O'Brien, Robert. *Marriott, The J. Willard Marriott Story*. Salt Lake City, Nev.: Desert Book Company, 1977. 336 p.

MARSH AND MCLENNAN COMPANIES

"Founding Fathers: The History of Marsh and McLennan Companies." *M 8* (September 1981) : 1-8.

Souder, William F., Jr. *Marsh and McLennan: A Century of Insurance Service 1871-1971*. New York, N.Y.: Newcomen Society in North America, 1971. 20 p. (Newcomen address)

MARSH SUPERMARKETS, INC.

Lasting Values: The First Half-Century of Marsh Supermarkets, Inc. Yorktown, Ind.: The Company, 1984. 214 p.

MARTIN MARIETTA CORPORATION

Cunningham, Mary. *Powerplay: What Really Happened at Bendix*. New York, N.Y.: Linden Press/Simon & Schuster, 1984. 286 p.

Hartz, Peter F. *Merger; The Exclusive Inside Story of the Bendix-Martin-Marietta Takeover War*. New York, N.Y.: Morrow, 1985. 418 p.

Lambert, Hope. *Till Death Do Us Part: Bendix vs. Martin Marietta*. San Diego, Calif.: Harcourt Brace Jovanovich, 1983. 264 p.

Sloan, Allan. *Three Plus One Equals Billions: The Bendix-Martin Marietta War*. New York, N.Y.: Arbor House, 1983. 270 p.

MARTINELLI (S.) AND COMPANY

Groves, Martha. "A Cider-Maker's Sparkling Success." *Los Angeles Times*, 30 October 1990, sec. D, p. 1.

MARY KAY COSMETICS

Ash, Mary Kay. *Mary Kay.* Cambridge: Harper & Row, 1981. 206 p.

Ash, Mary Kay. *Mary Kay; The Success Story of America's Most Dynamic Businesswoman.* Rev. ed., New York, N.Y.: Perennial Library, 1986. 200 p.

Kingan, Adele. "Mary Kay Ash, Founder and Chairman of the Board, Mary Kay Cosmetics, Inc." *The Executive Female* (November/December 1982): 12-14.

MacPhee, William. "Mary Kay Ash of Mary Kay Cosmetics." In *Rare Breed: The Entrepreneur, An American Culture*, 21-36. Chicago, Ill.: Probus Publishing Company, 1987.

Shook, Robert L. "Mary Kay Ash." In *The Entrepreneurs: Twelve Who Took Risks and Succeeded*, 103-114. New York, N.Y.: Harper & Row, 1980.

Sobel, Robert, and David B. Sicilia. "Mary Kay Ash: The Pink Cadillac Approach." In *The Entrepreneurs: An American Adventure*, 38-41. Boston, Mass.: Houghton Mifflin Company, 1986.

Taylor, Russel R. "Mary Kay Ash: 'You Can Do It.'" In *Exceptional Entrepreneurial Women*, 65-71. New York, N.Y.: Quorum Books, 1988.

MASCO CORPORATION

Masco Corporation. *Masco 50: The First Fifty Years, 1929-79.* Taylor, Mich.: The Company, 1979. 15 p.

MASSON (PAUL) VINYARDS

Balzer, Robert L. *Uncommon Heritage; The Paul Masson Story.* Los Angeles, Calif.: Ward Richie Press, 1970. 118 p.

MATSON NAVIGATION COMPANY

Worden, William L. *Cargoes: Matson's First Century in the Pacific.* Honolulu: University of Hawaii, 1981. 192 p.

MATSUSHITA ELECTRIC CORPORATION OF AMERICA

Landman, Amos. *The Wisdom of the Many: The Story of 25 Years, Matsushita Electric Corporation of America.* Secaucus, N.J.: The Company, 1984. 148 p.

MATTEL, INC.

Handler, Elliot. *The Impossible Really is Possible: The Story of Mattel.* New York, N.Y.: Newcomen Society in North America, 1968. 28 p. (Newcomen address)

MAXWELL HOUSE COFFEE
SEE:
GENERAL FOODS CORPORATION

MAY AND SPEH DATA PROCESSING CENTER

"Story of a Service Bureau Survivor." *Data Management* 17 (October 1979): 18-19+

MAY DEPARTMENT STORES COMPANY

Parkhill, Forbes. *The May Story.* St. Louis, Mo.: The Company, n.d. 30 p.

MAYER (OSCAR) AND COMPANY

Mayer, Oscar G. *Oscar Mayer & Company: From Corner Store to National Processor.* New York, N.Y.: Newcomen Society in North America, 1970. 24 p. (Newcomen address)

MAYTAG COMPANY

Gorman, John. "Maytag Builds Success to Last, Without Repairs." *Chicago Tribune*, 8 September 1986, sec. 4, p. 1.

"Maytag." *Merchandiser* 27, no.2 (1982) (Anniversary issue)

Maytag Company. *Brief History of the Maytag Company.* Newton, Iowa: The Company, 1985. 3 p.

MAZDA NORTH AMERICA, INC.

Fucini, Joseph. *Working for the Japanese; Inside Mazda's American Auto Plant.* New York, N.Y.: Free Press, 1990. 258 p.

MCI COMMUNICATIONS CORPORATION

Kahaner, Larry. *On the Line; How MCI Took On AT&T, And Won!.* New York, N.Y: Warner Books, 1987. 344 p.

Kahaner, Larry. *On the Line; The Men of MCI--Who Took On AT&T, Risked Everything, And Won.* New York, N.Y.: Random House, 1986. 327 p.

Shook, Robert L. "William G. McGowen." In *The Entrepreneurs: Twelve Who Took Risks and Succeeded*, 139-156. New York, N.Y.: Harper & Row, 1980.

MEAD CORPORATION

Carr, William H.A. *Up Another Notch: Institution Building at Mead.* New York, N.Y.: McGraw-Hill, 1989. 256 p.

Maurer, Herrymon. *In Quiet Ways: George H. Mead, The Man and the Company.* Dayton, Ohio: The Company, 1970. 307 p.

Mead Corporation. *Mead Corporation History.* Dayton, Ohio: The Company, 1988. 6 p.

MEDIA NETWORKS, INC.

Shook, Robert L. "Dale W. Lang." In *The Entrepreneurs: Twelve Who Took Risks and Succeeded*, 53-65. New York, N.Y.: Harper & Row, 1980.

MEDTRONIC, INC.

Pine, Carol, and Susan Mundale. "Earl Bakken; Sparks of Life." In *Self-Made: The Stories of 12 Minnesota Entrepreneurs*, 39-54. Minneapolis, Minn.: Dorn Books, 1982.

U.S. Congress. House. Committee on Energy and Commerce. Subcommittee on Oversight and Investigation. *Failed Pacemaker Leads, Hearing Before the Subcommittee on Oversight and Investigation.* 98th Cong., 2d Sess., 13 March 1984.

MEIJER, INC.

Meijer, Hendrik G. *Thrifty Years: The Life of Hendrik Meijer.* Grand Rapids, Mich.: Erdmans, 1984. 246 p.

MELLON BANK

Hersh, Burton. *The Mellon Family, A Fortune in History.* New York, N.Y.: Morrow, 1978. 640 p.

Koskoff, David E. *The Mellons, The Chronicle of America's Richest Family.* New York, N.Y.: Crowell, 1978. 602 p.

McCullough, C. Hax. *One Hundred Years of Banking, The History of Mellon National Bank and Trust Company.* Pittsburgh, Pa.: The Company, 1969. 81 p.

MELLON STUART COMPANY

Mellon Stuart Company. *Mellon Stuart Company; 70 Years with a Future As Bright As Its Past.* Pittsburgh, Pa.: The Company, 1987. 16 p.

MELROE COMPANY

Karolevitz, Robert F. *"E.G.," Inventor by Necessity; The Story of E.G. Melroe and the Melroe Company.* Aberdeen, S.D.: North Plains Press, 1968. 160 p

MELVILLE SHOE CORPORATION

Rooney, Francis C., Jr. *Creative Merchandising in an Era of Change.* New York, N.Y.: Newcomen Society in North America, 1970. 24 p. (Newcomen address)

MEMPHIS LIGHT, GAS AND WATER DIVISION

Memphis Light, Gas and Water Division. *People You Can Count on Since 1939; A Historical Review.* Memphis, Tenn.: The Company, 1987. 16 p.

MENASHA WOODEN WARE COMPANY

Smith, Mowry, and Giles Clark. *One Third Crew, One Third Boat, One Third Luck. The Menasha Corporation (Menasha Wooden Ware Company) Story, 1849-1974.* Neenah, Wash.: The Company, 1974. 174 p.

MENTOR CORPORATION

Rudolph, Barbara. "The Up & Comers: Nice Guys Finish Last." *Forbes* 134 (22 October 1984): 114-115.

MERCANTILE NATIONAL BANK, DALLAS

Francis, J.D. *The Growing Story of the Mercantile National Bank.* New York, N.Y.: Newcomen Society in North America, 1972. 20 p. (Newcomen address)

MERCANTILE STORES COMPANY, INC.

Newcomb, William A. *Mercantile Stores Company, Inc.: A Profile of a Growing Retail Enterprise.* Wilmington, Del.: Mercantile Stores Co., Inc. 1975. 131 p.

MERCEDES-BENZ OF NORTH AMERICA, INC.

Kimes, Beverly Rae. *The Star and the Laurel, The Centennial History of Daimler, Mercedes and Benz, 1886-1986.* Montvale, N.J.: The Company, 1986. 268 p.

MERCHANTS NATIONAL BANK AND TRUST COMPANY OF INDIANAPOLIS

Frenzel, Otto N., Jr. *The City and the Bank 1865-1965: The Story of Merchants National Bank and Trust Company of Indianapolis.* New York, N.Y.: Newcomen Society in North America, 1965. 24 p. (Newcomen address)

Jarvis, Helen R. *The City and the Bank, 1865-1965; The Story of 100 Years in the Life of Indianapolis and the Merchants National Bank & Trust Company of Indianapolis.* Indianapolis, Ind.: Benham Press, 1965. 114 p.

MERCHANTS NATIONAL BANK AND TRUST COMPANY OF SYRACUSE

Melvin, Crandall. *A History of the Merchants National Bank and Trust Company of Syracuse, New York; One Hundred Eighteen Years.* Syracuse: Syracuse University, 1969. 158 p.

MERCK AND COMPANY, INC.

Merck and Company, Inc. *Fifty Years of Research; Merck Sharp & Dohme Research Laboratories.* Rahway, N.J.: The Company, 1983. 20 p.

Merck and Company, Inc. *The Merck Tradition.* Rahway, N.J.: The Company, 1969. 8 p. (Reprinted from *Resident and Staff Physician*, April, 1969.)

MERLE NORMAN COSMETICS

Fucini, Joseph J., and Suzy Fucini. "Merle N. Norman, Merle Norman Cosmetics: 'If They Like the Results They'll Buy the Product.'" In *Experience Inc.; Men and Women Who Founded Famous Companies After the Age of 40*, 160-166. New York, N.Y.: Free Press, 1987.

MERRELL DOW PHARMACEUTICALS

Enck, Henry Snyder. "William Stanley Merrell, Cincinnati Industrialist." Thesis, University of Cincinnati, 1965.

MERRILL BANKSHARES COMPANY

Grant, John F. *Merrill Bankshares Company: "--Business Talents and Devotion to Those Highest Commercial Principles Which Underlie the Truest and Most Enduring Success."* New York, Newcomen Society in North America, 1977. 22 p. (Newcomen publication; no. 1066)

MERRILL LYNCH

Regan, Donald T. *The Merrill Lynch Story*. New York, N.Y.: Newcomen Society in North America, 1981. 22 p. (Newcomen publication; no. 1142)

MERRILL TRANSPORT COMPANY

Merrill, Paul E. *Forty-Six Years a Truckman: The Story of Merrill Transport Company*. New York, N.Y.: Newcomen Society in North America, 1975. 26 p. (Newcomen publication; no. 1023)

MESA PETROLEUM COMPANY

Pickens, T. Boone. *Boone*. Boston, Mass.: Houghton Mifflin Co., 1987. 304 p.

MESSER (SONIA) COMPANY

"The Sonia Messer Company Does It All." *Agency Sales Magazine* 14 (January 1984): 4-7.

MESTA MACHINE COMPANY

O'Boyle, Thomas F. "Rise and Fall: Turnabout in Fortunes of Mesta Machine is History with a Moral; In Bankruptcy Now, Company Once Led [Rolling] Mill-Machinery Market." *Wall Street Journal* 202 (3 January 1984): 1+, and 202 (4 January 1984): 1+

METRO-GOLDWYN-MAYER, INC.

Cary, Gary. *All the Stars in Heaven, Louis B. Mayer's MGM*. New York, N.Y.: Dutton, 1981. 320 p.

Eames, John Douglas. *The MGM Story: The Complete History of Fifty Roaring Years*. New York, N.Y.: Crown Publishers, 1975. 400 p.

Easton, Carol. *The Search for Sam Goldwyn; A*

Biography. New York, N.Y.: Morrow, 1976, c1975. 304 p.

Marx, Arthur. *Goldwyn: A Biography of the Man Behind the Myth*. New York, N.Y.: Norton, 1976. 376 p.

Metro-Goldwyn-Mayer, Inc. *Corporate History*. Culver City, Calif.: The Company, 1978. 4 p.

METRO MOBILE CTS, INC.

Levitt, Mortimer. "George Lindermann: Filling an Old Prescription in a Lucrative New Way." In *How to Start Your Own Business Without Losing Your Shirt; Secrets of Seventeen Successful Entrepreneurs*, 177-185. New York, N.Y.: Atheneum, 1988.

METROMEDIA, INC.

Kluge, John W. *The Metromedia Story...* New York, N.Y.: Newcomen Society in North America, 1974. 18 p.

MEYER (MARY) CORPORATION

Warrock, Anna M. "The Meyers: 'A Matter of Survival: We Were Losing Money.'" *New England Business. Annual Report* (1988): 16VT.

MFA, INC.

Lay, Chuck. "The Evolution of an Idea: MFA Celebrates 75 Years." *Today's Farmer* (March 1989): 10-15.

MIAMI DOLPHINS

McLemore, Morris T. *The Miami Dolphins*. Garden City, N.Y.: Doubleday, 1972. 343 p.

MICHIGAN CREDIT UNION LEAGUE

Crews, Cecil Robert. *History of the Michigan Credit*

Union League. Detroit, Mich.: Wayne State University Press, 1971. 872 p.

MICHIGAN NATIONAL BANK

Poll, Richard D. *Howard J. Stoddard, Founder, Michigan National Bank*. East Lansing: Michigan State University Press, 1980. 257 p.

MICRON TECHNOLOGY, INC.

Gilder, George. "The Rise of Micron." In *The Spirit of Enterprise*, 218-244. New York, N.Y.: Simon and Schuster, 1984.

MICROSOFT CORPORATION

Brandt, Richard. "The Billion-Dollar Whiz Kid." *Business Week (Industrial/Technology Edition)* 2993 (13 April 1987): 68-76.

Van Gelder, Lindsy. "The Nerd Who Roars." *Business Month* 131 (April 1988): 56-60.

MIDLAND MUTUAL LIFE INSURANCE COMPANY

McIntosh, James B. *The Midland Mutual Life Insurance Company: "The Pearl of the Midwest."* New York, N.Y.: Newcomen Society in North America, 1972. 17 p. (Newcomen address)

MID-PACIFIC AIRLINES

Bekey, Michelle. "Hawaii's Friendly Skies." *Venture* 6 (January 1984): 100+

MIDSTATE AIRLINES

Midstate Airlines. *Midstate Airlines: More Than Two Decades of Service*. Stevens Point, Wis.: The

Company, 1985. 4 p.

MIDWAY AIRLINES

Midway Airlines. *The Midway Story*. Chicago, Ill.: The Company, 1985. 4 p.

MIKE-SELL'S POTATO CHIP COMPANY

Mapp, Leslie C. *"A Common Thing Done Uncommonly Well": The Story of the Mike-Sell's Potato Chip Company*. New York, N.Y.: Newcomen Society of the United States, 1985. 19 p. (Newcomen publication; no. 1236)

MILES LABORATORIES, INC.

Compton, Walter A. *Serving Needs in Health and Nutrition: The Story of Miles Laboratories, Inc.* New York, N.Y.: Newcomen Society in North America, 1973. 24 p.

Cray, William C. *Miles: A Centennial History, 1884-1984*. Englewood Cliffs, N.J.: Prentice-Hall, 1984. 277 p.

Miles Laboratories, Inc. *Miles: Our First Century, 1884-1984*. Elkhart, Ind.: The Company, 1984. 20 p.

MILK MARKETING, INC.

Milk Marketing, Inc. *"Pride and Cooperation": The MMI Story*. Strongsville, Ohio: The Company, n.d. 7 p.

MILLER (HERMAN) COMPANY

De Pree, Hugh. *Business As Unusual; The People and Principles at Herman Miller*. Zeeland, Mich.: Herman Miller Research Corporation, 1986. 197 p.

MILLER MANUFACTURING COMPANY, INC.

Mattison, Lewis C. *Forests, Wood Products, And Homes; The Story of the Miller Manufacturing Company, Inc., 1897-1972.* Richmond: Whittet and Shepperson, 1972. 56 p.

MILLIKEN AND COMPANY

"How Roger Milliken Runs Textiles' Premier Performer." *Business Week (Industrial Edition)* 2671 (18 January 1981): 62-65, 68, 73.

MILTON BRADLEY COMPANY
SEE:
BRADLEY (MILTON) COMPANY

MILTON ROY COMPANY

Sheen, Robert T. *The Milton Roy Story: From a Basement Workshop to a Professionally Managed Public Company.* New York, N.Y.: Newcomen Society in North America, 1972. 28 p. (Newcomen address)

MINIATURE PRECISION BEARINGS, INC.

Hill, Evan. *Beanstalk; The History of Miniature Precision Bearings, Inc., 1941-1966.* Keene, N.H.: The Company, 1966. 188 p.

MINNEAPOLIS STAR AND TRIBUNE COMPANY

Morison, Bradley L. *Sunlight on Your Doorsteps: The Minneapolis Tribune's First Hundred Years, 1867-1967.* Minneapolis, Minn.: Ross & Haines, Inc., 1966. 149 p.

MINNESOTA MINING AND MANUFACTURING

Minnesota Mining & Manufacturing Company. *Company History Covering 75 Years.* St. Paul, Minn.: The

Company, 1977. 130 p.

"The Tale of the Tape--50 Years of Innovation at 3M."
Office 92 (September 1980): 101-104.

MINNESOTA TRANSFER RAILWAY COMPANY

Stottlemyr, John M. *The First 100 Years: A History of the
Minnesota Transfer Railway Company.* Minnesota:
The Company, 1982. 16 p.

MINNESOTA VIKINGS

Diamond, Jeff. *The First Fifteen Years: Viking,
1961-1975.* Minneapolis, Minn.: Minnesota Vikings,
1976. 76 p.

MINOLTA CORPORATION

Kusomota, Sam. *My Bridge to America: Discovering the
New World for Minolta.* New York, N.Y.: Dutton,
1989. 340 p.

MINUTE MAID CORPORATION

Harris, Sara, and Robert Francis Allen. *The Quiet
Revolution: The Story of a Small Miracle in American
Life.* New York, N.Y.: Rawson Associates Publishers,
1978. 283 p.

MISSISSIPPI BANKERS ASSOCIATION

Mallory, Lewis F. *Mississippi Bankers Association: A
Century of Service.* New York, N.Y.: Newcomen
Society of the United States, 1989. 22 p. (Newcomen
publication; no. 1328)

MISSISSIPPI POWER COMPANY

Watson, A.J., Jr. *Electric Power and People Power: The
Story of the Mississippi Power Company.* New York,

N.Y.: Newcomen Society in North America, 1969. 24 p. (Newcomen address)

MISSOURI, KANSAS AND TEXAS RAILROAD COMPANY

Hofsommer, Donovan L. *Katy Northwest, The Story of a Branch Line Railroad.* Boulder, Colo.: Pruett Pub., 1976. 305 p.

Missouri-Kansas-Texas Railroad Company. *The Opening of the Great Southwest, 1870-1970.* The Company, 1970. 33 p.

MISSOURI PACIFIC CORPORATION

Jenks, Downing B. *The Missouri Pacific Story.* New York, N.Y.: Newcomen Society in North America, 1977. 15 p. (Newcomen publication; no. 1065)

Miner, H. Craig. *The Rebirth of the Missouri Pacific, 1956-1983.* College Station, Tex.: Texas A&M University Press, 1983. 236 p.

THE MISSOURI PUBLIC SERVICE COMPANY

Green, Richard C. *The Missouri Public Service Company: A Saga of Free Enterprise.* New York, N.Y.: Newcomen Society in North America, 1967. 28 p. (Newcomen address)

MITCHELL (ED.), INC.

Levitt, Mortimer. "Ed. Mitchell: A Retail Clothier Brings In the Crowds with a Warm Family Touch." In *How to Start Your Own Business Without Losing Your Shirt; Secrets of Seventeen Successful Entrepreneurs,* 171-176. New York, N.Y.: Atheneum, 1988.

MITRE CORPORATION

Meisel, Robert C., and John F. Jacobs. *MITRE, The First Twenty Years, A History of the MITRE Corporation, 1958-1978*. Bedford, Mass.: The Company, 1979. 288 p.

MOBIL OIL CORPORATION

Mobil Oil Corporation. *A Brief History of Mobil*. Fairfax, Va.: The Company, 1987. 8 p.

Socony Mobil Oil Company, Inc. *Mobil Oil Corporation; A Report to the Financial Community*. New York, N.Y.: The Company, 1966. 60 p.

Warner, Rawleigh, Jr. *Mobil Oil: A View from the Second Century*. New York, N.Y.: Newcomen Society in North America, 1966. 24 p. (Newcomen address)

MOLECULAR DEVICES CORPORATION

Kingston, Brett. "Gary Steele of Molecular Devices Corporation." In *The Dynamos: Who Are They Anyway?*, 137-142. New York, N.Y.: Wiley, 1987.

MONARCH CONSTRUCTION CORPORATION

Carper, Jean. *Not With a Gun*. New York, N.Y.: Grossman, 1973. 211 p.

THE MONARCH MACHINE TOOL COMPANY

The Monarch Machine Tool Company. *The Seventy-Fifth Year*. Sidney, Ohio: The Company, 1984. 8 p.

MONDAVI (ROBERT) WINERY

MacPhee, William. "Robert Mondavi of Robert Mondavi Winery." In *Rare Breed: The Entrepreneur, An American Culture*, 91-101. Chicago, Ill.: Probus

Publishing Company, 1987.

MONSANTO COMPANY

Forrestal, Dan J. *Faith, Hope, And $5,000: The Story of Monsanto: The Trials and Triumphs of the First 75 Years*. New York, N.Y.: Simon & Schuster, 1977. 185 p.

Levinson, Harry, and Stuart Rosenthal. "John W. Hanley." In *CEO: Corporate Leadership in Action*, 137-176. New York, N.Y.: Basic Books, 1984.

MONTANA-DAKOTA UTILITIES COMPANY

Montana-Dakota Utilities Company. *The First 50 Years*. Bismarck: The Company, 1979. 28 p.

MONTGOMERY WARD AND COMPANY

Herndon, Booton. *Satisfaction Guaranteed; An Unconventional Report to Today's Consumers*. New York, N.Y.: McGraw-Hill, 1972. 342 p.

Hersch, Linda. "Schwartz Recounts Montgomery Ward History at Marketing Council Confab." *Zip/Target Marketing* 8 (June 1985): 21-22.

Hoge, Cecil C. *First Hundred Years Are the Toughest; What We Can Learn from the Century of Competition Between Sears and Wards*. Berkeley, Calif.: Ten Speed Press, 1988. 192 p.

Latham, Frank Brown. *1872-1972: A Century of Serving Consumers; The Story of Montgomery Ward*. 2nd ed. Chicago, Ill.: The Company, 1972. 95 p.

Montgomery Ward and Company. *Montgomery Ward Facts; Chronological Fact Sheet*. Chicago, Ill.: The Company, 1989. 15 p.

Tedlow, Richard S. "Bringing the Mass Market Home: Sears, Montgomery Ward, and Their Newer Rivals." In *New and Improved: The Story of Mass Marketing in America*, 259-343. New York, N.Y.: Basic Books, 1990.

MOORE SPECIAL TOOL COMPANY, INC.

Moore Special Tool Company, Inc. *The First Half Century, 1924-1974*. Bridgeport, Conn.: The Company, 1974. 47 p.

MOORMAN MANUFACTURING COMPANY

Moorman Manufacturing Company. *A Century of Service: 1885-1985*. Quincy, Ill.: The Company, 1985. 16 p.

MORAN TOWING AND TRANSPORTATION COMPANY, INC.

Moran, Edmond J. *The Moran Story*. New York, N.Y.: Newcomen Society in North America, 1965. 24 p. (Newcomen address)

MORGAN, (J.P.) AND COMPANY

Chernow, Ron. *The House of Morgan: An American Banking Dynasty and the Rise of Modern Finance*. New York, N.Y.: Atlantic Monthly Press, 1990. 812 p.

Hoyt, Edwin P., Jr. *The House of Morgan*. New York, N.Y.: Dodd, Mead and Company, 1966. 428 p.

MORGAN STANLEY AND COMPANY, INC.

Morgan Stanley and Company, Inc. *Morgan Stanley 1970*. New York, N.Y.: The Company, 1971. 83 p.

Morgan Stanley and Company, Inc. *Morgan Stanley: The First Fifty Years*. New York, N.Y.: The Company, 1984? 14 p.

MORSE HARDWARE COMPANY

Heller, Ramon. *Sell 'Em Low--Send and Get More, A Centennial History of Morse Hardware Company.* Bellingham, Wash.: R. Heller, 1984. 88 p.

MORTIMER'S RESTAURANT

Levitt, Mortimer. "Glenn Bernbaum: Snob Appeal Made Mortimer's the Playpen for the Rich and Famous." In *How to Start Your Own Business Without Losing Your Shirt; Secrets of Seventeen Successful Entrepreneurs*, 105-112. New York, N.Y.: Atheneum, 1988.

MORTON POTTERY COMPANY

Hall, Doris, and Burdell Hall. *Morton's Potteries: 99 Years, 1877-1976: An Historical Sketch and Product Identification Guide for the Morton Potteries.* Morton, Ill.: D. Hall, 1982. 88 p.

MORTON THIOKOL, INC.

Morton Thiokol, Inc. *The Right Chemistry: A History of Morton Thiokol, Inc.* Chicago, Ill.: The Company, 1985. 15 p.

MOTORBOOKS INTERNATIONAL

Meyer, O.D. "Book Marque." *Road & Track* 42 (September 1990): 100+

MOTOROLA, INC.

Colletti, Jerome A. *Profit Sharing and Employee Attitudes; A Case Study of the Deferred Profit-Sharing Program at Motorola, Inc.* Madison, Wis.: Center for the Study of Productivity Motivation, University of Wisconsin, 1967. 96 p.

Petrakis, Harry Mark. *A Founder's Touch: The Life of Paul Galvin of Motorola.* New York, N.Y.: McGraw-Hill, 1965. 240 p.

MOTOWN RECORD CORPORATION

Benjaminson, Peter. *The Story of Motown.* New York, N.Y.: Grove Press, 1979. 180 p.

George, Nelson. *Where Did Our Love Go? The Rise and Fall of the Motown Sound.* New York, N.Y.: St. Martin's Press, 1985. 250 p.

Martin, Sandra Pratt. *Inside Motown; The Million Dollar Story of the Black Sound.* New York: Drake, 1974.

Morse, David. *Motown & The Arrival of Black Music.* London, England: Studio Vista, 1971. 110 p.

Taraborrelli, J. Randy. *Motown, Hot Wax, City Cool and Solid Gold.* Garden City, N.Y.: Doubleday, 1986. 213 p.

Waller, Don. *The Motown Story.* New York, N.Y.: C. Scribner, 1985. 256 p.

MOUNT HOPE FINISHING COMPANY

Davis, Burke. *A Fierce Personal Pride: The History of Mount Hope Finishing Company and Its Founding Family.* Butner, N.C.: the company, 1981. 167 p.

MOUNT WASHINGTON RAILWAY COMPANY

Teague, Ellen C. *Mount Washington Railway Company: World's First Cog Railway.* Mount Washington, New Hampshire. New York, N.Y.: Newcomen Society in North America, 1970. 28 p.

MOUNTAIN BELL

Blantz, Robert C. *Mountain Bell: Seventy-Five Years of Growth and Change.* New York, N.Y.: Newcomen Society of the United States, 1986, c1987. 23 p. (Newcomen publication; no. 1281)

Harden, H. "100 Years of Service." *Telephony* 196 (2 April 1979): 50-52.

MOUSE SYSTEMS CORPORATION

Kingston, Brett. "Steve Kirsch of Mouse Systems Corporation." In *The Dynamos: Who Are They Anyway?*, 77-83. New York, N.Y.: Wiley, 1987.

MPI INDUSTRIES, INC.

Ryan, Charles B. *Molding Its Future with Wood and Plastic: The Story of MPI Industries, Inc.* New York, N.Y.: Newcomen Society in North America, 1968. 24 p. (Newcomen address)

MRS. FIELDS COOKIES

Fields, Debbie. *"One Smart Cookie": How a Housewife's Chocolate Chip Recipe Turned into a Multimillion Dollar Business, The Story of Mrs. Fields Cookies.* New York, N.Y.: Simon and Schuster, 1987. 173 p.

MTV NETWORKS

Denisoff, R. Serge. *Inside MTV.* New Brunswick, N.J.: Transaction Books, 1988. 373 p.

MUNFORD, INC.

Munford, Dillard. *Munford, Inc.: A Brief History.* New York, N.Y.: Newcomen Society in North America, 1974. 16 p.

MURCHISON FAMILY
SEE:
DALLAS COWBOYS

MUSE AIR

Muse Air Corporation. Public Relations Department. *Muse Air: A Chronology*. Dallas, Tex.: The Company, 1984. 3 p.

THE MUSIC OF YOUR LIFE

Levitt, Mortimer. "Al Ham: A Musician's Virtuoso Venture into Radio Programming." In *How to Start Your Own Business Without Losing Your Shirt; Secrets of Seventeen Successful Entrepreneurs*, 165-170. New York, N.Y.: Atheneum, 1988.

MUTUAL ASSURANCE COMPANY

Lyons, L.J. "From Colonial Times to Today: The Green Tree." *National Underwriter; Property Casualty Edition* 89 (19 July 1985): 48-49.

MUTUAL BENEFIT LIFE INSURANCE COMPANY

Mutual Benefit Life Insurance Company. *A Brief History*. Newark, N.J.: The Company, 1966. 32 p.

NABISCO BRANDS, INC.

Cahn, William. *Out of the Cracker Barrel: The Nabisco Story From Animal Crackers to Zuzus*. New York, N.Y.: Simon and Schuster, 1969. 367 p.

NALCO CHEMICAL COMPANY

Nalco Chemical Company. *50 Years of Progress*. Oak Brook, Ill.: The Company, 1978. 13 p.

NASH FINCH COMPANY

Nash Finch Company. *100 Years: 1885-1985.* St. Louis Park, Minn.: The Company, 1984. 40 p.

NATIONAL AIRLINES, INC.

Cearley, George Walker, Jr. *National "Airlines of the Stars": An Illustrated History.* Dallas, Tex.: G.W. Cearley, Jr., 1985. 96 p.

Williams, Brad. *The Anatomy of an Airline.* New York, N.Y.: Doubleday, 1970. 233 p.

THE NATIONAL BANK OF COMMERCE OF SEATTLE

Marple, Elliot, and Bruce H. Olson. *The National Bank of Commerce of Seattle, 1889-1969; Territorial to Worldwide Banking in Eighty Years, Including the Story of the Marine Bancorporation.* Palo Alto, Calif.: Pacific Books, 1972. 277 p.

NATIONAL BANK OF COMMERCE TRUST AND SAVINGS ASSOCIATION

Yaussi, Glenn. *National Bank of Commerce: Seventy-Five Years of Service to Nebraska.* New York, N.Y.: Newcomen Society in North America, 1977. 18 p. (Newcomen publication; no. 1071)

NATIONAL BANK OF DETROIT

National Bank of Detroit. *History of NBD.* Detroit, Mich.: The Bank, 1985. 22 p.

NATIONAL BANK OF GEORGIA

Birnie, Joseph Earle. *The History of the National Bank of Georgia.* Atlanta, Ga.: The Bank, 1978. 124 p.

NATIONAL BANK OF MIDDLEBURY

National Bank of Middlebury. *The National Bank of Middlebury, Your Bank: 150th Anniversary, 1831-1981.* Middlebury, Vt.: The Bank, 26 p.

NATIONAL BISCUIT COMPANY
SEE
NABISCO BRANDS, INC.

NATIONAL BROADCASTING COMPANY

Campbell, Robert. *The Golden Years of Broadcasting, A Celebration of the First 50 Years of Radio and TV on NBC.* New York, N.Y.: Scribner, 1976. 256 p.

MacDonald, J. Fred. *One Nation Under Television: The Rise and Decline of Network TV.* New York, N.Y.: Pantheon. 1990. 335 p.

NATIONAL BULK CARRIERS, INC.

Shields, Jerry. *The Invisible Billionaire, Daniel Ludwig.* Boston, Mass.: Houghton, 1986. 401 p.

NATIONAL CAN CORPORATION

Stuart, Robert D. *The National Can Story; In an Historic Industry an Historic Company Organized for the Future.* New York, N.Y.: Newcomen Society in North America, 1971. 28 p. (Newcomen address)

NATIONAL CASH REGISTER COMPANY

Allyn, Stanley C. *My Half Century with NCR.* New York, N.Y.: McGraw-Hill, 1967. 209 p.

"Celebrating the Future, 1884-1984." In *NCR. Annual Report*, 10-32. Dayton, Ohio: The Company, 1983.

NATIONAL COMMERCE BANK AND TRUST COMPANY

Herzog, Lester W., Jr. *150 Years of Service and Leadership: The Story of National Commercial Bank and Trust Company.* New York, N.Y.: Newcomen Society in North America, 1975. 25 p. (Newcomen publication; no. 1018)

NATIONAL CONSUMER COOPERATIVE BANK

Richter, Jay. *Where Credit Was Due, The Creation of the National Consumer Cooperative Bank.* St. Paul, Minn.: Cooperative Foundation, 1985. 110 p.

NATIONAL FARMER'S BANK

Millett, Larry. *The Curve of the Arch: The Story of Louis Sullivan's Owatonna Bank.* St. Paul, Minn.: Minnesota Historical Society Press, 1985. 248 p.

NATIONAL GRANGE MUTUAL INSURANCE COMPANY

Colby, Kenneth P. *From an Idea to Reality: The Story of National Grange Mutual Insurance Company.* New York, N.Y.: Newcomen Society in North America, 1973. 22 p.

NATIONAL GYPSUM COMPANY

Hayes, John Patrick. *National Gypsum Company: The Power of Balance.* New York, N.Y.: Newcomen Society of the United States, 1985. 23 p. (Newcomen publication; no. 1263)

NATIONAL INTERGROUP, INC.

National Intergroup, Inc. *History.* Pittsburgh, Pa.: The Company, 1985. 2 p.

NATIONAL LABORATORIES - LEHN AND FINK DIVISION

"Fred Taylor: 50 Years at Lehn and Fink." *Aerosol Age* 20 (September 1975): 33+

NATIONAL LIBERTY CORPORATION

DeMoss, Arthur S. *National Liberty Corporation*. New York, N.Y.: Newcomen Society in North America, 1978. 14 p. (Newcomen publication; no. 1079)

NATIONAL LIFE AND ACCIDENT INSURANCE COMPANY, INC.

Stamper, Powell. *The National Life Story: A History of the National Life and Accident Insurance Company of Nashville, Tennessee*. New York, N.Y.: Appleton-Century-Crofts, 1968. 359 p.

NATIONAL MEDICAL ENTERPRISES, INC.

Eamer, Richard K. *The History of National Medical Enterprises, Inc. and the Investor-Owned Hospital Industry*. New York, N.Y.: Newcomen Society of the United States, 1989. 32 p. (Newcomen publication; no. 1333)

NATIONAL RAILROAD PASSENGER CORPORATION SEE: AMTRAK

NATIONAL REVENUE CORPORATION

Shook, Robert L. "Richard D. Schultz." In *The Entrepreneurs: Twelve Who Took Risks and Succeeded*, 127-137. New York, N.Y.: Harper & Row, 1980.

THE NATIONWIDE INSURANCE COMPANIES

Doss, Bowman. *People Working Together: The Story of the Nationwide Insurance Organization.* New York, N.Y.: Newcomen Society in North America, 1968. 24 p. (Newcomen address)

Jeffers, Dean W. *The Nationwide Story, Volume II: A Phenomenal Growth Period.* New York, N.Y.: Newcomen Society in North America, 1981. 19 p. (Newcomen publication; no. 1150)

NATIONWIDE MUTUAL INSURANCE COMPANY

Cosgrove, John. "Nationwide and Consumerism." *National Underwriter (Property/Casualty/Employee Benefits)* 92 (25 July 1988): 21-22.

NATOMAS TRANSPORTATION COMPANY
SEE:
AMERICAN PRESIDENT LINES, LTD.

NATORI COMPANY

Taylor, Russel R. "Josie Natori; She Made a Blouse into a Nightshirt." In *Exceptional Entrepreneurial Women*, 47-51. New York, N.Y.: Quorum Books, 1988.

NAUTILUS SPORTS MEDICINE INDUSTRIES, INC.

Nayak, P. Ranganath, and John M. Ketteringham. "Nautilus: The Unfinished Breakthrough." In *Breakthroughs!*, 260-285. New York, N.Y.: Rawson Associates, 1986.

NBC
SEE:
NATIONAL BROADCASTING COMPANY

NCNB

NCNB. *NCNB: A Brief History*. Charlotte, N.C.: The Company, 1984. 5 p.

NCR
SEE:
NATIONAL CASH REGISTER COMPANY

NEEDHAM HARPER WORLDWIDE, INC.

Harper, Paul. *Working the Territory: 60 Years of Advertising from the People of Needham Harper Worldwide, Inc.* Englewood Cliffs, N.J.: Prentice-Hall, 1985. 127 p.

SEE ALSO: DDB NEEDHAM WORLDWIDE, INC.

NEILS (J.) LUMBER COMPANY

Neils, Paul. *Julius Neils and the J. Neils Lumber Company*. Seattle, Wash.: F. McCaffrey, 1971. 87 p.

NEIMAN-MARCUS

Marcus, Stanley. *His & Hers; The Fantasy World of the Neiman-Marcus Catalogue*. New York, N.Y.: Viking Press, 1982. 200 p.

Marcus, Stanley. *Minding the Store, A Memoir*. Boston, Mass.: Little, Brown and Company, 1974. 383 p.

Marcus, Stanley. *Quest for the Best*. New York, N.Y.: Viking Press, 1979. 228 p.

NELSON (THOMAS) PUBLISHERS

Summer, B. "The Rise of Thomas Nelson." *Publishers Weekly* 237 (5 October 1990): 24+

NESTLE COMPANY, INC.

Heer, Jean. *World Events, 1866-1966: The First Hundred Years of Nestle*. White Plains, N.Y.: Nestle Co., Inc., 1966. 226 p.

Wolflisberg, Hans J. *A Century of Global Operations; The Flavorful World of Nestle*. New York, N.Y.: Newcomen Society in North America, 1966. 28 p. (Newcomen address)

NEW ENGLAND CONFECTIONERY COMPANY

Ehrenfeld, T. "Golden Wafers." *Boston* (November 1988): 89+

NEW ENGLAND MOXIE COMPANY

Moxie Encyclopedia, Vol. 1: The History. Vestal, N.Y.: Vestal Press, 1985.

Potter, Frank N. *The Moxie Mystique*. Virginia Beach, Va.: Donning Co., 1981.

NEW ENGLAND MUTUAL LIFE INSURANCE COMPANY

Collier, Abram T. *A Capital Ship: New England Life: A History of America's First Chartered Mutual Life Insurance Company, 1835-1985*. Boston, Mass.: The Company, 1985. 336 p.

NEW ENGLAND PATRIOTS

Fox, Larry. *The New England Patriots*. New York, N.Y.: Atheneum, 1979. 345 p.

McGuane, George. *New England Patriots: A Pictorial History*. Virginia Beach, Va.: JCP Corporation of Virginia, 1980. 208 p.

NEW YORK BANK FOR SAVINGS

New York Bank for Savings. *The Story of the New York Bank for Savings: The First 150 Years*. New York, N.Y.: The Bank, 1969. 21 p.

NEW YORK DAILY NEWS

Barron, James. "As City Shifted, News Lost Its Punch." *New York Times*, 31 October 1990, sec. B, P. 2

McGivena, Leo E. *The News: The First Fifty Years of New York's Picture Newspaper*. New York, N.Y.: New York Daily News, 1969. 428 p.

NEW YORK GIANTS

Stein, Fred. *Day by Day in Giants History*. New York, N.Y.: Leisure Press, 1985.

Terzian, James P. *New York Giants*. New York, N.Y.: Macmillan, 1973. 191 p.

NEW YORK HELICOPTER CORPORATION

New York Helicopter Corporation. *Biography of New York Helicopter Corporation*. New York, N.Y.: The Company, 1985. 2 p.

NEW YORK ISLANDERS

Wilner, Barry. *The New York Islanders: Countdown to a Dynasty*. New York, N.Y.: Leisure Press, 1983. 208 p.

NEW YORK LIFE INSURANCE COMPANY

Meares, Charles William Victor. *Looking Back; A Memoir of New York Life*. s.l.: s.n., 1985. 162 p.

New York Life Insurance Company. *New York Life: A Company on the Move*. New York, N.Y.: The

Company, 1969. 31 p.

NEW YORK METS

D'Agostino, Dennis. *This Date in New York Mets History: A Day by Day Listing of Events in the History of the New York National League Baseball Team.* New York, N.Y.: Stein and Day, 1981. 222 p.

Fishman, Lew. *New York's Mets: Miracle at Shea.* Englewood Cliffs, N.J.: Prentice Hall, 1974. 126 p.

Honig, Donald. *The New York Mets: The First Quarter Century.* New York: Crown, 1986.

Koppett, Leonard. *The New York Mets; The Whole Story.* rev. ed. New York, N.Y.: Macmillan, 1974. 384 p.

NEW YORK, RIO AND BUENOS AIRES LINE

O'Neill, Ralph A., with Joseph F. Hood. *A Dream of Eagles.* Boston, Mass.: Houghton Mifflin, 1973. 324 p.

THE NEW YORK STOCK EXCHANGE

Sobel, Robert. *The Last Bull Market: Wall Street in the 1960's.* New York, N.Y.: Norton, 1980. 242 p.

Sobel, Robert. *N.Y.S.E: A History of the New York Stock Exchange, 1935-1975.* New York, N.Y.: Weybright and Talley, 1975. 398 p.

NEW YORK TELEPHONE COMPANY

Ehrenberg, Ronald G. *The Regulatory Process and Labor Earnings.* New York, N.Y.: Academic Press, 1979. 204 p.

NEW YORK TIMES COMPANY

Cose, Ellis. "The Cathedral: The New York Times." In *The Press*, 185-279. New York, N.Y.: Morrow, 1989.

Levinson, Harry, and Stuart Rosenthal. "Arthur O. Sulzberger." In *CEO: Corporate Leadership in Action*, 219-258. New York, N.Y.: Basic Books, 1984.

Talese, Gay. *The Kingdom and the Power.* New York, N.Y.: World Publishing Company, 1969. 555 p.

Talese, Gay. *The Kingdom and the Power.* Garden City, N.Y.: Anchor Press, Doubleday, 1978. 590 p.

NEW YORK YANKEES

Bove, Vincent. *And on the Eighth Day God Created the Yankees.* Plainfield, N.J.: Haven Books, 1981. 174 p.

Frommer, Harvey. *Baseball's Greatest Rivalry: The New York Yankees and Boston Red Sox.* New York, N.Y.: Atheneum, 1982. 159 p.

Gallagher, Mark. *Day by Day in New York Yankees History.* New York, N.Y.: Leisure Press, 1983. 352 p.

Gallagher, Mark. *Fifty Years of Yankee All-Stars.* New York, N.Y.: Leisure Press, 1984. 224 p.

Honig, Donald. *The New York Yankees: An Illustrated History.* New York, N.Y.: Crown, 1981. 32 p.

Salant, Nathan. *This Date in New York Yankees History.* rev. ed., New York, N.Y.: Stein & Day, 1983. 418 p.

Sullivan, George, and John Powers. *Yankees: An Illustrated History.* Englewood Cliffs, N.J.: Prentice-Hall, 1982. 312 p.

NEWHALL LAND AND FARMING COMPANY

Dickson, James F. *The Newhall Land and Farming Company: Unlocking the Productivity of the Land.* New York, N.Y.: Newcomen Society in North America, 1983. 24 p. (Newcomen publication; no. 1210)

NEWMONT MINING CORPORATION

Ramsey, Robert Henderson. *Men and Mines of Newmont; A Fifty-Year History.* New York, N.Y.: Octagon Books, 1973. 344 p.

NEWPORT NEWS SHIPBUILDING AND DRY DOCK COMPANY

Campbell, Edward J. *A Century of Leadership: The Story of Newport News Shipbuilding and Dry Dock Company.* New York, N.Y.: Newcomen Society of the United States, 1986. 22 p. (Newcomen publication; no. 1271)

Hawkins, Van. *Dorothy and the Shipbuilders of Newport News, Designed by Edward Conner.* Norfolk, Va., Donning Company, 1976. 103 p.

NEWPORT PHARMACEUTICALS INTERNATIONAL

"FDA Rejects AIDS Drug, Raps Firm." *Los Angeles Times*, 22 February 1986, sec. IV, p. 1.

NEWPORT STEEL CORPORATION

Corwin, Nancy. *Industrial Development in Northern Kentucky: The Newport Steel Story.* Unpublished paper, 1985. 24 p. (On file at the Newport Steel Corporation).

NEXT, INC.

Meyer, Michael. "The Visionary." In *The Alexander Complex: The Dreams That Drive the Great Businessmen*, 15-51. New York, N.Y.: Times Books, 1989.

NICHOLS MORTGAGE COMPANY
SEE:
STOCKTON SAVINGS ASSOCIATION

NIELSEN (A.C.) COMPANY

Stavro, Barry. "Rating Nielsen." *Forbes* 134 (17 December 1984): 100-105.

NIKE, INC.

Eales, Roy. "Is Nike a Long Distance Runner?" *Multinational Business* 1 (1986): 9-14.

Nayak, P. Ranganath, and John M. Ketteringham. "A Teacher of Competitive Response." In *Breakthroughs!*, 236-259. New York, N.Y.: Rawson Associates, 1986.

Rhodes, Lucien. "Winning Is a State of Mind at Nike." *Inc.* 3 (August 1981): 52-57.

NIP MAGAZINE

"30 Years of Publishing: A Legacy of Excellence, 1955-1985." *NIP* (July 1985): 46-49.

NISSAN MOTOR CORPORATION IN U.S.A.

Egerton, John. *Nissan in Tennessee*. Smyrna, Tenn.: Nissan Motor Corporation, 1983. 127 p.

Rae, John Bell. *Nissan/Datson, A History of Nissan Motor Corporation in U.S.A., 1960-1980*. New York, N.Y.: McGraw-Hill, 1982. 331 p.

NISUS CORPORATION

Carroll, Paul B. "Luck, Planning Bring Success to Small Firm." *Wall Street Journal* (14 April 1982): 29+

NL INDUSTRIES

Nestor, Oscar W. *The Strike As an Investment to Increase Productivity.* New Brunswick, N.J.: Institute of Management and Labor Relations, Rutgers, State University of New Jersey, 1980. 75 p.

NON-LINEAR SYSTEMS, INC.

Wolff, Michael F. "Riding the Biggest Wave." *IEEE Spectrum* 21 (December 1984): 66-71.

NORRIS INDUSTRIES, INC.

Norris, Kenneth T. *The Story of Norris Industries, Inc.: From Job Shop to Industrial Giant.* New York, N.Y.: Newcomen Society in North America, 1973. 30 p.

NORTH AMERICAN ROCKWELL CORPORATION

Anderson, Robert. *Through Turbulent Times.* New York, N.Y.: Newcomen Society of the United States, 1984. 24 p. (Newcomen publication; no. 1233)

Atwood, John Leland. *North American Rockwell, Storehouse of High Technology.* New York, N.Y.: Newcomen Society in North America, 1970. 24 p. (Newcomen address)

Lay, Beirne. *Earthbound Astronauts, The Builders of Apollo-Saturn.* Englewood Cliffs, N.J.: Prentice Hall, 1971. 198 p.

SEE ALSO: ROCKWELL INTERNATIONAL

NORTH CAROLINA MUTUAL LIFE INSURANCE COMPANY

Alston, Roland. "North Carolina Mutual's Policy for Growth." *Black Enterprise* 20 (June 1990): 214-218.

Gloster, Jesse E. *North Carolina Mutual Life Insurance Company: Its Historical Development and Current Operations.* New York, N.Y.: Arno Press, 1976. 349 p.

Kennedy, William Jesse. *The North Carolina Mutual Story; A Symbol of Progress, 1898-1970.* Durham, N.C.: The Company, 1970. 308 p.

Weare, Walter B. *Black Business in the New South: A Social History of the North Carolina Mutual Life Insurance Company.* Urbana: University of Illinois Press, 1973. 312 p.

NORTH CAROLINA RAILROAD COMPANY

North Carolina. Department of Transportation. *Report on the North Carolina Railroad Company and Atlantic & North Carolina Railroad Company for the General Assembly of North Carolina, December 22, 1976.* Raleigh, N.C.: State of North Carolina, Department of Transportation, 1977. 98 p.

The Tree of Life; A History of the North Carolina Railroad. Compiled and designed by John F. Gilbert. Text by Grady B. Jefferys. Raleigh: North Carolina Railroad Company, 1972. 96 p.

NORTH CENTRAL AIRLINES, INC.

Serling, Robert J. *Ceiling Unlimited; The Story of North Central Airlines.* Marceline, Mo.: Walsworth Publishing Company, 1973. 245 p.

NORTH JERSEY RAPID TRANSIT COMPANY

Quinby, Edwin Jay. *Interurban Interlude; A History of the North Jersey Rapid Transit Company.* Ramsey, N.J.: Model Crafts, 1968. 92 p.

NORTH PACIFIC COAST RAILROAD COMPANY

Dickinson, A. Bray. *Narrow Gauge to the Redwoods; The Story of the North Pacific Coast Railroad and San Francisco Bay Paddle-Wheel Ferries.* Costa Mesa, Calif.: Trans-Anglo Books, 1970. 168 p.

NORTH-EAST AIRLINES

Larcom, Paul S. "Eastward Ho by Air: A History of Boston-Maine and Central Vermont Airways." (With an early history of their successor North-East Airlines.) *American Aviation Historical Society Journal* 25, no.4 (1980) 242-250.

NORTHEAST AIRLINES, INC.

Mudge, Robert W. *Adventures of a Yellowbird: The Biography of an Airline.* Boston, Mass.: Branden Press, 1969. 374 p.

NORTHERN ILLINOIS GAS COMPANY

Chandler, Marvin. *An Energetic Distributor of the Energy of the Future: The Story of Northern Illinois Gas Company.* New York, N.Y.: Newcomen Society in North America, 1966. 28 p. (Newcomen address)

NORTHERN OHIO TRACTION AND LIGHT COMPANY

Blower, James M. *Northern Ohio Traction Revisited.* Akron, Ohio: The Company, 1968. 181 p.

Blower, James M., and Robert S. Korach. *The NOT&L Story.* Chicago, Ill.: Center Electric Railfans Association, 1966. 268 p.

NORTHERN TRUST BANK

Fox, David W. *The Northern Trust Company Celebrates 100 Years: 1889/1989.* New York, N.Y.: Newcomen Society of the United States, c1989, 1990. 20 p. (Newcomen publication; no. 1336)

"History in the Making: The Northern Trust Marks Its 95th Anniversary." *Bank News* 37 (14 August 1984): 1-3.

NORTHROP CORPORATION

Northrop Corporation. *Northrop Corporation Historical Background.* Los Angeles, Calif.: The Company, 1985. 5 p.

NORTHWEST AIRLINES, INC.

Mills, Stephen E. *A Pictorial History of Northwest Airlines.* New York, N.Y.: Bonanza Books, 1980, c1972. 192 p.

Ruble, Kenneth Douglas. *Flight to the Top, How a Home Town Airline Made History--And Keeps on Making It: The Absorbing 60 Year Story of Northwest Airlines.* New York, N.Y.: Viking Press, 1986. 271 p.

Yenne, Bill. *Northwest Orient.* New York, N.Y.: Gallery Books, 1986. 112 p.

NORTHWEST BANCORPORATION

Chucker, Harold. *Banco at Fifty: A History of Northwest Bancorporation 1929-1979.* Minneapolis, Minn.: The Bank, 1979. 82 p.

NORTHWEST G.F. MUTUAL INSURANCE COMPANY

Fischer, David C. *Northwest G.F. Mutual Insurance Company, Eureka, South Dakota, 75th Anniversary, 1897-1972*. Eureka, S. Dak.: The Company, 1972. 39 p.

NORTHWEST ORIENT AIRLINES

Mills, Stephen E. *More Than Meets the Sky: A Pictorial History of the Founding and Growth of Northwest Airlines*. Seattle, Wash.: Superior Publishing Company, 1972. 192 p.

Northwest Orient Airlines. *Northwest Orient Airlines: A Brief History*. St. Paul, Minn.: The Company, 1985. 13 p.

NORTHWESTERN BELL TELEPHONE COMPANY

Rippey, James Crockett. *Goodbye, Central--Hello, World: A Centennial History of Northwestern Bell: The Diary of a Dream*. Omaha, Nebr.: Published for the Telephone Pioneers of America by Northwestern Bell, 1975. 344 p.

NORTHWESTERN MUTUAL LIFE INSURANCE COMPANY

Gurda, John. *The Quiet Company: A Modern History of Northwestern Mutual Life*. Milwaukee, Wis.: The Company, 1983. 334 p.

NORTHWESTERN NATIONAL BANK OF MINNEAPOLIS

Northwestern National Bank of Minneapolis. *100 Years of Service, 1872-1972*. Minneapolis, Minn.: The Bank, 1972. 14 p.

NORTHWESTERN PACIFIC RAILROAD COMPANY

Fox, Wesley. *Northwestern Pacific Pictorial.* Naperville, Ill.: W. Fox, 1983. 80 p.

Stindt, Fred A., and Guy L. Dunscomb. *The Northwestern Pacific Railroad, Redwood Empire Route.* Redwood City, Calif.: Stindt Books, 1964-1985. 2 Vols.

NORTON COMPANY

Cheape, Charles W. *Family Firm to Modern Multinational: Norton Company, A New England Enterprise.* Cambridge, Mass.: Harvard University Press, 1985. 424 p. (Harvard studies in business history; vol. 36)

Purcell, Theodore Vincent. *Institutionalizing Corporate Ethics: Case History.* New York, N.Y.: Presidents Association, Chief Executive Officers' Division of American Management Association, 1979. 32 p.

NORTON SIMON, INC.

Mahoney, David J. *Growth and Social Responsibility: The Story of Norton Simon, Inc.* New York, N.Y.: Newcomen Society in North America, 1973. 23 p. (Newcomen address)

NOVA FINANCIAL SERVICES, INC.

Anderson, George. "Making the Branch System Work." *Credit* 16 (May/June 1990): 26, 28.

NOXELL CORPORATION

Goldwasser, Thomas. "Hallmark: Caring Enough to Send the Very Best." In *Family Pride; Profiles of Five of America's Best-Run Family Businesses*, 45-84. New York, N.Y.: Dodd, Mead and Company, 1986.

Witt, Norbert A. *The Noxzema Story.* New York, N.Y.: Newcomen Society in North America, 1967. 24 p. (Newcomen address)

NUCOR CORPORATION

Fortney, David. "The Little Steel Mill That Could." *Reader's Digest* 127 (August 1985): 110-114.

NUCOR Corporation. *History of NUCOR Corporation.* Charlotte, N.C.: The Company, 1970. 3 p.

NUTRASWEET COMPANY

McCann, Joseph E. *Sweet Success: How Nutrasweet Created a Billion Dollar Business.* Homewood, Ill.: Dow Jones Irwin, 1990. 300 p.

NYNEX

Staley, Delbert C. *Nynex in a New Age.* New York, N.Y.: Newcomen Society of the United States, 1988. 18 p. (Newcomen publication; no. 1294)

OAK INDUSTRIES, INC.

Oak Industries, Inc. *Fifty Years.* Rancho Bernard, Calif.: The Company, 1982. 16 p.

OAKLAND ATHLETICS

Shea, John, and John Hickey. *Magic by the Bay: How the San Francisco Giants and Oakland Athletics Captured the Baseball World.* Berkeley, Calif.: North Atlantic, 1990. 334 p.

OAKLAND RAIDERS

Hession, Joseph, and Steve Cassady. *The Raiders from Oakland to Los Angeles.* San Francisco, Calif.: Foghorn Press, 1987. 200 p.

Peterson, James A., and Gray L. Miller. *The Year of the Raiders*. New York, N.Y.: New America Library, 1984. 256 p.

OCCIDENTAL LIFE INSURANCE COMPANY OF CALIFORNIA

Occidental Life Insurance Company of California. *A Star in the West; The Occidental Story*. Los Angeles, Calif.: The Company, 1970. 119 p.

OCCIDENTAL PETROLEUM CORPORATION

Bryson, John. *The World of Armand Hammer*. New York, N.Y.: Abrams, 1985. 255 p.

Weinberg, Steve. *Armand Hammer: The Untold Story*. Boston, Mass.: Little Brown, 1989. 501 p.

OCEAN SPRAY CRANBERRIES, INC.

Ocean Spray Cranberries, Inc. *The History of Ocean Spray Cranberries, Inc*. Plymouth, Mass.: The Company, 1981. 9 p. (Three articles published in Ocean Spray's *Harvest Magazine:* Spring 1980, Fall 1980, and Spring 1981 issues)

OCTAGON CORPORATION

Jones, Arthur. "Practice Profiles: The Four Musketeers." *Financial Planning* 13 (December 1984): 141-145.

ODELL ASSOCIATES, INC.

Rook, Benjamin T. *Odell Associates, Inc.: Planners, Architects, Engineers: The Legacy of Architecture*. New York, N.Y.: Newcomen Society of the United States, 1987, c1988. (Newcomen publication; no. 1290)

OGDEN STANDARD-EXAMINER

Hatch, Wilda Gene. *A Pioneer in Communications: The History of Ogden Standard-Examiner and the Electronic Advancements of the Standard Corporation*. New York, N.Y.: Newcomen Society in North America, 1972. 27 p. (Newcomen address)

OGILVY AND MATHER INTERNATIONAL, INC.

Ogilvy, David. *Blood, Brains & Beer: The Autobiography of David Ogilvy*. New York, N.Y.: Atheneum, 1978. 181 p.

OGLEBAY NORTON COMPANY

Jonovic, Donald J. *Iron Industry and Independence; A Biographical Portrait of Courtney Burton, Jr., American Industrialist and Patriot*. Cleveland, Ohio: Jamieson Press, 1985. 269 p.

OHIO BELL TELEPHONE COMPANY

Ohio Bell Telephone Company. *A Brief History of the Ohio Bell Telephone Company*. Cleveland, Ohio: The Company, 1975. 24 p.

OHIO CASUALTY GROUP

"A Story of Success." *Motor Travel* 39 (November 1966): 8-12. (Official publication of the Butler County Automobile Club)

OHIO FARMERS INSURANCE COMPANY

Condon, George E. *History of Ohio Farmers Insurance Company, 1848-1984*. Westfield Center, Ohio: Westfield Companies, 1985. 275 p.

OHIO VALLEY ELECTRIC CORPORATION

Waterman, Merwin Howe. *Ohio Valley Electric Corporation; A Case Study in Developing and Financing Private Power for a Public Purpose.* Ann Arbor, Mich.: Bureau of Business Research, Graduate School of Business, University of Michigan, 1966. 95 p. (Michigan business studies, vol.17, no.3)

OKLAHOMA GAS AND ELECTRIC COMPANY

Kennedy, Donald S. *Pioneers in Public Service: The Story of Oklahoma Gas and Electric Company.* New York, N.Y.: Newcomen Society in North America, 1972. 28 p. (Newcomen address)

Oklahoma Gas and Electric Company. *The Story of Oklahoma Gas and Electric Company, 1902-1983.* Oklahoma City, Okla.: The Company, 1983. 32 p.

OKLAHOMA PUBLISHING COMPANY

Gaylord, E.K. *The Oklahoma Publishing Company.* New York, N.Y.: Newcomen Society in North America, 1971. 28 p. (Newcomen address)

OKONITE COMPANY

Okonite Company. *The Okonite Company, 1878-1978, Our One-Hundredth Year Serving the Electrical Industry for Over 100 Years.* Ramsey, N.J.: The Company, 1979. 70 p.

OMNICOM GROUP
SEE:
DDB NEEDHAM WORLDWIDE

THE ONE BANCORP AND MAINE SAVINGS BANK

Masterton, Robert R. *The One Bancorp and Maine*

Savings Bank: Not Survival, But Progress. New York, N.Y.: Newcomen Society of the United States, 1986, c1987. 22p. (Newcomen publication; no. 1282)

ONEIDA LTD.

Carden, Maren L. *Oneida: Utopian Community to Modern Corporation.* Baltimore, Md.: Johns Hopkins University Press, 1969. 228 p.

ONTARIO CORPORATION

Nelton, Sharon. "Lessons of Leadership: The Right Man at the Right Time." *Nation's Business* 72 (June 1984): 84-86.

Ontario Corporation. *Ontario Corporation--A History (1955-1981): Including the History of Ontario Silver Company and Ontario Manufacturing Company, Inc., Predecessor Companies (1895-1955).* Muncie, Ind.: The Company, 1981. 128 p.

SEE ALSO: PYROMET, INC

OPM LEASING SERVICES

Fenichell, Stephen. *Other People's Money; The Rise and Fall of OPM Leasing Services.* Garden City, N.Y.: Doubleday, 1985. 256 p.

Gandossy, Robert P. *Bad Business: The OPM Scandal and the Education of the Establishment.* New York, N.Y.: Basic Books, 1985. 262 p.

ORFA CORPORATION OF AMERICA

Brammer, Rhonda. "A Touch of Alchemy? How to Turn Trash into $90 Million." *Barron's* 66 (20 January 1986): 16-20.

ORTHO DIVISION
SEE:
CHEVRON CHEMICAL COMPANY - ORTHO DIVISION

ORVILLE REDENBACHER
SEE:
REDENBACHER (ORVILLE)

OSBORNE COMPUTER CORPORATION

Osborne, Adam, and John Dvorak. *Hypergrowth: The Rise and Fall of Osborne Computer Corporation.* Berkeley, Calif.: Idthekkethan, 1984. 204 p.

OSCAR MAYER AND COMPANY
SEE:
MAYER (OSCAR) AND COMPANY

OTTENHEIMER PUBLISHERS

Carter, R.A. "100 Years of Ottenheimer." *Publishers Weekly* 237 (14 December 1990): 26+

OUTBOARD MARINE CORPORATION

Cleary, David Powers. "Evinrude Outboard Motors; I'll Take Care of Your Books, Ole." In *Great American Brands: The Success Formulas That Made Them Famous*, 80-86. New York, N.Y.: Fairchild Publications, 1981.

Outboard Marine Corporation. *Outboard Marine Corporation.* Waukeegan, Ill.: The Company, 1965.

OVERLAND MAIL COMPANY

Lee, Wayne C., and Howard C. Raynesford. *Trails of the Smoky Hill: From Coronado to the Cow Towns.* Caldwell, Idaho: Caxton Printers, 1980. 235 p.

OWENS-CORNING FIBERGLASS CORPORATION

Owens-Corning Corporation. *The History of Owens-Corning Fiberglass Corporation: A Capsule Look.* Toledo, Ohio: The Company, 1982. 14 p.

OWENS-ILLINOIS, INC.

Owens-Illinois, Inc. *Brief History of Owens-Illinois, Inc.* Toledo, Ohio: The Company, 1985. 2 p.

OZARK AIR LINES

Kidd, Glennon. "Wings Over the Ozarks: A History of Ozark Air Lines." *American Aviation Historical Society Journal* 22 (Fall 1977): 181-187.

PACCAR, INC.

"History." In *Paccar, Inc. Annual Report*, 4-17. Bellevue, Wash.: The Company, 1979.

PACIFIC ELECTRIC RAILWAY COMPANY

Crump, Spencer. *Ride the Big Red Cars: The Pacific Electric Story.* Glendale, Calif.: Trans-Anglo Books, 1988. 256 p.

PACIFIC GAS AND ELECTRIC COMPANY

Pacific Gas and Electric Company. *P.G. and E. Country.* San Francisco, Calif.: The Company, 1966.

Roe, David. *Dynamos and Virgins.* New York, N.Y.: Random House, 1984. 218 p.

PACIFIC INVESTMENT MANAGEMENT COMPANY

Gropper, Diane Hal. "The PIMCO Powerhouse." *Institutional Investor* 20 (January 1986): 97-102.

PACIFIC LIGHTING CORPORATION

Hornby, Robert A. *Pacific Lighting Corporation: A Giant of Energy*. New York, N.Y.: Newcomen Society in North America, 1968. 24 p. (Newcomen address)

PACIFIC LUMBER COMPANY

Wilkerson, Hugh. *Life in the Peace Zone; An American Company Town*. New York, N.Y.: Macmillan, 1971. 158 p.

PACIFIC MUTUAL LIFE INSURANCE COMPANY OF CALIFORNIA

Nunis, Doyce B. *Past is Prologue: A Centennial Profile of Pacific Mutual Life Insurance Company*. Los Angeles, Calif.: The Company, 1968. 72 p.

PACIFIC POWER AND LIGHT COMPANY

Dierdorff, John. *How Edison's Lamp Helped Light the West; The Story of Pacific Power & Light Company and Its Pioneer Forebears*. Portland: The Company, 1971. 313 p.

Pacific Power and Light Company. *The Pacific Power Story: 75 Years of Service*. Portland, Oreg.: The Company, 1985. 56 p.

PACIFIC SOUTHWEST AIRLINES

"Exit Smiling." *Los Angeles Times*, 8 April 1988, sec. IV, p. 1.

"PSA to Fade from Skies in Merger." *Los Angeles Times*, 8 December 1987, sec. I, p. 31.

PACIFICORP

Frisbee, Don C. *The PacifiCorp Story: 75 Years of*

Service and Partnership. New York, N.Y.: Newcomen
Society of the United States, 1985. 24 p. (Newcomen
publication; no. 1232)

PACKARD BELL

Weiner, Steve. "Computers/Communications: New Wine
in Vintage Bottles." *Forbes* 145 (14 May 1990): 122-
123.

PACKARD MOTOR CAR COMPANY

Aiken, Michael. *Economic Failure, Alienation and
Extremism*. Ann Arbor: University of Michigan Press,
1968. 213 p.

Kimes, Beverly Rae. *Packard, A History of the Motor Car
and the Company*. Princeton, N.J.: Princeton
Publishing, distributed by E.P. Dutton, 1978. 828 p.

Scott, Michael G. H. *Packard: The Complete Story*. Blue
Ridge Summit, Pa.: Tab Books, 1985. 201 p.

Turnquist, Robert E. *The Packard Story; The Car and the
Company*. New York, N.Y.: A.S. Barnes, 1965. 286 p.

PACOLET MANUFACTURING COMPANY

Webb, J.A. *The History of New Holland, Georgia, and
Pacolet Manufacturing Company*. Roswell, Ga.: W.H.
Wolfe Associates, 1985. 445 p.

PADEN CITY GLASS MANUFACTURING
COMPANY

Barnett, Jerry. *Paden City, The Color Company*. s.l.:
Barnett, 1978. 96 p.

PAN AMERICAN WORLD AIRWAYS, INC.

Bender, Marylin, and Selig Altschul. *Chosen Instrument:*

Pan Am, Juan Trippe, The Rise and Fall of an American Enterprise. New York, N.Y.: Simon and Schuster, 1982. 605 p.

Brock, Horace. *More About Pan Am: A Pilot's Story Continued*. Lunenberg, Vt.: Stinehour Press, 1980. 101 p. (Supplement to: *Flying the Oceans: A Pilot's Story of Pan Am*, 1935-1955)

Daley, Robert. *An American Saga; Juan Trippe and His Pan Am Empire*. New York, N.Y.: Random House, 1980. 529 p.

Mahoney, Lawrence. *The Early Birds; A History of Pan Am's Clipper Ships*. Miami, Fla.: Pickering Press, 1987. 112 p.

Norris, William. *Willful Misconduct: An Untold Story*. New York, N.Y: Norton, 1984. 290 p.

"Pan Am Has a History of Being First." *Los Angeles Times*, 11 December 1987, sec. IV, p. 1.

PANHANDLE EASTERN PIPELINE COMPANY

Panhandle Eastern Pipe Line Company. *Panhandle 50*. Houston, Tex.: The Company, 1979. 28 p.

PANTHEON BOOKS

Streitfeld, David. "Pantheon and the War of Words." *Washington Post*, 18 March 1990, sec. WBK, p. 15.

PARAMOUNT PICTURES, INC.

Eames, John Douglas. *The Paramount Story*. New York, N.Y.: Crown, 1985. 368 p.

Edmonds, I.G., and Reiko Mimura. *Paramount Pictures and the People Who Made Them*. San Diego, Calif.: A.S. Barnes, 1980. 272 p.

Halliwell, Leslie. *Mountain of Dreams, The Golden Years of Paramount Pictures.* New York, N.Y.: Stonehill, Distributed by Farrar, Straus & Giroux, 1976. 196 p.

PARISIAN, INC.

Hess, Emil C. *Parisian: Celebrating a Century of Service.* New York, N.Y.: Newcomen Society of the United States, 1986, c1987. 24 p. (Newcomen publication; no. 1278)

PARKE-DAVIS AND COMPANY

Parke-Davis and Company. *Parke-Davis at 100: Progress in the Past--Promise for the Future.* Detroit, Mich.: The Company, 1966.

PARKER BROTHERS, INC.

Parker Brothers, Inc. *90 Years of Fun, 1883-1973; The History of Parker Brothers.* Salem, Mass.: The Company, 1973. 71 p.

Wojahn, Ellen. *Playing by Different Rules.* New York, N.Y.: American Management Association, 1988. 306 p.

SEE ALSO: TONKA CORPORATION

PARKER DRILLING COMPANY

Parker Drilling Company. *Fifty Years of Drilling, 1934-1984.* Tulsa, Okla.: The Company, 1984. 16 p.

PARKER HANNIFIN CORPORATION

Parker, Patrick S. *Parker Hannifin Corporation.* New York, N.Y.: Newcomen Society in North America, 1980. 26 p. (Newcomen publication; no. 1107)

PARKER PEN COMPANY

Cleary, David Powers. "Parker Pens; 'Our Pens Can Write in Any Language.'" In *Great American Brands: The Success Formulas That Made Them Famous*, 223-231. New York, N.Y.: Fairchild Publications, 1981.

"The Pen Is Still Mighty at Parker--But." *Dun's Review* 116 (October 1980): 45-46.

PARMORAND PUBLICATIONS

Nicolaides, Louis. *The Production Company*. 2nd ed. Beverly Hills, Calif.: Parmorand Publications, 1983. 175 p.

PARSER MINERAL CORPORATION

"Parser Mineral Corporation Celebrates 100th Anniversary." *Lapidary Journal* 32 (July 1978): 986+.

PARSONS AND WHITTEMORE ORGANIZATION

Landegger, Karl F. *Growing with the Paper Industry Since 1853...: The Parsons and Whittemore Organization and the Black Clawson Company*. New York, N.Y.: Newcomen Society in North America, 1968. 24 p. (Newcomen address)

PARSONS BRINCKERHOFF, INC.

Bobrick, Benson. *Parsons Brinckerhoff: The First 100 Years*. New York, N.Y.: Van Nostrand Reinhold, 1985. 276 p.

PARSONS, BRINCKERHOFF, QUADE AND DOUGLAS, INC.

Douglas, Walter S. *An Enduring Heritage: Ninety Years of Progress in Engineering, Planning, and*

Architecture. New York, N.Y.: Newcomen Society in North America, 1975. 17 p. (Newcomen publication; no. 1019)

PATHMARK
SEE:
SUPERMARKETS GENERAL CORPORATION

PAUL MASSON VINYARDS
SEE:
MASSON (PAUL) VINYARDS

PAYCHEX

Barrier, Michael. "The Power of a Good Idea." *Nation's Business* 78 (November 1990): 34, 36.

PAYTON (BOB)

Copetas, A. Craig. "Payton's Place." *Inc.* 6 (October 1984): 135-144.

PC'S LIMITED

Kingston, Brett. "Michael Dell of PC's Limited." In *The Dynamos: Who Are They Anyway?*, 129-134. New York, N.Y.: Wiley, 1987.

PEABODY HOLDING COMPANY, INC.

"Peabody Celebrates First 100 Years in the Coal Business." *Coal Age* 88 (June 1983): 22-23.

PEAT, MARWICK, MITCHELL AND COMPANY

Hanson, Walter E. *Peat, Marwick, Mitchell and Company: 80 Years of Professional Growth.* New York, N.Y.: Newcomen Society in North America, 1978. 19 p. (Newcomen publication; no. 1075)

Wise, T.A. *Peat, Marwick, Mitchell & Co.: 85 Years.*

New York, N.Y.: The Company, 1982. 107 p.

PENN CENTRAL COMPANY

Daughen, Joseph R., and Peter Binzen. *The Wreck of the Penn Central.* Boston, Mass.: Little, Brown, 1971. 365 p.

Gartner, Michael. *Riding the Pennsy to Ruin; A Wall Street Journal Chronicle of the Penn Central Debacle.* Princeton, N.J.: Dow Jones Books, 1971. 90 p.

Salsbury, Stephen. *No Way to Run a Railroad: The Untold Story of the Penn Central Crisis.* New York, N.Y.: McGraw-Hill, 1982. 363 p.

Sobel, Robert. *The Fallen Colossus: The Penn Central and the Metamorphosis of American Capitalism.* New York, N.Y.: Weybright and Talley, 1976. 370 p.

U.S. Congress. House. Committee on Banking and Currency. *The Penn Central Failure and the Role of Financial Institutions,* Staff Report, 92nd Cong., 1st Sess. Washington, D.C.: GPO, 1972. 375 p.

U.S. Securities and Exchange Commission. *The Financial Collapse of the Penn Central Company; Staff Report to the Special Subcommittee on Investigations, Of the Committee on Interstate and Foreign Commerce, U.S. House of Representatives.* Washington, D.C.: GPO, 1972. 392 p.

SEE ALSO: AMTRAK

PENN SQUARE BANK

Singer, Mark. *Funny Money.* New York, N.Y.: Knopf, 1985. 256 p.

Zweig, Phillip L. *Belly Up; The Collapse of the Penn*

Square Bank. New York, N.Y.: Crown Publishers, 1985. 500 p.

PENNBANCORP

Roemer, William F. *Pennbancorp: A Merger Success Story.* New York, N.Y.: Newcomen Society of the United States, 1988. 24 p. (Newcomen publication; no. 1292)

PENNEY (J.C.) COMPANY, INC.

Batten, William M. *The Penney Idea: Foundation for the Continuing Growth of the J.C. Penney Company.* New York, N.Y.: Newcomen Society in North America, 1967. 24 p. (Newcomen address)

J.C. Penney Company, Inc. *Background on the J.C. Penney Company, Inc.* New York, N.Y.: The Company, 1985. 10 p.

J.C. Penney Company, Inc. *J.C. Penney Milestones.* New York, N.Y.: The Company, 1983. 4 p.

PENNSYLVANIA POWER AND LIGHT COMPANY

Nash, John Rumm, and Craig Orr. *Pennsylvania Power & Light Company: A Guide to the Records.* Wilmington: Hagley Museum and Library, 1985. 226 p.

Pennsylvania Power & Light Company. *Pennsylvania Power & Light Company Profile: Statistical Review, 1966-1976.* Discussion of current issues. Allentown, Pa.: The Company, 1977. 48 p.

PENNSYLVANIA POWER COMPANY

Pennsylvania Power Company. *50 Years, 1931-1981.* New Castle, Pa.: The Company, 1981. 23 p.

PENNSYLVANIA STATE EMPLOYEES CREDIT UNION

Condon, Mark R. "A Sleeping Giant Awakens." *Credit Union Magazine* 51 (December 1985): 94-98.

PENNZOIL COMPANY

Coll, Steve. *The Taking of Getty Oil: The Full Story of the Most Spectacular--And Catastrophic--Takeover of All Time.* New York, N.Y.: Atheneum, 1987. 528 p.

Meyer, Henry I. *Corporate Financial Planning Models.* New York, N.Y.: Wiley, 1977. 218 p.

Petzinger, Thomas, Jr. *Oil and Honor, The Texaco-Pennzoil Wars.* New York, N.Y.: Putnam, 1987. 416 p.

Shannon, James. *Texaco and the $10 Billion Jury.* Englewood Cliffs, N.J.: Prentice Hall, 1988. 545 p.

PENOBSCOT SAVINGS BANK

Penobscot Savings Bank. *100 Years, Penobscot Savings Bank; Bangor and the World, 1869-1969.* Bangor, Maine: The Bank, 1969. 23 p.

PENTAIR, INC.

Fucini, Joseph J., and Suzy Fucini. "Murray J. Harpole, Pentair, Inc.: 'I Decided--I Would Give It Five Years No Matter How Tough It Got.'" In *Experience Inc.; Men and Women Who Founded Famous Companies After the Age of 40,* 153-159. New York, N.Y.: Free Press, 1987.

PEOPLE EXPRESS AIRLINES, INC.

Rhodes, Lucien. "That Daring Young Man and His Flying Machines." *Inc.* (January 1984): 42-52.

Walsh, John. "The People's Co-Op Takes Flight." *The Director* 37, no.3 (October 1983): 43-44.

PEOPLES BANK OF BLOOMINGTON

Crissey, Elwell. *Peoples Bank of Bloomington: First 100 Years, 1869-1969.* Bloomington, Ill.: Pantagraph Press, 1969. 153 p.

PEOPLE'S SAVINGS BANK--BRIDGEPORT

Hawley, Samuel W. *People's Savings Bank--Bridgeport: A Story of Private Thrift and Public Service.* New York, N.Y.: Newcomen Society in North America, 1974. 26 p. (Newcomen publication; no. 1001)

PEPSICO, INC.

Enrico, Roger. *The Other Guy Blinked: How Pepsi Won the Cola Wars.* New York, N.Y.: Bantam, 1986. 280 p.

Louis, J.C. *The Cola Wars.* New York, N.Y: Everest House, 1980. 386 p.

Mack, Walter, and P. Buckley. *No Time Lost.* New York, N.Y.: Atheneum, 1982. 211 p.

PepsiCo, Inc. *PepsiCo: The First Twenty Years.* Purchase, N.Y.: The Company, 1985. 8 p.

Pepsi-Cola Company. *The Pepsi-Cola Story.* Purchase, N.Y.: The Company, 1984. 14 p.

Sculley, John. *Odyssey: Pepsi to Apple: A Journey of Adventure, Ideas, And the Future.* New York, N.Y.: Harper, 1987. 450 p.

"Slice: Case Study of a Setback." *New York Times*, 15 July 1988, sec. D, p. 1.

Tedlow, Richard S. "The Great Cola Wars: Coke Vs. Pepsi." In *New and Improved: The Story of Mass Marketing in America*, 22-111. New York, N.Y.: Basic Books, 1990.

PEQUEGNAT (ARTHUR) CLOCK COMPANY

Varkaris, Jane, and Costas Varkaris. *The Pequegnat Story: The Family and the Clocks*. Dubuque, Iowa: Kendall/Hunt, 1982. 187 p.

PERDUE FARMS, INC.

Perdue Farms, Inc. *A Biography of Frank Perdue, Chairman of the Board, Perdue Farms Incorporated*. Salisbury, Md.: The Company, 1986?. 6 p.

Perdue Farms, Inc. *Historical Highlights*. Salisbury, Md.: The Company, 1988. 4 p.

Sobel, Robert, and David B. Sicilia. "Frank Perdue: The Man of 270 Million Chickens." In *The Entrepreneurs: An American Adventure*, 77-81. Boston, Mass.: Houghton Mifflin Company, 1986.

Whiteside, Thomas. "Not Just a Commodity Anymore; Frank Perdue Is One Reason Chickens Are No Longer Anonymous." *FarmFutures; The Farm Business Magazine* (January 1988): 26-27.

Whiteside, Thomas. "Pitching Chickens: How Frank Perdue Found Fame As a Poultry Pioneer." *FarmFutures; The Farm Business Magazine* (February 1988): 12H-12I.

PERKIN-ELMER CORPORATION

"History." In *Perkin-Elmer Corporation. Background Information*, 32-33. Norwalk, Conn.: The Company, 1985.

PEROT SYSTEMS CORPORATION

Mason, Todd. *Perot: An Unauthorized Biography.* Homewood, Ill.: Dow Jones-Irwin, 1990. 316 p.

PERRY DRUG STORES

Razzano, Rhonda. "Jack Robinson: Perry Drug's Monday Morning Autocrat." *Chain Store Age Executive* 61 (November 1985): 21-23.

PET, INC.

Pet, Inc. *Creating a Masterpiece, The First 100 Years of Pet, Incorporated.* St. Louis, Mo.: The Company, 1985. 47 p.

PETER PAUL, INC.

Elston, Lloyd W. *Peter Paul, Inc.: Quality Candy Since 1919.* New York, N.Y.: Newcomen Society in North America, 1971. 24 p. (Newcomen address)

PETROLANE, INC.

Munzer, R.J. *Petrolane, Inc.* New York, N.Y.: Newcomen Society in North America, 1979. 17 p. (Newcomen publication; no. 1097)

PFIZER, INC.

Mines, Samuel. *Pfizer: An Informal History.* New York, N.Y.: The Company, 1978. 248 p.

Pratt, Edmund T. *Pfizer: Bringing Science to Life.* New York, N.Y.: Newcomen Society of the United States, 1985. 24 p. (Newcomen publication; no. 1247)

PHELPS DODGE CORPORATION

Durham, G. Robert. *Phelps Dodge Corporation: "Proud*

of Its Past, Prepared for the Future." New York,
N.Y.: Newcomen Society of the United States, 1989.
24 p. (Newcomen publication; no. 1325)

THE PHILADELPHIA PHILLIES

Bilovsky, Frank, and Richard Westcott. *The Phillies
Encyclopedia.* New York, N.Y.: Leisure Press, 1984.
541 p.

Dolson, Frank. *The Philadelphia Story: A City of
Winners.* South Bend, Ind.: Icarus Press, 1981. 318 p.

Lewis, Allen. *The Philadelphia Phillies.* New York, N.Y.:
Simon and Schuster, 1982.

Lewis, Allen. *The Philadelphia Phillies: A Pictorial
History.* Virginia Beach: JCP Corporation of Virginia,
1981. 176 p.

Lewis, Allen. *This Date in Philadelphia Phillies History:
A Day by Day Listing of Events in the History of the
Philadelphia National League Baseball Team.* New
York, N.Y.: Stein and Day, 1979. 273 p.

THE PHILADELPHIA RAPID TRANSIT COMPANY

Cox, Harold E. *Utility Cars of Philadelphia, 1892-1971.*
Forty Fort, Pa.: The Company, 1971. 132 p.

THE PHILADELPHIA '76ERS

Williams, Pat, and Bill Lyons. *We Owed You One: The
Uphill Struggle of the Philadelphia '76ers.*
Wilmington, Del.: Tri Mark Publishing Company,
1983. 220 p.

THE PHILADELPHIA STOCK EXCHANGE

Wetherill, Elkins. *The Story of the Philadelphia Stock
Exchange.* New York, N.Y.: Newcomen Society in

North America, 1976. 19 p. (Newcomen publication; no. 1036)

PHILIP MORRIS, INC.

Hunter, Sam. *Art in Business: The Philip Morris Story.* New York, N.Y.: Published under the auspices of Business Committee for the Arts by Abrams, 1979. 200 p.

Philip Morris, Inc. *Philip Morris History.* New York, N.Y.: Communications Research Dept., Philip Morris, Inc., 1982. 22 p.

Philip Morris, Inc. *Philip Morris History Highlights.* New York, N.Y.: The Company, 1985. 29 p.

PHILIPS INDUSTRIES, INC.

Philips Industries, Inc. *25th Year; Twenty-Five Years of Growth.* Dayton, Ohio: The Company, 1982. 22 p.

PHILLIPS PETROLEUM COMPANY

Finney, Robert. *Phillips, The First 66 Years.* Bartlesville, Okla.: The Company, 1983. 219 p.

Wallis, Michael. *Oil Man; The Story of Frank Phillips and the Birth of Phillips Petroleum.* Forward by John Gibson Phillips, Jr. New York, N.Y.: Doubleday, 1988. 480 p.

THE PHOENIX GAZETTE

Pulliam, Eugene C. *Is There a Fighter in the House?* New York, N.Y.: Newcomen Society in North America, 1966. 24 p. (Newcomen address)

PICA SYSTEMS

Gite, Lloyd. "One-Stop Processing." *Black Enterprise*

(January 1985): 35.

PICKARD, INC.

Platt, Dorothy Pickard. *The Story of Pickard China.* Hanover, Pa.: Printed by Everybody's Press, 1970. 85 p.

PIEDMONT

Davis, Thomas H. *The History of Piedmont: Setting a Special Pace.* New York, N.Y.: Newcomen Society in North America, 1982. 24 p. (Newcomen publication; no. 1160)

PIEDMONT AND NORTHERN RAILWAY

Fetters, Thomas T., and Peter W. Swanson. *The Piedmont and Northern; The Great Electric System of the South.* San Marino, Calif.: Golden West Books, 1974. 175 p.

THE PILLSBURY COMPANY

Powell, William J. *Pillsbury's Best: A Company History from 1869.* Minneapolis, Minn.: The Company, 1985. 252 p.

PINKERTON'S NATIONAL DETECTIVE AGENCY

Barrier, Michael. "Tom Wathen's Security Blanket." *Nation's Business* 78 (May 1990): 26-30.

Glasheen, Leah. "We Never Sleep--Fifty Years of Pinkerton's at the Smithsonian." *Security Management* 25 (November 1981): 45-6.

Horan, James D. *The Pinkertons, The Detective Dynasty That Made History.* New York, N.Y.: Crown Publishing Company, 1967. 564 p.

Morn, Frank. *The Eye That Never Sleeps: A History of the Pinkerton National Detective Agency.* Bloomington: Indiana University Press, 1982. 244 p.

"Pinks--A Colorful Part of U.S. History." *Los Angeles Times*, 22 December 1987, sec. IV, p. 3.

PIONEER HI-BRED INTERNATIONAL, INC.

Hunger, J. David. "Pioneer Hi-Bred International, Inc." *Journal of Management Case Studies* 3 (Spring 1987): 2-26.

PIONEER NATURAL GAS COMPANY

Pioneer Natural Gas Company. *The History of the Pioneer Natural Gas Company.* Amarillo, Tex.: The Company, 1965. 6 p.

PIPER AIRCRAFT CORPORATION

Cleary, David Powers. "Piper Aircraft--Because Air Is Everywhere." In *Great American Brands: The Success Formulas That Made Them Famous*, 232-238. New York, N.Y.: Fairchild Publications, 1981.

Francis, Devon E. *Mr. Piper and His Cubs.* Ames: Iowa State University Press, 1973. 256 p.

Piper, W.T. *From Club to Navajo: The Story of Piper Aircraft Corporation.* New York, N.Y.: Newcomen Society in North America, 1970. 31 p. (Newcomen address)

PITTSBURGH AND LAKE ERIE RAILROAD

McLean, Harold H. *Pittsburgh and Lake Erie R.R.* San Marino, Calif.: Golden West Books, 1980. 236 p.

PITTSBURGH-DES MOINES CORPORATION

Versteeg, Jean D. *The History of Pittsburgh-Des Moines Corporation, 1892-1982*. Pittsburgh, Pa.: The Company, 1982. 77 p.

THE PITTSBURGH PIRATES

Eckhouse, Morris, and Carl Mastrocola. *This Date in Pittsburgh Pirates History*. New York, N.Y.: Stein and Day, 1980. 272 p.

PITTSBURGH STEELERS

Didinger, Ray. *Pittsburgh Steelers*. New York, N.Y.: Macmillan, 1974. 192 p.

Oates, Bob. *Pittsburgh's Steelers: The First Half Century*. Los Angeles, Calif.: Published for the Pittsburgh Steelers by Rosebud Books, 1982. 95 p.

PITTSTON COMPANY

Pittston Company. *Pittston, Yesterday, Today, And Tomorrow*. Greenwich, Conn.: The Company, 1980. 32 p.

Stern, Gerald M. *The Buffalo Creek Disaster, How the Survivors of One of the Worst Disasters in Coal-Mining History Brought Suit Against the Coal Company--And Won*. New York, N.Y.: Vintage Books, 1977. 307 p. (Reprint of the 1976 ed., published by Random House)

PIZZA INN, INC.

Pizza Inn, Inc. *Pizza Inn: The First Twenty-Five Years*. Dallas, Tex.: The Company, 1984. 9 p.

PLANNING ALTERNATIVES
SEE:
OCTAGON CORPORATION

PLATINUM TECHNOLOGY, INC.

Richman, Tom. "Recruiting Affiliates." *Inc.* 12 (December 1990): 157-158.

PLAYBOY ENTERPRISES, INC.

Lownes, Victor. *The Day the Bunny Died.* Secaucus, N.J.: Lyle Stuart, 1983. 190 p.

Miller, Russel. *Bunny, The Real Story of Playboy.* New York, N.Y.: Holt, Rinehart & Winston, 1985, c1984. 352 p.

Tully, Shawn. "Playboy Makes the Boss's Daughter Boss." *Fortune* 106 (23 August 1982): 105-118.

Weyr, Thomas. *Reaching for Paradise: The Playboy Vision of America.* New York, N.Y.: NYT Books, 1978. 324 p.

PLAYWRIGHTS PRODUCING COMPANY

Wharton, John Franklin. *Life Among the Playwrights, Being Mostly the Story of the Playwrights Producing Company, Inc.* New York, N.Y.: Quadrangle/New York Times Book Company, 1974. 336 p.

PLUMLY INDUSTRIES

Fucini, Joseph J., and Suzy Fucini. "George W. Plumly, Plumly Industries: 'People Will Always Say It Can't Be Done, Until Someone Comes Along and Does It.'" In *Experience Inc.; Men and Women Who Founded Famous Companies After the Age of 40*, 207-214. New York, N.Y.: Free Press, 1987.

POCKET BOOKS, INC.

Fucini, Joseph J., and Suzy Fucini. "Robert F. De Graff, Pocket Books, Inc.: 'People Would Buy More Books If They Were Cheaper.'" In *Experience Inc.; Men and Women Who Founded Famous Companies After the Age of 40*, 129-135. New York, N.Y.: Free Press, 1987.

POE (MCDONALD)

Poe, McDonald, Sr. *Fifty Years of Law Practice*. Waldron, Ark.: Donald Poe, 1976. 404 p.

POLAROID CORPORATION

National Council of the Churches of Christ in the United States of America. Corporate Information Center. *The Polaroid "Experiment" in South Africa*. New York, N.Y.: Office of Resource Studies, Division of Christian Life and Mission, National Council of Churches, 1971. 14 p.

Nossiter, Daniel D. "No Instant Success, But New Focus Brightens the Picture at Polaroid." *Barron's* 67 (5 July 1982): 11, 16, 20.

Olshaker, Mark. *Instant Image; The Polaroid Story, Edwin Land and the Polaroid Experience*. New York, N.Y.: Stein & Day, 1978. 277 p.

Polaroid Corporation. *Polaroid Corporation: A Chronology*. Cambridge, Mass.: The Company, 1983. 10 p.

Wensberg, Peter C. *Land's Polaroid; A Company and the Man Who Invented It*. Boston, Mass.: Houghton Mifflin, 1987. 258 p.

POPULAR SCIENCE PUBLISHING COMPANY

Heyn, Ernest V. *A Century of Wonders: 100 Years of Popular Science*. New York, N.Y.: Doubleday, 1972. 320 p.

PORTLAND GENERAL ELECTRIC COMPANY

Dillin, Carol A. "A Century of Investor-Owned Electric Service--A Utility History." *Public Utilities Fortnightly* 124 (31 August 1989): 9-12.

POSTAL INSTANT PRESS

Fucini, Joseph J., and Suzy Fucini. "Bill Levine, Postal Instant Press: 'I Saw a Good Opportunity and I Jumped in.'" In *Experience Inc.; Men and Women Who Founded Famous Companies After the Age of 40*, 16-22. New York, N.Y.: Free Press, 1987.

POTLATCH CORPORATION

Madden, Richard B. *"Tree Farmers and Wood Converters": The Story of Potlatch Corporation*. New York, N.Y.: Newcomen Society in North America, 1975. 24 p. (Newcomen publication; no. 1010).

Peterson, Keith. *Company Town; Potlatch, Idaho, And the Potlatch Lumber Company*. Pullman, Wash.: Washington State University Press; Moscow, Idaho: Latah County Historical Society, 1987. 284 p.

PPG INDUSTRIES

PPG Industries. *PPG: A Century of Achievement*. Pittsburgh, Pa.: The Company, 1983. 31 p. (Published as vol. 91, no.2, of: *PPG Products Magazine*)

THE PRAIRIE FARMER

Evans, James F. *Prairie Farmer and WLS: The Burridge*

D. Butler Years. Urbana: University of Illinois Press, 1969. 329 p.

PRECISION RUBBER PRODUCTS CORPORATION

Allen, Robert E. *"O" Rings Make History*. Dayton, Ohio: Otterbein Pub. Co.: 1969. 156 p.

PRICE WATERHOUSE AND COMPANY

"Price Waterhouse Review Anniversary Issue Commemorating the Seventy-Fifth Anniversary of Price Waterhouse & Company." *Price Waterhouse Review* 10 (Autumn 1965): 1-71.

PRITZKER AND PRITZKER

Bender, Marylin. "The Very Private Pritzkers." In *At the Top; Behind the Scenes with the Men and Women Who Run America's Corporate Giants*, 300-328. Garden City, N.Y.: Doubleday, 1975.

PROCTER AND GAMBLE COMPANY

Cleary, David Powers. "Ivory Soap; 99 44/100% Pure--It Floats." In *Great American Brands: The Success Formulas That Made Them Famous*, 172-181. New York, N.Y.: Fairchild Publications, 1981.

Crain, Rance, and Fred Danzig. "Patience and Perspective." *Advertising Age* 58 (20 August 1987): 148-160.

Freeman, Laurie. "The House That Ivory Built." *Advertising Age* 58 (20 August 1987): 4-14, 162-200.

Millman, Nancy F. "Saga of P&G's Ivory Soap: Keeping a Brand Afloat 100 Years." *Advertising Age* 50 (2 July 1979): 24-27.

"Procter and Gamble at 150 Years Old; A Special Report."

Cincinnati Enquirer, 16 August 1987, sec. J, p.1.

Procter and Gamble Company. *Procter and Gamble: Celebrating 150 Years of Excellence*. Cincinnati, Ohio: The Company, 1987. 25 p.

Procter and Gamble Company. *The Story of Procter and Gamble*. Cincinnati, Ohio: The Company, 1972. 48 p.

Schisgall, Oscar. *Eyes on Tomorrow: The Evolution of Procter and Gamble*. Chicago, Ill.: J.G. Ferguson Publishing Company, 1981. 295 p.

Schisgall, Oscar. "P&G: Past Is Prolog." *Advertising Age* 53 (11 January 1982): 47-48, 52, 55.

PROTECTIVE INDUSTRIAL INSURANCE COMPANY OF ALABAMA, INC.

McCall, Nathan. "B.E. Insurance Company of the Year: Premium Profits." *Black Enterprise* 16 (June 1986): 182-186.

PROTECTIVE LIFE INSURANCE COMPANY

Rushton, William J., III. *A Sense of Quality, A Sense of Protective Life*. New York, N.Y.: Newcomen Society in North America, 1976. 22 p. (Newcomen Publication; no. 1049)

PROTOCOM DEVICES

Kingston, Brett. "Raphael Collado and Ramon Morales of Protocom Devices." In *The Dynamos: Who Are They Anyway?*, 35-44. New York, N.Y.: Wiley, 1987.

PROVIDENCE JOURNAL COMPANY

Byrnes, Garrett D., and Charles H. Spilman. *The Providence Journal: 150 Years*. Providence, R.I.: The Company, 494 p.

PROVIDENT LOAN SOCIETY OF NEW YORK

Schmed, Peter. *God Bless Pawnbrokers.* New York, N.Y.: Dodd, Mead, 1975. 217 p.

PROVINCETOWN-BOSTON AIRLINE, INC.

Hartman, Charles. "Provincetown-Boston Airlines: A Tale of Two Airlines." *Inc.* (5 February 1983): 51-53+

"PBA History" *Air Transportation World* 22 (January 1985): 76-77.

PRUDENTIAL INSURANCE COMPANY OF AMERICA

Carr, William H.A. *From Three Cents a Week--The Story of the Prudential Insurance Company of America.* Englewood Cliffs, N.J.: Prentice-Hall, 1975. 316 p.

PUBLIC SERVICE COMPANY OF COLORADO

Fisher, Ellen Kingman. *One Hundred Years of Energy: Public Service Company of Colorado and Its Predecessors, 1869-1969.* New York, N.Y.: Garland, 1989. 517 p.

PUBLIC SERVICE COMPANY OF INDIANA

Blanchar, Carroll H. *Indiana and the Electric Age: The Story of Public Service Company of Indiana.* New York, N.Y.: Newcomen Society in North America, 1969. 28 p. (Newcomen address)

Public Service Company of Indiana. *Indiana and the Electric Age: The Story of Public Service Indiana.* Plainfield, Ind.: The Company, 1982. 20 p.

PUBLIC SERVICE ELECTRIC AND GAS COMPANY

Conniff, James C.G., and Richard Conniff. *The Energy People: A History of PSE&G.* Newark, N.J.: The Company, 1978. 392 p.

Smith, Robert I. *A Cycle of Service: The Story of Public Service Electric and Gas Company.* New York, N.Y.: Newcomen Society in North America, 1980. 24 p. (Newcomen publication; no. 1121)

PUBLISHERS WEEKLY

Grannis, C.B. "1872-1972; Celebrating 100 Years of Publishers Weekly and the American Book Trade." *Publishers Weekly* 201 (17 January 1972): 28-36.

PUBLIX SUPER MARKETS

Jenkins, George W. *The Publix Story.* New York, N.Y.: Newcomen Society in North America, 1978. 23 p. (Newcomen publication; no. 1098)

Watters, Pat. *Fifty Years of Pleasure, The Illustrated History of Publix Super Markets, Inc.* Lakeland, Fla.: The Company, 1980. 263 p.

PUGET SOUND POWER AND LIGHT COMPANY

Wing, Robert C. *A Century of Service; The Puget Power Story.* Bellevue, Wash.: The Company, 1987. 178 p.

PULITZER PUBLISHING COMPANY

Pulitzer, Joseph. *Pulitzer Publishing Company: Newspapers and Broadcasting in the Public Interest.* New York, N.Y.: Newcomen Society of the United States, 1989. 27 p. (Newcomen publication; no. 1322)

PULLMAN, INC.

Adelman, William. *Touring Pullman, A Study in Company Paternalism; A Walking Guide to the Pullman Community in Chicago, Illinois.* 2d ed. Chicago, Ill.: Illinois Labor History Society, 1977. 46 p.

Bender, Marylin. "Pullman's Journey to the East." In *At the Top; Behind the Scenes with the Men and Women Who Run America's Corporate Giants,* 95-120. Garden City, N.Y.: Doubleday, 1975.

McKissack, Pat. *A Long Hard Journey; The Story of the Pullman Porter.* New York, N.Y.: Walker, 1989. 144 p.

Pullman, Inc. *Portrait at 100.* Chicago, Ill.: The Company, 1976. 16 p.

PYROMET, INC.

Du Bois, William, Jr. *Pyromet, Inc., A History (1950-1983), Including Information on the History of CDS Engineering of San Jose, California, and Pyromet Industries of Muncie, Indiana.* Muncie, Ind.: Ontario Corporation, 1983. 160 p.

SEE ALSO: ONTARIO CORPORATION

QUAKER OATS COMPANY

Marquette, Arthur F. *Brands, Trademarks, and Good Will: The Story of the Quaker Oats Company.* New York, N.Y.: McGraw-Hill, 1967. 274 p.

QUAKER OATS COMPANY - ROCKFORD PET FOODS DIVISION

Quaker Oats Company. Rockford Pet Foods Division. *Rockford; The Pet Food Story, 1923-1987.* Rockford,

Ill.: The Company, 1987. 98 p.

QUAKER STATE OIL

Wood, Quentin E. *Quaker State Roots Go Deep into the World's First Oil Field*. New York, N.Y.: Newcomen Society of the United States, 1986. 24 p. (Newcomen publication; no. 1277)

QUICK FROZEN FOODS

Williams, E.W. "Biography of an Industry and the Magazine That Grew Up with It: The History of Frozen Foods, 1938-1968." *Quick Frozen Foods* 31 (August 1968): 49-105.

R&J CORVETTE PARTS, INC.

Souder, William. "Dream Machine." *Inc.* 7 (May 1985): 129-134.

RADIO SHACK
SEE:
TANDY CORPORATION

RALSTON PURINA COMPANY

Cleary, David Powers. "Ralston Purina Foods & Feeds; Find the Right Foundations and Build on Them." In *Great American Brands: The Success Formulas That Made Them Famous*, 239-245. New York, N.Y.: Fairchild Publications, 1981.

Ralston Purina Company. *Ralston Purina Vignettes*. St. Louis, Mo.: The Company, 1970. 9 p.

RAMADA HOTEL GROUP

Fucini, Joseph J., and Suzy Fucini. "Marion W. Isbell, Ramada Inns: 'All of My Life I Tried to Get Ahead by Outworking the Guy Next to Me.'" In *Experience*

Inc.; Men and Women Who Founded Famous Companies After the Age of 40, 192-199. New York, N.Y.: Free Press, 1987.

Ramada Hotel Group. *Ramada Hotel Group. Fact Sheet*. Phoenix, Ariz.: The Company, 1990. 2 p.

RAND CORPORATION

Rand Corporation. *Rand 25th Anniversary Volume*. Santa Monica, Calif.: The Company, 1973. 239 p.

Smith, Bruce L.R. *The Rand Corporation; Case Study of a Nonprofit Advisory Corporation*. Cambridge, Mass.: Harvard University Press, 1966. 332 p.

RANGER BOATS
SEE:
WOOD MANUFACTURING COMPANY

RANSOME AIRLINES

Feldman, Joan M. *The Ransome Airline Story*. Philadelphia, Pa.: The Company, 1977.

RAVEIS (WILLIAM) REAL ESTATE

Levitt, Mortimer. "William Raveis: 'Scratch an Entrepreneur and You Will Find an Ego.'" In *How to Start Your Own Business Without Losing Your Shirt; Secrets of Seventeen Successful Entrepreneurs*, 157-163. New York, N.Y.: Atheneum, 1988.

RAYOVAC

Ruble, Kenneth Douglas. *The RAYOVAC Story--The First 75 Years*. Madison, Wis.: The Company, 1981. 207 p.

RAYTHEON COMPANY

Nayak, P. Ranganath, and John M. Ketteringham. "The

Microwave Oven: Tis Black Magic!" In *Breakthroughs!*, 179-207. New York, N.Y.: Rawson Associates, 1986.

Scott, Otto J. *The Creative Ordeal: The Story of Raytheon*. New York, N.Y: Atheneum, 1974. 429 p.

Warsh, David. "How Raytheon Flourished Without Corporate Fads." *Boston Globe*, 20 May 1990, sec. A, p. 1.

RCA CORPORATION

Bilby, Kenneth. *The General: David Sarnoff and the Rise of the Communications Industry*. New York, N.Y.: Harper and Row, 1986. 326 p.

Cleary, David Powers. "RCA TV/Radio/Stereo; It Is the Use to Which the New Invention Is Put, And Not the Invention Itself, That Determines Its Value to Society." In *Great American Brands: The Success Formulas That Made Them Famous*, 246-255. New York, N.Y.: Fairchild Publications, 1981.

Dreher, Carl. *Sarnoff: An American Success*. New York, N.Y.: Quadrangle/New York Times, 1977. 282 p.

Radio Corporation of America. *RCA: A Historical Perspective, 1919-1984*. Princeton, N.J.: The Company, 1985. 86 p.

RCA: A Collection of Five Articles About RCA. Moorestown, N.J.: The Company, 1971. 36 p.

Sobel, Robert. RCA. New York, N.Y.: Stein & Day, 1986. 282 p.

READER'S DIGEST ASSOCIATION, INC.

Wood, James Playsted. *Of Lasting Interest: The Story of Reader's Digest*. Garden City, N.Y.: Doubleday,

1967. 270 p.

READING COMPANY

Carleton, Paul. *Memories of Reading Company Power, 1833-1976*. Dunnellon, Fla.: D. Carleton Railbooks, 1985. 144 p.

RED RIVER LUMBER COMPANY

Hanft, Robert M. *Red River: Paul Bunyan's Own Lumber Company and Its Railroads*. Chico, Calif.: Center for Business and Economic Research, California State University, Chico, 1980. 304 p.

REDCOM LABORATORIES, INC.

"All About Redcom." *Telephone Engineering & Management (Part 2)* 92 (1 May 1988): 10-11.

REDENBACHER (ORVILLE)

Moore, Frazier. "A Corn for Connoisseurs." *Madison Avenue* 27 (May 1985): 14-18.

REDGATE COMMUNICATIONS CORPORATION

Kingston, Brett. "Ted Leonsis of Redgate Communications Corporation." In *The Dynamos: Who Are They Anyway?*, 217-223. New York, N.Y.: Wiley, 1987.

REEBOK INTERNATIONAL LTD.

Reebok International Ltd. *Backgrounder: Reebok Brands Today*. Stoughton, Mass.: The Company, 1989. 6 p.

REEVE ALEUTIAN AIRWAYS

Ogle, Janice R. *The History of Reeve Aleutian Airways: Fifty Years of Service, 1932-1982*. Anchorage, Alaska: The Company, 1982. 18 p.

REEVES TELECOM CORPORATION

Moore, Harrison L. "Better Off Dead." *Inc.* 1 (December 1979): 50-54.

REGENT CORPORATION

Kingston, Brett. "Avy Stein of Regent Corporation." In *The Dynamos: Who Are They Anyway?*, 65-74. New York, N.Y.: Wiley, 1987.

REHAB (C.P.) CORPORATION

Levitt, Mortimer. "Dean Sloane: Delivering Sophisticated Health Care in a Profitable New Way." In *How to Start Your Own Business Without Losing Your Shirt; Secrets of Seventeen Successful Entrepreneurs*, 97-103. New York, N.Y.: Atheneum, 1988.

RELIABLE LIFE INSURANCE COMPANY

McMahon, Helen Griffin. *Portals to Protection; A History of the Reliable Life Insurance Company from the Perspective of Helen Griffin McMahon*. St. Louis, Mo.: The Company, 1972. 181 p.

REMINGTON ARMS COMPANY

West, Bill. *Remington Arms and History*. 2nd ed., Glendora, Calif.: B. West, 1988. (2 volumes: vol. 1, 1816-1934; vol. 2, to 1989)

REMINGTON PRODUCTS, INC.

Kiam, Victor. *Live to Win: Achieving Success in Life and Business*. New York, N.Y.: Harper and Row, 1989. 258 p.

RENAL SYSTEMS, INC.

Pine, Carol, and Susan Mundale. "Louis Cosentino; Doing

Something Right." In *Self-Made: The Stories of 12 Minnesota Entrepreneurs*, 87-99. Minneapolis, Minn.: Dorn Books, 1982.

REPUBLIC AIRLINES

"Birth of a Major Airline." *Air International* (November 1982): 1-8.

REPUBLICBANK CORPORATION

RepublicBank Corporation. *Republic Bank Corporation.* Dallas, Tex.: The Bank, 1985. 9 p.

REPUBLIC FINANCIAL SERVICES, INC.

Perry, Russell H. *Republic Financial Services, Inc.: Since 1903--A Story of Progress Under the American Free Enterprise System.* New York, N.Y.: Newcomen Society in North America, 1976. 24 p. (Newcomen publication; no. 1042)

RESORTS INTERNATIONAL, INC.

Mahon, Gigi. *The Company That Bought the Boardwalk: A Reporter's Story of How Resorts International Came to Atlantic City.* New York, N.Y.: Random House, 1980. 262 p.

RESTAURANT DEVELOPMENT CORPORATION

Poe, Richard. "Franchise Gold 100--First Place Winners: Grow Up or Die." *Success* 37 (November 1990): 78-92.

RETIREMENT PROGRAM SERVICES

Levitt, Mortimer. "Julian Brodie: Expert Counseling for the New Retiree Market, At Wholesale." In *How to Start Your Own Business Without Losing Your Shirt; Secrets of Seventeen Successful Entrepreneurs*, 69-76.

New York, N.Y.: Atheneum, 1988.

REVLON, INC.

Bender, Marylin. "That Man Revson Leads, But Who Will Follow?" In *At the Top; Behind the Scenes with the Men and Women Who Run America's Corporate Giants*, 124-143. Garden City, N.Y.: Doubleday, 1975.

Tobias, Andrew P. *Fire and Ice: The Story of Charles Revson, The Man Who Built the Revlon Empire*. New York, N.Y.: W. Morrow, 1976. 22 p.

REYNOLDS AND REYNOLDS COMPANY

Meyer, Robert Henry. *The Reynolds and Reynolds Company, "A Peoples Company."* New York, N.Y.: Newcomen Society in North America, 1973. (Newcomen address)

Reynolds and Reynolds Company. *Historical Highlights of the Reynolds and Reynolds Company Founded in 1866*. Dayton, Ohio: The Company, 1985. 26 p.

Reynolds and Reynolds Company. *Timeline--Company History*. Dayton, Ohio: The Company, 1987. 8 p.

REYNOLDS METALS COMPANY

Reynolds Metals Company. *Reynolds Aluminum and the People Who Make It*. Richmond: The Company, 1975. 24 p.

REYNOLDS (R.J.) INDUSTRIES, INC.

Cleary, David Powers. "Camel Cigarettes; Don't Look for Premiums or Coupons..." In *Great American Brands: The Success Formulas That Made Them Famous*, 40-52. New York, N.Y.: Fairchild Publications, 1981.

Reynolds, Patrick. *The Gilded Leaf: Triumph, Tragedy, And Tobacco: Three Generations of the R.J. Reynolds Family and Fortune*. Boston, Mass.: Little, Brown, 1989. 353 p.

R.J. Reynolds Industries. *Our 100th Anniversary, 1875-1975*. Winston-Salem, N.C.: The Company, 1975. 32 p.

Sticht, J. Paul. *The RJR Story: The Evolution of a Global Enterprise*. New York, N.Y.: Newcomen Society in North America, 1983. 28 p. (Newcomen publication; no. 1190)

Tilley, Nannie May. *R.J. Reynolds Tobacco Company*. Chapel Hill: University of North Carolina Press, 1985. 720 p.

SEE ALSO: RJR NABISCO, INC.

RICH (MARK) INTERNATIONAL

Copetas, A. Craig. *Metal Men; Mark Rich and the 10-Billion-Dollar Scam*. New York, N.Y.: Putnam, 1985. 224 p.

RICH PRODUCTS CORPORATION

Rich Products Corporation. *Introduction*. Buffalo, N.Y.: The Company, 1986. 2 p.

RICHARDS FARMS, INC.

Shook, Robert L. "William J. Richards." In *The Entrepreneurs: Twelve Who Took Risks and Succeeded*, 81-91. New York, N.Y.: Harper & Row, 1980.

RICHARDS GROUP

Cooper, Ann. "Steering to Dallas, Tex.: Stan Richards'

Agency Heats Up Texas Ad Scene." *Advertising Age* 57 (27 February 1986): 4-5.

RICHFIELD OIL CORPORATION

Jones, Charles S. *From the Rio Grande to the Arctic; The Story of the Richfield Oil Corporation.* Norman: University of Oklahoma Press, 1972. 364 p.

RICH'S, INC.

Sibley, Celestine. *Dear Store: An Affectionate Portrait of Rich's.* Garden City, N.Y.: Doubleday, 1967. 143 p.

RICKENBACKER INTERNATIONAL CORPORATION

Smith, Richard R. *The History of Rickenbacker Guitars.* Fullerton, Calif.: Centerstream Publications, 1987. 246 p.

RIGGS NATIONAL BANK OF WASHINGTON, D.C.

Carr, Roland T. *32 President's Square.* Forward by Richard Walsh. Washington, D.C. Acropolis Books, 1980.

RJR NABISCO, INC.

Burrough, Bryan. *Barbarians at the Gate: The Fall of RJR Nabisco.* New York, N.Y.: Harper & Row, 1990. 528 p.

Eblen, Tom, and L. Eric Elie. "The RJR Nabisco Story: A History of Dedication to Growth." *Atlanta Constitution*, 21 October 1988, sec. C, p. 8.

Lampert, Hope. *True Greed: What Really Happened in the Battle for RJR Nabisco.* New York, N.Y.: New American Library, 1990.

SEE ALSO: REYNOLDS (R.J.) INDUSTRIES

RKO RADIO PICTURES, INC.

Jewell, Richard B. *The RKO Story*. New York, N.Y.: Arlington House, 1982. 320 p.

ROBBINS AND MYERS, INC.

Robbins & Myers, Inc. *Highlights From Our History, 1878-1978.* Dayton, Ohio: The Company, 1978. 11 p.

Wall, Fred G. *The Standard of the Industry: The Story of Robbins and Myers, Inc.* New York, N.Y.: Newcomen Society in North America, 1978. 16 p. (Newcomen publication; no. 1080)

ROBERTSON (H.H.) COMPANY

Jones, Douglas A. *H.H. Robertson: A Unique International Company.* New York, N.Y.: Newcomen Society in North America, 1966. 24 p. (Newcomen address)

ROBINS (A.H.) COMPANY

A.H. Robins Company. *A.H. Robins: 1866-1978.* Richmond: The Company, 1978. 32 p.

Englemayer, Sheldon D. *Lord's Justice*. Richmond, Va.: Anchor Press, Doubleday, 1985. 300 p.

Mintz, Morton. *At Any Cost: Corporate Greed, Women, And the Dalkon Shield.* New York, N.Y.: Pantheon/Random House, 1985. 308 p.

Robins, E. Clairborne. *"Making Today's Medicines with Integrity--Seeking Tomorrow's with Persistence": The Story of A.H. Robins Company.* New York, N.Y.: Newcomen Society in North America, 1966. 20 p. (Newcomen address)

ROBINSON NUGENT, INC.

Robinson Nugent, Inc. *In Recognition of J.D. Robinson, 1904-1981: From Local Garage to International Manufacturing Facilities.* New Albany, Ind.: The Company, 1983. 6 p.

ROCHESTER AND PITTSBURGH COAL COMPANY

Cooper, Eileen Mountjoy. *Rochester and Pittsburgh Coal Company: The First One Hundred Years.* Indiana, Pa.: The Company, 1982. 224 p.

ROCHESTER TELEPHONE CORPORATION

Howe, F.L. *This Great Contrivance, The First Hundred Years of the Telephone in Rochester.* Rochester, N.Y.: The Company, 1979. 124 p.

ROCKEFELLER GROUP, INC.

Rockefeller Group, Inc. *The Center: A History and Guide to Rockefeller Center.* New York, N.Y.: The Company, 1982. 128 p.

Rockefeller Group, Inc. *The Story of Rockefeller Center; From Facts to Fine Arts.* New York, N.Y.: The Company, 1987. 48 p.

ROCKFORD PET FOODS DIVISION
SEE:
QUAKER OATS COMPANY

ROCKWELL INTERNATIONAL

Braband, Ken C. *The First 50 Years: A History of Collins Radio Company and the Collins Divisions of Rockwell International.* Cedar Rapids, Iowa: Communications Dept., Avionics Group, Rockwell International, 1983. 218 p.

Rockwell International Corporation. *History*. Pittsburgh, Pa.: The Company, 1979. 11 p.

SEE ALSO: NORTH AMERICAN ROCKWELL CORPORATION

ROCKWELL INTERNATIONAL--GRAPHIC SYSTEMS DIVISION

Kogan, H. "Gross--100 Years of Service to Newspapers." *Editor and Publisher Fourth Estate* 118 (4 May 1985): 82-83.

ROCKY MOUNTAIN FUEL COMPANY

Resigno, Richard. "No Final Chapter: The Amazing Story of a Company's Three Decades in Bankruptcy." *Barron's* 61 (20 April 1981): 11, 47-49.

RODDIS PLYWOOD CORPORATION

Huston, Harvey. *The Roddis Line; The Roddis Lumber & Veneer Company Railroad and the Dells & Northeastern Railway*. Winnetka, Ill.: The Company, 1972. 150 p.

RODDY MANUFACTURING COMPANY

Roddy, Pat. *75 Years of Refreshment*. Knoxville, Tenn.: The Company, 1983. 290 p.

ROHM AND HAAS COMPANY

Hochheiser, Sheldon. *Rohm and Haas: History of a Chemical Company*. Philadelphia, Pa.: University of Pennsylvania Press, 1985. 300 p.

ROHR CORPORATION

Austin, Edwin T. *Rohr: The Story of a Corporation*. Chula Vista, Calif.: The Company, 1969. 118 p.

ROPER CORPORATION

Roper Corporation. *Roper Corporation 100, 1874-1974: A Century of Quality*. Kankakee, Ill.: The Company, 1974. 9 p.

RORER, INC.

"Rorer: Civil War to Today, A Pioneer in Health Care." *Drug Topics* 127 (20 June 1983): 72-73.

ROSEBURG LUMBER COMPANY

"A Lumberman's Dream--40 Years of Growth." *Roseburg Woodsman* 22 (March 1976). Special fortieth anniversary issue.

ROSTENBERG, LEONA

Rostenberg, Leona, and Madeleine B. Stern. *Old & Rare; Thirty Years in the Book Business*. New York, N.Y.: A. Schram, 1974. 234 p.

ROTARY CLUB, CHARLOTTE, N.C.

Green, Harold K. *The Rotary Club of Charlotte; 50 Years of "Service Above Self."* Charlotte, N.C.: The Club, 1966. 80 p.

ROTARY CLUB, LAKELAND, FLA.

Lay, Chester Frederic. *Fifty Golden Years, 1918-1968; A Brief History of Lakeland Rotary*. Lakeland, Fla.: The Club, 1968. 69 p.

ROTARY CLUB, OAKLAND, CALIF.

Rotarily Yours; A History of the Rotary Club of Oakland. Oakland, Calif.: The Club, 1969. 224 p.

ROTARY CLUB, PALO ALTO, CALIF.

Rotary Club, Palo Alto, Calif. *The First Fifty Years of the Rotary Club of Palo Alto, 1922-1972; A Chronological Narrative of the Palo Alto Rotary Club's Contributions to Group Fellowship, Community Service, Vocational Ethics, and International Understanding.* Palo Alto, Calif.: The Club, 1972. 96 p.

ROTARY CLUB, TRENTON

History of the Trenton Rotary Club, 1914-1969; Fifty-Five Years of Civic and Social Activities. Prepared under the joint authorship of J. Lewis Unsworth and others. Trenton, N.J.: Published under the auspices of the Trenton Historical Society, 1970. 214 p.

ROTARY INTERNATIONAL

Rotary International. *The World of Rotary.* Elliott McCleary, ed. Evanston, Ill.: The Club, 1975. 144 p. (Rotary International publication; no. 88)

ROTO-ROOTER, INC.

Phalon, Richard. "Roto-Rooter's New Drill." *Forbes* 144 (11 December 1989): 176, 178.

ROUSE COMPANY

Gibbons, Boyd. *Wye Island.* Baltimore, Md.: Published for Resources for the Future by Johns Hopkins University Press, 1977. 227 p.

Meyer, Michael. "The Spiritualist." In *The Alexander Complex: The Dreams That Drive the Great Businessmen*, 107-156. New York, N.Y.: Times Books, 1989.

RUDER FINN, INC.

Finn, David. "Confessions of a Family Company CEO." *Across the Board* 27 (September 1990): 54-58.

RUST-OLEUM CORPORATION

Edwards, H. Wallace. *Gift O' the Sea; The Story of Rust-Oleum*. Evanston, Ill.: The Company, 1971. 151 p.

RYAN AERONAUTICAL COMPANY

Carpenter, Dorr B., and Mitch Mayborn. *Ryan Guidebook, Fifty Years of Ryan Airplanes (1925-1975), Described in Detail Including the Classic S-T, The PT-22, Spirit of St. Louis, Bluebird, Navion, and Broughams*. 2nd ed., Dallas, Tex.: Flying Enterprise Pub., 1976. 120 p.

Cassagneres, Ev. *The Spirit of Ryan*. Blue Ridge Summit, Pa.: Tab Books, 1982. 250 p.

Wagner, William. *Ryan Broughams and Their Builders*. Temple City, Calif.: Historical Aviation Album, 1974. 98 p.

Wagner, William. *Ryan, The Aviator: Being the Adventures and Ventures of Pioneer Airman and Businessman T. Claude Ryan*. New York, N.Y.: McGraw-Hill, 1971. 253 p.

SAFECO INSURANCE COMPANIES

Copeland, Sid. *The Safeco Story, 1923-1980*. Seattle, Wash.: The Companies, 1981. 247 p.

SAFETY-KLEEN CORPORATION

Flax, Steven. "The Little Red Washtub." *Forbes* 127 (27 April 1981): 96, 101.

SAFEWAY STORES

"Ending Our Fiftieth Year: The First Decade." *Safeway News* 31 (February/ March 1976): 1+

"Ending Our Fiftieth Year: The Second Decade." *Safeway News* 31 (April 1976): 7-12.

"Ending Our Fiftieth Year: The Third Decade." *Safeway News* 31 (May/June 1976): 4-10.

"Ending Our Fiftieth Year: The Fourth Decade." *Safeway News* 31 (July 1976): 8-12.

"Ending Our Fiftieth Year: The Fifth Decade." *Safeway News* 31 (August/ September 1976): 5-9.

"Ending Our Fiftieth Year: The Sixth Decade." *Safeway News* 31 (October 1976): 1-12.

Safeway Stores, Inc. *Our 50th Year.* Oakland: The Company, 1975. 25 p. (Published as part of the 1975 annual report).

SAGA CORPORATION

"Corporate History." In *Saga Corporation. Fact Book*, 4-7. Menlo Park, Calif.: The Company, 1984.

ST. JUDE MEDICAL

Pine, Carol, and Susan Mundale. "Manuel Villafana; The Heart of the Matter." In *Self-Made: The Stories of 12 Minnesota Entrepreneurs*, 161-172. Minneapolis, Minn.: Dorn Books, 1982.

ST. LOUIS CAR COMPANY

Lind, Alan R. *From Horsecars to Streamliners: An Illustrated History of the St. Louis Car Company*. Park Forest, Ill.: Transportation History Press, 1978.

400 p.

ST. LOUIS CARDINALS

Broeg, Bob. *Bob Broeg's Redbirds, A Century of Cardinal's Baseball.* St. Louis, Mo.: River City Publishers, 1981.

Leptich, John, and Dave Barnowski. *This Date in St. Louis Cardinals History.* New York, N.Y.: Stein and Day, 1983. 353 p.

ST. PAUL AND TACOMA LUMBER COMPANY

Morgan, Murray Cromwell. *The Mill on the Boot: The Story of the St. Paul and Tacoma Lumber Company.* Seattle, Wash.: University of Washington Press, 1982. 286 p.

ST. REGIS PAPER COMPANY

Amigo, Eleanor, and M. Neuffer. *Beyond the Adirondacks: The Story of St. Regis Paper Company.* Westport, Conn.: Greenwood Press, 1980. 219 p. (Contributions in economics and economic history no. 35)

ST. VINCENT HOSPITAL AND HEALTH CARE CENTER, INC.

Farris, Bain J. *St. Vincent Hospital and Health Care Center, Inc.: Present, Past and Future.* New York, N.Y.: Newcomen Society of the United States, 1988. 24 p. (Newcomen publication; no. 1307)

SALOMON BROTHERS

Lewis, Michael M. *Liar's Poker: Rising Through the Wreckage on Wall Street.* New York, N.Y.: Norton, 1989. 249 p.

Sobel, Robert. *Salomon Brothers, 1910-1985: Advancing to Leadership*. New York, N.Y.: The Company, 1986. 240 p.

SALT LAKE TRIBUNE

Malmquist, O.N. *The First 100 Years: A History of the Salt Lake Tribune, 1871-1971*. Salt Lake City: Utah State Historical Society, 1971. 454 p.

SALT RIVER PROJECT

Salt River Project. *A Valley Reborn: The Story of the Salt River Project*. Phoenix, Ariz.: The Company, 1987. 24 p.

SAMBO'S RESTAURANTS, INC.

Bernstein, Charles. *Sambo's: Only a Fraction of the Action; The Inside Story of a Restaurant Empire's Rise and Fall*. Burbank, Calif.: National Literary Guild, 1984. 197 p.

SAN DIEGO AND CORONADO FERRY COMPANY

San Diego and Coronado Ferry Company. *Pathway Through the Bay*. San Diego, Calif.: The Company, 1969. 8 p.

SAN DIEGO GAS AND ELECTRIC COMPANY

"Centennial Edition, 1881-1981." *News Meter Quarterly* 57, no.1 (1981): 1-47.

SAN FRANCISCO FORTY-NINERS

Peters, Nick. *San Francisco Giants Almanac: Thirty Years of Baseball by the Bay*. Berkeley, Calif.: North Atlantic, 1988. 200 p.

Sullivan, John. *Day by Day in San Francisco Forty-Niners*

History. New York, N.Y.: Leisure Press, 1984. 240 p.

Tuckman, Michael W., and Jeff Schultz. *San Francisco Forty Niners: Team of the Decade; The Inside Story of How They Came from Nowhere to Win Four Super Bowls, Updated to Include the 1989-90 Championship Season*. Rev. ed. Crescent City, Calif.: Prime Publishing Comm., 1990. 280 p.

SAN FRANCISCO GIANTS

Mandel, Mike. *SF Giants, An Oral History*. Santa Cruz: Mandel, 1979. 256 p.

Shea, John, and John Hickey. *Magic by the Bay: How the San Francisco Giants and Oakland Athletics Captured the Baseball World*. Berkeley, Calif.: North Atlantic, 1990. 334 p.

Stein, Fred, and Nick Peters. *Day by Day in Giants History*. New York, N.Y.: Leisure Press, 1985. 304 p.

Stein, Fred, and Nick Peters. *Giants Diary: A Century of Giants Baseball in New York and San Francisco*. Berkely, Calif.: North Atlantic, 1987. 350 p.

SAN JOAQUIN AND EASTERN RAILROAD

Johnston, Hank. *The Railroad That Lighted Southern California*. Los Angeles, Calif.: Trans-Anglo Books, 1965. 128 p.

SANDERS ASSOCIATES, INC.

Sanders Associates, Inc. *Background Information*. South Nashua, N.H.: The Company, 1984. 13 p.

SANDY HILL CORPORATION

Juckett, J. Walter. *In Retrospect*. Burlington, Vt.: G. Little Press, 1982. 376 p.

SANTA FE, PRESCOTT, AND PHOENIX RAILWAY

Sayre, John W. *Santa Fe, Prescott, And Phoenix Railway: The Scenic Line of Arizona.* Boulder, Colo.: Pruett, 1990.

SATCORP

Kingston, Brett. "Jeff Moritz of SATCORP." In *The Dynamos: Who Are They Anyway?*, 23-30. New York, N.Y.: Wiley, 1987.

THE SATURDAY EVENING POST

Friedrich, Otto. *Decline and Fall: The Struggle for Power at a Great American Magazine, The Saturday Evening Post.* New York, N.Y.: Harper and Row, 1970. 499 p.

SEE ALSO: CURTIS PUBLISHING COMPANY

SAUNDERS LEASING SYSTEM, INC.

Saunders, Harris. *Top Up or Down? The Origin and Development of the Automobile and Truck Renting and Leasing Industry--56 Years, 1916-1972.* Birmingham, Ala.: The Company, 1972. 306 p.

SAUNDERS (W.B.) COMPANY

Dusseau, John L. *Informal History of W.B. Saunders Company on the Occasion of Its Hundredth Anniversary.* Philadelphia, Pa.: The Company, 1988. 269 p.

SAVINGS AND LOAN BANK OF THE STATE OF NEW YORK

Eldridge, Charles, John Wilson, and Edward H. Leete. *The Bank That Led the Way: Savings and Loan Bank of the State of New York; The First Fifty Years, 1915-1965*. New York, N.Y.: The Bank, 1966. 258 p.

SAVINGS BANK OF NEW LONDON

Noyes, Gertrude Elizabeth. *The Savings Bank of New London at 150, 1827-1977*. New London, Conn.: The Bank, 1977. 110 p.

SCANA CORPORATION

Warren, John A. *SCANA Corporation: A History of Service*. New York, N.Y.: Newcomen Society of the United States, 1987. 24 p. (Newcomen publication; no. 1296)

SCANDINAVIAN DESIGN, INC.

Rutigliano, Anthony J. "Bob Darvin Is Sitting Pretty." *Management Review* 75 (April 1986): 15-17.

SCHAAK ELECTRONICS

Pine, Carol, and Susan Mundale. "Richard Schaak; The Battler." In *Self-Made: The Stories of 12 Minnesota Entrepreneurs*, 127-143. Minneapolis, Minn.: Dorn Books, 1982.

SCHEDULED SKYWAYS

Quastler, I.E. "A Short History of Scheduled Skyways." In *Air Midwest: The First Twenty Years*, 245-270. San Diego, Calif.: Airline Press of California, 1985.

SCHERING PLOUGH-KENILWORTH NJ

"Schering: The War Baby." *Drug Topics* 127 (18 July 1983): 62-63.

SCHJELDAHL (G.T.) COMPANY
SEE:
SHELDAHL COMPANY

SCHLITZ (JOS) BREWING COMPANY

Rowen, James. "Corporate Lore: The Case of Schlitz." *Across the Board* 21 (September 1984): 55-57.

SCHLUMBERGER LIMITED

Auletta, Ken. *The Art of Corporate Success: The Story of Schlumberger.* New York, N.Y.: Putnam, 1984. 184 p.

SCHNUCK MARKETS, INC.

Partch, Ken. "Schnuck's at 50; The Third Generation Digs In." *Supermarket Business* 45 (January 1990): 17-26, 47.

Schnuck Markets, Inc. *Schnuck's Fact Sheet; Company History.* Bridgeton, Mo.: The Company, 1988. 5 p.

SCHUYLKILL FISHING COMPANY

Wainwright, Nicholas B. *The Schuylkill Fishing Company of the State in Schuylkill, 1732-1982.* Philadelphia, Pa.: The Company, 1982. 150 p.

SCHWAB (CHARLES) AND COMPANY, INC.

Willis, Rod. "Charles Schwab: High-Tech Horatio Alger?" *Management Review* 75 (September 1986): 17-20.

SCHWAN'S SALES ENTERPRISES

Pine, Carol, and Susan Mundale. "Marvin Schwan; The Emperor of Ice Cream." In *Self-Made: The Stories of 12 Minnesota Entrepreneurs*, 57-67. Minneapolis, Minn.: Dorn Books, 1982.

SCOTT AVIATION CORPORATION

Scott, Earle M. *The Saga of Scott Aviation Corporation.* Buffalo: Printed by Artcraft Printers and Lithographers, 1973. 249 p.

SCOTT PAPER COMPANY

Momyer, Robert K. "ScotTowels at 50." *Marketing Communications* 6 (July 1981): 40-41, 45.

SCOTTISH AMERICAN INVESTMENT COMPANY LIMITED

Weir, Ronald B. *A History of the Scottish American Investment Company Limited, 1873-1973.* Edinburgh, Scotland: The Company, 1973. 36 p.

SCRIPPS HOWARD

"History." In *Scripps Howard*, 2-3. Cincinnati, Ohio: The Company, 1987.

Scripps Howard. *Heritage: The Scripps Family Story.* Cincinnati, Ohio: The Company, 1988. 16 p.

SEA ISLAND COMPANY

Gilbert, John. *Sea Island Company, 1930-1980: Alfred W. Jones of Sea Island.* New York, N.Y.: Newcomen Society in North America, 1981. 32 p. (Newcomen publication; no. 1132)

SEABOARD LUMBER AND SHIPPING

Perrault, E.G. *Wood & Water: The Story of Seaboard Lumber and Shipping.* Seattle, Wash.: University of. Washington Press, 1985. 320 p.

SEABORD AIR LINE RAILWAY

Prince, Richard E. *Seabord Air Line Railway: Steam Boats, Locomotives and History*. Green River, Wyo.: The Company, 1969. 268 p.

SEALED AIR CORPORATION

Dunphy, Thomas Joseph Dermot. *Sealed Air Corporation: "Our Products Protect Your Products": A Story of Modern Day Protective Packaging*. New York, N.Y.: Newcomen Society in North America, 1982. 20 p. (Newcomen publication; no. 1173)

SEALED POWER CORPORATION

"History--Chronology of Growth." In *Sealed Power Corporation. Fact File*, 17-18. Muskegon, Mich.: The Company, 1985.

Tuttle, Robert D. *A Tradition of Achievement: The Story of Sealed Power Corporation*. New York, N.Y.: Newcomen Society of the United States, 1986. 24 p. (Newcomen publication; no. 1273)

SEARS, ROEBUCK AND COMPANY

Bjorncrantz, C. Eduard. "Sears' Big Book: Dinosaur or Phoenix." *Direct Marketing* 49 (July 1986): 71-74.

Hoge, Cecil C. *First Hundred Years Are the Toughest; What We Can Learn from the Century of Competition Between Sears and Wards*. Berkeley, Calif.: Ten Speed Press, 1988. 192 p.

Katz, Donald R. *The Big Store: Inside the Crisis and Revolution at Sears*. New York, N.Y.: Viking, 1987. 604 p.

Lawrence, B.H. "Sears' Discounting Gamble." *Washington Post*, 26 March 1989, sec. H, p. 1.

Sears, Roebuck and Company. *Merchant to the Millions, A Brief History of Origins and Development of Sears, Roebuck and Company*. Chicago, Ill.: The Company, 1978. 28 p.

Steck, Robert N. "American Entrepreneurs: Cataloging Success." *D&B Reports* 38 (July/August 1990): 16+

Tedlow, Richard S. "Bringing the Mass Market Home: Sears, Montgomery Ward, And Their Newer Rivals." In *New and Improved: The Story of Mass Marketing in America*, 259-343. New York, N.Y.: Basic Books, 1990.

Weil, Gordon Lee. *Sears, Roebuck, U.S.A.: The Great American Catalog Store and How It Grew*. Briarcliff Manor, N.Y.: Stein and Day, 1977. 277 p.

Worthy, James C. *Shaping an American Institution; Robert E. Wood and Sears, Roebuck*. Urbana: University of Illinois Press, 1984. 344 p.

SEE ALSO: ALLSTATE INSURANCE COMPANY

SEASCOPE SYSTEMS, INC.

Simon, Jane. "Fantasies Come True: Classic Yacht Sailing That's Tax Deductible." *New England Business* 7 (3 June 1985): 48-53.

SEATTLE-FIRST NATIONAL BANK

Scates, Shelby. *Firstbank: The Story of Seattle-First National Bank*. Seattle, Wash.: The Bank, 1970. 130 p.

THE SECOND CITY

Sweet, Jeffrey. *Something Wonderful Right Away*. New York, N.Y.: Avon Books, 1978. 383 p.

SECURITY BENEFIT LIFE INSURANCE COMPANY

Smith, Dean L. *Eleven Men and Eleven Dollars.* Topeka, Kans.: The Company, 1976. 196 p.

Smith, Dean L. *A Nickel a Month.* St. Louis, Mo.: MidAmerica Pub., 1979. 239 p.

SECURITY MUTUAL LIFE INSURANCE COMPANY

Baker, William Gary. "A History of the Security Mutual Life Insurance Company, 1895-1971." Ph.D. diss., University of Nebraska, 1975. 268 p.

Doll, Michael G., and Anita Knopp Doll. *Building on a Century of Service: The History of Security Mutual Life Insurance Company of New York, 1886-1986.* New York, N.Y.: The Company, 1987. 97 p.

SECURITY PACIFIC NATIONAL BANK

Larkin, Frederick G., Jr. *Security Pacific Bank's 100 Years of Keeping Faith with the Community.* New York, N.Y.: Newcomen Society in North America, 1971. 27 p. (Newcomen address)

SECURITY STORAGE COMPANY OF WASHINGTON, D.C.

Gore, Philip Larner. *Around the Corner or Around the World--Move with Security: The Story of Security Storage Company of Washington.* New York, N.Y.: Newcomen Society in North America, 1976. 23 p. (Newcomen publication; no. 1054)

SELZNICK INTERNATIONAL

Behlmer, Rudy. *Memo from David O. Selznick.* New York, N.Y.: Viking Press, 1972. 549 p.

SEVEN OAKS INTERNATIONAL

Fucini, Joseph J., and Suzy Fucini. "Sam A. Sarno, Seven Oaks International: 'The Market Was Wide Open--You Could Not Help But Make Money.'" In *Experience Inc.; Men and Women Who Founded Famous Companies After the Age of 40*, 119-125. New York, N.Y.: Free Press, 1987.

THE 7 SANTINI BROTHERS

Buchholz, Barbara B., and Margaret Crane. "The 7 Santini Brothers, Bronx, NY." In *Corporate Blood Lines: The Future of the Family Firm*, 92-110. New York, N.Y.: Carol Publishing Group, 1989.

SEVENSON CONSTRUCTION CORPORATION

Posner, Bruce G. "Private Lives: Profiles from the Inc. 500--#54: Sevenson Construction Corp." *Inc.* 7 (December 1985): 77-80.

SHAKLEE CORPORATION

Shook, Robert L. *The Shaklee Story*. New York, N.Y.: Harper & Row, 1982. 188 p.

SHAWMUT BANK OF BOSTON

Knowles, Asa S. *Shawmut: 150 Years of Banking, 1836-1986*. Boston, Mass.: Houghton Mifflin, 1986. 533 p.

SHEARSON LOEB RHOADES

Carrington, Tim. *The Year They Sold Wall Street*. Boston, Mass.: Houghton, 1985. 384 p.

SEE ALSO: AMERICAN EXPRESS COMPANY
SEE ALSO: LEHMAN BROTHERS

SHELDAHL COMPANY

Pine, Carol, and Susan Mundale. "G.T. Schjeldahl; A Life of Pure Events." In *Self-Made: The Stories of 12 Minnesota Entrepreneurs*, 69-84. Minneapolis, Minn.: Dorn Books, 1982.

SHELL OIL COMPANY

Beaton, Kendall. *Enterprise in Oil; A History of Shell in the United States*. New York, N.Y.: Appleton-Century-Crofts, 1967. 515 p.

Bridges, Harry. *The Americanization of Shell: The Beginnings and Early Years of Shell Oil Company in the United States*. New York, N.Y.: Newcomen Society in North America, 1972. 26 p. (Newcomen address)

Wells, Barbara. *Shell at Deer Park: The Story of the First Fifty Years*. Houston, Tex.: The Company, 1972. 139 p.

SHENANDOAH LIFE INSURANCE COMPANY

Herbert, Hiram J. *Shenandoah Life, The First Fifty Years, 1916-1966*. Roanoke, Va.: The Company, 1966. 102 p.

SHERWIN-WILLIAMS COMPANY

Cleary, David Powers. "Sherwin-Williams Paints--Not Just to Produce Paints, But to Contribute to Brighter, More Colorful Living." In *Great American Brands: The Success Formulas That Made Them Famous*, 256-260. New York, N.Y.: Fairchild Publications, 1981.

Sherwin-Williams Company. *Century Past Century Future*. Cleveland, Ohio: The Company, 1966.

SHREVE, CRUMP AND LOW COMPANY

Shreve, Crump & Low Co. *Selling Quality Jewels Since 1800; A History of Shreve, Crump & Low Co.* Boston, Mass.: The Company, 1974. 72 p.

SIDLEY AND AUSTIN

Kogan, Herman. *Traditions and Challenges, The Story of Sidley & Austin.* Crawfordsville, Ind.: R.R. Donnelley & Sons, 1983. 464 p.

SIEBERT (MURIEL) AND COMPANY

Taylor, Russel R. "Muriel Siebert; Rebel of Wall Street." In *Exceptional Entrepreneurial Women*, 59-64. New York, N.Y.: Quorum Books, 1988.

SIERRA PACIFIC POWER COMPANY

Stedham, Austin W. *Sierra Pacific Power Company: A Partnership Commitment to Nevada's Future.* New York, N.Y.: Newcomen Society of the United States, 1989. 27 p. (Newcomen publication; no. 1326)

SIFCO INDUSTRIES, INC.

Smith, Charles H. *SIFCO Industries, Inc.: "Forging Ahead."* New York, N.Y.: Newcomen Society in North America, 1984. 23 p. (Newcomen publication; no. 1204)

SIGNODE INDUSTRIES, INC.

Soltow, James H. *Signode: 75 Years and Beyond.* Glenview, Ill.: The Company, 1985. 65 p.

SIKORSKY AIRCRAFT

Siuru, Bill. "Igor Sikorsky: Aviation Pioneer and Engineering Entrepreneur." *Mechanical Engineering*

112 (August 1990): 60-63.

THE SILVER PALATE

Levitt, Mortimer. "Julee Rosso and Sheila Lukins: Gourmet Takeout, Palatable at Any Price." In *How to Start Your Own Business Without Losing Your Shirt; Secrets of Seventeen Successful Entrepreneurs*, 188-194. New York, N.Y.: Atheneum, 1988.

SIMMONS COMPANY

Cleary, David Powers. "Simmons Beautyrest Mattresses; Bedding is Dull and Unappreciated. In Fact, No One Even Sees It; It's Usually Covered with Sheets." In *Great American Brands: The Success Formulas That Made Them Famous*, 261-268. New York, N.Y.: Fairchild Publications, 1981.

SIMON AND SCHUSTER, INC.

Schwed, Peter. *Turning the Pages: An Insider's Story of Simon & Schuster, 1924-1984*. New York, N.Y.: Macmillan, 1984. 300 p.

SIMPLOT (J.R.) COMPANY

Gilder, George. "A Patch of Sand." In *The Spirit of Enterprise*, 23-41. New York, N.Y: Simon and Schuster, 1984.

MacPhee, William. "J.R. (Jack) Simplot of J.R. Simplot Company." In *Rare Breed: The Entrepreneur, An American Culture*, 117-130. Chicago, Ill.: Probus Publishing Company, 1987.

SIMPSON INVESTMENT COMPANY

Simpson Investment Company. *Simpson: A History of Simpson*. Seattle, Wash.: The Company, 1989. 6 p.

SIMPSON LOGGING COMPANY

James, David A. *Grisdale, Last of the Logging Camps; A Photo Story of Simpson Camps from 1890 into 1986: Centennial Supplement, An Album of Big Logs and Old Locomotives*. Washington State centennial edition. Fairfield, Wash.: Ye Galleon Press, 1988. 142 p.

SINCLAIR OIL COMPANY

Sinclair Oil Company. *A Great Name in Oil: Sinclair Through Fifty Years*. New York, N.Y.: F.W. Dodge Company, 1966. 102 p.

SINGER SEWING COMPANY

Brandon, Ruth. *A Capitalist Romance: Singer and the Sewing Machine*. Philadelphia, Pa.: Lippincott, 1977. 244 p.

Cleary, David Powers. "Singer Sewing Machines; If the Purchase Price is a Problem, Why Not Let Her Buy the Machine with Monthly Rental Fees?" In *Great American Brands: The Success Formulas That Made Them Famous*, 269-279. New York, N.Y.: Fairchild Publications, 1981.

SKADDEN, ARPS, SLATE, MEAGHER AND FLOM

Stevens, Mark. "Making Money, Making Rain." In *Power of Attorney: The Rise of the Giant Law Firms*, 101-127. New York, N.Y.: McGraw Hill, 1987.

Wilson, Chase DeKay. "Managing for Success at Skadden, Arps." *International Financial Law Review* 3 (November 1984): 31-35.

SKELLY OIL COMPANY

Ironside, Roberta. *An Adventure Called Skelly; A History of Skelly Oil Company Through Fifty Years,*

1919-1969. New York, N.Y.: Appleton-Century-Crofts, 1970. 147 p.

SKI VIEW, INC.

Levitt, Mortimer. "Joseph Kohler: A 'Burma Shave' Advertising Twist Worth $2.5 Million." In *How to Start Your Own Business Without Losing Your Shirt; Secrets of Seventeen Successful Entrepreneurs*, 61-68. New York, N.Y.: Atheneum, 1988.

SLOPPY JOE'S BAR

Wells, Sharon. *Sloppy Joe's Bar; The First Fifty Years*. Key West, Fla.: Key West Saloon, Inc., 1983. 56 p.

SMITH AND WESSON, INC.

Jinks, Roy G. *History of Smith Wesson: Nothing of Importance Will Come Without Effort*. North Hollywood, Calif.: Beinfeld Publishing Company, 1977. 290 p.

SMITH FARMS

Buchholz, Barbara B., and Margaret Crane. "Smith Farms, Chula, MO." In *Corporate Blood Lines: The Future of the Family Firm*, 127-144. New York, N.Y.: Carol Publishing Group, 1989.

SMITH, HINCHMAN AND GRYLLS ASSOCIATES, INC.

Meathe, Philip J. *Smith, Hinchman & Grylls Associates, Inc., Architects, Engineers, Planners*. New York, N.Y.: Newcomen Society in North America, 1979. 30 p. (Newcomen publication; no. 1106)

SMITH TOOL

Schlee, B. Carolyn. *From Blacksmith to Blackgoldsmiths,*

The Story of Smith Tool. Newport Beach, Calif.: The Company, 1977. 101 p.

SMITHKLINE CORPORATION

Marion, John Francis. *The Fine Old House: SmithKline Corporation's First 150 Years.* Philadelphia, Pa.: The Company, 1980. 251 p.

SEE ALSO: BECKMAN INSTRUMENTS

SMITH'S TRANSFER CORPORATION

Brown, Charles D. *Fifty Years Down the Road: The Story of Smith's Transfer 1930-1980.* Verona, Va.: McClure Press, 1981. 128 p.

SMUCKER (J.M.) COMPANY

Ellis, William Donohue. *With a Name Like--.* Orville, Ohio: The Company, 1987. 161 p.

SNAP-ON TOOLS CORPORATION

Snap-On Tools Corporation. *Snap-On Tools Corporation, 1920-1980's.* Kenosha, Wis.: The Company, 1984. 28 p.

SOFT SHEEN PRODUCTS INC.

Solomon, Kenneth I., Peter F. Cieslak, and Boris Weisman. "Soft Sheen Products, Inc.: 'The Miracle on 87th Street.'" *Perspective* 9 (1983): 24-28.

SOLOMON EQUITIES

Kingston, Brett. "David Solomon of Solomon Equities." In *The Dynamos: Who Are They Anyway?*, 145-151. New York, N.Y.: Wiley, 1987.

SONOCO PRODUCTS COMPANY

Coker, Charles W. *The Story of SONOCO Products Company*. New York, N.Y.: Newcomen Society in North America, 1976. 23 p. (Newcomen publication; no. 999)

SONOCO Products Company. *A Commitment to Values, The SONOCO Tradition*. Hartsville, S.C.: The Company, 1985. 15 p.

SOO LINE RAILROAD COMPANY

Abbey, Wallace W. *The Little Jewel: Soo Line Railroad Company and the Locomotives That Make It Go*. Pueblo, Colo.: Pinion Productions, 1984. 216 p.

SOTHEBY PARKE BERNET, INC.

Faith, Nicholas. *Sold: The Rise and Fall of the House of Sotheby*. New York, N.Y.: Macmillan, 1985. 269 p.

Herrmann, Frank. *Sotheby's: Portrait of an Auction House*. New York, N.Y.: Norton, 1981, c1980. 468 p.

Hogrefe, Jeffrey. *"Wholly Unacceptable": The Bitter Battle for Sotheby's*. New York, N.Y.: W. Morrow, 1986. 238 p.

Norton, Thomas E. *100 Years of Collecting in America; The Story of Sotheby Parke Bernet*. New York, N.Y.: H.N. Abrams, 1984. 240 p.

SOUTH CAROLINA NATIONAL BANK

Lindley, James G. *South Carolina National: The First 150 Years*. New York, N.Y.: Newcomen Society of the United States, 1985. 24 p. (Newcomen publication; no. 1245)

Rogers, George C. *The South Carolina National Bank; The First One Hundred and Fifty Years.* Columbia, S.C.: The Bank, 1984. 99 p.

SOUTH CENTRAL BELL IN MISSISSIPPI

Edmonds, N. Frank. *South Central Bell in Mississippi.* New York, N.Y.: Newcomen Society in North America, 1981. 24 p. (Newcomen publication; no. 1128)

SOUTH JERSEY INDUSTRIES, INC.

Gemmel, William A. *From Small Beginnings: A History of South Jersey Industries, Inc. and South Jersey Gas Company, 1910-1985.* Folsom, N.J.: W.A. Gemmel, 1987. 256 p.

SOUTHERN BANCORPORATION OF ALABAMA

Gaffey, Guy H., Jr. *Southern Bancorporation of Alabama: A Story of Safety, Service, Integrity, Innovation, and Growth.* New York, N.Y.: Newcomen Society in North America, 1975. 18 p. (Newcomen publication; no. 1026)

SOUTHERN BELL TELEPHONE AND TELEGRAPH COMPANY

Park, David G., Jr. *Good Connections, A Century of Service by Men and Women of Southern Bell.* St. Louis, Mo.: The Company, 1984. 300 p.

Southern Bell. *Legacy and Promise: The Story of Southern Bell.* Atlanta, Ga.: The Company, 1984. 64 p.

SOUTHERN CALIFORNIA EDISON COMPANY

Myers, William A. *Iron Men and Copper Wires: A Centennial History of the Southern California Edison*

Company. Glendale, Calif.: Trans-Anglo Books, 1983. 255 p.

Whitaker, James B. *Strategic Planning in a Rapidly Changing Environment.* Lexington, Mass.: Lexington Books, 1978.

THE SOUTHERN COMPANY

Branch, Hallee, Jr. *Alabama Power Company and the Southern Company.* New York, N.Y.: Newcomen Society in North America, 1967. 24 p. (Newcomen address)

SOUTHERN PACIFIC RAILROAD COMPANY

Hofsommer, Donovan L. *The Southern Pacific, 1901-1985.* College Station, Tex.: Texas A&M University Press, 1986. 373 p.

SOUTHERN PINE LUMBER COMPANY

Walker, Lawrence C. *Axes, Oxen, and Men: A Pictorial History of the Southern Pine Lumber Company.* Diboll, Tex.: Angelina Free Press, 1975. 73 p.

THE SOUTHERN RAILWAY COMPANY

Davis, Burke. *The Southern Railway: Road of the Innovators.* Chapel Hill, N.C.: University of North Carolina Press, 1985. 309 p.

SOUTHERN SAW SERVICE, INC.

Brown, Edmund D. *1594 Evans Drive, S.W.: A History of Southern Saw Service, Inc., And the Atlanta Saw Service.* Atlanta, Ga.: The Company, 1983. 213 p.

SOUTHERN UNION GAS COMPANY

Chesnutt, N.P. *Southern Union.* El Paso, Tex.: Mangan

Books, 1979. 216 p.

SOUTHLAND CORPORATION

Liles, Allen. *Oh Thank Heaven! The Story of the Southland Corporation.* Dallas, Tex.: The Company, 1977. 264 p.

SOUTHWEST AIRLINES

Southwest Airlines. *Southwest Airlines History.* Dallas, Tex.: The Company, 1984. 31 p.

Walker, Tom. "Southwest: The First Ten Years." *Southwest Airlines Magazine* 10 (June 1981): 1-13.

SOUTHWIRE COMPANY

Cumming, Joseph B. *Roy Richards: The Man--The Legend--The Legacy.* Carrollton, Ga.: The Company, 1987. 24 p.

Richards, Roy. *A Southern Adventure in Free Enterprise: The Story of Southwire Company.* New York, N.Y.: Newcomen Society in North America, 1966. 24 p. (Newcomen address)

SPALDING AND EVENFLO COMPANIES, INC.

Cleary, David Powers. "Spalding Sporting Goods; Spalding Has Gone into the Baseball Business." In *Great American Brands: The Success Formulas That Made Them Famous,* 280-286. New York, N.Y.: Fairchild Publications, 1981.

SPARKMAN AND STEPHENS

Kinney, Francis S. *"You Are First": The Story of Olin and Rod Stephens of Sparkman & Stephens, Inc.* New York, N.Y.: Dodd, Mead, 1978. 327 p.

SPENCER STUART AND ASSOCIATES

Stuart, Spencer R. *Spencer Stuart & Associates, 25 Years of Professional Leadership in Executive Search Consulting.* New York, N.Y.: Newcomen Society in North America, 1982. 24 p. (Newcomen publication; no. 1163)

SPERRY RAND CORPORATION

Lundstrom, David H. *A Few Good Men from Univac.* Cambridge, Mass.: MIT Press, 1987. 227 p. (MIT Press series in the history of computing)

SPIEGEL, INC.

Cornell, James, Jr. *The People Get the Credit: The First One Hundred Years of the Spiegel Story, 1865-1965.* Chicago, Ill.: The Company, 1965. 171 p.

Smalley, Orange A. *The Credit Merchants; A History of Spiegel, Inc.* Introduction by: Harold F. Williamson. Carbondale: Southern Illinois University Press, 1973. 336 p.

SPIRAL PRESS, INC.

Blumenthal, Joseph. *Typographic Years, A Printer's Journey Through a Half-Century, 1925-1975.* New York, N.Y.: F.C. Bell, 1982. 153 p.

Pierpont Morgan Library. *The Spiral Press Through Four Decades; An Exhibition of Books and Ephemera; With a Commentary by Joseph Blumenthal.* New York, N.Y.: Pierpont Morgan Library, 1966. 66 p.

SPIR-IT, INC.

Koselka, Rita. "Stirring Story." *Forbes* 146 (12 November 1990): 308, 310.

SPRAGUE (C.H.) AND SON COMPANY

Powers, Henry M. *C.H. Sprague and Son Company: A New England Colossus.* New York, N.Y.: Newcomen Society of the United States, 1985. 24 p. (Newcomen publication; no. 1252)

SPRINGS INDUSTRIES, INC.

"Colonel's Different Kind of Company." *Textile World* *125* (December 1975): 51+

SQUARE D COMPANY

Square D Company. *About Square D.* Paletine, Ill.: The Company, 1985. 20 p.

Stead, Jerre L. *Square D: Profits, Dividends for 54 Consecutive Years: Global Leader in Industrial Controls and Electrical Distribution.* New York, N.Y.: Newcomen Society of the United States, 1990. 24 p. (Newcomen publication; no. 1343)

SQUIBB CORPORATION

Furlaud, Richard M. *Squibb Corporation: Its First Four Years.* New York, N.Y.: The Company, 1971.

STALEY (A.E.) MANUFACTURING COMPANY

Forrestal, Dan J. *The Kernel and the Bean; The 75-Year Story of the Staley Company.* New York, N.Y.: Simon & Schuster, 1982. 315 p.

STANDARD CORPORATION, OGDEN, UTAH

Hatch, Wilda Gene. *A Pioneer in Communications; The History of the Ogden Standard-Examiner and the Electronic Advancements of the Standard Corporation.* New York, N.Y.: Newcomen Society in North America, 1972. 27 p.

STANDARD FRUIT AND STEAMSHIP COMPANY

Karnes, Thomas L. *Tropical Enterprise: The Standard Fruit and Steamship Company in Latin America.* Baton Rouge: Louisiana State University Press. 1978. 332 p.

SEE ALSO: CASTLE AND COOKE, INC.

STANDARD LIFE INSURANCE COMPANY

Newman, W.R., III. *"Bucking Like a Mule": The Story of Standard Life.* New York, N.Y.: Newcomen Society in North America, 1972. 24 p. (Newcomen address)

STANDARD OIL COMPANY

Destler, Chester McArthur. *Roger Sherman and the Independent Oil Men.* Ithaca, N.Y.: Cornell University Press, 1967. 305 p.

Gray, Edmund R., and C. Ray Gullett. *Employee Representation at Standard Oil Company of New Jersey: A Case Study.* Baton Rouge: Division of Research, College of Business Administration, Louisiana State University, 1973. 40 p.

STANDARD OIL COMPANY OF CALIFORNIA

Haynes, Harold J. *Standard Oil Company of California: 100 Years Helping to Create the Future.* New York, N.Y.: Newcomen Society in North America, 1980. 22 p. (Newcomen publication; no. 1115)

Standard Oil Company of California. *The First 100 Years.* San Francisco, Calif.: The Company, 1979. 10 p.

STANDARD OIL COMPANY OF INDIANA

Dedmon, Emmett. *Challenge and Response; A Modern History of the Standard Oil Company (Indiana).*

Chicago, Ill.: Mobium Press, 1984. 324 p.

STANDARD OIL COMPANY OF NEW JERSEY

Gray, Edmund R., and C. Ray Gullett. *Employee Representation at Standard Oil Company of New Jersey: A Case Study*. Baton Rouge: Division of Research, College of Business Administration, Louisiana State University, 1973. 40 p.

History of Standard Oil Company (New Jersey). New York, N.Y.: Harper, 1955-1971. 3 volumes.

Wall, Bennett H., and George S. Gibb. *Teagle of Jersey Standard*. New Orleans, La.: Tulane University, 1974. 386 p.

SEE ALSO: EXXON CORPORATION

STANDARD RATE AND DATA SERVICE, INC.

Myers, Kenneth H. *SRDS: The National Authority Serving the Media-Buying Function*. Evanston, Ill.: Northwestern University Press, 1968. 335 p.

STANDARD SCREW COMPANY

Taylor, James A. *"Minding Our Business": The Story of Standard Screw Company*. New York, N.Y.: Newcomen Society in North America, 1969. 32 p. (Newcomen address)

THE STANLEY WORKS

Davis, Donald W. *The Stanley Works: A 125 Year Beginning*. New York, N.Y.: Newcomen Society in North America, 1969. 24 p. (Newcomen address)

STAR PIN COMPANY OF SHELTON, CONN.

Heusser, Audrey E. "The First One-Hundred Years of a

People Oriented Company." *Connecticut Industry* 44 (September 1966): 6-7+

STATE AUTOMOBILE MUTUAL INSURANCE COMPANY

Gingher, Paul R. *Running Mates: The Story of State Automobile Mutual Insurance Company and Columbus Mutual Life Insurance Company.* New York, N.Y.: Newcomen Society in North America, 1978. 30 p. (Newcomen publication; no. 1090)

STATE BANK OF ROSHOLT, WIS.

Rosholt, Malcolm Leviatt. *76th Anniversary of the State Bank of Rosholt, 1904-1980.* Rosholt, Wis.: The Bank, 1980. 16 p.

STATE MUTUAL LIFE ASSURANCE COMPANY OF AMERICA

State Mutual Life Assurance Company of America. *25 Years, 1957-1982.* Worcester, Mass.: The Company, 1982. 28 p. (*Intercom* special issue)

STATE NATIONAL BANK OF EL PASO

Sonnichsen, Charles Leland. *The State National Since 1881: The Pioneer Bank of El Paso.* El Paso, Tex.: Texas Western Press, 1971. 171 p.

STATEN ISLAND RAPID TRANSIT RAILWAY

Staten Island Rapid Transit Railway. *Staten Island Rapid Transit Railway: 1860-1965.* Brooklyn, N.Y.: Silver Leaf Rapid Transit, 1965. 63 p.

STEIFF

Bohlin, Virginia. "Rare Steiff Dolls Sell for $1,500 to $8,000." *Boston Globe*, 1 April 1990, sec. B, p. 43.

STEVENS (J.P.) AND COMPANY

Conway, Mimi. *Rise Gonna Rise: A Portrait of Southern Textile Workers*. Garden City, N.Y.: Anchor Press, 1979. 228 p.

Ferguson, Lloyd C. *From Family Firm to Corporate Giant; J.P. Stevens and Company, 1813-1963*. Braintree, Mass.: D.H. Mark Publishing Company, 1970. 33 p.

STICKLEY (L&J G), INC.

Machan, Dyan. "Rescuing a Proud Name." *Forbes* 145 (5 February 1990): 132-136.

STOCKTON SAVINGS ASSOCIATION

Kingston, Brett. "Brett Davis of Stockton Savings Association/Troy and Nichols Mortgage Company." In *The Dynamos: Who Are They Anyway?*, 11-20. New York, N.Y.: Wiley, 1987.

STONE AND WEBSTER ENGINEERING CORPORATION

Allen, William F., Jr. "Evolution in an Industry--As Seen by an Engineer." *Public Utilities Fortnightly* 124 (20 July 1989): 15-20.

Allen, William F., Jr. *Stone & Webster: A Century of Service*. New York, N.Y.: Newcomen Society of the United States, 1989, c1990. 26 p. (Newcomen publication; no. 1338)

STONE CONTAINER CORPORATION

Stone, Marvin N. *Stone Container Corporation: A Story of Growth in the American Tradition*. New York, N.Y.: Newcomen Society in North America, 1975. 24 p. (Newcomen publication; no. 1004)

STONE MANUFACTURING COMPANY

Stone, Eugene E. *Stone Manufacturing Company: The First Half-Century of Clothing a Changing World.* New York, N.Y.: Newcomen Society of the United States, 1985. 22 p. (Newcomen publication; no. 1222)

STONEYFIELD FARM (N.H.)

Kummer, C. "Yogurt Moguls." *New England Monthly* (June 1989): 24+

STORY MAGAZINE

Foley, Martha. *The Story of Story Magazine: A Memoir.* New York, N.Y.: Norton, 1980. 288 p.

STP CORPORATION

Brufke, Edward F. *The Racer's Edge; Andy Granatelli and the STP Corporation.* Braintree, Mass.: D.H. Mark Publishing Company, 1971. 28 p.

STRAUS-FRANK COMPANY

Lanzone, John A. *Horse, Next to Woman, God's Greatest Gift to Man; A History of the Straus-Frank Company.* San Antonio: The Company, 1970. 72 p.

STRAWBRIDGE AND CLOTHIER

Lief, Alfred. *Family Business: A Century in the Life and Times of Strawbridge and Clothier.* New York, N.Y.: McGraw-Hill, 1968. 343 p.

Veale, Frank R. *Family Business: Strawbridge and Clothier; The Momentous Seventies.* Philadelphia, Pa.: The Company, 1981. 224 p.

STUDEBAKER CORPORATION

Cannon, William A. *Studebaker: The Complete Story.* Blue Ridge Summit, Pa.: Tab Books, 1981. 368 p.

Hall, Asa E., and Richard M. Langworth. *The Studebaker Century: A National Heritage.* Contoocook, N.H.: Dragonwyck Publications, 1983. 192 p.

Langworth, Richard M. *Studebaker: The Postwar Years.* Osceola, Wis.: Motorbooks International, 1979. 195 p.

Mayborn, Mitch. *Studebaker: The Last Years of Studebaker, 1952-1966.* 2d ed. Dallas, Tex.: Highland Enterprises, 1974. 52 p.

SUBARU OF AMERICA, INC.

Posner, Bruce G., and Steven Pearlstein. "Auto Entrepreneur Harvey Lamm." *Inc.* 10 (June 1988): 44-54.

SUBURBAN PROPANE GAS CORPORATION

Anton, Mark J. *Suburban Propane Gas Corporation: The Development of a Selectively Positioned Energy Company.* New York, N.Y.: Newcomen Society in North America, 1982. 20 p. (Newcomen publication; no. 1167)

SUBURBAN TRUST COMPANY

Sherwood, J. Robert. *The Story of Suburban Trust Company: A Bank with Vision.* New York, N.Y.: Newcomen Society in North America, 1968. 28 p. (Newcomen address)

SUN COMPANY

Johnson, Arthur M. *The Challenge: The Sun Oil Company, 1947-1977.* Columbus: Ohio State

University Press, 1983. 481 p.

Sun Company. *Celebrating a Century of Energy, 1886-1986.* Radner, Pa.: The Company, 1985. 72 p.

SUN MICROSYSTEMS

Kingston, Brett. "Andreas Bechtolsheim, Vinod Khosla, Bill Joy, and Scott McNealy of the SUN Microsystems Team." In *The Dynamos: Who Are They Anyway?*, 49-60. New York, N.Y.: Wiley, 1987.

SUN OIL COMPANY
SEE:
SUN COMPANY

SUNDSTRAND CORPORATION

Sundstrand Corporation. *A History of the Company.* Rockford, Ill.: The Company, 1985. 10 p.

SUNDT (M.M.) CONSTRUCTION COMPANY

Sundt, M. Eugene, and W.E. Naumann. *M.M. Sundt Construction Company: "From Small Beginnings--."* New York, N.Y.: Newcomen Society in North America, 1975. 36 p. (Newcomen publication; no. 993)

SUNFLOWER FOOD STORES

Lewis, Morris, Jr. *Wholesaler--Retailer: The Story of Lewis Grocer Company and the Sunflower Food Stores.* New York, N.Y.: Newcomen Society in North America, 1975. 21 p. (Newcomen publication; no. 1021)

SUNKIST GROWERS, INC.

"Part I--History." In *The Sunkist Adventure*, 5-18. Washington, D.C.: U.S. Department of Agriculture,

Farmer Cooperative Service, 1975. (FCS Information no. 94)

SUNLITE, INC.

Luke, Robert. "Sunlite Is Stepping Out of the Shade to Try a New Tactic." *Atlanta Constitution*, 5 July 1989, sec. E, p. 2.

SUNSET MAGAZINE

Lane, L.W., Jr. *The Sunset Story, To Serve the Westerner--And No One Else...* New York, N.Y.: Newcomen Society of the United States, 1973. 29 p. (Newcomen publication; no. 966)

SUNSHINE STATE BANK

Adams, James Ring. "Darkness at Sunshine State." In *The Big Fix: Inside the S&L Scandal: How an Unholy Alliance of Politics and Money Destroyed America's Banking System*, 125-142. New York, N.Y.: Wiley, 1990.

SUNSWEET GROWERS, INC.

Couchman, Robert. *The Sunsweet Story; A History of the Establishment of the Dried Fruit Industry in California and of the 50 Years of Service of Sunsweet Growers, Inc.* San Jose, Calif.: The Company, 1967. 139 p.

SUPERMARKETS GENERAL CORPORATION

"Happy Birthday, Everybody! Pathmark is Ten Years Old." *Pathmark News* (September 1978): 1-4.

SUPERSCOPE, INC.
SEE:
MARANTZ CORPORATION

SUPREME LIFE INSURANCE COMPANY

Puth, Robert C. *Supreme Life: The History of a Negro Life Insurance Company.* New York, N.Y.: Arno Press, 1976, c1968. 293 p. (Originally presented as the author's thesis, Northwestern University, 1967)

SVERDRUP CORPORATION

Franzwa, Gregory M. *Challenge: The Sverdrup Story Continues.* St. Louis, Mo.: Patrice Press, 1988. 204 p.

Franzwa, Gregory M. *Legacy, The Sverdrup Story.* St. Louis, Mo.: The Company, 1978. 286 p.

SWAN LAND AND CATTLE COMPANY

Mothershead, Harmon Ross. *The Swan Land and Cattle Company, Ltd.* Norman, Okla.: University of Oklahoma Press, 1971. 203 p.

SWEET ADELINES, INC.

Parsons, Sandra. *30 Years of Harmony, Sweet Adelines, Inc., 1947-1977.* Tulsa, Okla.: The Company, 1978. 162 p.

SWIFT AND COMPANY

Darby, Edwin. "Swift." In *The Fortune Builders*, 117-135. Garden City, N.Y.: Doubleday and Company, Inc., 1986.

SWIFTE AIR LINES

Quastler, I.E. *Swifte Air Lines, 1969-1979: The History of an American Commuter Airline.* San Diego, Calif.: Commuter Airlines Press, 1979. 126 p.

SYNTEX CORPORATION

"The Roots of Syntex." In *About Syntex Corporation*, 2-3. Palo Alto, Calif.: The Company, 1982.

SYSCO CORPORATION

Sysco Corporation. *The Sysco Story*. Houston, Tex.: The Company, n.d. 16 p.

SYSCO/FROST-PACK FOOD SERVICES, INC.

Geelhoed, E. Bruce. *The Thrill of Success: The Story of SYSCO/Frost-Pack Food Services, Inc.* Muncie, Ind.: Bureau of Business Research, College of Business and Department of History, Ball State University, 1983. 96 p. (Ball State University business history series; no.2)

SYSTEM DEVELOPMENT CORPORATION

Baum, Claude. *The System Builders: The Story of SDC*. Santa Monica, Calif.: The Company, 1981. 302 p.

T&K ROOFING COMPANY

Hyatt, Joshua. "Inc. 500: Out of the Ordinary." *Inc.* 12 (December 1990): 110-120.

T-BAR, INC.

Eisenberg, Evan, and Howard Eisenberg. "A Firm That Integrity Built." *Small Business Report* 9 (September 1984): 79-83.

TAFT BROADCASTING COMPANY

Taft Broadcasting Company. *History of Taft Broadcasting Company*. Cincinnati, Ohio: The Company, 1985. 16 p.

TALKEETNA AIR SERVICE

Greiner, James. *Wager the Wind: The Don Sheldon Story*. Chicago, Ill.: Rand McNally, 1974. 255 p.

TANDEM COMPUTERS

Isaac, Debra. "Tandem's Twofold Task." *Management Today* (November 1984): 70-73, 153-156.

TANDY CORPORATION

Lappen, Alyssa A. "Tandy Corp.: 'We're Still Here.'" *Forbes* 146 (26 November 1990): 191-195.

West, James L. *Tandy Corporation: "Start on a Shoe String."* New York, N.Y.: Newcomen Society in North America, 1968. 24 p. (Newcomen address)

TANNER (O.C.) COMPANY

Tanner, Obert C. *Commitment to Beauty*. New York, N.Y: Newcomen Society in North America, 1982. 23 p. (Newcomen publication; no. 1146) .

TCBY ENTERPRISES, INC.

Fucini, Joseph J., and Suzy Fucini. "Frank D. Hickingbotham; TCBY Enterprises, Inc.: 'The Time Was Right for a National Frozen Yogurt Chain.'" In *Experience Inc.; Men and Women Who Founded Famous Companies After the Age of 40*, 9-15. New York, N.Y.: Free Press, 1987.

TDINDUSTRIES, INC.

Rosenstein, Joseph. "TDIndustries: An Employee-Owned Company." *Journal of Management Case Studies* 3 (Spring 1987): 80-89.

TDK USA CORPORATION

"TDK; Portrait of a Company in Fast Forward." *Audio* 68 (August 1984). (Special advertising supplement)

TEC, INC.

TEC, Inc. *Background of TEC, Inc.* Tucson: The Company, 1981. 4 p.

TECO ENERGY, INC.

Culbreath, H.L. *The TECO Energy Story: Fueling Growth for 90 Years.* New York, N.Y.: Newcomen Society of the United States, 1988. 23 p. (Newcomen publication; no. 1315)

TEELING AND GALLAGHER

"Service and Continuity Are the Keys to Success." *Agency Sales Magazine* 17 (March 1987): 4-9.

TELERATE, INC.

Stein, Jon, and Ginger Szala. "Neal Hirsch; Tim Slater." *Futures: The Magazine of Commodities and Options (Profiles Issue)* 17 (July 1988): 25-29.

TENNECO, INC.

Tenneco, Inc. *Tenneco's First 35 Years.* Houston, Tex.: The Company, 1978. 16 p.

TEXACO, INC.

Coll, Steve. *The Taking of Getty Oil: The Full Story of the Most Spectacular and Catastrophic Takeover of All Time.* New York, N.Y.: Atheneum/Macmillan Pub., 1987. 528 p.

Petzinger, Thomas, Jr. *Oil and Honor, The Texaco-Pennzoil Wars.* New York, N.Y.: Putnam, 1987. 416 p.

Shannon, James. *Texaco and the $10 Billion Jury.* Englewood Cliffs, N.J.: Prentice Hall, 1988. 545 p.

Texaco, Inc. *A Short History of Texaco, Inc., 1902-1984.* White Plains, N.Y.: The Company, 1984. 33 p.

TEXAS AND PACIFIC RAILWAY

Collias, Joe G. *The Texas and Pacific Railway: Super-Power to Steamliners, 1925-1975.* Crestwood, Mo.: M.M. Books, 1989. 159 p.

TEXAS COMMERCE BANCSHARES, INC.

Stuart, Alexander. "Ben Love Conquers All in Houston." *Fortune* 100 (19 November 1979): 122-132.

TEXAS EASTERN CORPORATION

Bufkin, I. David. *Texas Eastern Corporation, "A Pioneering Spirit."* New York, N.Y.: Newcomen Society in North America, 1983. 24 p. (Newcomen publication; no. 1187)

TEXAS GULF SULPHUR COMPANY, INC.

Patrick, Kenneth G. *Perpetual Jeopardy, The Texas Gulf Sulphur Affair, A Chronicle of Achievement and Misadventure.* New York, N.Y: Macmillan, 1972. 363 p.

Shulman, Morton. *The Billion Dollar Windfall.* New York, N.Y.: Morrow, 1970, c1969. 239 p.

TEXAS INSTRUMENTS

Bagamery, Ann. "Texas Instruments in Mid-Life." *Forbes*

129 (15 March 1982): 64-69.

Texas Industrial Commission. *Texas Instruments: Global Growth from Seismology to Space Age Technology*. Dallas, Tex.: The Company, 1971.

Texas Instruments. *A Brief History of Texas Instruments*. Dallas, Tex.: The Company, 1982. 3 p.

TEXAS RANGERS

Rodgers, Phil. *Impossible Takes a Little Longer: The Texas Rangers from Pretenders to Contenders*. Dallas, Tex.: Taylor Pub., 1990. 232 p.

TEXASGULF

Fogarty, Charles F. *The Story of Texasgulf: A Story of People Dedicated to Finding, Developing, And Conserving Natural Resources Essential to a Higher Standard of Living for Everyone*. New York, N.Y.: Newcomen Society in North America, 1976. 40 p. (Newcomen publication; no. 1033)

TEXTRON, INC.

Eisenhauer, Robert S. *Textron--From the Beginning*. Providence: The Company, 1979. 147 p.

Little, Royal. *How to Lose $100,000,000 and Other Valuable Advice*. Boston, Mass.: Little, Brown, 1979. 334 p.

Textron, Inc. *The Royal Little Story*. Providence, R.I.: The Company, 1966.

T.G.&Y. STORES

Faulk, Odie B. *The Making of a Merchant: R.A. Young and T.G.&Y Stores*. Oklahoma City, Okla.: Western Heritage Books, 1980. 284 p.

THOMAS BROTHERS MAP COMPANY

"The Thomas Bros. Map Company." *Los Angeles* (April 1986): 121+

THOMAS (S.N.) SONS

Thomas, Leon S. *S.N. Thomas' Sons and Norman Shirtmakers: "A Family Affair."* New York, N.Y.: Newcomen Society in North America, 1979. 20 p. (Newcomen publication; no. 1105)

THOMPSON (J.) WALTER

Millman, Nancy. In *Emperors of Adland; Inside the Advertising Revolution*, 159-176. New York, N.Y.: Warner Books, 1988.

Morgan, Richard. *J. Walter Takeover: From Divine Right to Common Stock*. Homewood, Ill.: Business One IRWIN, 1990. 254 p.

THOUSAND TRAILS, INC.

Rhodes, Lucien. "How Thousand Trails Got Out of the Woods." *Inc.* 3 (November 1981): 78-88.

3M CORPORATION
SEE:
MINNESOTA MINING AND MANUFACTURING CORPORATION

TICOR

Loebbecke, Ernest J. *Serving the Nation's Needs for Diversified Financial Services: The Story of the T.I.Corporation of California*. New York, N.Y.: Newcomen Society in North America, 1973. 23 p. (Newcomen publication; no. 983)

TIDY CAR, INC.

Shook, Robert L. "Gary Goranson." In *The Entrepreneurs: Twelve Who Took Risks and Succeeded*, 93-101. New York, N.Y.: Harper & Row, 1980.

TIFFANY AND COMPANY

Carpenter, Charles, and Janet Zapata. *The Silver of Tiffany & Co., 1850-1987*. Boston, Mass.: Museum of Fine Arts, 1987. 63 p.

Loring, John. *Tiffany's, One Hundred and Fifty Years*. New York, N.Y.: Doubleday, 1987. 240 p.

Purtell, Joseph. *The Tiffany Touch*. New York, N.Y.: Pocket Books, 1973. 390 p.

Schneirla, Peter. *Tiffany, 150 Years of Gems and Jewelry*. New York, N.Y: The Company, 1987. 10 p.

TIGER INTERNATIONAL, INC.

"The First Thirty Years." *Tiger Spirit* 1 (April 1978): 11-27.

TII INDUSTRIES, INC.

Fucini, Joseph J., and Suzy Fucini. "Alfred J. Roach, TII Industries, Inc.: 'There are Still So Many New Ideas to Be Tried.'" In *Experience Inc.; Men and Women Who Founded Famous Companies After the Age of 40*, 30-36. New York, N.Y.: Free Press, 1987.

TIME, INC.

Byron, Christopher. *The Fanciest Drive: What Happened When the Media Empire of Time/Life Leaped Without Looking into the Age of High-Tech*. New York, N.Y.: W.W. Norton, 1986. 280 p.

Prendergast, Curtis. *The World of Time, Inc.; The Intimate History of a Changing Enterprise, Volume Three: 1960-1980.* New York, N.Y.: Atheneum, 1986. 590 p.

Swanberg, W.A. *Luce and His Empire.* New York, N.Y.: Scribner's, 1972. 529 p.

TIMES MIRROR CORPORATION

Cose, Ellis. "The Contender: Times Mirror." In *The Press*, 120-184. New York, N.Y.: Morrow, 1989.

Hart, Jack R. *The Information Empire: The Rise of the Los Angeles Times and Times Mirror Corporation.* Washington, D.C.: University Press of America, 1981. 410 p.

Kreig, Andrew. *Spiked; How Chain Management Corrupted America's Oldest Newspaper.* Old Saybrook, Conn.: Peregrine Press, 1987. 237 p.

TIMEX CORPORATION

Timex Corporation. *The Timex Story.* Waterbury, Conn.: The Company, 1988. 2 p.

THE TIMKEN COMPANY

The Timken Company. *History of the Timken Company.* Canton, Ohio: The Company, 1978. 22 p.

TODD SHIPYARDS CORPORATION

Gilbride, John L. *Todd Shipyards: In Peace and War.* New York, N.Y.: Newcomen Society in North America, 1966. 28 p. (Newcomen address)

Mitchell, C. Bradford. *Every Kind of Shipwork: A History of Todd Shipyards Corporation, 1916-1981.* New York, N.Y.: The Company, 1981. 320 p.

TOFUTTI BRANDS, INC.

Fucini, Joseph J., and Suzy Fucini. "David Mintz, Tofutti Brands, Inc.: 'A Little Voice Kept Whispering, Keep Going.'" In *Experience Inc.; Men and Women Who Founded Famous Companies After the Age of 40*, 66-71. New York, N.Y.: Free Press, 1987.

TOKHEIM CORPORATION

Lee, Bob. *Tokheim Pump Company, Ft. Wayne, Indiana, An Illustrated History, 1901-1980*. Detroit, Mich.: Harlo; Dearborn Heights, Mich.: B. Lee, 1980. 153 p.

TONKA CORPORATION

Tonka Corporation. *Tonka Update: Tonka Corporation Chronology*. Minneapolis, Minn.: The Company, 1989. 5 p.

TOOTSIE ROLL INDUSTRIES, INC.

Boas, Nancy. "How Sweet It Is: Tootsie, A Mom-And-Pop Industry, Doesn't Fudge on Its Charming Product or Rich Past." *Across the Board* 21 (December 1984): 13-16.

TOPPS CHEWING GUM, INC.

Leptich, John. "Topps Baseball Cards Were, Naturally, A Smart Kid's Idea." *Chicago Tribune*, 23 October 1989, sec. 3, p. 2.

TORCHMARK CORPORATION

Samford, Frank Park. *Torchmark Corporation: A History of a New Company*. New York, N.Y.: Newcomen Society of the United States, 1984. 26 p. (Newcomen publication; no. 1226)

TOTINO'S (MRS.) PIZZA

Pine, Carol, and Susan Mundale. "Rose Totino; Big Business in the Kitchen." In *Self-Made: The Stories of 12 Minnesota Entrepreneurs*, 145-159. Minneapolis, Minn.: Dorn Books, 1982.

Taylor, Russel R. "Rose Totino; The Loving Queen of Pizza." In *Exceptional Entrepreneurial Women*, 93-102. New York, N.Y.: Quorum Books, 1988.

TOUCHE ROSS AND COMPANY

Swanson, Theodore. *Touche Ross: A Biography; The Life and Services of a Multinational Partnership in the Expanding Profession of Accounting and Management Consulting.* New York, N.Y.: The Company, 1972. 96 p.

TOYOTA MOTOR SALES, U.S.A.

Toyota Motor Sales, U.S.A. *Toyota, The First Twenty Years in the U.S.A.* Torrance, Calif.: The Company, 1977. 134 p.

Toyota Motor Sales, U.S.A. *Toyota USA: The First Fifteen Years*. Torrance, Calif.: The Company, 1973. 48 p.

TRACY COLLINS BANK AND TRUST COMPANY

Arrington, Leonard J. *Tracy Collins Bank & Trust Company: A Record of Responsibility, 1884-1984.* Midvale, Utah: Eden Hill, 1984. 252 p.

TRAILER TRAIN COMPANY

Buford, Curtis D. *Trailer Train Company: A Unique Force in the Railroad Industry.* New York, N.Y.: Newcomen Society in North America, 1982. 24 p. (Newcomen publication; no. 1159)

TRAMMELL CROW COMPANY

Sobel, Robert. *Trammell Crow, Master Builder: The Story of America's Largest Real Estate Empire.* New York, N.Y.: Wiley, 1989. 254 p.

TRANS UNION CORPORATION

Owen, William M. *Autopsy of a Merger; Trans Union: The Deal That Rocked the Corporate World.* Deerfield, Ill.: William M. Owen, 1986. 341 p.

TRANS WORLD AIRLINES, INC.

Bartlett, Donald L., and James B. Steele. *Empire: The Life, Legend, And Madness of Howard Hughes.* New York, N.Y.: W.W. Norton, 1979. 687 p.

Moore, G. "Legacy of Leadership: The Story of Trans-World Airlines." *Aerospace* (December 1979): 14-22.

Serling, Robert J. *Howard Hughes' Airline: An Informal History of TWA.* New York, N.Y.: St. Martin's/Marek, 1983. 338 p.

Tinn, David B. *Just About Everybody Vs. Howard Hughes.* Garden City, N.Y.: Doubleday, 1973. 462 p.

Trans World Airlines, Inc. *A History of TWA Aircraft.* New York, N.Y.: The Company, 1985. 17 p.

Trans World Airlines, Inc. Flight Operations Department. *Legacy of Leadership: A Pictorial History of Trans World Airlines.* Marceline, Mo.: Walsworth Publishing Company, 1971. 224 p.

SEE ALSO: HUGHES AIRCRAFT COMPANY

TRANS-CARIBBEAN AIRWAYS

"Oscar Roy Chalk." In *1971 Current Biography Yearbook,*

85-87. New York, N.Y.: H.W. Wilson, 1972.

TRANSCONTINENTAL GAS PIPELINE CORPORATION

Transcontinental Gas Pipeline Corporation. *History of Transcontinental.* Houston, Tex.: The Company, 1968. 18 p.

THE TRAVELERS INSURANCE COMPANIES

Beach, Morrison H. *"A Century of Security": The Story of the Travelers Insurance Companies.* New York, N.Y.: Newcomen Society in North America, 1973. 29 p. (Newcomen address)

Hendron, William E., and Frank D. Campbell. *Travelers in the Economy, 1978-1982.* Hartford, Conn.: The Company, Corporate Research Division, 1977. 100 p.

The Travelers Insurance Company. *The History of Insurance in America Reads Like A History of the Travelers.* Hartford, Conn.: The Company, 1981. 37 p.

Travelers Insurance Company. *The Story of the Travelers.* Rev. ed. Hartford, Conn.: The Company, 1976. 29 p.

TREND LINE CORPORATION

Hogg, William T. *In the Sun Belt--At the Right Time--With The Right People: The Story of Trend Line in Central Mississippi.* New York, N.Y.: Newcomen Society in North America, 1977. 20 p. (Newcomen publication; no. 1063)

TROPICANA JUICE

Fucini, Joseph J., and Suzy Fucini. "Anthony T. Rossi, Tropicana Juice: 'Control--That Is the Most Important Thing.'" In *Experience Inc.; Men and Women Who*

Founded Famous Companies After the Age of 40, 137-180. New York, N.Y.: Free Press, 1987.

THE TRUMP GROUP, INC.

Trump, Donald J. *Trump: Surviving at the Top.* New York, N.Y.: Random House, 1990. 256 p.

Tuccille, Jerome. *Trump.* New York, N.Y.: Donald I. Fine, 1987. 272 p.

Tuccille, Jerome. *Trump, The Saga of America's Most Powerful Real Estate Baron.* New York, N.Y.: Donald I. Fine, 1985. 243 p.

TRUST COMPANY OF GEORGIA

Martin, Harold H. *Three Strong Pillars; The Story of Trust Company of Georgia.* 2nd ed. Atlanta, Ga.: The Company, 1981. 154 p.

TRW

Mettler, Ruben F. *The Little Brown Hen That Could: The Growth Story of TRW, Inc.* New York, N.Y.: Newcomen Society in North America, 1982. 24 p. (Newcomen publication; no. 1172)

TRW. *The Little Brown Hen That Could.* Cleveland, Ohio: The Company, 1984. 24 p.

TRW - REDA PUMP DIVISION

TRW. Reda Pump Division. *Memories, A Story of People and a Company Called TRW Reda.* Bartlesville, Okla.: The Division, 1980. 126 p.

TUPPERWARE NORTH AMERICA

Clifford, M. "Come to My Party." *Country Living* (March 1989): 138+

McCarthy, Rebecca. "In Homage to Tupperware." *Atlanta Journal*, 23 July 1989, sec. M, p. 1.

TURNER BROADCASTING SYSTEMS, INC.

Meyer, Michael. "Glory." In *The Alexander Complex: The Dreams That Drive the Great Businessmen*, 197-234. New York, N.Y.: Times Books, 1989.

Whittemore, Hank. *CNN the Inside Story*. Boston, Mass.: Little, Brown, 1990. 319 p.

Williams, Christian. *Lead, Follow or Get Out of the Way: The Story of Ted Turner*. New York, N.Y.: Times Books, 1981. 282 p.

SEE ALSO: ATLANTA BRAVES

TWENTIETH CENTURY-FOX FILM CORPORATION

Dunne, John Gregory. *The Studio*. New York, N.Y.: Farrar, Straus & Giroux, 1969. 255 p.

Silverman, Stephen M. *The Fox That Got Away; The Last Days of the Zanuck Dynasty at Twentieth Century-Fox*. Secaucus, N.J.: Lyle Stuart, 1988. 356 p.

Solomon, Aubrey. *Twentieth Century-Fox: A Corporate and Financial History*. Metuchen, N.J.: Scarecrow Press, 1988. 285 p.

Thomas, Tony, and Aubrey Solomon. *The Films of 20th Century-Fox: A Pictorial History*. Secaucus, N.J.: Citadel Press, 1985. 492 p.

TWIN CITY RAPID TRANSIT COMPANY

Lowry, Goodrich. *Streetcar Man: Tom Towry and the Twin City Rapid Transit Company*. Minneapolis, Minn.: Lerner Publications, 1979. 177 p.

TYSON FOODS, INC.

"Doing Business Just for You: Yesterday." In *Tyson Foods, Inc. Annual Report*, 4-8. Springdale, Ark.: The Company, 1984.

MacPhee, William. "Don Tyson of Tyson Foods, Inc." In *Rare Breed: The Entrepreneur, An American Culture*, 145-161. Chicago, Ill.: Probus Publishing Company, 1987.

TYZ-ALL PLASTICS, INC.

Levitt, Mortimer. "Gene Ballin: 'A True Entrepreneur Invents His Own Opportunities.'" In *How to Start Your Own Business Without Losing Your Shirt; Secrets of Seventeen Successful Entrepreneurs*, 133-141. New York, N.Y.: Atheneum, 1988.

UAL, INC.

Carlson, Edward E. *UAL, Inc.: United Airlines and Western International Hotels, Partners in Travel*. New York, N.Y.: Newcomen Society in North America, 1975. 15 p. (Newcomen publication; no. 1030)

Johnson, Robert Elliott. *Airway One: A Narrative of United Airlines and Its Leaders*. Chicago, Ill.: The Company, 1974. 208 p.

Stitch, Rodney. *The Unfriendly Skies: An Aviation Watergate*. Alamo, Calif.: Diablo Western Press, 1980. 372 p.

Taylor, Frank J. *"Pat" Patterson*. Menlo Park, Calif.: Lane Magazine and Book Company, 1967. 160 p.

UGI CORPORATION

UGI Corporation. *UGI Corporation, the First 100 Years*.

Valley Forge, Pa.: The Company, 1982. 96 p.

UGLY DUCKLING RENT-A-CAR SYSTEM, INC.

Fucini, Joseph J., and Suzy Fucini. "Tom Duck, Ugly Duckling Rent-A-Car System, Inc.: 'Some People Just Take a Little Bit Longer Than Others to Get There.'" In *Experience Inc.; Men and Women Who Founded Famous Companies After the Age of 40*, 185-191. New York, N.Y.: Free Press, 1987.

UNC RESOURCES

UNC Resources. *UNC Resources History*. Falls Church, Va.: The Company, 1983. 10 p.

UNIFIED SERVICES, INC.

Buchholz, Barbara B., and Margaret Crane. "Unified Services, Inc., Washington, D.C." In *Corporate Blood Lines: The Future of the Family Firm*, 229-244. New York, N.Y.: Carol Publishing Group, 1989.

UNION BANK, LOS ANGELES

Volk, Harry J. *Union Bank: Sixty Years of Quality Banking*. New York, N.Y.: Newcomen Society in North America, 1974. 23 p. (Newcomen publication; no. 1006)

UNION CARBIDE CORPORATION

Baxi, Uprendra, and Thomas Paul. *Mass Disasters and Multinational Liability, The Bhopal Case*. Bombay, India: N.M. Tripathi, 1986. 230 p.

Bhopal, Its Setting, Responsibility, And Challenge. Delhi, India: Ajunta Publications, 1985. 98 p.

Bogard, William. *The Bhopal Tragedy: Language, Logic and Politics in the Production of a Hazard*. Boulder,

Colo.: Westview Press, 1989. 154 p.

Cherniack, Martin. *The Hawk's Nest Incident: America's Worst Industrial Disaster.* New Haven, Conn.: Yale University Press, 1986. 210 p.

De Grazia, Alfred. *A Cloud Over Bhopal, Causes, Consequences and Constructive Solutions.* Bombay, India; New York, N.Y.: Kalos Foundation for the India-American Committee for the Bhopal Victims, 1985. 145 p.

Union Carbide Corporation. *Our History.* Danbury, Conn.: The Company, 1976. 15 p.

UNION CENTRAL LIFE INSURANCE COMPANY

Union Central Life Insurance Company. *Splendid Century; A Centennial History of the Union Central Life Insurance Company of Cincinnati, Ohio, 1867-1967.* Cincinnati, Ohio: The Company, 1967. 161 p.

UNION ELECTRIC COMPANY

Union Electric Company. *A History of Union Electric Company.* St. Louis, Mo.: The Company, 1984. 5 p.

UNION EQUITY CO-OPERATIVE EXCHANGE

Union Equity Co-operative Exchange. *Union Equity: A Story of Growth and Performance.* Enid, Okla.: The Company, 1986?. 13 p.

UNION INSURANCE COMPANY

Union Insurance Company. *100 Years of Service.* Lincoln, Nebr.: The Company, 1986. 30 p.

UNION MUTUAL LIFE INSURANCE COMPANY

Lane, Carleton G. *A Maine Heritage: A Brief History of*

Union Mutual Life Insurance Company, 1848-1968. New York, N.Y.: Newcomen Society in North America, 1968. 28 p. (Newcomen address)

UNION NATIONAL BANK AND TRUST COMPANY OF SOUDERTON

Ruth, John L. *The History of the Indian Valley and Its Bank.* Souderton, Pa.: The Bank, 1976. 209 p.

THE UNION NATIONAL BANK, LOWELL, MASSACHUSETTS

Bourgeois, Homer W. *The Union National Bank: The Story of an All American Bank in an All American City.* New York, N.Y.: Newcomen Society in North America, 1972. 24 p. (Newcomen address)

UNION OIL COMPANY OF CALIFORNIA

Hartley, Fred L. *"The Spirit of 76": The Story of the Union Oil Company of California.* New York, N.Y.: Newcomen Society in North America, 1976. 20 p. (Newcomen publication; no. 1053)

Hutchinson, William Henry. *Oil, Land, and Politics: The California Career of Thomas Robert Bard.* Norman: University of Oklahoma Press, 1965. 2 v.

Union Oil Company of California. *Sign of the 76: The Fabulous Life and Times of the Union Oil Company of California.* Los Angeles, Calif.: The Company, 1976. 424 p.

Wetly, Earl M. *The 76 Bonanza: The Fabulous Life and Times of the Union Oil Company of California.* Menlo Park, Calif.: Lane Magazine and Book Company, 1966. 351 p.

UNION PACIFIC CORPORATION

Cook, William Sutton. *Building the Modern Union Pacific.* New York, N.Y.: Newcomen Society of the United States, 1984. 24 p. (Newcomen publication; no. 1228)

Kenefick, John C. *Union Pacific and the Building of the West.* New York, N.Y.: Newcomen Society of the United States, 1985. 18 p. (Newcomen publication; no. 1251)

Klein, Maury. *Union Pacific, Vol.2: The Rebirth, 1894-1969.* New York, N.Y.: Doubleday, 1990. 720 p.

Union Pacific Corporation. *Union Pacific Corporation: Energy, Transportation, Natural Resources.* New York, N.Y.: The Company, 1979. 28 p.

UNION PACIFIC RAILROAD COMPANY

Ames, Charles E. *Pioneering the Union Pacific; A Reappraisal of the Builders of the Railroads.* New York, N.Y.: Appleton, 1969. 608 p.

Athearn, Robert G. *Union Pacific Country.* Chicago, Ill.: Rand McNally, 1971. 480 p.

Baily, Ed H. *The Century of Progress: A Heritage of Service, Union Pacific, 1869-1969.* New York, N.Y.: Newcomen Society in North America, 1969. 24 p. (Newcomen publication; no. 866)

UNION TRUST COMPANY OF MARYLAND

Cooper, Elliot T. *A Documentary History of the Union Trust Company of Maryland, Baltimore, And Its Predecessor Institutions: Bank of Baltimore and the National Bank of Baltimore, 1795-1969.* Baltimore, Md.: The Company, 1970. 281 p.

UNIROYAL, INC.

Vila, George R. *The Story of UNIROYAL: 75 Years of Progress.* New York, N.Y.: Newcomen Society in North America, 1968. 24 p. (Newcomen address)

UNITED AIR LINES, INC.
SEE:
UAL, INC.

UNITED ARTISTS

Balio, Tino. *United Artists: The Company Built by the Stars.* Madison: University of Wisconsin Press, 1976. 323 p.

Balio, Tino. *United Artists: The Company That Changed the Film Industry.* Madison, Wis.: University of Wisconsin Press, 1987. 446 p.

Bergan, Ronald. *The United Artists Story.* New York, N.Y.: Crown Publishers, 1986. 352 p.

UNITED BANK OF ARIZONA

Simmons, James P. *Banking on Arizona's Future: The Story of United Bank of Arizona.* New York, N.Y.: Newcomen Society in North America, 1980. 27 p. (Newcomen publication; no. 1124)

UNITED BANKS OF COLORADO, INC.

Hart, N. Berne. *United Banks of Colorado, Inc.: A Proud History of Service to Colorado.* New York, N.Y.: Newcomen Society in North America, 1981. 19 p. (Newcomen publication; no. 1139)

UNITED FRUIT COMPANY

McCann, Thomas P. *An American Company: The Tragedy of United Fruit.* New York, N.Y.: Crown,

1976. 244 p.

Melville, John H. *The Great White Fleet*. New York, N.Y.: Vantage Press, 1976. 275 p.

UNITED PARCEL SERVICE OF AMERICA

United Parcel Service of America. *This is United Parcel Service*. Greenwich, Conn.: The Company, 1976. 36 p.

UNITED PRESS INTERNATIONAL, INC.

Gordon, Gregory, and Ronald E. Cohen. "The Sinking of UPI." *Washington Post*, 10 December, 1989. sec. WMAG, p. 31.

Quigg, H.D. "UPI; As It Was and As It Is." *Editor and Publisher, The Fourth Estate* 115 (25 September 1982): 16-18.

UNITED REFINING COMPANY

United Refining Company. *History of United Refining Company*. Warren, Pa.: The Company, 1977. 17 p.

U.S. BORAX AND CHEMICAL CORPORATION

Travis, Norman J. *The Tinical Trail: A History of Borax*. London: Harrap, 1984. 311 p.

Travis, Norman J., and C.L. Randolph. *United States Borax & Chemical Corporation: The First One Hundred Years*. New York, N.Y.: Newcomen Society in North America, 1973. 24 p.

U.S. INDUSTRIAL CHEMICALS COMPANY

Barnes, Harry C. *From Molasses to the Moon: The Story of U.S. Industrial Chemicals Company*. New York, N.Y.: The Company, 1975. 160 p.

U.S. NEWS AND WORLD REPORT, INC.

Gordon, Richard L. "U.S. News Values Its Past--And Future." *Advertising Age* 55 (5 March 1984): 4, 68-69.

UNITED STATES RUBBER COMPANY

Babcok, Glenn D. *History of the United States Rubber Company: A Case Study in Corporate Management.* Bloomington, Ind.: Bureau of Business Research, Graduate School of Business, Indiana University, 1966. 495 p.

UNITED STATES SAVINGS BANK OF NEWARK, N.J.

United States Savings Bank of Newark, N.J. *History of the United States Savings Bank of Newark, N.J.* Newark, N.J.: The Bank, 1976. 92 p.

UNITED STATES STEEL CORPORATION

Kulkosky, Edward. "The Rebirth of U.S. Steel." *Financial World* 148 (15 September 1979): 17-21.

Voorhees, Enders McClumpha. *Financial Policy in a Changing Economy.* Lebanon, Pa.: Sowers Printing Company, 1970. 232 p.

UNITED STATES SUGAR CORPORATION

McGovern, Joseph J. *United States Sugar Corporation: The First Fifty Years.* Clewiston, Fla.: The Company, 1981. 45 p.

UNITED STATES WATCH COMPANY

Muir, William. *Marion, A History of the United States Watch Company.* Columbia, Pa.: National Association of Watch and Clock Collectors, Inc., 1985. 216 p.

UNITED TECHNOLOGIES CORPORATION

Fernandez, Ronald. *Excess Profits; The Rise of United Technologies*. Reading, Mass.: Addison-Wesley, 1983. 320 p.

UNITED TELECOMMUNICATIONS, INC.

Henson, Paul H. *United Telecommunications, Inc.: A Rose by Any Other Name--*. New York, N.Y.: Newcomen Society in North America, 1972. 22 p. (Newcomen address)

UNITED TILE COMPANY OF DALLAS

United Tile Company of Dallas. *Dependability for Twenty Years, 1947-1967*. Dallas, Tex.: The Company, 1967.

UNIVERSAL FOODS CORPORATION

Universal Foods Corporation. *Universal Foods: The First 100 Years*. Milwaukee, Wis.: The Company, 1982. 46 p.

UNIVERSAL PICTURES COMPANY, INC.

Fitzgerald, Michael G. *Universal Pictures: A Panoramic History in Words, Pictures, And Filmographies*. New Rochelle, N.Y.: Arlington House, 1976. 766 p.

UOP (UNIVERSAL OIL PRODUCTS COMPANY)

Logan, John O. *UOP--Technology in Action*. New York, N.Y.: Newcomen Society in North America, 1975. 16 p. (Newcomen publication; no. 1017)

UPS
SEE:
UNITED PARCEL SERVICE OF AMERICA

U.R.M. STORES, INC.

U.R.M. Stores, Inc. *The First Fifty Years Are the Hardest*. Spokane, Wash.: The Company, 1971. 58 p.

USA NETWORK

Reiss, Craig. "Kay Koplovitz: A Cable Innovator Whose Legendary Bouts at the Negotiating Table Foresaw a Revolution." *Advertising Age* 56 (5 December 1985): 4-6.

USA TODAY

Neuharth, Allen. *Confessions of an S.O.B.* New York, N.Y.: Doubleday, 1989. 372 p.

Prichard, Peter. *The Making of McPaper: The Inside Story of USA Today*. Kansas City, Kans.: Andrews, McMeel & Parker, 1987. 370 p.

USAIR

USAir. *USAir History*. Pittsburgh, Pa.: The Company, 1980. 3 p.

Woolsey, James P. "USAir, Inc.: First in Pittsburgh, First in the World." *Air Transport World* 20 (June 1983): 32-37.

USLIFE CORPORATION

Crosby, Gordon E., Jr. *USLIFE Corporation: Meeting Changing Consumer Needs Through Diversified Financial Services*. New York, N.Y.: Newcomen Society in North America, 1972. 19 p. (Newcomen address)

USM CORPORATION

Brewster, William S. *USM Corporation: Our First 75*

Years. New York, N.Y.: Newcomen Society in North America, 1974. 20 p. (Newcomen publication; no. 989)

UTAH-IDAHO SUGAR COMPANY

Arrington, Leonard J. *Beet Sugar in the West, A History of the Utah-Idaho Sugar Company, 1891-1966*. Seattle, Wash.: University of Washington Press, 1966. 234 p.

VALLEYDALE PACKERS, INC.

Valleydale Packers, Inc. *Valleydale Packers, Inc. History*. Salem, Va.: The Company. 1988. 2 p.

VAL-PAK DIRECT MARKETING SYSTEMS, INC.

Kane, Sid. "The King of Coupons." *Venture* 6 (October 1984): 96-104.

VAN DORN COMPANY

Van Dorn Company. *Responding to the Times, A History Since 1872*. Cleveland, Ohio: The Company, 1984. 24 p.

VAUGHN (L.) COMPANY

Hyatt, Joshua. "Succession: Splitting Heirs." *Inc.* 10 (March 1988): 102-110.

VECTOR GRAPHIC, INC.

Benner, Susan. "Next Stop Wall Street." *Inc.* 3 (March 1981): 36-41.

VENTURE

Scardino, Albert. "The Magazine That Lost Its Way." *New York Times*, 18 June 1989, sec. 3, p. 1.

VERNON (LILLIAN)

Taylor, Russel R. "Lillian Vernon Katz; Queen Mother of Mail Order." In *Exceptional Entrepreneurial Women*, 19-24. New York, N.Y.: Quorum Books, 1988.

VERRILL AND DANA

Putnam, Roger A. *Verrill and Dana: Faith in the Future--Pride in the Past*. New York, N.Y.: Newcomen Society of the United States, 1987. 20 p. (Newcomen publication; no. 1288)

VICORP

Kochak, J. "The History of VICORP." *Restaurant Business* 84 (10 April 1985): 282+

VICTOR COMPTOMETER CORPORATION

Darly, Edwin. *It All Adds Up; The Growth of Victor Comptometer Corporation*. Chicago, Ill.: The Company, 1968. 243 p.

VICTORIA BANK AND TRUST COMPANY

Johnson, Laurence S. *A Century of Service, The Concise History of Victoria Bank and Trust Company*. Victoria, Tex.: The Company, 1979. 92 p.

VIKINGS INDUSTRIES, INC.

Cunningham, Connie. "From Its Humble Beginnings, Vikings Industries Now a Force." *Atlanta Constitution*, 20 April 1989, sec. XG, p. 4.

VIRGINIA ELECTRIC AND POWER COMPANY

Will, Erwin H. *The Past--Interesting, The Present--Intriguing, The Future--Bright: A Story of Virginia Electric and Power Company*. New York, N.Y.:

Newcomen Society in North America, 1965. 24 p. (Newcomen address)

VITAGRAPH COMPANY OF AMERICA

Slide, Anthony, and Alan Gevinson. *The Big V; A History of the Vitagraph Company*. Metuchen, N.J.: Scarecrow Press, 1987. 332 p.

VON FURSTENBERG (DIANE), LTD.

Taylor, Russel R. "Diane Von Furstenberg; She Relies on Intuition." In *Exceptional Entrepreneurial Women*, 53-58. New York, N.Y.: Quorum Books, 1988.

VOUGHT CORPORATION

Moran, Gerard P. *Aeroplanes Vought, 1917-1977*. Temple City, Calif.: Historical Aviation Album, 1978. 164 p.

VULCAN MATERIALS COMPANY

Blount, W. Houston. *The Past As a Challenge to the Future*. New York, N.Y.: Newcomen Society of the United States, 1984. 20 p. (Newcomen publication; no. 1184)

WABASH VALLEY BANK AND TRUST COMPANY

Life, Carlos A. *Wabash Valley Bank and Trust Company, 75th Anniversary, 1904-1979, A Commemorative History*. Peru, Ind.: The Bank, 1979. 77 p.

WACHOVIA CORPORATION

Wachovia Corporation. *Wachovia: 1879-1979*. Winston-Salem, N.C.: The Company, 1979. 21 p.

WACO AIRCRAFT COMPANY

Brandly, Raymond H. *Waco Airplanes: Ask Any Pilot:*

The Authentic History of Waco Airplanes and the Biographies of the Founders, Clayton J. Bruckner and Elwood J. Sam Junkin. Dayton: R.H. Brandly, 1979. 163 p.

Schreiner, Herm. "The Waco Story, Part I: Clayton Bruckner and the Founding Years. *American Aviation Historical Society. Journal* 25 (Winter 1980): 281-299.

WAINWRIGHT (H.C.) AND COMPANY

Jacker, Corinne. *H.C. Wainwright & Co., 1868-1968, A Centennial.* New York, N.Y.: The Company, 1967. 77 p.

WAKEFIELD SEAFOODS

Blackford, Mansel G. *Pioneering a Modern Small Business: Wakefield Seafoods and the Alaskan Frontier.* Greenwich, Conn.: JAI Press, 1979. 210 p. (Industrial development and the social fabric; vol. 6)

WALDEN BOOK COMPANY, INC.

Frank, Jerome P. "Waldenbooks at 50." *Publishers Weekly* 223 (29 April 1983): 36-41.

WALGREEN COMPANY

Kogan, Herman, and Rick Kogan. *Pharmacist to the Nation: A History of Walgreen Co., America's Leading Drug Store Chain.* Deerfield, Ill.: The Company, 1989. 288 p.

"Seventy-Five Years of Walgreen Progress." *Walgreen World* 43 (September-October 1976): 1-28. (75th anniversary issue)

WALL DRUG STORE

Jennings, Dana Close. *Free Ice Water; The Story of Wall Drug*. Aberdeen, S.D.: North Plains Press, 1969. 95 p.

WALL INDUSTRIES

Fortenbaugh, Samuel B., Jr. *The Wall Ropery, 1800-1980*. Beverly, N.J.: The Company, 1980. 63 p.

WALL STREET JOURNAL

Caliam, Carnegie Samuel. *The Gospel According to the Wall Street Journal*. Atlanta, Ga.: John Knox Press, 1975. 114 p.

Neilson, Winthrop, and Frances Neilson. *What's News--Dow Jones: Story of the Wall Street Journal*. Radnor, Pa.: Chilton Book Company, 1973. 171 p.

Rosenberg, Jerry M. *Inside the Wall Street Journal: The History and the Power of Dow Jones & Company and America's Most Influential Newspaper*. New York, N.Y.: Macmillan, 1982. 328 p.

Scharff, Edward E. *Worldly Power: The Making of the Wall Street Journal*. New York, N.Y.: Beaufort Books, 1986. 305 p.

Wendt, Lloyd. *The Wall Street Journal: The Story of Dow Jones & the Nation's Business Newspaper*. Chicago, Ill.: Rand McNally, 1982. 448 p.

SEE ALSO: DOW, JONES AND COMPANY

WALLACE-MURRAY CORPORATION

Raach, Fred R. *Wallace-Murray Corporation*. New York, N.Y.: Newcomen Society in North America, 1972. 23 p. (Newcomen address)

WAL-MART STORES, INC.

Bowermaster, Jon. "When Wal-Mart Comes to Town." *New York Times*, 2 April 1989, sec. 6, part 2, p. 28.

Trimble, Vance H. *Sam Walton: The Inside Story of America's Richest Man*. New York, N.Y.: Dutton, 1990. 319 p.

Wal-Mart Stores, Inc. *Wal-Mart Stores Fact Sheet*. Bentonville, Ariz.: The Company, 1985. 3 p.

WALTERS (JIM) CORPORATION

Williams, Randall, and Hilda Dent. "Billion Dollar Shell Game." *Southern Exposure* 8, no.1 (1980): 86-91.

WANG LABORATORIES

Wang, An. *Lessons: An Autobiography*. Reading, Mass.: Addison-Wesley, 1986. 248 p.

WARING AND LAROSA

Kanner, B. "Water Under the Bridge." *New York* 23 (23 July 1990): 14+

WARNACO

Field, John W. *Fig Leaves and Fortunes: A Fashion Company Named Warnaco*. West Kennebunk, Maine: Phoenix Publishing, 1990. 160 p.

WARNER BROTHERS COMPANY

Freedland, Michael. *The Warner Brothers*. New York, N.Y.; London, England: St. Martins Press/Harrap, 1983. 240 p.

Guy, Rory. *Fifty Years of Film, 1923-1973*. Burbank, Calif.: Warner Brothers Records, 1973. 56 p.

Higham, Charles. *Warner Brothers.* New York, N.Y.: Scribner's, 1975. 232 p.

Hirschhorn, Clive. *The Warner Brothers Story.* New York, N.Y.: Crown Pub., 1979. 480 p.

Silke, James R. *Here's Looking at You, Kid: 50 Years of Fighting, Working and Dreaming at Warner Bros.* Boston, Mass.: Little, Brown, 1976. 317 p.

Stuart, Jerome. *Those Crazy, Wonderful Years When We Ran Warner Bros.* Secaucus, N.J.: Lyle Stuart, 1983. 285 p.

Woollay, Lynn, Robert W. Malsbary, and Robert G. Strange. *Warner Bros. Television, Every Show of the Fifties and Sixties, Episode-By-Episode.* Jefferson, N.C.: McFarland, 1985. 296 p.

WARNER COMMUNICATIONS

Bender, Marylin. "From Caskets to Cable: Warner Communications." In *At the Top; Behind the Scenes with the Men and Women Who Run America's Corporate Giants*, 271-299. Garden City, N.Y.: Doubleday, 1975.

WARREN RUPP COMPANY

Rupp, Warren E. *The Warren Rupp Company: Innovative Pumps Foster Success.* New York, N.Y.: Newcomen Society in North America, 1983. 23 p. (Newcomen publication; no. 1195)

WASHINGTON GAS LIGHT COMPANY

Bittinger, Donald S. *Washington Gas Light Company: A Potpourri of Past, Present, and Future.* New York, N.Y.: Newcomen Society in North America, 1971. 24 p. (Newcomen address)

Hamilton, Martha M. "Created by Congress, Company Brought D.C. Out of the Dark." *Washington Post*, 23 January 1989, sec. WBIZ, p. 35.

WASHINGTON NATIONAL CORPORATION

Washington National Corporation. *The People Business: A Brief History of the Washington National Organization.* Evanston, Ill.: The Company, 1978. 12 p.

WASHINGTON POST

Cose, Ellis. "The Underdog." In *The Press*, 27-119. New York, N.Y.: Morrow, 1989.

Davis, Deborah. *Katherine the Great: Katherine Graham and the Washington Post.* New York, N.Y.: Harcourt Brace Jovanovich, 1979. 280 p.

Roberts, Chalmers McGeagh. *The Washington Post: The First 100 Years.* Boston, Mass.: Houghton Mifflin, 1977. 495 p.

WASHINGTON PUBLIC POWER SUPPLY SYSTEM

Leigland, James, and Robert Lamb. *WPP$$, Who is to Blame for the WPPSS Disaster.* Cambridge, Mass.: Ballinger Publishing Company, 1986. 253 p.

WASHINGTON REDSKINS

Denlinger, Ken. *Redskin Country: From Baugh to the Super Bowl.* New York, N.Y.: Leisure Press, 1983. 224 p.

Denlinger, Ken. *Washington Redskins; The Allen Triumph.* Englewood Cliffs, N.J.: Prentice-Hall, 1973. 144 p.

Denlinger, Ken, and Paul Allner. *Day by Day in*

Washington Redskins History. New York, N.Y.: Leisure Press, 1984. 320 p.

WASHINGTON STATE FERRIES

Demoro, Harre W. *The Evergreen Fleet: A Pictorial History of Washington State Ferries*. San Marino, Calif.: Golden West Books, 1971. 136 p.

WASHINGTON STEEL CORPORATION

Fitch, T.S. *Washington Steel Was Born South of Columbus*. New York, N.Y.: Newcomen Society in North America, 1967. 24 p. (Newcomen address)

WASHINGTON-VIRGINIA RAILWAY COMPANY

Merriken, John E. *Old Dominion Trolley Too: A History of the Mount Vernon Line*. Dallas, Tex.: L.O. King, Jr., 1987. 142 p.

WASHINGTONIAN

Trueheart, Charles. "Washingtonian's Sterling Secrets." *Washington Post*, 25 September 1990, sec. C, p. 1.

WAVERLY, INC.

Waverly, Inc. *A Century of Progress, 1890-1990*. Baltimore, Md.: The Company, 1989. 131 p.

Waverly Press. *Three Quarters of a Century Plus Ten, 1890-1975*. Baltimore, Md.: Waverly Press, Williams and Wilkins, 1975. 71 p.

WEAN UNITED, INC.

Wean, R.J., Jr. *Teamwork and Technology: The Story of Wean United*. New York, N.Y.: Newcomen Society in North America, 1969. 24 p. (Newcomen address)

WEATHERBY (FIREARMS), INC.

MacPhee, William. "Roy Weatherby of Weatherby (Firearms), Inc." In *Rare Breed: The Entrepreneur, An American Culture*, 165-185. Chicago, Ill.: Probus Publishing Company, 1987.

WEATHERHEAD COMPANY

Grabner, George J. *The Weatherhead Company; A Cycle Completed--A Commitment to the Future*. New York, N.Y.: Newcomen Society in North America, 1970. 20 p. (Newcomen address)

WEBB AND KNAPP, INC.

Zeckendorf, William, with Edward McCreary. *The Autobiography of William Zeckendorf*. New York, N.Y.: Holt, 1970. 312 p.

WEBSTER INDUSTRIES, INC.

Nordholt, John B., Jr. *Webster Industries, Inc.: One Hundred Years of Trail, Travail, and Triumph*. New York, N.Y.: Newcomen Society in North America, 1976. 22 p. (Newcomen publication; no. 1044)

WEDTECH CORPORATION

Thompson, Marilyn W. *Feeding the Beast: How Wedtech Became the Most Corrupt Little Company in America*. New York, N.Y.: Scribner, 1990. 337 p.

Traub, James. *Too Good to Be True; The Outlandish Story of Wedtech*. New York, N.Y.: Doubleday, 1990. 568 p.

WEIL BROTHERS COTTON

Bush, George S. *An American Harvest: The Story of Weil Brothers Cotton*. Englewood Cliffs, N.J.: Prentice-

Hall, 1982. 495 p.

WELCH GRAPE JUICE COMPANY, INC.

Chzanof, William. *Welch's Grape Juice: From Corporation to Co-Operative.* Syracuse, N.Y.: Syracuse University Press, 1977. 407 p.

WELLS, FARGO AND COMPANY

Jackson, William Turrentine. *Portland: Wells Fargo's Hub for the Pacific Northwest.* Portland: Oregon Historical Society, 1985. 36 p. (Reprinted from the Oregon Historical Quarterly, Fall 1985)

Loomis, Noel M. *Wells Fargo.* New York, N.Y.: Clarkson N. Potter, Inc., 1968. 340 p.

Under Cover for Wells Fargo: The Unvarnished Recollections of Fred Dodge. Boston, Mass.: Houghton Mifflin, 1969. 280 p.

Wells Fargo and Company. *In July 1852 a "Newcomer" Made Its Appearance on Montgomery Street in San Francisco--.* San Francisco, Calif.: The Company, 1977. 17 p.

WELLS RICH GREENE, INC.

Wolfe, John. "Guard Changes at Era's Hot Shop: Mary Wells Starred in the 'Golden Years' of US Advertising." *Advertising Age* 61 (23 April 1990): 46+

WENDY'S INTERNATIONAL, INC.

Wendy's International, Inc. *Wendy's: A Tradition of Quality.* Dublin, Ohio: The Company, 1984. 99 p.

WEST PENN POWER COMPANY

Van Atta, Robert B. *50 Years--At Your Service: The Origins and Development of West Penn Power Company.* Greensburgh, Pa.: The Company, 1965. 64 p.

WEST POINT-PEPPERELL, INC.

West Point-Pepperell, Inc. *The History of West Point-Pepperell.* West Point, Ga.: The Company, 1984. 6 p.

WEST SIDE LUMBER COMPANY

Ferrell, Mallory Hope. *West Side, Narrow Gauge in the Sierra.* Edmonds, Va.: Pacific Fast Mail, 1979. 319 p.

WESTERN AIRLINES, INC.

"Kirk Kerkorian." In *1975 Current Biography Yearbook,* 219-221. New York, N.Y.: H.W. Wilson, 1976.

Serling, Robert J. *The Only Way to Fly: The Story of Western Airlines, America's Senior Air Carrier.* Garden City, N.Y.: Doubleday, 1976. 494 p.

WESTERN COMPANY OF NORTH AMERICA

Chiles, H.E. *The Western Company of North America: 44 Years of Pacesetting in the Oil Business.* New York, N.Y.: Newcomen Society of the United States, 1984. 28 p. (Newcomen publication; no. 1205)

WESTERN COSTUME COMPANY

Cerone, Daniel. "Western Costume: Preserving Fabric of Hollywood History." *Los Angeles Times,* 14 March 1989, sec, V, p. 1.

WESTERN ELECTRIC COMPANY

Balzer, Richard. *Clockwork: Life in and Outside an American Factory*. Garden City, N.Y.: Doubleday, 1976. 333 p.

Gorman, Paul A. *Century One--A Prologue*. New York, N.Y.: Newcomen Society in North America, 1969. 24 p.

McKinsey and Company. *A Study of Western Electric's Performance; A Report*. New York, N.Y.: AT&T, 1969. 251 p.

Smith, George David. *Anatomy of a Business Strategy: Bell, Western Electric and the Origins of the American Telephone Industry*. Baltimore, Md.: Johns Hopkins University Press, 1985. 237 p.

SEE ALSO: AMERICAN TELEPHONE AND TELEGRAPH COMPANY

WESTERN GEAR CORPORATION

Bannan, Thomas J. *From Cogwheels to Space-Age Systems: The Story of Western Gear Corporation*. New York, N.Y.: Newcomen Society in North America, 1969. 24 p. (Newcomen address)

WESTERN INTERNATIONAL HOTELS, INC.

Carlson, Edward E. *UAL, Inc.: United Airlines and Western International Hotels: Partners in Travel*. New York, N.Y.: Newcomen Society in North America, 1975. 15 p. (Newcomen publication; no. 1030)

WESTERN PACIFIC RAILROAD

Western Pacific Railroad. *Perlman, Alfred E., Western Pacific Railroad: "The Feather River Route."* New

York, N.Y.: Newcomen Society in North America, 1975. 16 p. (Newcomen publication; no. 1014)

WESTERN SAVINGS AND LOAN ASSOCIATION

Driggs, Douglas H. *The Path We Came by: The Story of Western Savings and Loan Association.* New York, N.Y.: Newcomen Society in North America, 1969. 32 p. (Newcomen address)

WESTERN-SOUTHERN LIFE INSURANCE COMPANY

Moore, Gerald E. *Making an Idea Succeed; The Western-Southern Story.* Cincinnati, Ohio: The Company, 1988. 177 p.

WESTERN UNION CORPORATION

Western Union Corporation. *Western Union: From Wire to Westar.* Upper Saddle River, N.J.: The Company, 1985. 20 p.

WESTERN UNION INTERNATIONAL, INC.

Gallagher, Edward A. *Getting the Message Across: The Story of Western Union International, Inc.* New York, N.Y.: Newcomen Society in North America, 1971. 24 p. (Newcomen address)

WESTERN UNION TELEGRAPH CORPORATION

McFall, Russell W. *Making History by Responding to Its Forces.* New York, N.Y.: Newcomen Society in North America, 1971. 20 p. (Newcomen address)

WESTERN WORLD INSURANCE, INC.

Jennings, John. "Western World Marks Its 25th Anniversary." *National Underwriter (Property/Casualty/Employee Benefits)* 93 (18

September 1989): 17, 44-45.

WESTFIELD COMPANIES

Condon, George E. *History of Ohio Farmers Insurance Company, 1848-1984.* Westfield Center, Ohio: The Company, 1985. 274 p.

WESTINGHOUSE ELECTRIC CORPORATION

Schatz, Ronald W. *The Electrical Workers: A History of Labor at General Electric and Westinghouse, 1923-1960.* Urbana: University of Illinois Press, 1983. 279 p.

WESTWARD SAVINGS AND LOAN ASSOCIATION

Adams, James Ring. "The Biggest Scam in History." In *The Big Fix: Inside the S&L Scandal: How an Unholy Alliance of Politics and Money Destroyed America's Banking System*, 17-33. New York, N.Y.: Wiley, 1990.

WETTERAU, INC.

"Wetterau Incorporated; 120 Years of Progress, 1869-1989." In *Wetterau, Inc. Annual Report.* Hazelwood, Mo.: The Company, 1989. (Unnumbered insert)

WEYERHAEUSER COMPANY

Jones, Alden H. *From Jamestown to Coffin Rock; A History of Weyerhaeuser Operations in Southwest Washington.* Tacoma, Wash.: The Company, 1974. 346 p.

Twining, Charles Edwin. *Phil Weyerhaeuser, Lumberman.* Seattle, Wash.: University of Washington Press, 1985. 401 p.

Weyerhaeuser, George H. *"Forests for the Future": The*

Weyerhaeuser Story. New York, N.Y.: Newcomen Society in North America, 1981. 24 p. (Newcomen publication; no. 1141)

WFC CORPORATION

Adams, James Ring. "The Road to Washington." In *The Big Fix: Inside the S&L Scandal: How an Unholy Alliance of Politics and Money Destroyed America's Banking System*, 71-86. New York, N.Y.: Wiley, 1990.

WHEATON INDUSTRIES

"Wheaton Industries: 100 Years of Pride." *Wheaton Industries Centennial Newsletter* (October 1987-February 1989). A series of articles commemorating the 100th anniversary of Wheaton.

WHITE CASTLE SYSTEMS, INC.

Gelfand, M. Howard. "One Square Burger that's Gotten Around: Since 1921 White Castle Has Warmed the Heart's and Plates of Many." *Advertising Age* 54 (21 November 1983): sec 2, M24-M25.

White Castle Systems, Inc. *White Castle; 60 Years at Sixth and Broadway.* Cincinnati, Ohio: The Company, 1987. 4 p.

WICKER GARDEN

Taylor, Russel R. "Pamela Scurry: 'I Think It Is Okay to Want It All.'" In *Exceptional Entrepreneurial Women*, 87-92. New York, N.Y.: Quorum Books, 1988.

WICKES CORPORATION

Bush, George. *The Wide World of Wickes: An Unusual Story of an Unusual Growth Company.* New York, N.Y.: McGraw-Hill, 1976. 486 p.

WIEN AIR ALASKA

Harkey, Ira. *Pioneer Bush Pilot: The Story of Noel Wien.*
Seattle, Wash.: University of Washington Press, 1974.
307 p.

WIFFLE BALL, INC.

Fucini, Joseph J., and Suzy Fucini. "David Mullany,
Wiffle Ball, Inc.: 'I Wanted to Control My Own
Company.'" In *Experience Inc.; Men and Women
Who Founded Famous Companies After the Age of
40*, 23-29. New York, N.Y.: Free Press, 1987.

WILBUR-ELLIS COMPANY

Wilbur-Ellis Company. *The First Fifty Years: 1921-1971.*
San Francisco, Calif.: The Company, 1971. 37 p.

SEE ALSO: CONNELL BROS. COMPANY, LTD.

WILEY (JOHN) AND SONS, INC.

Anthony, Carolyn T. "John Wiley at 175." *Publishers
Weekly* 222 (24 September 1982): 42-46.

Moore, John Hammond. *Wiley: One Hundred Seventy
Five Years of Publishing.* New York, N.Y.: Wiley,
1982. 279 p.

WILLAMETTE INDUSTRIES, INC.

Baldwin, Catherine A. *Making the Most of the Best:
Willamette Industries' Seventy-Five Years.* Portland,
Oreg.: The Company, 1982. 172 p.

WILLIAMSON-DICKIE MANUFACTURING
COMPANY

Williamson, C. Dickie. *Williamson-Dickie Manufacturing
Company: A Partnership for Progress.* New York,

N.Y.: Newcomen Society of the United States, 1985.
20 p. (Newcomen publication; no. 1250)

WILSON (DOUG) STUDIOS

Kingston, Brett. "Doug Wilson of Doug Wilson Studios."
In *The Dynamos: Who Are They Anyway?*, 199-205.
New York, N.Y.: Wiley, 1987.

WINNEBAGO INDUSTRIES, INC.

Fucini, Joseph J., and Suzy Fucini. "John K. Hanson,
Winnebago Industries, Inc.: 'Learning the Lessons of
Small Business.'" In *Experience Inc.; Men and
Women Who Founded Famous Companies After the
Age of 40*, 59-65. New York, N.Y.: Free Press, 1987.

Winnebago Industries, Inc. *Winnebago: A Proud History,
A Dynamic Future*. Forest City, Iowa: The Company,
1981. 8 p.

WISCONSIN DAIRIES

"25 Years of Making Our Future Come True." *Dairy
Express* (July-December 1988). A series of articles in
the July-December issues of the company's magazine.

WISCONSIN POWER AND LIGHT COMPANY

"WP&L's 60th Anniversary." *Concepts; For Employees of
Wisconsin Power and Light Company* 10 (Spring
1984): 1-27.

WITCO CHEMICAL CORPORATION

Wishnick, William. *The Witco Story*. New York, N.Y.:
Newcomen Society in North America, 1976. 34 p.
(Newcomen publication; no. 1029)

WITT COMPANY

The Witt Company. *Witt's 100; 1887-1987.* Cincinnati, Ohio: The Company, 1987. 40 p.

WIX CORPORATION

Sims, Allen H., and L.G. Alexander. *Wix Corporation.* New York, N.Y.: Newcomen Society in North America, 1974. 32 p. (Newcomen address)

WLS (RADIO STATION) CHICAGO

Evans, James F. *Prairie Farmer and WLS: The Burridge D. Butler Years.* Urbana: University of Illinois Press, 1969. 329 p.

WOOD MANUFACTURING COMPANY

MacPhee, William. "Forrest and Nina Wood of Ranger Boats." In *Rare Breed: The Entrepreneur, An American Culture*, 189+. Chicago, Ill.: Probus Publishing Company, 1987.

WOODSTOCK AND SYCAMORE TRACTION COMPANY

Robertson, William E. *The Woodstock and Sycamore Traction Company.* Delavan, Wis.: National Bus Trader, 1985. 56 p.

WOODWARD, BALDWIN AND COMPANY

Baer, Mary Baldwin. *A History of Woodward, Baldwin and Company.* Annapolis, Md.: Baer, 1977. 72 p.

WOOLWORTH (F.W.) COMPANY

Brough, James. *The Woolworth's.* New York, N.Y.: McGraw-Hill, 1982. 224 p.

F.W. Woolworth Company. *100th Anniversary: 1879-1979.* New York, N.Y.: The Company, 1979. 55 p.

Nichols, John Peter. *Skyline Queen and the Merchant Prince; The Woolworth Story.* New York, N.Y.: Trident Press, 1973. 144 p.

Thompson, Donald N. "Brascan Vs. Woolworth--It Would Have Been the Largest Hostile Takeover in History." *Business Quarterly: Canada's Management Magazine* 44 (Autumn 1979): 69-79.

WORCESTER COUNTY NATIONAL BANK

Tymeson, Mildred McClary. *Worcester Bankbook: From County Barter to County Bank, 1804-1966.* Worcester, Mass.: The Bank, 1966. 183 p.

WORCESTER TELEGRAM AND GAZETTE

Stoddard, Robert W. *The Evening Gazette: 100 Years--A Consistent Story.* New York, N.Y.: Newcomen Society in North America, 1966. 24 p.

WORLD CARPETS

Shaheen, Shaheen. *World Carpets: The First Thirty Years.* Dalton, Ga.: The Company, 1984. 121 p.

WORLD JOURNAL TRIBUNE

Sage, Joseph. *Three to Zero: The Story of the Birth and Death of the World Journal Tribune.* New York, N.Y.: American Newspaper Publishers Association, 1967. 82 p.

WORTHEN BANK AND TRUST COMPANY

Walsh, Mary Phyllis. *In the Vaults of Time.* Little Rock, Ark.: The Bank, 1976. 179 p.

WORTHINGTON FOODS, INC.

Worthington Foods, Inc. *Putting Good Taste Into Good Nutrition; Yesterday and Today.* Worthington, Ohio: The Company, 1984. 12 p.

WORTHINGTON INDUSTRIES

McConnell, John H. *"--And We've Only Scratched the Surface": The Growth Story of Worthington Industries.* New York, N.Y.: Newcomen Society in North America, 1981. 20 p. (Newcomen publication; no. 1138)

WQXR (RADIO STATION) NEW YORK CITY

Sanger, Elliot M. *Rebel in Radio; The Story of WQXR.* New York, N.Y.: Hastings House, 1973. 190 p.

WRIGHT AIRLINES

Wright Airlines. *Wright's History.* Cleveland, Ohio: The Company, 1983. 2 p.

WRIGHT (J.A.) AND COMPANY

Proper, David R. *The Story of Wright's Silver Cream 1873-1973.* Keene, N.Y.: The Company, 1973. 41 p.

WRIGLEY (WM) JR COMPANY

Angle, Paul McClelland. *Philip K. Wrigley: A Memoir of a Modest Man.* Chicago, Ill.: Rand McNally, 1975. 192 p.

Cleary, David Powers. "Wrigley's Chewing Gum; Restraint in Regard to Immediate Profits." In *Great American Brands: The Success Formulas That Made Them Famous*, 287-294. New York, N.Y.: Fairchild Publications, 1981.

WVLK (RADIO STATION)

"WVLK: Central Kentucky's No.1 Radio Station for 28 Years." *Kincaid Towers* (1980): 32-35.

WWL (RADIO STATION) NEW ORLEANS

Pusateri, C. Joseph. *Enterprise in Radio: WWL and the Business of Broadcasting in America.* Washington, D.C.: University Press of America, 1980. 336 p.

WYATT (JOB P.) AND SONS COMPANY

Wyatt, Joann Carlson. *Through the Patience of Job.* Raleigh, N.C.: Edwards & Broughton Company, 1981. 107 p.

WYLE LABORATORIES

Graybill, Harry G., ed. *The Wyle Companies.* El Segundo, Calif.: The Company, 1972.

WYLY CORPORATION

Voth, Ben. *A Piece of the Computer Pie.* Houston, Tex.: Gulf Publishing Company, 1974. 182 p.

WYMAN-GORDON COMPANY

Carter, Joseph R. *Wyman-Gordon Company: 100 Years Committed to Challenge and Leadership.* New York, N.Y.: Newcomen Society in North America, 1983. 22 p. (Newcomen publication; no. 1194)

WYSE ADVERTISING

Taylor, Russel R. "Lois Wyse; She Writes Books on the Side." In *Exceptional Entrepreneurial Women,* 13-17. New York, N.Y.: Quorum Books, 1988.

XEROX CORPORATION

Alexander, Robert C. *Fumbling the Future: How Xerox Invented, Then Ignored the First Personal Computer.* New York, N.Y.: W. Morrow, 1988. 274 p.

Brooks, John. "Story of the Xerox Corporation." In *Business Adventures*, 145-175. New York, N.Y.: Weybright and Tally, 1969.

Day, Charles R., Jr. "A Lesson from the Past." *Industry Week* 225 (27 May 1985): 70-71.

Dessauer, John H. *My Years with Xerox: The Billions Nobody Wanted.* New York, N.Y.: Doubleday, 1971. 239 p.

Jacobson, Gary, and J. Hillkirk. *Xerox, American Samurai.* New York, N.Y.: Macmillan, 1986. 338 p.

Xerox Corporation. *The Story of Xerography.* Stamford, Conn.: The Company, 1978. 9 p.

YANKEE ATOMIC ELECTRIC COMPANY

Yankee Atomic Electric Company. *25 Years of Progress with Nuclear Power.* Farmingham, Mass.: The Company, 1985. 87 p.

YANKEE PUBLISHING, INC.

Trowbridge, C. Robertson. *Yankee Publishing Incorporated: Fifty Years of Preserving New England's Culture While Extending Its Influence.* New York, N.Y.: Newcomen Society of the United States, 1985, c1986. 28 p. (Newcomen publication; no. 1255)

YARNALL, BIDDLE AND COMPANY

West, Harold A. *Two Hundred Years, 1764-1964: The*

Story of Yarnall, Biddle and Company, Investment Bankers. Philadelphia, Pa.: The Company, 1965. 82 p.

YELLOW FREIGHT SYSTEMS, INC.

Filgas, James F. *Yellow in Motion: A History of Yellow Freight System, Inc.* Bloomington: Indiana University Press, 1971. 144 p.

YOUNGSTOWN SHEET AND TUBE COMPANY

Buss, Terry F., and F. Stevens Redburn. *Shutdown at Youngstown: Public Policy for Mass Unemployment.* Albany, N.Y.: State University of New York Press, 1983. 219 p. (SUNY Series on Urban Public Policy)

YOURDON, INC.

Desmond, John. "The Friendly Master." *Software Magazine* 8 (February 1988): 38-43.

THE ZALE CORPORATION

Stringer, Tommy Wayne. "The Zale Corporation: A Texas Success Story." Ph.D. diss., North Texas State University, 1984. 229 p.

ZIONS FIRST NATIONAL BANK

Simmons, Roy W. *Zions First National Bank: Growing into Its Second Hundred Years.* New York, N.Y.: Newcomen Society in North America, 1974. 23 p. (Newcomen publication; no. 979)

ZONDERVAN CORPORATION

Ruark, James E., and T.W. Engstrom. *The House of Zondervan.* Grand Rapids, Mich.: The Company, 1981. 162 p.

ZURN INDUSTRIES, INC.

Zurn, Everett F., and F.W. Zurn. *Zurn Industries, Inc.: The Evolution of Environmentalism.* New York, N.Y.: Newcomen Society in North America, 1973. 22 p. (Newcomen address)

INDEX BY INDUSTRY

ACCOUNTING

Anderson (Arthur) and Company
Haskins and Sells
Peat, Marwick, Mitchell and Company
Price Waterhouse and Company

ADVERTISING

Benton and Bowles, Inc.
Burnett (Leo) Company
Chiat/Day
DDB Needham Worldwide, Inc.
Doyle Dane Bernbach
Henderson Advertising
Hill Holliday Connors Cosmopulos
Interpublic Group Companies
JWT Group, Inc.
Needham Harper Worldwide, Inc.
Ogilvy and Mather International, Inc.
Richards Group
Ski View, Inc.
Thompson (J.) Walter USA
Waring and Larosa
Wells Rich Greene, Inc.
Wyse Advertising

AEROSPACE

Cade Industries
Raytheon Company

AIR CONDITIONING, HEATING AND REFRIGERATION

Carrier Corporation
Garrett Corporation

AIRCRAFT

Alexander Aircraft Company
Atlantic Aviation Corporation
Avtek Corporation
Beech Aircraft Corporation
Boeing Company
California Aero Company
Consolidated Aircraft Corporation
Douglas Aircraft Company
General Dynamics Corporation
Goodyear Aircraft Corporation
Granville Airplane Company
Grumman Corporation
Hughes Aircraft Company
Lear, Inc.
Lockhead Aircraft Corporation
Luscombe Airplane Corporation
McDonnell Douglas Corporation
Piper Aircraft Corporation
Rockwell International
Rohr Corporation
Ryan Aeronautical Company
Sikorsky Aircraft
United Technologies Corporation
Vought Corporation
Waco Aircraft Company

AIRLINES

Air Florida
Alaska Airlines
American Airlines, Inc.
Antilles Air Boats
Braniff Airways
Cascade Airways
Comair, Inc.
Command-Aire Corporation
Continental Airlines Corporation
Delta Airlines, Inc.
Eastern Airlines, Inc.
Empire Airlines (II)
Frontier Airlines
Golden Gate Airlines
Hawaiian Airlines
Horizon Air
Laker Airways
Mid-Pacific Airlines
Midstate Airlines
Midway Airlines
Muse Air
National Airlines
New York Helicopter Corporation
New York, Rio and Buenos Aires Line
North Central Airlines, Inc.
North-East Airlines
Northwest Airlines
Northwest Orient Airlines
Ozark Air Lines
Pacific Southwest Airlines
Pan American World Airways, Inc.
People Express Airlines, Inc.
Piedmont Airlines
Provincetown-Boston Airline, Inc.
Ransome Airlines
Reeve Aleutian Airways
Republic Airlines
Scheduled Skyways

Southwest Airlines
Swifte Air Lines
Talkeetna Air Service
Tiger International, Inc.
Trans-Caribbean Airways
Trans World Airlines, Inc.
UAL, Inc.
USAir
Western Airlines, Inc.
Wien Air Alaska
Wright Airlines

AMUSEMENT

Hard Rock Cafe
Sloppy Joe's Bar

APPAREL

Cluett, Peabody and Company, Inc.
Custom Shop
Farah Manufacturing Company
Genesco, Inc.
Haggar Company
Hardwick Clothes, Inc.
Hart Schaffner and Marx
Jantzen, Inc.
Kellwood Company
Levi Strauss and Company
Maidenform, Inc.
Mitchell (Ed.), Inc.
Natori Company
Stone Manufacturing Company
Thomas (S.N.) Sons
Von Furstenberg (Diane), Ltd.
Warnaco
West Point-Pepperell, Inc.
Western Costume Company
Williamson-Dickie Manufacturing Company

ARCHAEOLOGY

Garrow and Associates

ATHLETIC EQUIPMENT
SEE:
SPORTING GOODS

AUCTION HOUSES

Sotheby Parke Bernet, Inc.

AUTOMOTIVE SERVICES

Tidy Car, Inc.

BANKING

Alabama Bancorporation
Allied Bankshares
Amarillo National Bank
American Security Bank
Arizona Bank
BancOhio Corporation
Bank of Boston Corporation
Bank of New Mexico
Bank of New York
Bank of Virginia
BankAmerica Corporation
Bankers Trust Company
Bar Harbor Banking and Trust Company
Barnett Bank of Jacksonville
BayBanks
Boston Bank of Commerce
Bowery Savings Bank
Brown Brothers Harriman and Company
Buffalo Savings Bank
Butcher (Jacob F.)
Caldwell and Company
Capital National Bank

BEVERAGES

American Distilling Company
American Natural Beverage Corporation
Anheuser-Busch Companies
Brown-Forman Distillers Corporation
Coca-Cola
Coors (Adolph) Company
Dr. Pepper Company
Firestone Vineyard
Glen Ellen Winery
Gold Kist, Inc.
Heileman (G.) Brewing Company
Hills Brothers Coffee, Inc.
Hudepohl Brewing Company
Leisy Brewing Company
Makers Mark Distillery, Inc.
Martinelli (S.) and Company
Masson (Paul) Vinyards
Mondavi (Robert) Winery
Pepsi-Cola Company
Roddy Manufacturing Company
Schlitz (Jos) Brewing Company

BIOTECHNOLOGY

Genentech
Molecular Devices Corporation

BOOK STORES

Bookstop
Rostenberg, Leona
Walden Book Company

BUILDING MATERIALS

AFG Industries, Inc.
Certain-Teed Corporation
Manville Corporation

Masco Corporation
National Gypsum Company
Owens-Corning Fiberglass Corporation
Robertson (H.H.) Company
Wallace-Murray Corporation
Walter (Jim) Corporation

BUSINESS SERVICES

ARA
Carlson Companies, Inc.
Equifax, Inc.
Gelco Corporation
Little (Arthur D.)
Marketing Corporation of America
Paychex
Retirement Program Services
Safety-Kleen Corporation
Seascope Systems, Inc.
Seven Oaks International
Spencer Stuart and Associates
TDIndustries
Unified Services, Inc.

CABLE AND PAY TV SYSTEMS

Oak Industries, Inc.
Warner Communications

CEMENT, GYPSUM AND MASONRY

Gifford-Hill and Company
Hummel Industries, Inc.

CERAMICS
SEE:
STONE, CLAY, GLASS AND CONCRETE

CHEMICAL PRODUCTS

Adell Chemical Company (LESTOIL)
Air Products and Chemicals, Inc.
Alco Standard Corporation
Allied Corporation
Cabot Corporation
Cargille, Inc.
Celanese Corporation of America
Cevron Chemical Company-Ortho Division
Cor-Ago Company
Dexter Corporation
Dow Chemical Company
Du Pont de Nemours (E.I.) and Company
Ethyl Corporation
Farmland Industries, Inc.
GAF Corporation
Gore (W.L.) and Associates, Inc.
Grace (W.R.) and Company
Great Lakes Chemical Corporation
Halcon International, Inc.
Hercules, Inc.
Huber (J.M.) Corporation
Huntsman Chemical Corporation
International Minerals and Chemical Corporation
Loctite Corporation
Lord Corporation
Lubrizol Corporation
Monsanto Company
Morton Thiokol, Inc.
Nalco Chemical Company
PPG Industries
Rohm and Hass Company
STP Corporation
Union Carbide Corporation
U.S. Borax and Chemical Corporation
U.S. Industrial Chemicals Company
Vinings Industries, Inc.
Witco Chemical Corporation

CHILD CARE CENTERS

Kinder-Care Learning Centers, Inc.

CLOCKS AND WATCHES

Forestville Manufacturing Company
Howard Clock Products
Pequegnat (Arthur) Clock Company
United States Watch Company

CLUBS AND MEMBERSHIP ORGANIZATIONS

American Brush Manufacturers Association
American Farm Burea Federation
American Institute of Certified Public Accountants
Automobile Club of Southern California
Book-of-the-Month-Club
Cincinnati Country Club
Cotton Producers Association, Atlanta
East Texas Chamber of Commerce
Financial Executives Institute
Michigan Credit Union League
Mississipi Bankers Association
Rotary Club, Charlotte, N.C.
Rotary Club, Lakeland, Fla.
Rotary Club, Palo Alto, Calif.
Rotary Club, Trenton, N.J.
Rotary Club, Oakland, Calif.
Rotary International

COAL

Eastern Gas and Fuel Associates
Lehigh Coal and Navigation
Mapco, Inc.
Peabody Holding Company, Inc.
Pittston Company
Rochester and Pittsburgh Coal Company

COLLECTIBLES

Messer (Sonia) Company
Steiff Dolls
Topps Chewing Gum, Inc.

COMPUTER SERVICES

AccuRay Corporation
Comdisco, Inc.
Computer Science Corporation
Context Management Corporation
Electronic Data Systems Corporation
May and Speh Data Processing Center
OPM Leasing Services
Protocom Devices
System Development Corporation
Wyly Corporation

COMPUTER SOFTWARE

Egghead Discount Software
Da Vinci Systems Corporation
Intergraph Corporation
Interleaf, Inc.
MacNeal-Schwendler Corporation
Microsoft Corporation
Platinum Technology, Inc.
Yourdon, Inc.

COMPUTERS

Amdahl Corporation
Apple Computers
AST Research Corporation
Atari, Inc.
Borland International
Burroughs Corporation
CCT, Inc. (Concepts in Computer Technology)
CPT Corporation

Compaq Computer Corporation
Computer Memories, Inc.
Control Data Corporation
Convergent Technologies
Cray Computer Corporation
Data General Corporation
Digital Equipment Corporation
Electronic Data Systems Corporation
Hayes Microcomputer Products, Inc.
Honeywell, Inc.
International Business Machines Corporation
Lear Siegler, Inc.
Micron Technology, Inc.
Mouse Systems Corporation
National Cash Register Company
NeXt, Inc.
Non-Linear Systems, Inc.
Osborne Computer Corporation
Packard Bell
Perot Systems Corporation
PC's Limited
Sperry Rand Corporation
SUN Microsystems
Tandem Computers
Tandy Corporation
TEC, Inc.
Vector Graphics, Inc.
Wang Laboratories

CONFECTIONERY
SEE:
SUGAR

CONGLOMERATES

Alco Standard Corporation
Amfac
Carborundum Company
Figgie International Holdings, Inc.

FMC Corporation
Fuqua Industries
Greyhound Corporation
Gulf and Western Industries, Inc.
IC Industries
Litton Industries
Martin Marietta Corporation
Pritzker and Pritzker
RCA Corporation
RJR Nabisco
Regent Corporation
SCANA Corporation
Tenneco, Inc.
Textron, Inc.
TRW
Vulcan Materials Company

CONSTRUCTION

Atkinson (Guy F.) Company of California
Associated General Contractors of America
Austin Bridge Company
Austin Company
Bass (D.C.) and Sons Construction Company
Bechtel Corporation
Blount, Inc.
Centex Corporation
Champion Bridge Company
Cianbro Corporation
Foster Wheeler Corporation
Harbert Corporation
Hubbard Construction Company
Jones (J.A.) Construction Company
Kiewit (Peter) Sons, Inc.
Kimmins Corporation
Monarch Construction Corporation
Sevenson Construction Corporation
Sundt (M.M.) Construction Company
T&K Roofing Company

CONSUMER CREDIT

American Express Company
Associates Corporation of North America
Associates Investment Company
Beneficial Corporation
C.I.T. Financial Corporation
Diners Club
Gulf and Western Industries
Household Finance Corporation
Kentucky Finance Company, Inc.
NOVA Financial Services, Inc.
Provident Loan Society of New York

CONTAINERS

Anchor Hocking Glass Corporation
Ball Corporation
Brockway Glass Company, Inc.
Clark (J.L.) Manufacturing Company
National Can Corporation
Owens-Illinois, Inc.
Van Dorn Company

COSMETICS AND TOILETRIES

Arden (Elizabeth) Inc.
Avon Products, Inc.
Chesebrough-Pond's, Inc.
Jergens (Andrew) Company
Lauder (Estee)
Mary Kay Cosmetics
Merle Norman Cosmetics
Noxell Corporation
Soft Sheen Products, Inc.
Revlon, Inc.

COURIER SERVICES

Federal Express

CREDIT UNIONS
SEE:
SAVINGS AND LOAN ASSOCIATION

CUTLERY

The Forschner Group

DEFENSE SYSTEMS

General Dynamics Corporation
Ling-Temco-Vought, Inc.
Lockhead Corporation
Northrop Corporation
Raytheon Company
Scott Aviation Corporation

DEPARTMENT STORES, DRUG, AND SPECIALTY STORES

Allied Stores Corporation
Barneys New York
Beauty Store & More
Belk Stores Services
Bendel (Henri) Associates
Bloomingdale's
Businessland, Inc.
Carter Hawley Hale Stores, Inc.
Computerland Corporation
Dillard's Department Store
Drug Emporium, Inc.
Eckerd (Jack) Corporation
Elder Beerman Stores Corporation
Federated Department Stores
Grant (W.T.) Company
Great American Salvage Company
Halle Bros. Company

DIRECT MARKETING

DISTRIBUTORS

Teeling & Gallagher

DRUG STORES
SEE:
DEPARTMENT STORES

DRUGS
SEE:
PHARMACEUTICALS

ELECTRIC & GAS UTILITIES

Alabama Power Company
American Electric Power Company
Arizona Public Services Company
Atlanta Gas Light Company
Boston Edison Company
Brooklyn Union Gas
Central Hudson Gas and Electric Corporation
Central Illinois Public Service Company
Central Power and Light Company
Central Vermont Public Service Corporation
Cincinnati Gas and Electric Company
Citizens Gas and Coke Utility
Columbus and Southern Ohio Electric Company
Commonwealth Companies, Inc.
Commonwealth Edison Company
Community Public Service Company
Consolidated Edison Company of New York, Inc.
Consumers Power Company
Delta Natural Gas Company, Inc.
Detroit Edison Company
Duke Power Company
East Ohio Gas Company
Eastern Gas and Fuel Associates
El Paso Company
Florida Power Corporation
Houston Lighting and Power Company
Illinois Power Company
Indianapolis Power and Light Company

ELECTRIC EQUIPMENT AND SUPPLIES

Anderson Electric Corporation
AVX Corporation
Chance (A.B.) Company
Cutler-Hammer, Inc.
Emerson Electric Company
General Electric Company
Gould, Inc.
Grainger (W.W.), Inc.
Hobart Corporation
McGraw-Edison Company
Maytag Company
Plumly Industries
Rayovac
Remington Products, Inc.
Robbins and Myers, Inc.
Sheldahl Company
Sprague (C.H.) and Son Company
Square D Company
Union Electric Company
Westinghouse Electric Company

ELECTRONICS

Action Instruments, Inc.
Allen-Bradley Company
Coherent, Inc.
Cubic Corporation
Electropac Companies, Inc.
General Radio Company
Hazeltine Corporation
Hewlett Packard Company
Klipsch Loudspeaker Systems
Koss Corporation
Marantz Company, Inc.
Matsushita Electric Corporation of America
Redcom Laboratories
Robinson Nugent, Inc.
Schaak Electronics

T-Bar, Inc.
Tandy Corporation
TDK USA Corporation
Texas Instruments
Wyle Laboratories

EMPLOYMENT SERVICES

Careertrack

ENGINEERING

Albert Kahn Associates, Inc.
Benham-Blair and Affiliates, Inc.
Black and Veatch, Inc.
Bovay Engineers, Inc.
Camp Dresser and McKee, Inc.
Day and Zimmermann, Inc.
Ebasco Services, Inc.
Freese and Nichols, Inc.
Gibbs and Hill, Inc.
Harza Engineering Company
Henningson, Durham and Richardson
Jacobs Engineering Group, Inc.
Lockwood Greene Engineers, Inc.
Main (C.T.) Corporation
McKim, Mead and White
McMillen, Inc.
MITRE Corporation
Odell Associates, Inc.
Parsons Brinkerhoff, Inc.
Parsons Brinkerhoff, Quade and Douglas, Inc.
Smith, Hinchman and Crylls Associates, Inc.
Stone and Webster Engineering Corporation
Sverdrup Corporation

ENGINES

Baldwin-Lima-Hamilton Corporation

Baldwin Locomotive Works
Boeing Company
Briggs and Stratton Corporation
Continental Motors Corporation
Cummins Engine Companies, Inc.
Fairbanks-Morse Corporation
Johnson & Towers

ENTERTAINMENT

Corporation for Entertainment and Learning
Disney (Walt) Productions
Motown Record Corporation
Music of Your Life
Playboy Enterprises, Inc.
Playwrights Producing Company
The Second City
Sloppy Joe's Bar

ENVIRONMENT

Environmental Systems Company

FARMS

Bob Evans Farms
Deerfoot Farms Company
Grove Farm Company, Inc.
High Tor Vineyards
King Ranch, Inc.
Koch Matador Cattle Company
Limoniera Company
Perdue Farms, Inc.
Richards Farms, Inc.
Smith Farms
Stoneyfield Farm
Swan Land and Cattle Company
Wyatt (Job P.) and Sons Company

FEEDS AND FEED INGREDIENTS

Agway, Inc.
Central Soya Company, Inc.

FINANCIAL SERVICES

American Express Company
American Stock Exchange
The Associates Corporation of North America
The Associates Investment Company
AVCO Corporation
Baldwin (D.H.) Company
Brighton Financial Planning, Inc.
COAP Planning Company
Deak-Perera Group
Financial Services Corporation
Leucadia National
National Revenue Corporation
New York Stock Exchange
Octagon Corporation
Philadelphia Stock Exchange
Republic Financial Services, Inc.
TICOR

FIREARMS

Colt Industries
Marlin Firearms Company
Remington Arms Company
Weatherby (Firearms), Inc.

FISHING

Schuylkill Fishing Company

FLOOR COVERING

American Olean Tile Company

Armstrong World Industries, Inc.
United Tile Company of Dallas

FOOD AND FOOD PROCESSING

Amfac
American Agronomics
Anderson, Clayton and Company
Archer Daniels Midland Company
Beatrice Food Company
Birds Eye Frozen Foods
Bob Evans Farms
Borden Company
Bruno's, Inc.
Bryan Foods, Inc.
Campbell Soup Company
Carnation Company
Castle and Cooke, Inc.
CFS Continental
Chelsea Milling Company
Consolidated Foods
Del Monte Corporation
Di Giorgio Fruit Corporation
Doskocil Companies, Inc.
Famous Amos Choclate Chip Company
Foremost-McKeeson, Inc.
General Foods Corporation
General Mills, Inc.
Gerber Products Company
Hebrew National Kosher Foods, Inc.
Heinz (H.J.) Company
Herbalife International
Hershey Foods Corporation
Heublein Corporation
Iowa Beef Processors, Inc.
Jennie-O Foods
Jeno's, Inc.
Kellogg Company
Lance, Inc.
Land O'Lakes Creamories, Inc.

FOOTWEAR
SEE:
LEATHER PRODUCTS

FOREST PRODUCTS

Anderson-Tully Company
Baskahegan Company
Boise Cascade Corporation
Diamond Match Company
Georgia-Pacific Corporation
Kellogg (L.D.) Lumber Company
Louisiana-Pacific
Ludwig (Daniel)
Mead Corporation
Menasha Wooden Ware Company
Miller Manufacturing Company
Neils (J.) Lumber Company
Pacific Lumber Company
Potlatch Corporation
Red River Lumber Company
Roddis Plywood Corporation
St. Paul and Tacoma Lumber Company
Seaboard Lumber and Shipping
Simpson Logging Company
Southern Pine Lumber Company
West Side Lumber Company
Weyerhaeuser Company
Willamette Industries, Inc.

FREIGHT TRANSPORTATION

American President Lines, Ltd.
Bekins Van Lines Company
Consolidated Freightways, Inc.
Emery Air Freight Corporation
Federal Express Corporation
Keeshin Transport System, Inc.
United Parcel Service of America
Yellow Freight System, Inc.

FUEL AND ICE DEALERS

Brown (K.J.) and Company

FUNERAL SERVICES

Blake-Lamb Funeral Homes

FURNITURE

Amedco, Inc.
Chasen (N.) and Son, Inc.
Haverty Furniture Companies, Inc.
Hill-Rom Company
Hillenbrand Industries
Keller Manufacturing Company
Lane Company
Levitz Furniture Corporation
MPI Industries, Inc.
Scandinavian Design, Inc.
Simmons Company
Stickley (L&J), Inc.
Wickes Corporation

GLASS
SEE:
STONE

GROCERY AND CONVENIENCE STORES

Acme Markets, Inc.
Alpha Beta Company
Associated Grocers, Inc.
Atlantic and Pacific Tea Company
Grace's Marketplace
Jitney Jungle Stores of America
Kroger Company
Lewis Grocer Company
Marsh Supermarkets, Inc.

Munford, Inc.
Publix Super Markets
Safeway Stores
Schnuck Markets, Inc.
Southland Corporation
Sunflower Food Stores
Supermarkets General Corporation

HARDWARE

Ace Hardware Corporation
Atlanta Saw Company
Black and Decker Manufacturing Company
Cotter and Company
Hoe (R.) and Company
Kenrick (Archibald) and Sons
Knox Industrial Supplies
Morse Hardware Company
Southern Saw Service, Inc.
Standard Screw Company
Stanley Works

HEALTH SERVICES

Frontier Nursing Service, Inc.
Humana, Inc.
Lifetime Corporation

HOME BUILDERS

Champion Home Builders Company
Kaufman and Broad, Inc.

HOSPITALS

Alachua General Hospital, Inc.
Bayfront Medical Center
Humana, Inc.
National Medical Enterprises, Inc.
Rehab (C.P.) Corporation

Renal Systems, Inc.
St. Vincent Hospital and Health Care Center, Inc.

HOTELS

Broadmoor Hotel, Inc.
Chase Hotel-St. Louis
Dunes Hotels and Casino's, Inc.
Grand Hotel
Holiday House
Holiday Inns of America, Inc.
Howard Johnson
Hyatt Corporation
Inter-Continental Hotels
Marriott Corporation
Ramada Inns
Western International Hotels, Inc.

HOUSEHOLD PRODUCTS

Amway
Cuisinart, Inc.
Hoover Company
Johnson (S.C.) and Sons, Inc.
Magic Chef, Inc.
Maytag Company
Norris Industries
Oneida Ltd.
Pickard, Inc.
Roper Corporation
Shaklee Corporation
Tupperware

INSTRUMENTATION

Ballantine Laboratories, Inc.
ISCO, Inc.

INSURANCE

Aetna Life and Casualty
Allstate Insurance Company
American General Insurance Company
American International Group
Atlanta Life Insurance Company
Atlantic Mutual Insurance Company
Bankers Life and Casualty Company
Bankers Security Life Insurance Society
Bowman (E.G.) Company
Business Men's Assurance Company of America
Cincinnati Financial Corporation
Cofederation Life Insurance Company
Columbus Mutual Life Insurance Company
Combined Insurance Company of America
Commonwealth Life Insurance Company
Connected Mutual Life Insurance Company
Continental Assurance Company
Continental Insurance Company
CUNA Mutual Insurance Society
East Augusta Mutual Fire Insurance Company
Employee Insurance of Wausau Mutual Company
Equitable Life Assurance Society of the United States
Equitable Life Insurance Company of Iowa
Erie Insurance Exchange
Federal Deposit Insurance Corporation
Festersen (Fred) and Associates
Fidelity Union Life Insurance Company
First American National Securities
First Executive Life
Government Employees Insurance Company
Guarantee Mutual Life Company
Hartford Steam Boiler Inspection and Insurance Company
Home Insurance Company
Hospital Corporation of America
Independent Life and Accident Insurance Company
Insurance Company of North America
The Kemper Group
Kentucky Central Life Insurance Company

Westfield Companies
Western-Southern Life Insurance Company
Western World Insurance, Inc.

INVESTMENT

Affiliated Fund, Inc.
Babson (David L.) and Company
Bache Halsey Stuart
Brown Brothers, Harriman and Company
Butcher and Company
Chicago Research and Trading Group
City Securities Corporation
Clark Estates, Inc.
Drexel Burnham Lambert
Drysdale Government Securities, Inc.
Equity Funding Corporation of America
Fiduciary Trust Company
Garrett (Robert) and Sons, Inc.
Geldermann, Inc.
Goldman, Sachs and Company
Grange Mutual Casualty Company
Grigsby Branford Powell, Inc.
Hutton (E.F.) Group, Inc.
Investors Overseas Services
Jordan Company
Kidder, Peabody, and Company
Kuhn, Loeb and Company
Lehman Brothers Kuhn Loeb
Leland O'Brien Rubinstein Associates
Levine and Company
Lord, Abbet and Company
Merrill Lynch
Morgan Stanley and Company, Inc.
Pacific Investment Management Company
Rich (Mark) International
Salomon Brothers
Schwab (Charles) and Company
Scottish American Investment Company Limited
Shearson Loeb Rhoades

Siebert (Muriel) amd Company
Telerate, Inc.
Yarnall, Biddle and Company

JEWELERS

Bixler's
Caldwell (J.E.) and Company
Gouterman and Sheffey, Inc.
Shreve, Crump and Low Company
Tanner (O.C.) Company
Tiffany and Company
Zale Corporation

LAW AND LEGAL SERVICES

Baker and McKenzie
Cummings and Lockwood
Finley, Kumble, Wagner, Heine, Underberg, Manley and Casey
Fitch Miller and Tourse
Gaston, Snow and Ely, Bartlett
Hinkley and Singley
Jones, Day, Reavis and Poque
Kelley Drye and Warren
McNair Law Firm, P.A.
Sidley and Austin
Skadden, Arps, Slate, Meagher & Flom
Verrill and Dana

LAWN AND TREE SERVICES

ChemLawn
Davey Tree Expert Company

LEASING
SEE:
RENTING AND LEASING

LEATHER AND FOOTWEAR

Admos Shoe Corporation
Barry (R.G.) Corporation
Brown Group, Inc.
Endicott Johnson Corporation
Interco, Inc.
Melville Shoe Corporation
Nike, Inc.

LEISURE TIME

Brunswick Corporation
Dickerson (Charles W.) Field Music, Inc.
Kentucky Hills Industries
Leddy's (M.L.) Boot and Saddlery
Lionel Train Company
Resorts International

LUMBER
SEE:
FOREST PRODUCTS

MACHINE TOOLS

Acme-Cleveland Corporation
Cincinnati Milacron
Houdaille Industries
Monarch Machine Tool Company
Moore Special Tool Company, Inc.

MACHINERY AND EQUIPMENT

Allis-Chalmers Corporation
Babcock and Wilcox Company
Baker International Corporation
Barber-Greene Company
Bissell Carpet Sweepers
Black Clawson Company
Bodine Corporation

Briggs and Stratton
Bucyrus-Erie Company
Caterpillar Tractor Company
Clark Equipment Company
Colt Industries, Inc.
Combustion Engineering, Inc.
Cooper Industries
Data Card Corporation
Dayton Reliable Tool and Manufacturing Company
Deere and Company
Ex-Cell-O Corporation
Fellows Gear Shaper Company
Ferracute Machine Company
Figgie International Holdings, Inc.
Goss Printing Press Company
Harnischfeger Corporation
Hesston Corporation
Joy Manufacturing Company
McNally Pittsburgh
Melroe Company
Miniature Precision Bearings, Inc.
Norton Company
Parker Hannifin Corporation
Sandy Hill Corporation
Singer Sewing Company
Smith Tool
Sundstrand Corporation
Tokheim Corporation
TRW-Reda Pump Division
USM Corporation
Warren Rupp Company
Wean United, Inc.
Western Gear Corporation
Wyman-Gordon Company

MAIL ORDER

Bean (L.L.), Inc.
Berry (L.M.), Inc.

Horchow Collection
JS&A Group, Inc.
Montgomery Ward and Company
Penney (J.C.) Company, Inc.
Sears, Roebuck and Company
Spiegel, Inc.

MANAGEMENT SERVICES
SEE:
BUSINESS SERVICES

MARKET RESEARCH

BrainReserve
Nielsen (A.C.) Company

MEASURING AND CONTROL

Cutler-Hammer, Inc.
Datum, Inc.
Fluke (John) Manufacturing Company, Inc.
Perkin-Elmer Corporation

MEAT PACKING AND PROCESSING

Bob Evans Farms
CR Industries
Darling-Delaware Company
Hormel (George A.) and Company
Iowa Beef Processsors, Inc.
Mayer (Oscar) and Company
Tyson Foods, Inc.

MEDICAL AND DENTAL EQUIPMENT AND SUPPLIES

Abbott Laboratories
Alcon Laboratories
American Hospital Supply Corporation
Cardiac Pacemakers, Inc. (CPI)
Johnson and Johnson

Medtronic
Mentor Corporation
Milton Roy Company
St. Jude Medical

MEMBERSHIP ORGANIZATIONS
SEE:
CLUBS

METAL PRODUCTS

Aluminum Company of America
Aztec Manufacturing Company
Ball Corporation
Charlotte Pipe and Foundry Company
Clow Corporation
Eastern Company
Elano Corporation
Eli Bridge Company
Gilbert and Bennett Manufacturing Company
Gorham Company
Griffin Wheel Company
Illinois Tool Works, Inc.
International Silver Company
J.P. Industries
Kaman Corporation
Kennametal, Inc.
Kerite Company
Lunkenheimer Company
Marlin Firearms Company
Mesta Machine Company
Okonite Company
Ontario Corporation
Pyromet, Inc.
SIFCO Industries, Inc.
Signode Industries, Inc.
Southwire Company
Victor Comptometer Corporation
Youngstown Sheet and Tube Company

MINING AND MINERALS

Aluminum Company of America
AMAX, Inc.
American Brass Company
American Zinc Company
Anglo American Corporation of South Africa
Calumet and Hecla, Inc.
Chisos Mining Company
Cleveland-Cliffs Iron Company
Cold Spring Granite Company
Copper Range Company
Cyprus Minerals Company
Dixon (Joseph) Crucible Company
Homestake Mining Company
Hunt International Resources Corporation
Kaiser Aluminum and Chemical Corporation
Kerr-McGee Nuclear Corporation
Newmont Mining Corporation
Oglebay Norton Company
Parser Mineral Corporation
Phelps Dodge Corporation
Reynolds Metals Company
Rocky Mountain Fuel Company
Texas Gulf Sulphur Company
Texasgulf

MOBIL HOMES

Coachmen Industries
Fuqua Industries, Inc.
Winnebago Industries, Inc.

MOTION PICTURE AND THEATRE

Columbia Pictures
Disney (Walt) Productions
Imagine Films Entertainment
Metro-Goldwyn-Mayer, Inc.
Paramount Pictures, Inc.

Mercedes-Benz of North America, Inc.
Nissan Motor Corporation in U.S.A.
PACCAR, Inc.
Studebaker Corporation
Packard Motor Car Company
Subaru of America, Inc.
Toyota Motor Sales, U.S.A.

MUSICAL INSTRUMENTS

Estey Organ Company
Kimball International
Rickenbacker International Corporation

NATURAL GAS

American Natural Resources Company
Columbia Gas System Service Corporation
Consolidated Natural Gas Company
Delta Natural Gas Company
Indiana Gas Company
Lone Star Gas Company
Northern Illinois Gas Company
Panhandle Eastern Pipeline Company
Pioneer Natural Gas Company
South Jersey Industries, Inc.
Southern Union Gas Company
Suburban Propane Gas Corporation
Texas Eastern Corporation
Transcontinental Gas Pipeline Corporation

NEWSPAPERS

Arizona Republic
Baltimore Sun
Birmingham News
Boston Globe
Chicago Tribune
Cincinnati Enquirer
Cincinnati Post

Evening Gazette
Fort Worth Star-Telegram
Gannett Company
Hartford Courant
Kansas City Star
Knight-Ridder
Los Angeles Times
Los Angeles Weekly
Louisville Courier Journal
Minneapolis Star and Tribune Company
New York Daily News
New York Times Company
Ogden Standard-Examiner
Phoenix Gazette
Salt Lake Tribune
Times Mirror Company
USA Today
Wall Street Journal
Worcester Telegram and Gazette
World Journal Tribune

OFFICE EQUIPMENT AND FURNITURE

Addressograph Multigraph Corporation
Art Metal, Inc.
Bruning (Charles) Company
Faber-Castell Corporation
Miller (Herman) Company
Reynolds and Reynolds Company
Xerox Corporation

OIL

Arabian American Oil Company
Ashland Oil
Atlantic Richfield Company
Barons Oil Ltd.
Charter Company
Continental Oil Company

Diamond Shamrock
Exxon Corporation
Getty Oil Company
Gulf Oil Company
Home-Stake Production Company
Hudson Oil Company
Husky Oil Company
Kerr-McGee Corporation
Kewanee Oil Company
Marathon Oil Company
Mesa Petroleum Company
Mobil Oil Corporation
Occidental Petroleum Corporation
Pennzoil Company
Phillips Petroleum Company
Quaker State Oil
Shell Oil Company
Sinclair Oil Company
Standard Oil Company
Sun Oil Company
Texaco, Inc.
Union Oil Company of California

OIL SERVICE AND EQUIPMENT

Case International Company
Dresser Industries
Foster Wheeler Corporation
Hughes Tool Company
Lufkin Industries, Inc.
NL Industries
Parker Drilling Company
Petrolane, Inc.
Pullman, Inc.
Schlumberger Limited
UOP (Universal Oil Products Company)
Western Company of North America

OPTICS
SEE:
PHOTO AND OPTICS

PACKAGING

Garlock Packaging Company
Sealed Air Corporation
Tyz-All Plastics, Inc.

PAINT

Rust-Oleum Corporation
Sherwin-Williams Company

PAPER

Avery International
The Chesapeake Corporation of Virginia
Crane and Company
Crown Zellerbach Corporation
Federal Paper Board Company, Inc.
Hammermill Paper Company
Kimberly-Clark Corporation
MacMillan Bloedel Limited
Mead Corporation
Parsons and Whittemore Organization
Pentair, Inc.
St. Regis Paper Company
Scott Paper Company
SONOCO Products Company
Stone Container Corporation

PENS, PENCILS, ETC.

Binney & Smith, Inc.
Parker Pen Company

PERIODICALS

The Banker Magazine
Buildings; the Construction and Building Management Journal Cornell
Hotel and Restaurant Administration Quarterly
Electronic News
Forbes Magazine
Life Magazine
McClure's Magazine
NIP Magazine
Popular Science Publishing Company
Prairie Farmer
Publishers Weekly
Quick Frozen Foods
Reader's Digest Association, Inc.
Saturday Evening Post
Story Magazine
Sunset Magazine
U.S. News and World Report
Venture
Washingtonian

PHARMACEUTICALS

Abbott Laboratories
Burroughs Wellcome Company
Carter-Wallace, Inc.
Dorsey Laboratories
Gilpin (Henry B.) Company
Lilly (Eli) and Company
Miles Laboratories, Inc.
Newport Pharmaceuticals International
Parke-Davis and Company
Pfizer, Inc.
Robins (A.H.) Company
Rorer, Inc.
Schering Plough-Kenilworth NJ
SmithKline Corporation
Squibb Corporation

PHOTO AND OPTICAL

American Optical Corporation
Bell and Howell Company
Duncan Electric Company
Fox Photo, Inc.
Kodak (Eastman) Company
Lazzara Optical
Minolta Corporation
Polaroid Corporation

PLASTICS
SEE:
RUBBER AND PLASTICS

POLLUTION CONTROL

Browning-Ferris Industries
Zurn Industries, Inc.

PRINTING AND ENGRAVING

American Greetings Corporation
Barouh-Eaton Allen Corporation
Beck Engraving Company, Inc.
Dataco, Inc.
Dietrich-Post Company
Gibson Greeting Cards, Inc.
Hallmark Cards, Inc.
Hederman Brothers
Hennegan Company
Krueger (W.A.) Company
Kwik-Kopy Corporation
Lasky Company
Postal Instant Press
Waverly, Inc.

PROFESSIONAL ORGANIZATIONS
SEE:
CLUBS

PROTECTIVE SERVICES

Brink's, Inc.
Pinkerton's National Detective Agency

PUBLIC RELATIONS

Dudley-Anderson-Yutzy Public Relations, Inc.
Ruder Finn, Inc.

PUBLIC UTILITIES
SEE:
ELECTRIC AND GAS UTILITIES

PUBLISHING

Able (Richard) and Company
Bantam Books, Inc.
Best (A.M.) Company
Bobbs-Merrill Company
Cliffs Notes, Inc.
Coward, McCann and Geoghan
Curtis Publishing Company
Dartnell Corporation
Davis (F.A.) Company
Donnelley (R.R.) and Sons
Dow, Jones and Company
Field Enterprises Educational Corporation
Graves (Earl G.) Ltd.
Grolier, Inc.
Harper and Row, Publishers, Inc.
Hearst Corporation
Houghton Mifflin Company
Johnson Publishing
Lane Publishing Company
Lea and Febiger

RADIO AND TELEVISION

Turner Broadcating Systems, Inc.
United Press International
USA Network Cable
WLS (Radio Station) Chicago
WVLK (Radio Station) Lexington, Ky.
WWL (Radio Station) New Orleans

RAILROADS

Amtrak
Baltimore and Ohio Railroads
Bessemer and Lake-Erie Railroad Company
Burlington Northern, Inc.
Central Pacific Railway Company
The Chesapeake and Ohio Railway
The Chessie System, Inc.
Chicago and Alton Railroad Company
Chicago and North Western Railway Company
Chicago, Burlington and Quincy Railroad Company
Consolidated Rail Corporation (ConRail)
Delaware and Hudson Railroad
Denver and Rio Grande Western Railroad Company
Duluth, Missable and Iron Range Railway Company
Erie Railroad
GATX Corporation
Guilford Transportation Industries, Inc.
Florida East Coast Railway (FEC)
Hagerstown and Frederick Railway Company
Illinois Central Railroad
Interstate Public Service Company
Jonesboro, Lake City and Eastern Railroad
Kansas City Southern Railway Company
Louisville and Nashville Railroad Company
Maine Central Railroad
Minnesota Transfer Railway Company
Missouri, Kansas and Texas Railroad Company
Missouri Pacific Corporation
Mount Washington Railway Company
North Carolina Railroad Company
North Pacific Coast Railroad Company

Northwestern Pacific Railroad Company
Pacific Electric Railway Company
Penn Central Company
Piedmont and Northern Railway
Pittsburgh and Lake Erie Railroad
Reading Company
San Joaquin and Eastern Railroad
Santa Fe, Prescott, and Phoenix Railway
Seabord Airline Railway
Soo Line Railroad Company
Southern Pacific Railroad Company
Southern Railway Company
Staten Island Rapid Transit Railway
Texas and Pacific Railway
Trailer Train Company
Trans Union Corporation
Union Pacific Railroad Company
Washington-Virginia Railway Company
Western Pacific Railroad

REAL ESTATE

Bach Realty, Inc.
Birtcher Realty Corporation
Coldwell Banker Real Estate Group, Inc.
Elyachar Real Estate
First Realty Reserve
Friendswood Development Company
Galbreath (John W.) and Company
Goodtab Management Company
Helmsley-Noyes Company, Inc.
Leavell Company
Lincoln Property Company
Luckman Partnership, Inc.
Newhall Land and Farming Company
Raveis (William) Real Estate
Rouse Company
Sea Island Company
Solomon Equities

Sunlite, Inc.
Trammell Crow Company
The Trump Group, Inc.
Webb and Knapp, Inc.

RECORDING

A&M Records, Inc.
Atlantic Recording Corporation
Commodore Records
Geffen Records
Motown Record Corporation

RECREATION

Bass Pro Shops
Coleman Company, Inc.
Colorado Mountain Club
Delta Queen Steamboat Company
Fitness Finders, Inc.
Heldor Industries
Outboard Motors Corporation
Parker Brothers
Spalding and Evenflo Companies, Inc.
Sparkman and Stephens
Thousand Trails, Inc.

RENTING AND LEASING SERVICES

Leasco Data Processing Equipment Corporation
Saunders Leasing Systems, Inc.
Ugly Duckling Rent-A-Car System, Inc.

RESEARCH AND DEVELOPMENT

American Institute of Steel Construction, Inc.
Batelle Memorial Institute
Beckman Instruments, Inc.
Rand Corporation

RESTAURANTS

Benihana National Corporation
Burger King Corporation
Chic-Fil-A Corporation
Domino's Pizza
Hardee's Food Systems
I Can't Believe It's Yogurt
Kentucky Fried Chicken
McDonald's Corporation
Mortimer's Restaurant
Payton (Bob)
Pizza Inn, Inc.
Restaurant Development Corporation
Saga Corporation
Sambo's Restaurants, Inc.
The Siver Palate
TCBY Enterprises, Inc.
VICORP
Wendy's International, Inc.
White Castle System, Inc.

RESTORATION

Bedford-Stuyvesant Restoration Corporation
Mansions and Millionaires, Inc.

ROBOTS

Condec Corporation

RUBBER AND PLASTICS

Armstrong Rubber Company
Bandag, Inc.
Cooper Tire and Rubber Company
Dayco Corporation
Firestone Tire and Rubber Company
General Tire and Rubber Company

Goodyear Tire and Rubber Company
Kelly-Springfield Tire Company
Precision Rubber Products Corporation
Spir-it, Inc.
Tupperware
UNIROYAL, Inc.
United States Rubber Company

SAVINGS AND LOAN

Buckeye Federal Savings and Loan Association
California Federal Savings and Loan Association
Chevy Chase Savings and Loan, Inc.
Citizens Federal Savings and Loan Association
Empire Savings and Loan
Farm and Home Savings and Loan Association
First Federal Savings and Loan Association of Jackson
First Federal Savings and Loan Association of Minneapolis
First Federal Savings and Loan Association of St. Petersburg
Gibralter Savings and Loan Association
Glendale Federal Savings and Loan
Home State Savings and Loan
Lincoln Savings and Loan of Irvine
Pennsylvania State Employee Credit Union
Stockton Savings Association
Western Savings and Loan Association
Westwood Savings and Loan Association
WFC Corporation

SECURITY SERVICES
SEE:
PROTECTIVE SERVICES

SEEDS

Burpee Seed Company
Pioneer Hi Bred International, Inc.

SHIP BUILDING AND SHIPPING

American Ship Building Company
Cunard Steamship Company
Delta Steamship Lines
Ellam (Patrick), Inc.
Herreshoff Manufacturing Company
Howard Ship Yard and Dock Company
Litton Industries
Matson Navigation Company
Newport News Shipbuilding and Dry Dock Company
Todd Shipyards Corporation

SHOES
SEE:
LEATHER AND FOOTWEAR

SOAPS AND CLEANERS

Armour and Company
Clorox Company
Colgate-Palmolive Company
Economics Laboratory, Inc.
Procter and Gamble Company
Wright (J.A.) and Company

SPORTING GOODS

Blumenfeld Sports Net
Lannon Manufacturing Company
MacGregor Golf Company
Nautilus Sports Medicine Industries, Inc.
Spalding and Evenflo Companies, Inc.

SPORTS CLUBS

Atlanta Braves
Baltimore Orioles
Boston Celtics

Boston Red Sox
California Angels
Chicago Bears
Chicago Cubs
Chicago White Sox
Cincinnati Bengals
Cincinnati Reds
Cleveland Browns
Cleveland Indians
Dallas Cowboys
Denver Broncos
Detroit Tigers
Green Bay Packers
Kansas City Chiefs
Los Angeles Dodgers
Los Angeles Rams
Miami Dolphins
Minnesota Vickings
New England Patriots
New York Giants
New York Islanders
New York Mets
New York Yankees
Oakland Raiders
Philadelphia Phillies
Philadelphia '76ers
Pittsburgh Pirates
Pittsburgh Steelers
St. Louis Cardinals
San Francisco Forty-Niners
San Francisco Giants
Texas Rangers
Washington Redskins

STEEL

Armco Steel Corporation
Atlantic Steel Company
Bethlehem Steel Corporation
Bliss and Laughlin Industries

United Telecommunications, Inc.
Western Electric Company
Western Union

TELEVISION
SEE:
RADIO

TEXTILES

Amoskeag Manufacturing Company
Avondale Mills
Bancroft (Joseph) and Sons Company
Burlington Industries, Inc.
Dan River, Inc.
Fieldcrest Mills, Inc.
Glen Raven Mills, Inc.
Greenwood Mills
Milliken and Company
Mount Hope Finishing Company
New England Moxie Company
Springs Industries, Inc.
Stevens (J.P.) and Company
Wall Industries
Webster Industries
Weil Brothers Cotton
Woodward, Baldwin and Company

TIRES
SEE:
RUBBER AND PLASTICS

TOBACCO

American Tobacco Company
Liggert Group
Philip Morris, Inc.
Reynolds (R.J.) Industries, Inc.

TOYS

Bradley (Milton) Company
Coleco Industries, Inc.
Discovery Toys
Hasbro, Inc.
Lionel Train Company
Mattel, Inc.
Meyer (Mary) Corporation
Parker Brothers, Inc.
Wiffle Ball, Inc.

TRADE
SEE:
WHOLESALE TRADE

TRANSPORTATION

Dayton, Covington, and Piqua Traction Company
Denver Tramway Corporation
Greyhound Corporation
Ithaca Street Railway Company
North Jersey Rapid Transit Company
Overland Mail Company
Philadelphia Rapid transit Company
Pullman, Inc.
Twin City Rapid Transit Company
Wells Fargo and Company
Woodstock and Sycamore Traction Company

TRANSPORTATION EQUIPMENT

A-P-A Transport
Columbia Manufacturing Company
Idex Corporation

TRAVEL AGENCIES

Casto Travel

TROPHIES AND AWARDS

Champion Awards, Inc.

TRUCKING

Aero Mayflower Transit Company, Inc.
Coles Express
Consolidated Freightways, Inc.
Hunt (J.B.) Transport, Inc.
Merrill Transport Company
Security Storage Company of Washington, D.C.
The 7 Santini Brothers
Smith's Transfer Corporation

WASTE MANAGEMENT, REFUSE, AND SEWERAGE

Browning-Ferris Industries, Inc.
Combustion Engineering, Inc.
Industrial Services of America, Inc.
Marine Shale Processors, Inc.
ORFA Corporation of America

WATER PURIFICATION PRODUCTS

Culligan International Company
Krofta Waters, Inc.

WATER TRANSPORTATION

Alexander and Baldwin, Inc.
Foss Company
Goodrich Transit Company
Joy Line
Moran Towing and Transportation Company, Inc.
National Bulk Carriers, Inc.
San Diego and Coronado Ferry Company
Washington State Ferries

WATER UTILITY

Consumer Water Company
Elizabethtown Water Company
Hackensack Water Company
Indianapolis Water Company

WHOLESALE TRADE

Amtorg Trading Corporation
Amway Corporation
FCX, Inc.
Foremost-McKesson, Inc.
Grabar Electric Company
Gross, Kelly and Company, Inc.

WINDOWS

Anderson Corporation

WINERY
SEE:
BEVERAGES

WOOD PRODUCTS

Vaughn (L.) Company

INDEX BY AUTHOR

478

INDEX BY EXECUTIVE OFFICER

APPENDIX A

COLLECTED WORKS OF CORPORATE HISTORIES

Adams, James Ring. *The Big Fix: Inside the S&L Scandal: How an Unholy Alliance of Politics and Money Destroyed America's Banking System.* New York, N.Y.: Wiley, 1990. 308 p.

Bender, Marylin. *At The Top; Behind the Scenes with the Men and Women Who Run America's Corporate Giants.* Garden City, N.Y.: Doubleday, 1975.

Brooks, John. *Business Adventures.* New York, N.Y.: Weybright and Talley, 1969. 400 p.

Buchholz, Barbara B., and Margaret Crane. *Corporate Bloodlines: The Future of the Family Firm.* New York, N.Y.: Carol Publishing Group, 1989. 290 p.

Cleary, David Powers. *Great American Brands: The Success Formulas That Made Them Famous.* New York, N.Y.: Fairchild Publications, 1981. 307 p.

Cose, Ellis. *The Press.* New York, N.Y.: Morrow, 1989. 380 p.

Darby, Edwin. *The Fortune Builders.* Garden City, N.Y.: Doubleday, 1986. 276 p.

Ehrlich, Judith Ramsey. *The New Crowd: The Changing of the Jewish Guard on Wall Street.* Boston: Little, Brown, 1989. 444 p.

Fucini, Joseph J., and Suzi Fucini. *Experience, Inc.; Men and Women Who Founded Famous Companies After the Age of 40.* New York, N.Y.: Free Press, 1987. 244 p.

Gilder, George. *The Spirit of Enterprise.* New York, N.Y.: Simon & Schuster, 1984. 274 p.

Goldwasser, Thomas. *Family Pride; Profiles of Five of America's Best-Run Family Businesses.* New York, N.Y.: Dodd, Mead and Company, 1986.

Kingstone, Brett. *The Dynamos: Who Are They Anyway?* New York: Wiley, 1987. 256 p.

Levinson, Harry, and Stuart Rosenthal. *CEO; Corporate Leadership in Action.* New York: Basic Books, 1984. 308 p.

Levitt, Mortimer. *How to Start Your Own Business Without Losing Your Shirt; Secrets of Seventeen Successful Entrepreneurs.* New York, N.Y.: Atheneum, 1988. 213 p.

MacPhee, William. *Rare Breed: The Entrepreneur, An American Culture.* Chicago, Ill.: Probus Publishing Company, 1987. 224 p.

Meyer, Michael. *The Alexander Complex; The Dreams That Drive the Great Businessmen.* New York, N.Y.: Times Books, 1989. 258 p.

Millman, Nancy. *Emperors of Adland; Inside the Advertising Revolution*. New York, N.Y.: Warner Books, 1988. 225 p.

Nayak, P. Ranganath. *Breakthroughs!* New York: Rawson Associates, 1986. 371 p.

Pine, Carol, and Susan Mundale. *Self-Made: The Stories of 12 Minnesota Entrepreneurs*. Minneapolis, Minn.: Dorn Books, 1982. 223 p.

Shook, Robert L. *The Entrepreneurs: Twelve Who Took Risks and Succeeded*. New York: Harper & Row, 1980. 181 p.

Sobel, Robert, and David B. Sicclia. *The Entrepreneurs: An American Adventure*. Boston: Houghton Mifflin Company, 1986. 278 p.

Stevens, Mark. *Power of Attorney: The Rise of America's Best-Run Family Business*. New York, N.Y.: Dodd, Mead & Company, 1986. 187 p.

Taylor, Russel R. *Exceptional Entrepreneurial Women*. New York: Quorum Books, 1988. 178 p.

Tedlow, Richard S. *New and Improved: The Story of Mass Marketing in America*. New York, N.Y.: Basic Books, 1990. 481 p.